Galatians and the Rhetoric of Crisis

Lynn,
Thanks for
your friendship.
Nina

Galatians and the Rhetoric of Crisis

Demosthenes ◆ Cicero ◆ Paul

RHETORICÆ GRATOS SERMONI ASTVTA COLORES,
QVO DVICIVS FLVAT IS AD AVREIS ADYCIT.

Nina E. Livesey

POLEBRIDGE PRESS
Salem, Oregon

Cover illustration: Rhetorica by Dutch artist Frans Floris, engraved by
Cornelis Cort in 1565 as part of a series entitled, "The Seven Liberal Arts."
Wikimedia Commons.

> The illustration depicts the female personification Oratory instructing two
> figures. She holds a winged caduceus, the symbol of Hermes or Mercury who
> was considered by rhetoricians to be a patron of their art. On the floor are
> books by the traditional rhetorical authorities, Cicero, Isocrates, Demosthenes
> and Quintilian. The birds on the left are a parrot and a tit, symbolizing
> eloquence. The caption reads: "Rhetoricae gratos sermoni astuta colores quo
> dulcius fluat is ad aureis adjicit" ("She cleverly adds the pleasing hues of
> rhetoric to speech, by which it flows more sweetly to the ears").

Cover and interior design by Robaire Ream

Polebridge Press is the publishing arm of the Westar Institute, a non-
profit, public-benefit research and educational organization that bridges
the gap between scholarship about religion and the perception of religion
in popular culture. To learn more, visit westarinstitute.org.

Library of Congress Cataloging-in-Publication Data
Names: Livesey, Nina E., 1953- author.
Title: Galatians and the rhetoric of crisis : Demosthenes - Cicero - Paul /
  by Nina E. Livesey.
Description: Farmington, Minnesota : Polebridge Press, 2016. | Includes
  bibliographical references and index.
Identifiers: LCCN 2016022570 | ISBN 9781598151749 (alk. paper)
Subjects: LCSH: Bible. Galatians--Socio-rhetorical criticism. | Bible.
  Galatians--Criticism, interpretation, etc. | Demosthenes--Influence. |
  Cicero, Marcus Tullius--Influence.
Classification: LCC BS2685.52 .L58 2016 | DDC 227/.4066--dc23
LC record available at https://lccn.loc.gov/2016022570

Contents

Preface

This book would not have come to fruition without the help and support of many people. Associate Dean Martha Banz, Dean James Pappas of the University of Oklahoma (OU) College of Liberal Studies, and the larger OU granting committee approved a year-long sabbatical (2014–2015). That long stretch of uninterrupted time was invaluable to the completion of this project. Early on, a generous Junior Faculty Summer Fellowship from the College of Arts and Sciences at OU, supported by OU Director of the Religious Studies Program Charles Kimball, made possible several months of dedicated time and financial resources necessary to develop my ideas, to create a general outline for the book, and to produce drafts of several chapters. While on leave in France, OU History of Science graduate student Nathan Kapoor scanned and emailed needed articles. Professor of Classics Christine Shea read an early draft of the entire manuscript and offered helpful comments. New Testament Professor *Emeritus* Bernard B. Scott carefully reviewed drafts of the beginning chapters and made many valuable suggestions, especially for how best to introduce my subject.

The manuscript took on its present shape and became a unified whole in France, at "my place" at the window in *La Bibliothèque d'Agglomération de Saint-Omer* (fall 2014–spring 2015). I am convinced that my window location overlooking an inner garden courtyard in the *Salle des Archives* was magical. My muse met me there nearly every day. The room was very often silent. Often the only sounds were the clicks of my own keyboard. When occupied, I could for the most part ignore the nearby French conversations. The graciousness and professionalism of the staff, Matthieu Bécuwe, Sophie Barrère, Julie Ballanfat, and Laurence Bacart, fostered an atmosphere conducive for study and work. I thank them for their assistance and friendship. Library director Françoise Ducroquet cordially welcomed me into "the library family." Very special appreciation, however, goes to Rémy Cordonnier,

Responsable du fonds ancien de la Bibliothèque d'Agglomération de Saint-Omer, who took a personal interest in my research. While in Saint-Omer, I conformed my work schedule to the library's hours of operation; it gave me a necessary routine. I even benefitted from the library's strictly enforced noontime breaks, when everyone was without exception or delay cast out for an hour. Yet the brisk walk back and forth to the apartment for lunch and the return stop at the local espresso bar for a chat and a shot were revitalizing.

Working with Polebridge Press Publisher Larry Alexander has been a privilege. Larry was there for me whenever I needed his advice. He gave my entire first draft a thorough reading, while also making helpful suggestions. His questions forced me to clarify my points. Polebridge Press Editor Cassandra Farrin has taken a keen interest in my work and helped with the manuscript's public presentation and overall style. I especially thank Barbara Hampson for her copyediting. I am fairly certain my lengthy endnotes gave her fits, yet she diligently worked through them. Char Matejovsky and Robaire Ream put their artistic talents and expertise into the manuscript's final publish-ready form. The publishing team at Polebridge Press is superb.

More than anyone else I wish to thank my companion, best friend, and lifelong mate Steven Livesey for his moral support, patience, and encouragement. Over the course of this project, I encountered several sticking places, arguments that were difficult to work out and to then clearly articulate. Steve kept me on a steady course and encouraged me to press on. Those many walks to and from the library in Saint-Omer with him by my side gave me a chance to work through my ideas and kept me sane. This book is dedicated to him.

Abbreviations

Apol.	Plato, *Apologia*
Att.	Cicero, *Epistulae ad Atticum*
BAGD	Baur, Arndt, Gingrich and Danker. *Greek-English Lexicon of the New Testament and Other Early Christian Literature*
BDB	Brown-Driver-Briggs. *A Hebrew and English Lexicon of the Old Testament*
Cic.	Plutarch, *Cicero*
CIG	*Corpus Inscriptionum Graecarum*
Cod. Just.	Codex Justinianus
1, 2 Cor	1, 2 Corinthians
De. or.	*De oratore*
Deut	Deuteronomy
Eloc.	Demetrius, *De elocutione*
Ep.	Isocrates, *Epistulae*
Exod	Exodus
Fam.	Cicero, *Epistulae ad familiares*
Gal	Galatians
Gen	Genesis
Hist.	Herodotus, *Historiae*
hyp.	Libanius, *Hypotheses to the Orations of Demosthenes*
Inst.	Quintilian, *Institutio oratoria*
Isa	Isaiah
Jas	James
JBL	Journal of Biblical Literature
Jer	Jeremiah
Judg	Judges
LSJ	Liddell, Scott and Jones. *A Greek-English Lexicon*
LXX	Septuagint
Magn.	Ignatius, *To the Magnesians*
Mic	Micah
MT	Masoretic Text
OED	Oxford English Dictionary

Or.	Oration
Phil	Philippians
Phil.	*Philippic*
Phld.	Ignatius, *To the Philadelphians*
Rhet. ad Her.	Quintilian, *Rhetorica ad Herennium*
Rom	Romans
1 Sam	1 Samuel
Sir	Sirach
Tab. Defix. Aud.	*Defixionum Tabellae quotquot innotuerunt*
TDNT	*Theological Dictionary of the New Testament*
TLL	*Thesaurus linguae latinae*
Zech	Zechariah

Bible Versions

ASV	American Standard Version
NAB	New American Bible
NIV	New International Version
NRSV	New Revised Standard Version
SV	Scholar's Version

Introduction

> The "crisis," of course, is not simply produced by external circumstances, but it is, in part, brought into being by [the authors'] portrayal of certain events as threatening and calling for immediate response. (Bailey, *Philippics 1–6*, xxxi)

Projects often start with a question and this one is no exception. My question is why Paul (fl. mid-first century CE) rails against the circumcision of the gentiles/nations[1]/non-Jews, as they seek to join the Jesus community. As is evident in Paul's letter to the Galatians, the Galatian non-Jewish males Paul addressees anticipated, or perhaps were already undergoing, the procedure of circumcision (Gal 5:2–12), a basic Jewish rite often considered the necessary final step before joining the people of Israel.[2] Why would Paul, himself a Jew, be against their doing so?

My question—not unique in Pauline scholarship[3]—becomes acute now because of recent advances in Pauline scholarship.[4] In the more recent scholarship, Paul is widely understood to have been a lifelong Jew.[5] In this scholarship, he retains his allegiance to the God of Israel. Pamela Eisenbaum, for example, calls Paul a "radical Jewish monotheist."[6] Paul's extant writings confirm his fundamentally Jewish orientation. In Galatians and elsewhere, Paul relies heavily on Hebrew writings, albeit in their Greek form (LXX). Indeed, he is so thoroughly steeped in these writings that they are his language and greatly influence his worldview. Furthermore, the situation of the letter as it is generally understood in the more recent scholarship runs as follows: in Galatians the Jew Paul addresses non-Jewish Galatians and seeks to convince them of their already existing status as people of the God of Israel, without the prerequisites of circumcision (Gal 2:3, 9; 5:2–3) and works of Torah (Gal 2:15–16; 3:2–5; 5:4, 18).[7] The recent scholarship calls attention to and makes more acute a tension between

1

Paul's Jewish orientation / his status as a lifelong Jew and his mission.

In the traditional interpretation, Paul's rejection of circumcision and other Jewish rituals (works of Torah) is not a problem. By contrast, it serves productively to define Paul and his mission. According to the tradition, Paul is known as someone who claims to be no longer a Jew and to no longer practice Jewish rites. Indeed, Paul becomes a Christian. The Augustinian-Lutheran reading of Paul is the basis of the traditional view. At risk of over-simplification, the Augustinian-Lutheran understanding of Paul concerns itself primarily with the question of how persons are saved. Paul's primary concern is salvation and he comes to believe that God saves all persons not by works of law (Torah), but by faith alone, faith in Jesus Christ. Paul rejects works of Torah and circumcision because they are inadequate as a means of salvation. This perspective draws hard and fast distinctions between Christianity, identified as a religion of grace and faith, and Judaism, interpreted as a religion of non-grace-producing works. In this interpretation, Christianity very much supersedes Judaism and it is often Paul's statements against works of Torah and circumcision that are drawn upon to warrant such an understanding.

The more recent scholarship began in earnest in the last quarter of the twentieth century. Precipitated in large part by *Ha-Shoah* (the Jewish holocaust), two leading New Testament scholars, Krister Stendahl (1921–2008), Dean of Harvard Divinity School and then Lutheran Bishop of Stockholm, and E. P. Sanders (1937–) took up a much-needed reassessment of Paul and of ancient Judaism, and their groundbreaking work founds the recent and newer perspectives on Paul. Stendahl and Sanders challenge the basic underlying assumptions of the Augustinian-Lutheran view of Paul, and thereby significantly weaken its viability. Stendahl convincingly demonstrated that Paul[8] did not convert from Judaism to another faith, as the Augustinian-Lutheran perspective maintained, but that he instead remained a lifelong Jew.[9] Stendahl's interpretation is based on the simple observation that Paul in Galatians does not speak of conversion but instead of being called by the

God of Israel on a mission (Gal 1:15). Indeed, recent advances in the study of early Christianity confirm Stendahl's assessment. Paul could not have converted to Christianity, as no such entity or concept existed in the first century.[10] Furthermore, through his methodical analysis of Paul's writings, Stendahl convincingly argued that the notion of justification by faith or justification by faith alone, as was forcibly advanced in the highly influential exegesis of the sixteenth-century German Reformer Martin Luther (1483–1546), is anachronistic to the first-century Paul and instead reflects *later*—namely, Luther's own—theological concerns.[11]

As an Augustinian monk, Luther believed that humans were inherently sinful. Human sin, understood as "Original Sin," made it impossible for anyone to perform any good deeds or works through their own power. Good works were possible only by means of God's grace. Thus, when in Galatians Paul wrote that "a person is justified not by works of law but through faith in Jesus Christ" (NRSV, Gal 2:16), Luther interpreted Paul to say that works of law (Torah) are ineffective as a means of salvation because intrinsic human sinfulness makes the accomplishment of good works impossible. Moreover, those obedient to Torah sinned because in working to merit grace through Torah observance, they relied not on God but on their own human (and sinful) efforts. According to Luther, the Torah functioned in a positive sense only in so far as it made apparent human sinfulness and the subsequent need for salvation *outside of it, through Christ*. Commenting on Gal 2:16, Luther writes:

> Now the true meaning of Christianity is this: that a man [sic] first acknowledge, through the Law, that he is a sinner, for whom it is impossible to perform any good work. For the Law says: "You are an evil tree. Therefore everything you think, speak, or do is opposed to God. Hence you cannot deserve grace by your works. But if you try and do so, you make the bad even worse; for since you are an evil tree, you cannot produce anything except evil fruit, that is sins. 'For whatever does not proceed from faith is sin' (Rom 14:23)." Trying to

merit grace by preceding works, therefore, is trying to placate God with sins, which is nothing but heaping sins upon sins, making fun of God, and provoking His wrath.[12]

Stendhal rightly perceived that justification by faith alone as understood by Martin Luther was based on the assumption that Paul was searching for forgiveness and for a gracious God (i.e., salvation), that which he (Paul) was unable to find within traditional Judaism. Faith in Christ fulfilled a deep need that could not be satisfied in any other way. Yet as Stendahl notes, *it was not Paul but rather Luther himself who was in need of forgiveness and God's grace.* Burdened by the demands imposed on Augustinian monks—acute and ever-present reminders of the overriding need for penance and repentance from sins, Luther, not Paul, was searching for a God who could and would release him from his own burdensome and guilt-ridden works-oriented *Augustinian* system.[13] Based on his analysis of Paul's letters, Stendahl demonstrates that Paul did not suffer from angst or guilt, nor did he exhibit a need for forgiveness. Paul showed no signs whatsoever of struggling to find a forgiving and gracious God. Stendhal writes:

> Contrast Paul, a very happy and successful Jew, one who can, even when he thinks about it from his Christian perspective, say in his Epistle to the Philippians ". . . as to the righteousness under the law (I was) blameless" (Phil 3:6). That *is* what he says. He experiences no troubles, no problems, no qualms of conscience, and no feelings of shortcomings. He is a star pupil, the student to get the thousand dollar graduate scholarship in Gamaliel's Seminary, if we can trust Acts (22:3)—both for character and for achievements of scholarship—a very happy Jew. Nowhere in Paul's writings is there any indication that he had any difficulties in fulfilling what he as a Jew understood to be the requirements of the law.[14]

While Stendahl significantly destabilized the Augustinian-Lutheran interpretation of Paul, Sanders overturned its understanding of ancient Judaism. Sanders set out to determine whether or not "works-righteousness," the sense in which ancient Jews obeyed Torah for the purpose of becoming righteous and to merit God's grace and thereby become "saved," exemplified ancient Judaism. In his 1977 work titled *Paul and Palestinian Judaism: A Comparison of Patterns of Religion*, Sanders surveyed ancient Jewish texts dating from 200 BCE to 200 CE, works of the Dead Sea Scrolls, Jewish Apocrypha and Pseudepigrapha, and the Tannaitic litera-ture, and persuasively demonstrated that Palestinian Judaism was not at base legalistic. Taken together, the texts support the view that while obedience to Torah is essential, ancient Jews obeyed its commandments not in order to earn salvation but instead to secure their place within the covenant. According to Sanders, Jews considered Torah as a means of "getting in and staying in" the covenantal relationship forged with God.[15] Sanders coined the term "covenantal nomism" to describe Israel's relationship to God. He explains:

> Covenantal nomism is the view that one's place in God's plan is established on the basis of the covenant and that the covenant requires as the proper response of man his [sic] obedience to its commandments, while providing means of atonement for transgression.[16]

In ancient Judaism, God grants grace freely; persons did not work to earn it. The Torah provides the means of atonement and for-giveness. While God punishes evildoers, God's mercy on the righ-teous outweighs God's punishment of transgressions.[17]

While Stendahl, with his reanalysis of Paul, and Sanders, with his research on ancient Judaism, rendered the basis of the Augustinian-Lutheran position indefensible, neither scholar pro-vided a satisfactory explanation for why Paul counseled against circumcision and Torah adoption. Moreover, Stendahl's and Sanders's refutation of the Augustinian-Lutheran perspective on Paul did not entail a consequent denial of the importance of faith in Christ in Paul's theology, only the rejection of its grim and dis-torted understanding of ancient Judaism. Indeed, in their own evaluations of Paul, they too draw sharp distinctions between faith in Jesus and Torah and ironically both continue to express the notion that Paul is centrally concerned with the question of salvation. Stendahl reasoned that Paul understood that Christ opened a new path for salvation "equally open to Jews and Gentiles,"[18] yet one that is not based on Torah.[19] According to him, Paul found that the Torah, even with its provisions for forgiveness and grace, was no longer a valid alternative for salvation for gentiles and Jews alike.[20] Sanders, in his 1983 monograph *Paul, the Law, and the Jewish People*, concludes that according to Paul salvation is only possible through Jesus Christ and not through Torah.[21] Paul understood that God never intended to make gentiles righteous through the Torah.[22] Thus, and especially at the early stages of this newer understanding of Paul, remnants of the traditional view of Paul remain.

At present, Mark Nanos is one of the most influential Pauline scholars among those adopting the new view of Paul. Nanos, rightly so, keeps a Jewish Paul at the forefront of all of his work.[23] According to him, Paul was not only a Jew but continued with Jewish practices throughout his life.[24] Nanos resolves the tension between the Jewish Paul and his mission by adopting what can be termed a "universalist" solution. Paul was against non-Jews becoming circumcised because such an action limits God's domain to one group, to Jews. Nanos comments that God's oneness is compromised unless the one God is God of both Jews and non-Jews.[25] A universalistic approach to Paul, however, is unsatisfactory not just because of its anti-Jewish roots,[26] but because Paul does not evince dissatisfaction over the issue of Jewish particularity. Not only is that specific concern not evident in his writings, but Paul is also not systematic in his approach.[27] All of his letters, with the possible exception of Romans, address local and particular issues concerning groups of Jesus followers.

Another highly influential approach[28] to Paul's rejection of circumcision is that of Pamela Eisenbaum. Influenced by the earlier work of Paula Fredriksen, Eisenbaum explains that the Jewish Paul faced the question of how to bring the nations, non-Jews, to the God of Israel as history draws to a close.[29] Prophetic texts of the Hebrew scriptures, such as Isa 2:2–4, Mic 4:1–3, and Zech 8:21–23, guide and influence Paul to believe that in the last days all nations will come to the God of Israel as nations, as non-Jews.[30]

For Eisenbaum, as too for Nanos, Paul's strong stance against circumcision and works of Torah pertains exclusively to non-Jews. According to Eisenbaum, Paul's position can be explained by the fact that he is following these earlier prophetic visions. In this view, Paul aligns a situation on the ground, so to speak, with prophetic dictates. This scenario, however, does not accord well with Paul's strong rhetoric against circumcision and works of Torah. It flounders too, because Paul is not bound by the specific demands of Hebrew scriptures, as I indicate in the chapters that follow, but instead freely manipulates them to serve his own purposes. Rather than evince fidelity to scriptures, Paul instead charts his own course.

To come at this issue of Paul and his stance on circumcision, I do not take up directly and exclusively the subject of the ancient rite of circumcision—as this is an issue I have dealt with in an earlier work.[31] Rather, in the chapters that follow, I explore Paul through the lens of his rhetoric. Paul in Galatians adopts a highly rhetorical style with a strong theatrical emphasis. Thus the rhetorical[32] character of his arguments should be the lens[33] through which we view Paul's rejection of circumcision and Torah observance for non-Jews.

In Galatians, in which the topic of the circumcision of non-Jewish males surfaces, Paul self-presents as heated, angry, and as highly insistent regarding his own views. His arguments appear to be forced: when closely analyzed, many make little logical sense. While he raises the issue of circumcision elsewhere in his writings,[34] the forcefulness by which he forbids this practice occurs only in his letter to the Galatians, affirming that the situation and context condition his arguments. The sheer quantity and diversity of his arguments against circumcision and Torah adoption undermine their individual significance, as they bombard the hearer/reader in a seemingly endless and disconnected stream. The large number of diverse arguments against Torah and circumcision suggest that Paul is trying by whatever means necessary to push his own agenda forward,[35] and that something other than Torah and circumcision is at issue. In addition, there is the looming presence of Paul's opponents[36] or competitors, those

urging the Galatians to become circumcised. Paul addresses his
competitors with scathing rebuke (Gal 5:12). He not only provokes
his audience's emotions against them but also deploys and creates
numerous binary oppositions, which function to create a firm distinction between himself and his views and his opponents and
theirs.[37] By means of his many created oppositions, he establishes
a choice between two mutually exclusive alternatives: his views
and his good news or the views of his opponents/competitors.[38]
Shaye Cohen[39] aptly highlights the important component of competition in Paul's statements regarding Torah. Cohen remarks:

> Paul's negative assessment of the Torah and those who fol-
> low it is striking: he insists that the Torah does not come from
> God (3.19–20); no longer has a salvific role, and perhaps never
> did (3.21–22); and its observance is akin to the worship of the
> Greek gods (4.9–10). He furthermore claims that the Jewish
> people are neither the true seed of Abraham (3.16) nor the
> Israel of God (6.16). . . .
>
> Competition prompted this extreme negativity toward the
> Torah and Jewish distinctiveness.[40]

In agreement with Cohen, I argue that the issue of Paul's opponents[41] is central to his arguments on the issues of circumcision
and works of Torah. To make my position clear, while in Galatians
Paul argues vigorously against circumcision and Torah adoption
for non-Jews, he is not anti-Jewish nor is he against Torah per se.

In the chapters that follow, I employ an interpretive model defined by the classicist Cecil Wooten[42] and called the "rhetoric of crisis"[43] as a heuristic tool to analyze Paul's arguments in
Galatians. The rhetoric-of-crisis lens makes apparent the extent
and shape of Paul's rhetoric. More importantly for my purposes,
the rhetoric-of-crisis model makes possible the uncovering of a
viable explanation—and one that can be confirmed by the text itself—for Paul's stance regarding circumcision and Torah adoption
of non-Jews. My analysis involves a comparison among structural
units within the speeches of Demosthenes and Cicero and Paul's

letter to the Galatians. A comparison facilitates an understanding of the model's functioning and provides the necessary basis for viewing Galatians from this perspective.

Wooten coined the term "rhetoric of crisis" in the course of his analysis of the Philippic orations of Demosthenes (384–322 BCE) and Marcus Tullius Cicero (106–43 BCE). The rhetoric of crisis brings a present situation into a state of urgent concern by the way in which it portrays events.[44] It exaggerates an external situation, so as to make it appear threatening, as one that demands an immediate response from the audience/hearers. Historical accuracy and truth are secondary to the desired end, that is, the author's own position. Authors aim to gain support for their own perspective over that of their rivals by developing a highly favorable self-image. Through the use of "exaggeration, illustrative comparisons and graphic descriptions,"[45] the rhetoric-of-crisis authors arouse their audiences' emotions often for the purpose of evoking moral outrage. They offer clear-cut alternatives to their crisis—developing a contest between good and evil[46]—with no middle ground. In so doing, they force a choice between two options or points of view, their own "correct" position, or the "incorrect" one of their opponents. Political rivals are at the forefront of the rhetoric-of-crisis model.[47] Indeed, each leg of the model involves authorial engagement with rivals. In discussing the rhetoric of crisis more generally, Wooten relates the following:

> To him [the orator] the contest is black and white, the struggle of good against evil, and what is at stake, he argues, is the very existence of the civilization he is defending. He tries to convince the members of his audience that the history of their state has reached a fundamental crisis in which its very existence as they know it and everything that it represents are in danger. He then presents the situation as a clear choice between mutually exclusive and fundamentally opposed systems by means of what may be called the disjunctive mode. This determines many aspects of the orator's style–sentence patterns, arguments, presentation of character, structure of speeches, and images.[48]

Generally[49] speaking, the rhetoric of crisis employs four dominant means of persuasion: 1) the creation of a sense of urgency, 2) the author's own moral character or ethos, 3) the use of emotive language or pathos, and 4) the employment of disjunctive argumentation. Authors employ the rhetoric of crisis to encourage swift action toward a specific position (their own) and the avoidance of an alternative one. The Philippic orations of Demosthenes and Cicero exemplify this rhetoric, and also, as I will argue, so too does Paul in his letter to the Galatians.

Demosthenes[50] delivered his *First Philippic* in 351 BCE,[51] and this speech also marked the first time he opened a political debate.[52] The name "Philippic" refers to Philip II of Macedon (382–336 BCE). There are nine extant speeches by Demosthenes[53] against Philip, yet not all of them bear the name "Philippic" in their title.[54] Philip was the father of Alexander the Great (356–323 BCE) and ruled Macedon from 359–336 BCE. During his reign, he greatly expanded Macedonian territory and built the nation into the leading Hellenic power.[55] With regard to the historical background of Demosthenes' Philippic orations, the situation is as follows. Philip had been at war with Athens since he seized the former Athenian territory of Amphipolis in 357. His more recent incursions around Greece made it appear by some as though the situation for Athens was becoming dire. In 352, Philip was victorious at the battle of the Crocus Field and continued moving southwards in the direction of the pass of Thermopylae to Athens' north.[56] During 352–351, Philip waged a military campaign in Thrace to the northeast of Macedon.[57] These aggressive military actions brought Philip and his Macedonian forces very close to Chersonese and the Hellespont. The latter was a vital sea route between the Aegean and the Black Sea and was Athens' main route for imported food supplies.[58]

In his Philippic orations, Demosthenes, unlike his political opponents, took a hardline approach against Philip in an attempt to convince his Athenian audience to engage in a full-scale attack against him.[59] Wooten writes, "From 351 right through to the

Macedonian king's death in 336 Demosthenes used his oratorical and diplomatic skills in support of his unrelenting belief that Philip was a dire threat to the freedom of the Greek world in general and of the Athenians in particular and should be resisted." The position Demosthenes advanced, however, was largely based on his self-interest; he was preserving a system and a way of life in which he could best flourish. Wooten remarks, "Having created for himself a major role both as a courtroom advocate and as a politician in the democratic city-state that he so admired, Demosthenes was determined to defend at all costs the system in which he could best function, that is, in which he could use oratory to his greatest advantage." E. Badian goes further than Wooten and maintains that Demosthenes simply sought to be a leader.[60] Defending his own perspective meant that he was always at odds with his political foes in the Athenian senate.[61] Indeed, throughout his Philippic orations, Demosthenes is critical of those Athenians—his political rivals—who believe that Philip could be trusted and who seek to curry Philip's favor. While there is a looming but still somewhat distant military threat from Philip, Demosthenes employs this situation for his own political advantages, to safeguard his way of life, and to further his political career.

Like Demosthenes, Cicero too desired to preserve a way of life to which he had become accustomed.[62] He speaks of preserving the Republic and its "liberties," those he feels have been compromised first by the tyrannical rule of Julius Caesar (100–44 BCE) and now with his immediate successor Mark Antony (83–30 BCE).[63] Like Demosthenes, Cicero wished to make a name for himself,[64] and he too used oratory to further that goal. Indeed, Cicero closely studied the orations of Demosthenes and desired to emulate him. Gesine Manuwald[65] remarks that Cicero tried to prove himself the "Roman Demosthenes."[66] By intentionally naming his own speeches against his political foe Antony[67] "Philippics" after Demosthenes, he not only signaled his debt and connection to Demosthenes, but also helped to facilitate a comparison between Philip and Antony.[68]

Cicero's Philippic orations consist of fourteen speeches[69] and date from September 44 to April 43 BCE. His *Third Philippic* (December 44 BCE) is his first-delivered speech of this series and marks the official and public start of his campaign against Mark Antony. Manuwald comments, "Historically, the *Philippics* are part of the struggle for power in Rome after Caesar's assassination; in this process Cicero too was involved using all his rhetorical powers to support his cause."[70] Cicero makes the declaration of Antony as a public enemy (*hostis*)[71] the goal of all his Philippic[72] orations. "Cicero's whole campaign is based on one fundamental disjunctive pair: 'either Antonius is consul and his opponents must be punished, or Antonius is a public enemy and his opponents have acted rightly.'"[73]

Mark Antony was, like Cicero, a Roman politician at consular rank. In the immediate aftermath of Julius Caesar's assassination (15 March 44 BCE, the Ides of March), it was Antony who forged a compromise position within the Roman senate and assured the continuing legality of Caesar's legislation. It was Antony too who assumed leadership of the Republic.[74] Cicero, however, distrusted Antony.[75] Shortly after the Ides of March, Cicero wrote to his friend Atticus, "We have killed the tyrant, but tyranny persists."[76] According to Cicero, tyranny continued in the person of Antony.[77]

Henriette van der Blom explains that there was a deep philosophical and political divide between Cicero and Antony.[78] Antony was primarily a soldier, while Cicero was a writer and thinker.[79] Differences in their social status also play a role in their rivalry: Antony was born into nobility and Caesar's patronage enabled his rise to power.[80] Cicero, on the other hand, was always considered a "new man,"[81] and as such, he had to work hard to prove his worth.[82] Thus, when Cicero discovered Demosthenes' speeches against Philip, he found in them not only a way to make a name for himself, but also a model by which he could wage an effective campaign against his archrival Antony. In his fight against Antony, Cicero threw his support behind the then-young (nineteen year-old) Octavian (Augustus), not because he was enamored with the latter, but on account of his opposition to the former.[83]

Cicero eventually succeeded in having Antony declared a public enemy. But seven months later (November 43), Octavian formed a ruling coalition of the Republic with Antony and Marcus Aemelius Lepidus, known as the Second Triumvirate (Nov. 43–Dec. 33 BCE). Antony's return to power cost Cicero his life, as Antony's men hunted down and killed Cicero.[84]

While Paul's situation is different from both of these orators, the force with which he advances his views and his control over his rhetoric is nevertheless as strong in Galatians as it is in the writings of these earlier orators. Although Paul does not explicitly identify his opponents, he constructs his position as though they were present and out of a sense of animosity for them, creating and developing two separate and opposing positions. He makes sharp distinctions that did not otherwise exist between himself and his opponents. As is the case with Demosthenes and Cicero, Paul fashions scenarios and stretches the truth. He pulls from his source texts (LXX) with precision and high selectivity, and then makes modifications to his sources to fit his situation. For Paul, as for Demosthenes and Cicero, the end justifies the means.[85] The commonalities of rhetorical techniques, as seen in the rhetoric-of-crisis model, across all three authors suggest a shared underlying motivation for its use. As mentioned above, this method of analysis brings to light the extent to which Paul in Galatians is rhetorical and provides an intelligible method of analysis—that comports with the text and the compositional styles of ancient authors—for resolving the issue of why he counsels against the circumcision of non-Jews.

For clarification, I do not argue that Paul intentionally patterned his letter to the Galatians after either Demosthenes' or Cicero's Philippic orations, nor am I insisting that Paul's letter to the Galatians is a deliberative speech.[86] In making a comparison across compositional units of these three authors, I focus not on the overall species of the speeches or letter, but instead on the individual rhetorical techniques within the units. There is also, as I indicate, considerable flexibility in the ways in which these authors employ the model. Furthermore, my arguments do not rest

on the assumption that Paul was formally schooled in the art of
rhetoric, yet a growing body of scholarship[87] suggests that Paul
would not necessarily have needed such an education in order
to effectively employ rhetorical tropes. Finally, I often follow and
depend upon the details (the fine matter) in Hans Dieter Betz's
rhetorical commentary on Galatians. Yet when it comes to issues
of Paul's overall purpose or even on how best to distinguish between logical units, I often deviate from him.[88]

Individual chapters are dedicated to one of the four main components of the rhetoric-of-crisis model. Each of the four central chapters compares the particular rhetorical devices of the component
across the compositions of all three authors.

In chapter one I indicate how Demosthenes, Cicero, and Paul
develop a situation into a crisis. Short clipped phrases, rhetorical questions, and the repetition of key words and expressions
typify urgency. Audience rebuke and expressions and references
to time are other methods common to all three authors in their
development of urgency. The goal of urgency is to make a present
situation pressing. The techniques employed serve to bring the
situation to the attention of audiences and force a decision regarding the situation as it is being developed. Demosthenes forcefully
urges his audience to take immediate action against Philip (*First
Phil.* 10). A sense of urgency is particularly apparent in the work
of Cicero's *Third Philippic* given to persuade the Roman senate to
act against Antony. Nearly every phrase of the *exordium* (opening
section) of the speech contains a reference to time, a technique
that renders the present pregnant with significance. Short phrases
that coax action, the repetition of key words and expressions,
words that denote time and audience rebuke typify three central
passages (Gal 1:6–9; 3:1–5; 5:2–6) of Paul's letter to the Galatians, a
letter intended to coax the audience to Paul's side and away from
his opponents.

Chapter two takes up the motif of positive self-fashioning or
argumentation from moral character (ethos). An accomplished
rhetorical style is one way in which each author impresses his
audience. Audience castigation, feigned openness, foresight, and

exaggeration are other methods by which these authors promote a lofty and authoritative sense of self. In his *Second Philippic*, Demosthenes, for example, impresses his audience by his sophisticated style, exhibiting firm control over his discourse. Yet firm control over the discourse—especially with regard to what each author chooses to reveal about himself—is evident in the compositions of all three authors. All three authors exaggerate their prestige. Cicero intentionally conflates a public demonstration given in his honor with a triumph reserved for military heroes. From the first words of his letter to the Galatians, Paul establishes a lofty and highly authoritative ethos. He lets it be known that two divine beings have commissioned his apostleship. His angry tone, observable as early as the salutation, contributes to his sense of authority. As in the other legs of the model, opponents play a role in each authors' self-characterizations.

Chapter three regards the various ways in which Demosthenes, Cicero, and Paul provoke audience emotions against their opponents. Emotive language can take various forms: direct reprimand, repetition, irony, and sarcasm, and graphic images and/or highly descriptive language. Largely through the abundant use of place names, Demosthenes spreads an atmosphere of fear of Philip. Demosthenes also characterizes Philip as a non-human, a trope Cicero takes up and employs to characterize his enemy Antony. In his *Third Philippic*, Cicero employs graphic imagery to make Antony's tyrannical nature all the more vivid. Through his use of exclamatory language and repetition, that is itself emotionally evocative, Paul curses his opponents, casting them into a malevolent realm. And through an extended narrative or allegory, he draws a rather lurid connection between those of Torah, representative of his opponents, and sexual relations with a slave woman.

Chapter four deals with what can easily be considered the heart of the rhetoric of crisis, namely, the use of disjunctive argumentation. Through the use and creation of multiple oppositional pairs, Demosthenes, Cicero, and Paul offer their audiences clearcut and mutually exclusive alternatives. They create what Wooten refers to as "simplicity of decision-making."[89] All three authors employ the antithetical pair slavery/freedom, commonly used in

ancient polemics,[90] yet each author employs this common polemical opposition to designate something different and unique to his
own situation. Each author also creates his own unique oppositional pairs—such as, trust/mistrust, many/one, public enemy/
respected councilman, works of Torah/trust, and flesh/promise—
those that again fit his own particular circumstances. Paul in particular makes abundant use of binary oppositions, most of which
are self-developed.

This work tells three stories, those of Demosthenes, Cicero,
and Paul. Beginning with the earliest author (Demosthenes), each
chapter moves in a chronological fashion. For each component
of the model, Demosthenes and Cicero point the way for understanding Paul in his letter to the Galatians as operating similarly,
as employing comparable rhetorical tools in order to bring about
the objective of the component. While the individual life narratives and external situations of each author differ one from the
other, their like method of argumentation indicates their similarities of purpose.

1

Creating a Sense of Urgency

La langue est la matière qui s'offre à l'écrivain,
comme le marbre au sculpteur; mots et tours
existent en dehors de lui, indépendamment de lui,
ce n'est pas en eux qu'il faut chercher la trace de
sa personnalité. Le style est au contraire la marque
qu'il imprime à cette matière impersonnelle,
l'intégrant en quelque sorte à lui-même.
(Ronnet, *Étude sur le style de Démosthène*, 9)

Language is the material that offers itself to the
writer, as marble to a sculptor; words and towers
exist outside of him, independently of him, it is not in
them that one must look for a trace of his personality.
By contrast, the style is the mark that he imprints
onto this impersonal material, incorporating it in a
way to himself. (Translation is my own.)

Explicit and implicit references to a need to act immediately are
what one would expect to find in the rhetoric of crisis, as this rhetoric aims to urge hearers to act quickly and without hesitation.
Urgency does not exist in and of itself, instead authors engineer
it; they bring it about. Through rhetorical techniques that promote
urgency—the sense in which the present situation is pressing
and demands immediate attention and action—authors utilize a
situation at hand that is not necessarily pressing and fashion it

into one of immediate concern. Urgency aims to unsettle an audience.

In oral discourse urgency is more apparent—as auditors readily ascertain and react to a raised voice and rapid speech—than in written compositions. Often because of how the linear stream of words appears on a written page, these same characteristics, although implied and even signaled, are often overlooked. This chapter aims to make urgency apparent in the compositions of Demosthenes, Cicero, and Paul.

Urgency is more an art than a science. Certain rhetorical techniques bring about a sense of urgency, such as short clipped phrases, rhetorical questions, and the repetition of key words and expressions, but these techniques are not set in stone.[1] While Demosthenes, Cicero, and Paul all employ these techniques, they also use other rhetorical devices—those that suit their own purposes and rhetorical situations—to bring about urgency, as indicated in the sample units below. Short clipped phrases move the discourse along. They employ words that denote time in a targeted fashion to bring an audience's attention around to the present situation. They engage in audience rebuke—often through rhetorical questions—to push their audiences to immediate action. Demosthenes' audience criticisms are often scathing and sarcastic.

While repetition is very important in the development of urgency, it is by no means unique to it. Repetition contributes to every component of the rhetoric-of-crisis model. Ancient authors relied heavily on repetition because in oral cultures hearers did not have the luxury of contemplating the semantic meaning of words and phrases.[2] To signal importance, ancient authors relied upon repetition. John Foley remarks that repetition recreates meaning.[3] In their monograph *Sound Mapping the New Testament*, Margaret Lee and Bernard Scott emphasize that repetition serves to structure how an audience understands oral discourse.[4]

While this chapter and the three that follow discuss the basic components of the rhetoric of crisis—urgency, authorial self-fashioning, emotive language, and disjunctive mode, these categories are not hermetically sealed. There is instead an intermingling and overlapping of rhetorical tropes among the four components of the model. For example, tropes that elicit emotions also play a role in the promotion of urgency as well as in the creation of a strong self-image.

Urgency in Demosthenes

Demosthenes' *First Philippic* not only marks his debut into the political arena but also signals a turning point in Greek oratory. As George Kennedy observes, with Demosthenes' *First Philippic* "a new vigor appears which is unlike anything in Greek oratory since the fifth century and which involves a return to focus on a single form of argument."[5] The intense focus functions to not just present arguments that suggest the best course of action for the Athenian senators but also to present them as necessary and urgent. Demosthenes provides his audience with no alternatives but that of taking action. The tone he adopts in his *First Philippic* is emotional, brought about through his "highly patterned" language and his use of figurative speech. He often employs rhetorical questions and *hyperbaton* (the separation of words and phrases that are normally found together). Instances of the latter—whose purpose is to emphasize one or both of the elements being separated—occur in much higher percentage in his *First Philippic* than in his earlier speeches and exist in a more exaggerated or "violent" form.[6] That is, instead of a single word separating an adjective from its noun, one finds the insertion of several words between elements that would naturally go together. Finally, his *First Philippic* includes three instances of dramatic dialogue (1.10–11, 25–26, 44). These dialogues serve to provide a sense of "spontaneity, immediacy, and urgency."[7]

A sense of urgency is so apparent in Demosthenes' Philippic-cycle speeches that Donat Taddeo gave that technique the name "καιρός" ("the right moment").[8] According to Taddeo, καιρός denotes "an accumulation of highly variable incidents [that] produce a certain moment or occasion which is limited in time; one must take advantage of this opportunity quickly, before the limited time expires."[9] Although the term καιρός is not present in the passages that follow, the elements that constitute it are.

And as we will see in the following section, Cicero borrowed on Demosthenes' καιρός theme in his Philippic orations against Antony.[10]

An Authoritative Debut before the Senate

At first glance, the *proemium* (introduction or preamble) of Demosthenes' *First Philippic* appears to be rather gentle, that is, demanding little of his audience. Yet, as indicated below, many elements of urgency are present within it.

As a rule, Demosthenes' preambles form a strategic part of his speeches. Harvey Yunis remarks that in nearly every speech's opening, Demosthenes seeks to establish his "authority as an adviser and confirms the rectitude of his motives."[11] Demosthenes promotes himself at the expense of his opposing speakers and presents the situation at hand as being "vitally important."[12] As with many of his speeches, and the *Philippics* are no exception to this rule, Demosthenes' main strategy is to exaggerate and strengthen the danger Philip poses to Athens.[13]

As mentioned, this speech marks a turning point in Demosthenes' career: he dares for the first time to open the debate, a task normally assumed by elder statesmen.[14] Not only does he begin the debate, but he also does so with urgency and with an implied criticism of his opponents, those who, although they have been debating what to do about Philip's recent incursions around Athens, have not put forward any satisfactory proposals (ῥηθέντων) for stopping them.

From his opening line, Demosthenes creates a sense in which the present time demands attention. He makes the point that he can wait no longer. The speech's opening structure, however, is complex—as it includes embedded subordinating clauses—giving the impression of sluggishness rather than urgency. Yet the complexity of the sentence structure, as Wooten notes, would have functioned to hold the audience's attention and not detract from the situation at hand.[15] If his oratory had been too simple, he would have alienated the intelligent, but if too complex, his oration would have been lost on the ordinary hearer. Complexity signals, even to a large and seemingly unsophisticated audience, that Demosthenes was dealing with something important, and that alone peaks audience interest.[16] The first unit of the speech's opening follows.

1.1a Εἰ μὲν περὶ καινοῦ τινος πράγματος προυτίθετο, ὦ ἄνδρες Ἀθηναῖοι, λέγειν, ἐπισχὼν ἂν ἕως οἱ πλεῖστοι τῶν εἰωθότων γνώμην ἀπεφήναντο,
    1.1b εἰ μὲν ἤρεσκέ τί μοι τῶν ὑπὸ τούτων ῥηθέντων,
        1.1c ἡσυχίαν ἂν ἦγον,
    1.1d εἰ δὲ μή,
        1.1e τότ᾽ ἂν αὐτὸς ἐπειρώμην ἃ γιγνώσκω λέγειν.
1.1f ἐπειδὴ δ᾽ ὑπὲρ ὧν πολλάκις εἰρήκασιν οὗτοι πρότερον συμβαίνει καὶ νυνὶ σκοπεῖν,
    1.1g ἡγοῦμαι καὶ πρῶτος ἀναστὰς εἰκότως ἂν συγγνώμης τυγχάνειν.[17]
1.1h εἰ γὰρ ἐκ τοῦ παρεληλυθότος χρόνου τὰ δέονθ᾽ οὗτοι συνεβούλευσαν, οὐδὲν ἂν ὑμᾶς νῦν ἔδει βουλεύεσθαι.[18]

1.1a If some new matter were the topic of discussion, men of Athens, I would have waited until most of the regular speakers had given their opinion,
    1.1b and if anything they said pleased me,
        1.1c I would have kept quiet;
    1.1d if it did not,
        1.1e would I have ventured to state my own opinion.
1.1f But since we are dealing with matters that these men have often addressed on previous occasions,
    1.1g I think that I can reasonably be forgiven for standing up to speak first.
1.1h For if they had given the necessary advice in the past, there would be no need for you to be deliberating now.[19]

To gain his audience's attention, Demosthenes creates a sense of anticipation and suspense for his issue. He builds suspense by first telling his audience he is taking to the floor to speak (1.1a), but then by delaying what it is that he will speak about. His grammar bears this out: he leads off with a Greek particle μέν ("on the one hand"; 1.1a), and does not provide the anticipated δέ ("on the other"; marked in bold-faced type above) until 1.1f.[20] Prior to resolving the first μέν, he builds yet another layer of suspense and anticipation by inserting two more phrases with yet another (or internal) μέν and δέ pair (1.1b and 1.1d). Moreover, even when he resolves his issue grammatically (1.1f), suspense remains, as Demosthenes does not make explicit the reason why he addresses them. His audience only knows that prior proposals have failed.

Demosthenes deploys common signs of urgency. His phrases are often short, simple, and direct (1.1b, 1c, 1d, 1e) and thereby create movement by their punctuated or staccato[21] effect. No clashes of vowels or *hiatuses* (dissonance) stop the flow of the delivery.[22] Furthermore, he makes abundant use of repetition. There is a high instance of *anaphora* (the repetition of the leading word in successive phrases), with the repetition of the leading particle εἰ ("if") (1.1a, 1b, 1d, 1h), yet another way in which he builds suspense or anticipation for his subject.

Demosthenes makes use of contrary-to-fact conditional clauses to indicate that things are not as they should be. With them, he creates a pressing reason why he is addressing the Athenians at this time. Moreover, he employs what the writer of *On Invention* (175) called *antitheton* (a figure of thought that juxtaposes a hypothetical condition and an actual situation). With *antitheton*, he juxtaposes the hypothetical notion of his not addressing the senators (1.1b–1.1e), while at the same time standing before them to address them (1.1f–1.1g). The writer of *On Invention* remarks that no other figure of thought is as compelling, because the hypothetical situation "creates an expectation among the audience for the actual one [situation]."[23] Demosthenes' *antitheton* contains an added degree of interest in that his embedded conditional clauses (1.1b–1.1e) include a *chiasmus*:[24] a long protasis (the conditional phrase) (1.1b) followed by a short apodosis (the main clause of a condition; 1.1c), and then the reverse, a short protasis (1.1d), followed by a long apodosis (1.1e). Taken together, these contrary-to-fact and hypothetical conditional clauses create a sense of need and expectation for the subject at hand.

Demosthenes' political opponents play an important role in his promotion of urgency (1.1a, 1b, 1f, 1h).[25] He rises to speak because his opponents' solutions are ineffective. Through the use of consonance, the repetition of the final consonant sounds ὼν (marked in bold-faced type), Demosthenes forges a distinction between himself and his opponents. He describes himself with the Greek word ἐπισχὼν ("waited"; 1.1a); he is the one who has normally waited. The implication being that he is normally silent. By contrast, he refers to his opponents with the word εἰωθότων ("accustomed"; 1.1a). The repetition of the ending consonant ὼν suggests that Demosthenes is playing on these two words: there is similarity of sound but distinction in sense (a form of *paronomasia*).[26] It is his opponents, who are accustomed to speaking (τῶν ὑπὸ τούτων ῥηθέντων; 1.1b), but who have not given the necessary advice (1.1h). Furthermore, line 1.1f contains the expected δέ that resolves the μέν of line 1.1a, yet it also refers to the subject of Demosthenes' opponents (οὗτοι, "these"). By having line 1.1f begin with a non-customary word ἐπειδὴ ("since"), Demosthenes emphasizes the line itself, and as such calls attention to his opponents.[27]

Again through a play on similar-sounding words, Demosthenes makes an additional distinction between his opponents' advice and the counsel he offers. He refers to his opponents using the Greek word συνεβούλευσαν, a third-person aorist active verb that signifies a past action and means "advised" or "counseled," and employs a present middle infinitive verb, βουλεύεσθαι ("to deliberate") to refer to what the Athenians must now do (1.1h). In other words, his opponents' previously advanced policy (συνεβούλευσαν) has not worked, thus more deliberation (βουλεύεσθαι) is necessary. Both Greek words contain the same Greek root βούλευ, yet the two resultant words have different meanings. The similar sounds of the Greek root βούλευ draw an audience's attention, while they simultaneously conflict semantically.[28] Demosthenes strengthens the word play between συνεβούλευσαν and βουλεύεσθαι by creating yet another play on the Greek expression τὰ δέονθ᾽ ("things needed") and the Greek verb ἔδει ("needed"; 1.1h).[29] If his opponents had only previously given the needed advice (τὰ δέονθ᾽), there would be no need (ἔδει) for the Athenians to be deliberating now (νῦν; 1.1h). Their earlier but ineffective policy has shaped and contributed to the current crisis, which he and the Athenians must now work to rectify.

Questioning the Athenians to Action

A second passage (1.10a–1.11c) also from his *First Philippic* contains signs of urgency in the form of short clipped phrases, rhetorical questions, and the repetition of key words and expressions.[30] Rebuke in the form of rhetorical questions is one of the primary ways seen here in which Demosthenes prods his audience to action. With a series of rhetorical questions involving suppositions that cannot be denied, Demosthenes blasts his hearers.[31] He insists that his audience take stock of the present situation. They are at a carpe diem moment in time. Are they unaware that Philip (the unnamed Macedonian) is threatening their borders? Will they remain inactive and allow this threat to go unanswered? Here we see Demosthenes agitating his audience into taking action by over-questioning them.

   Prior to this instance of audience rebuke, Demosthenes encourages (1.2) and even praises his audience for their past actions (1.3). Audience chastisement is, however, his stock-in-trade,[32] as Gilberte Ronnet summarizes, "*Démosthène a plus souvent à blamer qu'à louer.*" ("Demosthenes wants more often to condemn than to give praise.")[33] According to Gottfried Mader, continuous audience castigation functioned to legitimate the need for the type of advice he offered.[34] Demosthenes often also uses the example of his enemy Philip to shame his Athenian audience to action.[35] Here he accuses the Athenians of being slow and apathetic (διὰ τὴν ὑμετέραν βραδυτῆτα καὶ ῥᾳθυμίαν; 1.8), which he claims accounts for the present crisis.[36] In the following passage audience chastisement occurs in abundance.

1.10a πότ᾽ οὖν, ὦ ἄνδρες Ἀθηναῖοι, **πότε** ἃ χρὴ πράξετε;

1.10b ἐπειδὰν τί γένηται;

1.10c ἐπειδὰν νὴ Δί᾽ **ἀνάγκη** τις ᾖ.

1.10d **νῦν δὲ** τί χρὴ τὰ γιγνόμενα ἡγεῖσθαι;

    1.10e ἐγὼ **μὲν** γὰρ οἴομαι τοῖς ἐλευθέροις μεγίστην **ἀνάγκην** τὴν ὑπὲρ τῶν πραγμάτων **αἰσχύνην** εἶναι.

1.10f ἢ βούλεσθε, εἰπέ μοι, περιόντες αὐτῶν πυνθάνεσθαι, "λέγεταί τι **καινόν**;"

    1.10g γένοιτο γὰρ ἂν τι **καινότερον** ἢ Μακεδὼν ἀνὴρ Ἀθηναίους καταπολεμῶν καὶ τὰ τῶν Ἑλλήνων διοικῶν;[37]

1.10a **When**, men of Athens, **when** will you do **what** is needed?

1.10b **What** are you waiting for?

1.10c For some **necessity** to arise, by Zeus?

1.10d **What then** should we call the present developments?

    1.10e For, I believe, the strongest **necessity** for free men is **shame** at their situation.

1.10f Or, tell me, do you wish to go around asking each other, "Is there any **news**?"

    1.10g What could be **graver news** than that a Macedonian is waging war on Athens and is in control of the affairs of Greece?[38]

Unlike the opening section, section 10 of Demosthenes' *First Philippic* is a dramatic one-sided dialogue. The dialogue form itself serves to capture the audience's attention and, according to Wooten, provides an "aura of spontaneity, immediacy, and urgency."[39] Four leading short and to-the-point questions (1.10a, 10b, 10d, 10f) drive his harsh one-sided conversation. "What are you waiting for?" he prods. The indented lines above are the responses to the questions posed, but two out of the three responses (1.10c, 10g) are themselves rhetorical questions. He sarcastically asks his audience if they are waiting perhaps from a sign from god, "by Zeus" (1.10c). He awakens his audience to a crisis with his barrage of questions and prods them to action.

As seen above in the speech's opening, here too Demosthenes leaves certain issues, such as what he calls the "shame" of their present situation, unresolved. Again, there is no corresponding δέ for the μέν introduced in 1.10e. According to Wooten, as used here, the rhetorical technique creates an "unfinished division," and a corresponding sense of spontaneity. It is typical of a passage in which the author is expecting more of his or her audience.[40]

The passage begins with and is characterized not only by questions but also by words and expressions that regard time, especially the present. Demosthenes begins with the Greek adverb πότε ("when"; 1.10a) and then repeats it for emphasis within the same line. The *scholion* (marginal comments) suggests that the second πότε was to have been pronounced with more emphasis than the first.[41] Thus, the phrase rendered with emphasis would have been spoken as, "When, men of Athens, *when*."[42] The πότε receives its answer only sometime later, in 1.10d, in which one finds another adverb of time, νῦν ("now"). Trevett translates the phrase in 1.10d νῦν δὲ idiomatically as "What, then," rather than the more literal "But now." The conjunction ἐπειδὰν ("whenever") starts two successive cola (an instance of *anaphora*; 1.10b, 10c). The first four phrases of the passage begin with words that denote time and they significantly contribute to the development of a situation at hand into one of present or immediate concern.

Demosthenes' repetition of key terms or their sounds also contributes to a sense of urgency. Demosthenes answers his hypothetical question of why the Athenians are waiting (1.10b) with the Greek word for necessity (ἀνάγκη; 1.10c, 10e). With ἀνάγκη, he signals that a necessity has arisen and is occurring now in their midst. He reinforces his point by creating a play on the Greek word ἀνάγκη ("necessity") and another similar-sounding Greek word, αἰσχύνην ("shame"; 1.10e).[43] As Wooten comments, the one word nearly defines the other.[44] Demosthenes' implication is that the Athenians are to feel shame at their own inaction with regard to the situation at hand, which is their necessity. In 1.10f and 1.10g, Demosthenes refers to the situation at hand with the word "news" (καινόν). Once again, he asks but then answers his own hypothetical question. With his answer, he repeats the Greek word for news but with its stronger comparative form καινότερον (literally, "newsier"; 1.10g). The comparative form functions to create a play on the word "news," but more importantly, because of this word's semantic range of meaning, Demosthenes makes the present situation itself *newsworthy*. With it, he creates the very news to which the Athenians need to pay attention. Only in the last line of the unit does he inform his audience that the news of note is Philip's threat, described here as an unnamed Macedonian man.[45]

In sum, a sense of urgency typifies these two units within Demosthenes' *First Philippic*. Demosthenes employs short clipped phrases, rhetorical questions, and the repetition of key words and expressions, typically found in units that promote urgency. Repetition in the form of word play prods his audience to action. Words that denote time also dot these units and because they occur at the head of their respective phrases, they receive extra emphasis. These time words function to call attention to the present and render it significant. As seen particularly in the opening passage, Demosthenes develops his crisis within the context of his political opponents. He pins the blame for the current "crisis" on them: had they given the necessary advice in the first place, there would be no issue of pressing concern now. With audience rebuke, Demosthenes does not hesitate to degrade and shame his audience into action.

Cicero: Urging on the Senators

Cicero delivered his first speech against Antony,[46] his third Philippic oration,[47] on December 20, 44 BCE at a meeting of the tribunes[48] (Roman officials) and plebs (the ordinary free citizens of Rome) that he had not initially planned on attending.[49] Cicero determined that the situation and time were right and ripe to launch his first full-scale attack against Antony. Senators were beginning to take sides either pro or contra Antony, and Cicero felt the need to weigh in. Antony himself had just recently fled Rome and was thereby not in attendance.

A recent dispatch concerning the Roman magistrate Decimus
Brutus and his governorship of the region of Cisalpine Gaul, a
region south of the Alps in modern-day France, also played a decisive role in precipitating Cicero's speech. In 46 BCE Julius Caesar
had granted the governorship of Gaul to Decimus Brutus under
the terms of the *Lex Iulia de provincii*. However, in June 44 and after
Caesar's assassination, Antony pushed through newer legislation
by means of the people of Rome, and not by the senate itself, that
reallocated the provinces and altered the duration of their gover-
norships.[50] Under this newer legislation, Antony reassigned the
province of Gaul to himself.

When Antony arrived in the Gallic province to assume leadership of the territory, Brutus refused to yield rule over to him,[51]
thereby disregarding the newer legislation Antony forged by
popular consent. In taking such a stance, Brutus directly contra-
vened Antony's ruling of July 44 that legalized the assignment of
that consular province to Dolabella and to Antony himself.[52] With
his speech, Cicero aimed to affirm the action of Brutus and obtain
a general ruling supporting those actions (see especially 3.37–39).
He made the argument that Antony's newer legislation was not
passed legally.[53] His larger purpose with the speech, however,
was to bring down Antony's rule.

Setting up the Crisis

A sense of urgency typifies the whole of Cicero's *Third Philippic*,[54]
and Taddeo remarks that to develop it, Cicero borrowed on
Demosthenes' "καιρός theme."[55] Indeed, the two develop urgency
using similar rhetorical techniques. Like Demosthenes' *exordium*
in his first Philippic-cycle speech against Philip, Cicero's opening
in his first Philippic discourse is filled, as indicated below, with a
sense of urgency.[56] Both its opening (*serius*, "later"), and the closing word (*celeritatis*, "speed")[57] refer to time. The closing word
rounds out and reinforces a sense of urgency in the opening passage. Cicero urges the senators to take immediate action against
Antony.[58] The *exordium* follows:

> 3.1a **Serius** omnino, patres conscripti, quam tempus rei pu-
> blicae postulabat,

3.1b **aliquando** tamen convocati sumus;

3.1c quod flagitabam equidem **cotidie,**

3.1d quippe cum bellum nefarium contra aras et focos, contra vitam fortunasque notras ab homine profligato ac perdito non comparari, sed geri **iam** viderem.

3.1e **Exspectantur Kalendae Ianuariae;**

3.1f quas non **exspectat** Antonius,

3.1g qui in provinciam D. Bruti, summi et singularis viri, cum exercitu impetum facere conatur;

3.1h ex qua se instructum et paratum ad urbem venturum esse minitatur.

3.2a Quae est igitur **exspectatio?**

3.2b aut quae vel **minimi dilatio temporis?**

3.2c Quamquam enim adsunt **Kalendae Ianuariae, tamen breve tempus longum est imparatis.**

3.2d **Dies** enim adfert vel **hora** potius, nisi provisum est, magnas saepe clades;

3.2e certus autem **dies** non ut sacrifici, sic consili **exspectari** solet.

3.2f Quod si aut **Kalendae Ianuariae** fuissent **eo die** quo primum ex urbe fugit Antonius, aut eae non essent **exspectatae,** bellum **iam** nullum haberemus.

3.2g Auctoritate enim senatus consensuque populi romani facile hominis amentis Fregissemus audaciam.

3.2h Quod confido equidem consules designatos, simul ut magitratum initerint, esse facturos;

3.2i Mea autem festinatio non victoriae solum avida est sed etiam **celeritatis.**

3.1a We have been called together, Members of the Senate, **later** than the crisis of the *Res publica* demanded;

3.1b but we meet **at last.**

3.1c I have been pressing **every day** for a meeting,

3.1d as I saw a wicked war not in preparation but **already** being waged by a profligate and desperate man against altars and hearths, against our lives and property.

3.1e The **Kalends of January are awaited;**

3.1f. but Antonius does not **wait** for them

3.1g he is attempting to invade the province of Decimus Brutus, a very noble and distinguished gentleman, with an army;

3.1h from there he threatens, when equipped and ready, to march on the city.

3.2a Why then the **waiting,**

3.2b Or why a **moment's delay?**

3.2c For even if the **Kalends of January** are nearly come, **still even a short time is long for the unready.**

3.2d For a **day,** or rather an **hour,** often brings great disasters if precautions have not been taken;

3.2e a decision is not like a sacrifice, for which a particular **day** is usually **awaited.**

3.2f But if either the **very day** when Antonius fled from the city had been the **Kalends of January,** or if those had not been **awaited,** we should not have a war **now.**

3.2g For we should easily have quelled the madman's insolence by the authority of the Senate and the consensus of the Roman people.

3.2h I am confident that the Consuls-Designate will do that as soon as they have come into office; for they have the best disposition, are of excellent judgment and show a remarkable harmony.

3.2i But my haste is eager not merely for victory, but also for **speed.**[59]

As mentioned, Cicero's *exordium* includes many of the common signs of urgency.[60] Moreover, words that refer directly to time (marked in bold-faced type above) abound and are present in nearly every phrase of the *exordium* (3.1a, 1b, 1c, 1d, 1e, 1f; 3.2a, 2b, 2c, 2d, 2e, 2f, 2i).[61] The short aphorism *tamen breve tempus longum est imparatis* ("even a short time is long for the unready") also refers to time (3.2c). As mentioned, the opening begins with *serius* (later) and ends or rounds out with *celeritatis* (speed), bringing about a general sense of urgency.[62] Short punctuated phrases (3.1a, 1b, 1c, 1e, 1f, 3.2a, 2b) fill the unit.[63] Lively rhetorical questions (3.2a, 2b),[64] and instances of *contentio* (a stretch between expressions), such as between *breve* ("short") and *logum* ("long"; 3.2c), by the progression from *dies* ("day") to *hora* ("hour"; 3.2d) and from *victoriae* ("victory") to *celeritatis* ("speed"; 3.2i)[65] also promote urgency.

Cicero makes ample use of repetition and with words that themselves refer to time. Forms of *exspectare* ("to wait for," "to expect") occur five times[66] and in a chiastic ABABC structure (3.1e, 1f, 3.2a, 2e, 2f). The chiasm emphasizes the contrast between the inactive senate and the busy Antony.[67] Three times Cicero refers to *Kalendae Ianuariae*,[68] the first of January (3.1e, 2c, 2f).[69] In doing so, he creates anticipation for this date, a time when he hopes the senators will make the more important rulings against Antony.

As with Demosthenes, Cicero also employs suspense but here also dread. Like Demosthenes in the unit above (1.10g), he too only indirectly refers to his foe. First he calls him a "profligate and desperate man" (3.1d) and only later (3.1f) clarifies that the person is Antony. By predicting that a wicked war is already beginning, Cicero creates the sense of impending doom (3.1d).[70]

In ways that are again similar to Demosthenes, Cicero engages in audience rebuke. Although much gentler with his audience than is Demosthenes, nonetheless Cicero leads off with a form of chastisement.[71] Beginning with the word *omnino* ("utterly," "altogether") of 3.1a, he accuses the senators of inaction; whether they were or not is beside the point. According to Manuwald, this speech is one of only three that begin with an adverb in the comparative that expresses criticism.[72] As though shaming his audience into action, he contrasts their inactivity with his own preparedness (3.1c) and with Antony's busyness (3.1f–h). His rhetorical questions, like those of Demosthenes, are meant to prod the senators to action (3.2a, 3.2b).

An Ending Exhortation

Cicero's *Third Philippic* builds to a pronounced plea for a change in course. Near its close, Cicero makes a final urgent request to not remain inactive but to rule instead against Antony (3.34–36). He calls upon the senators to rise to the occasion. He exaggerates both the positive and negative ramifications of the decisions the senators take, and remarks that by their inaction the Republic will come to an end.[73] He offers the senators two mutually exclusive alternatives, slavery or freedom,[74] to guide their choice of action. Before his final plea for immediate action, Cicero compliments his audience, praising them for their various past initiatives against Antony (3.3–14). He also appeals to their sense of reason, when he provides various explanations for why the senators should continue to oppose Antony (3.15–27).[75] As is the case with the speech's *exordium*, a sense of urgency is especially apparent in its conclusion.[76] The passage reads as follows.

3.34a Hanc igitur occasionem oblatam **tenete**, per deos immortalis, patres conscripti, et amplissimi orbis terrae consili principes vos esse aliquando **recordamini**!

3.34b **Signum date** populo romano sonsilium vestrum non deesse rei publicae, quoniam ille virtutem suam non defuturam esse profitetur.

3.34c Nihil est quod moneam vos.

3.34d Nemo est tam stultus qui non intellegat, si indormierimus huic tempori, non modo crudelem superbamque dominationem nobis sed ignominiosam etiam et flagitiosam ferendam.

3.35a nostis insolentiam Antoni, nostis amicos, nostis totam domum.

3.35b libidinosis, petualantibus, impuris, impudicis, aleatoribus, ebriis servire, ea summa miseria est summon dedecore coniuncta.

3.35c **Quod** si iam—**quod** di omen avertant!—fatum extremum rei publicae venit,

3.35d **quod** gladiators nobiles faciunt, ut honeste decumbant,

3.35e **faciamus** nos, principes orbis terrarum gentiumque omnium, ut cum dignitate potius **cadamus quam cum ignominia serviamus**.

3.36a **nihil** est detestabilius dedecore, **nihil** foedius servitute.

3.36b **ad** decus et **ad** libertatem nati sumus: **aut** haec **teneamus aut** cum **dignitate moriamur**.

3.34a Therefore, **seize** this proffered opportunity, by the immortal Gods!, Members of the Senate, and at long last **remember** that you are leaders of the most august council in the world.

3.34b **Give a signal** to the Roman people that your wisdom will not fail the *Res publica* [the Republic], since they declare that their courage will not be wanting.

3.34c There is no reason why I should advise you.

3.34d No man is so dull as not to realize that if we doze over this crisis we shall have to endure a despotism not only cruel and arrogant but ignominious and disgraceful.

3.35a You know Antonius' insolence, you know his friends, you know his whole retinue.

3.35b To be slave to libertines, bullies, foul profligates, gamblers, drunkards, that is the ultimate in misery joined with the ultimate in dishonor.

3.35c If—may the Gods avert the omen!—the final episode in the history of the *Res publica* has arrived,

3.35d let us behave like champion gladiators: they meet death honorably;

3.35e **let us**, who stand foremost in the world and all nations, see to it that **we fall** with dignity **rather than serve with ignominy.**

3.36a Nothing is more abominable than disgrace, nothing is uglier than slavery.

3.36b We were born for honour and freedom: **let us** either retain them or **die with dignity.**[77]

Cicero strongly urges the senators to "take advantage of the present moment." He does this through the use of direct exhortations (marked in bold-faced type above) to act and to act now (3.34a [2x], 34b, 35e [2x], 36b [2x]). Indeed, the passage opens with the second-person imperative *tenete* (seize) and with the expression that refers to time, "proffered opportunity" (*occasionem oblatam*; 3.34a).[78] He focuses his audience's attention on the present situation through his ample use of the second-person (you; 3.34a, *vos*; 34b *vestrum*; 34c, *vos*) and by calling his audience by

name, *patres conscripti* ("members [fathers] of the senate"; 3.34a).
Taddeo refers to line 3.34a—with its notion of seizing the opportunity at hand—as "the most striking parallel" of Demosthenes'
καιρός theme within Cicero's *Third Philippic*. Cicero is arguing
that if the Roman senate has any pride at all in their affairs, they
should take charge of the present situation and lead the Roman
people to reject the rule of Antony.[79]

Continuing with the καιρός theme and consistent with it,
Cicero claims that now is the time to act. To prod the senators to
action, he engages in exaggeration.[80] According to Cicero, Rome
is presently at a crucial time in history.[81] Cicero writes, *fatum extremum rei publicae venit* ("the final episode in the history of the *Res
publica* has arrived"; 3.35c).[82] The present moment is the best time
to act, *hanc igitur occasionem* ("now, at this occasion"; 3.34a). Cicero
cautions the senators of the risk of not acting against Antony. As
Taddeo remarks, for both Demosthenes and Cicero, "failure to
capitalize on the καιρός inevitably leads to undesirable results."[83]
In this case, the senators risk living under a cruel despot (3.34d)
and becoming his slaves. Cicero emphasizes the seriousness of the
situation through the repetition of words that pertain to serving or
slavery (*servire, serviamus, servitute*) (3.35b, 35e, 36a).[84] Short memorable phrases with repetitive words and clauses bring home his
points. He remarks, "To be slave to libertines, . . . is the ultimate
in misery joined with the ultimate in dishonor" (3.35b); "Nothing
is more abominable than disgrace, nothing is uglier than slavery"
(3.36a). According to Maximilian Braun, the references to slavery
and servitude recalled an ever-present reality and were therefore
very effective in argumentation.[85]

Finally, twice Cicero calls upon the gods (3.34a, 35c), a
technique also found in the καιρός theme of Demosthenes.[86]
Demosthenes reminds his Athenian audience of their god-given
blessings so as to provoke them to action. Taddeo suggests that
Cicero's invocation of the gods is meant to have that same effect:
to cause action out of appreciation.[87] While Manuwald calls the
expressions *per deos immortalis!* [88] ("by the immortal Gods!") and
quod di omen avertant! ("may the Gods avert the omen!") formulaic, they are at the same time emotionally charged.[89]

Repetition in the form of *anaphora* occurs often and is typical in these units containing other forms of urgency. Three times Cicero fires out, *nostis* ("you know"; 3.35a). Line 3.35a is short and the repetition both of the word and its identical placement within three successive clauses is striking and creates movement. Lines 3.35c and 3.35d contain the same type of successive phrases, yet now each begins with the conjunction *quod* (normally translated as "that"). In 3.36a, we see the same pattern with the noun *nihil* ("nothing") that starts two more phrases, and with the preposition *ad* ("to") and the conjunction *aut* ("or") in 3.36b. The series of similarly patterned phrases are rhythmic; they move. Moreover, Cicero employs four first-person plural subjunctive verbs, all of which contain the same *mus* ending (*homoioptoton*) to exhort the entire group, himself included, to action (3.35e, 36b).

In sum, signs of urgency dominate both the opening and closing passages of Cicero's *Third Philippic*, his first official Philippic oration before the Roman senate. He employs an abundance of the signature elements of urgency, such as short clipped phrases, rhetorical questions, and the repetition of key words and expressions. While he borrows on the καιρός theme from Demosthenes, he takes it into his own and new directions. References to time characterize his *exordium*—he takes this trope well beyond what is seen in Demosthenes—and a series of exhortations to act in the present against Antony typify the speech's close. Like Demosthenes, Cicero builds suspense. Developing urgency is crisis producing and in this closing unit Cicero employs exaggeration to magnify the current situation with Antony into a dire state of affairs. With hyperbole, Cicero speaks of the slave-like condition that will result under Antony's rule. Naming the present time as the "final episode in the history of the *Res publica*" (3.35c) is, from the standpoint of recent evaluations of the history of that time, ironic.[90]

Paul on Urgency

In Galatians, a sense of urgency is palpable,[91] and particularly apparent in Gal 1:6–9; 3:1–5; and 5:2–6, units spread rather evenly throughout the letter. Paul stirs his audience to action around

issues, namely, the good news (Gal 1:6–9), the means of righteousness (Gal 3:1–5), and circumcision (Gal 5:2–6). Rather than
detailing these issues with reasoned arguments, through the creation of oppositions, hyperbole, and high emotion, Paul builds
contention around them. That the Galatians adopt the "right" position with regard to these issues dominates Paul's discussions of
these issues. His emphasis on the "right" position, that is, on his
position, indicates that winning the Galatians to his side and from
the side of his competitors[92] is more significant than the issues
themselves. Like Demosthenes and Cicero, Paul employs many of
the rhetorical techniques common to the development of urgency,
namely, short clipped phrases, rhetorical questions, and the repetition of key words and expressions. Yet Paul also employs other
common tropes, audience rebuke and words that denote time, as
well as exclamations to prod his audience to action.

Defining the Issue and Creating a Crisis out of It (Gal 1:6–9)

After a very brief salutation (Gal 1:1–5), Paul comes right to the
point in verse 6. The unit defined by Gal 1:6–9 spells out the letter's purpose.[93] Betz and Joop Smit refer to this passage in terms
customarily employed for a speech, as an *exordium* (opening).[94]
Indeed Smit goes so far as to categorize Galatians as a deliberative speech.[95] Paul opens the body of his letter with suddenness
and harshness against his audience. His confrontational tone
and accompanying sense of drama is similar to what we saw in
Demosthenes (*Phil.* 1.10). Paul writes,

1:6 Θαυμάζω ὅτι οὕτως ταχέως μετατίθεσθε ἀπὸ τοῦ
καλέσαντος **ὑμᾶς** ἐν χάριτι [Χριστοῦ] εἰς ἕτερον
εὐαγγέλιον;
1:7a ὃ οὐκ ἔστιν ἄλλο,
1:7b εἰ μή τινές εἰσιν οἱ ταράσσοντες **ὑμᾶς** καὶ θέλοντες
μεταστρέψαι τὸ **εὐαγγέλιον** τοῦ Χριστοῦ.
1:8a ἀλλὰ καὶ ἐὰν ἡμεῖς ἢ ἄγγελος ἐξ οὐρανοῦ
εὐαγγελίζηται [ὑμῖν] παρ᾽ ὃ **εὐηγγελισάμεθα** ὑμῖν,
1:8b **ἀνάθεμα ἔστω.**
1:9a ὡς προειρήκαμεν καὶ ἄρτι πάλιν λέγω·

1:9b εἴ τις ὑμᾶς εὐαγγελίζεται παρ᾽ ὃ παρελάβετε,
1:9c ἀνάθεμα ἔστω.

1:6   I am amazed that **you** are so quickly changing from the one who called you in the grace [of the Anointed] to another **good news;**[96]
1:7a there is no other,
1:7b except some who trouble **you** and desire to alter the **good news** of the Anointed.
1:8a but even if we or an angel from heaven should **proclaim good news** [to you] contrary to what **we proclaimed** to you,
1:8b **let that one be accursed!**
1:9a as we have said before and now I say again:
1:9b if someone **proclaims to you good news** contrary to what you received,
1.9c **let that one be accursed!**[97]

With his first-person present Greek verb θαυμάζω ("I am amazed"), Paul starts his letter proper with a jolt (1:6). His exclamation—positioned as the first word of the unit—signals importance and urgency. Smit remarks that with it Paul brings his audience to a "state of alarm."[98]

Paul's θαυμάζω ("I am amazed") is also a form of audience rebuke, and an expression employed by ancient authors beyond those surveyed here.[99] Paul's rebuke—whether feigned,[100] ironic,[101] or neither one[102]—creates a sense of drama and raises the significance of the situation at hand. Using a present middle indicative verb μετατίθεσθε[103]—indicating present action—Paul accuses the Galatians of changing course (1:6). Betz translates the Greek verb as "deserting."[104] Regardless of whether or not the Galatians knew or intended to "desert" Paul, he characterizes their action as such and as verging on the irreversible. He also adds weighty significance to the ramifications of their future action: by changing to "another good news" (ἕτερον εὐαγγέλιον), the Galatians are affecting their relationship with God, they are departing "from the one who called them in grace" (Gal 1:6).[105]

As seen above in Demosthenes' *First Philippic* and in the *exordium* of Cicero's *Third Philippic*, Paul too makes use of words that refer to time to promote a sense of urgency. Adverbs for time mark the start and close of the unit: the adverb "quickly" (ταχέως; 1:6) occurs close to the unit's beginning and "now" (ἄρτι; 1:9a) resides at its end.[106] Through emphasis-producing techniques, Paul calls attention to each of these time words. The repetition of the ending consonant ως (*homoioteleuton*) in the two adjacent words οὕτως ταχέως ("so quickly"; 1:6)[107] adds significance to the phrase. The clash of ending and opening vowels in καὶ ἄρτι ("and now"; 1:9a) accentuates that second two-word expression, and creates cacophony.[108] References to time not only create movement in the discourse, but also serve to give the impression that the present is of utmost significance, pregnant with meaning.[109]

Paul employs repetition of key words and expressions throughout this unit to bring about a sense of urgency. He often repeats the Greek second-person plural pronoun ὑμᾶς ("you," marked in bold-faced type; 1:6, 7b, 9b). These second-person pronouns, like his θαυμάζω ("I am amazed"; 1:6), are attention grabbing. Words for "good news" (marked in bold-faced type) also occur with abundance throughout this short unit, in both nominal (εὐαγγέλιον; 1:6, 7b) and verbal forms (εὐαγγελίζηται, εὐηγγελισάμεθα, εὐαγγελίζεται; 1:8a [2x], 9b). An instance of *polyptoton*—repetition of the same word in a different form within close proximity—emphasizes the concept. While repetition of words for good news clearly marks them as significant, Paul leaves the content or the meaning of his good news unspecified.[110] Rather than providing a definition of it, he establishes two antithetical types of news, affirming the one as "good" and the other as no news at all, as essentially worthless (1:7a).[111] As Paul never describes his good news nor devotes time to detail it, the good news itself is of less significance compared to the necessity of simply choosing *it* over another type of news.[112]

More instances of repetition occur in the identical and twice-repeated expression (ἀνάθεμα ἔστω, "Let that one be accursed!"; 1:8b, 9c).[113] These emotionally charged[114] *exclamatios*—affective figures that consist of abrupt utterances[115]—function in and of themselves to give a sense of agitation or movement to the unit.[116] With them, Paul aims to discredit his competition.[117] Betz rightly observes Paul's employment here of demagoguery.[118] He issues the double curse—an extreme form of denouncement against his opponents—in the hearing of his Galatian audience. In doing so, Paul surrounds his opponents with evil, good's antithesis.

Short phrases or cola, as we have seen, add movement and provoke the audience to action. They become more apparent when shown not according to traditional versification but instead by how the composition would have been read aloud and heard.[119] The twice-repeated curses comprise two of the short phrases (1:8b, 9c) and function as bookends for two inner short emphatic phrases (1:9a, 9b). Taken together, all the phrases reinforce Paul's point made in 1:7a—itself a short phrase—that there is no other good news.

As is the case with both Demosthenes and Cicero, Paul's development of urgency regards his competition. He discusses his good news in seemingly the same breath as the news of his competitors. Rather than clarify the contents of his good news, he instead makes clear the negative consequence of changing or deserting from his good news to any other form of it (1:6). Indeed, Betz remarks that the term μετατίθεσθε ("you are changing" or "you are departing"; 1:6)—mentioned above—can be understood as a "political term."[120] Paul also strategically opposes two points of view, those that were not necessarily in direct opposition prior to his assessment, forcing a choice between two parties, Paul's and his competitors'. In 1:7b, Paul lays the blame for the crisis he develops at the feet of his competitors, those he assesses as troublemakers (ταράσσοντες).[121] He disparages his competitors as those who desire to "twist," "alter," or "turn around" (μεταστρέψαι)[122] the good news (1:7b). As mentioned, Paul twice curses his competition, harshly rebuking them in the hearing of his audience.

In sum, in Gal 1:6–9 Paul develops the situation in Galatia into a crisis using many of the common signs of urgency. Short cola keep the discourse alive and dynamic, encouraging the audience to take heed. Repetition cues the audience to important points. And with his identically phrased double curse, Paul creates an emotive atmosphere to engender audience agitation. The word for "good news" (εὐαγγέλιον) and its cognates receive particular attention, and because the word/expression is never explained, it instead peaks the audience's curiosity and anticipation. From the first word of the letter body, he abruptly rebukes his audience to gain their attention for his developing crisis (1:6). His second-person plural pronouns function to maintain it. Adverbs of time dot the unit, with the phrase "so quickly" present in the first verse of this unit and the expression "and now" occurring at its end; these adverbs contribute to a sense of urgency, as they focus attention on the here and now.

Paul assesses the situation, the crisis he creates, with considerable exaggeration, heightening its significance. He implies that by changing course, the Galatians are leaving the realm of God (1:6); he creates a binary opposition between his good news/agenda and that of his competitors; he strongly denies the value of his competitors' news; and, with much drama, he curses any and all competing forms of good news. The good news itself is of less significance, as Paul never spends time detailing it. Paul is more concerned that the Galatians not choose another good news than he is about the good news itself.

More Crisis Building to Gain the Galatians' Allegiance (Gal 3:1–5)

After a lengthy autobiographical section (1:10–2:21)—discussed in detail in chapter two[123]—Paul again engages more directly in the promotion of urgency in Gal 3:1–5.[124] He reprises the tone and many of the rhetorical tropes used to generate urgency in Gal 1:6–9.[125] Gal 3:1–5, and especially its opening interjection, function to bring the Galatians to their senses, to a state of alertness, and to Paul's developing crisis. The unit follows:

3:1a Ὦ ἀνόητοι Γαλάται,
3:1b τίς ὑμᾶς ἐβάσκανεν,
3:1c οἷς κατ᾽ ὀφθαλμοὺς Ἰησοῦς Χριστὸς προεγράφη
    ἐσταυρωμένος;

3:2a τοῦτο μόνον θέλω μαθεῖν ἀφ᾽ ὑμῶν·
3:2b **ἐξ ἔργων νόμου** τὸ **πνεῦμα** ἐλάβετε ἢ **ἐξ ἀκοῆς πίστεως;**
3:3a οὕτως **ἀνόητοί** ἐστε,
3:3b ἐναρξάμενοι **πνεύματι** νῦν σαρκὶ ἐπιτελεῖσθε;
3:4a τοσαῦτα ἐπάθετε **εἰκῆ;**
3:4b εἴ γε καὶ **εἰκῆ.**
3:5 ὁ οὖν ἐπιχορηγῶν ὑμῖν τὸ **πνεῦμα** καὶ ἐνεργῶν δυνάμεις ἐν ὑμῖν, **ἐξ ἔργων νόμου** ἢ **ἐξ ἀκοῆς πίστεως;**

3:1a **Oh senseless** Galatians!
3:1b Who has bewitched you?
3:1c [It was] before your eyes Jesus the Anointed was portrayed as crucified!
3:2a This alone I want to learn from you:
3:2b Did you receive the **spirit from works of Torah** or **from the hearing of faithfulness?**
3:3a Are you so **senseless,**
3:3b having begun in the **spirit,** are you now ending in the flesh?
3:4a Have you experienced such things **in vain?**
3:4b If [it was] really also **in vain.**
3:5 Thus, does [God] supply the **spirit** to you and work miracles among you **from works of Torah** or **from the hearing of faithfulness?**[126]

Like Gal 1:6–9, this unit too begins with exaggeration and a jolt. The phrase "Oh senseless Galatians!" (Ὦ ἀνόητοι Γαλάται; 3:1a) marks a dramatic transition from his autobiographical narrative that ends the previous chapter. As such, the transitional phrase is a classic example of *metabasis*, "an abrupt change of subject or the return to the subject from a digression."[127] With *metabasis*,[128] Paul recalls his audience to his crisis, while he also develops it.

As in Gal 1:6, Paul's abrupt interjection functions as audience rebuke.[129] His harsh reproach[130] of his audience is similar to Demosthenes', who with biting sarcasm asks his audience if they are perhaps waiting for a sign from Zeus before acting (*Phil.* 1.10b). Paul twice calls the Galatians "senseless" (ἀνόητοι; 3:1a, 3a).[131] Repetition strengthens the word's impact. Audience rebuke, which continues throughout the unit, reawakens his audience and alerts them to the crisis as he develops it. Like Demosthenes (*Phil.* 1.10), Paul's rebuke is in the form of rhetorical questions and with them, he bombards his audience.[132] With his rhetorical questions, he emotionally charges the atmosphere,[133] as through them he develops a sense of anger.[134] According to J. Van W. Cronjé, "questions enable the apostle to drive home his alarm more forcefully than by merely exhorting them not to do that again."[135] Moreover, with his rhetorical questions, Paul not only rebukes his audience but also establishes dichotomies—a rhetorical technique discussed in greater detail in chapter four—likely otherwise unknown to them. By creating harsh distinctions, he turns the present situation into a grave matter.[136] He distinguishes between the spirit (πνεῦμα; 3:2, 3, 5), assessed positively, and works of Torah (3:2b, 5) and flesh (σαρκὶ; 3:3b) depicted negatively. Through hierarchical arrangement, Paul creates two mutually exclusive alternative positions.

Repetition of key words and expressions (marked in bold-faced type above) is readily apparent within the unit. As mentioned, Paul twice repeats the pejorative term "senseless" (ἀνόητος; 3:1a, 3a). The adjective is in the identical form and location in each of its three-word short phrases. He repeats the expressions "from works of Torah" and "from hearing of faithfulness" (ἐξ ἔργων νόμου and ἐξ ἀκοῆς πίστεως) at the start of successive phrases (*anaphora*; 3:2b, 5), and with each instance opposes one to the other. As mentioned, the two antithetical phrases force a distinction between two alternative positions. The word εἰκῇ ("in vain") is found at the end of 3:4a and then again stands coupled with the longer expression "If [it was] really also in vain"[137] (εἴ γε καὶ εἰκῇ) in 3:4b, giving the impression of a sense of exasperation with his audience.[138] As mentioned, repetition, although not unique for the promotion of urgency, is nonetheless an important rhetorical device for promoting it. Repeated items signal issues deemed significant. Through repetition, Paul seeks to move his audience to his side and away from the side of his competitors.

Short clipped phrases typify Gal 3:1–5 as they do Gal 1:6–9. Short phrases function like repetitive mental punches (3:1a, 1b, 1c, 2a, 3a, 3b, 4a, 4b) to prod audience action. Paul often employs *hiatus* (a clash of vowel sounds) (3:1c, 2b, 3a, 3b, 4a, 4b), which creates dissonance, typical of authoritative speech.[139] Dissonance—because it breaks an harmonious sound pattern—attracts attention.

As is the case in Gal 1:6–9, here too competitors are in view. Paul makes the bold accusation—to be discussed in greater detail in the following chapter—that his competitors have "bewitched" (ἐβάσκανεν) the Galatians (3:1b). With this remark, he not only chastises the Galatians for being vulnerable to this type of attack,[140] but he also accuses his competitors for resorting to these evil tactics, thereby demeaning them.[141] By creating opposing and hierarchically arranged categories between "works of Torah," the side of his competition, and the "hearing of faithfulness" (3:2b, 5), his own position, Paul builds on the adversarial situation he is establishing between the two parties, and he brings to light a distinction that is otherwise not present.[142]

In sum, in Gal 3:1–5 Paul builds on the sense of urgency begun in Gal 1:6–9. With suddenness (Gal 3:1) and a string of rhetorical questions, Paul forcefully focuses his audience's attention onto the crisis as he develops it. Indeed, the exclamation in Gal 3:1 recalls the one in Gal 1:6, with each reinforcing the other. With his accusation of bewitchment aimed at his competitors, Paul maintains and now extends a distinction between himself and his competitors. He engages in a high degree of exaggeration. It is evident in his opening exclamation, in his accusation of bewitchment, but it is also present in the creation of opposing and mutually exclusive categories. Paul distinguishes between spirit and flesh, spirit and works of Torah, and the hearing of faithfulness and works of Torah. The oppositions, with one element of the pair assessed positively and the other negatively, turn a situation into a battle between two opposing sides. Through these techniques, Paul aims to draw the Galatians to his side and away from the side of his competitors.

Keeping the Crisis Front and Center (Gal 5:2–6)

In a third unit (Gal 5:2–6),[143] Paul once again directs his audience's attention to the crisis he begins more directly in Gal 1:6–9. Reading Galatians as a deliberative speech, Smit calls the section defined by Gal 4:21–5:6 the *enumeratio*,[144] the summation of the speech.[145] In this section, Paul warns the Galatians of the negative consequences[146] of adopting the recommendation of his competitors. The unit follows.

5:2a Ἴδε ἐγὼ Παῦλος λέγω ὑμῖν **ὅτι**
5:2b ἐὰν **περιτέμνησθε**, Χριστὸς ὑμᾶς οὐδὲν ὠφελήσει.
5:3a μαρτύρομαι δὲ πάλιν παντὶ ἀνθρώπῳ **περιτεμνομένῳ ὅτι**
5:3b ὀφειλέτης ἐστὶν **ὅλον τὸν νόμον** ποιῆσαι.
5:4   κατηργήθητε ἀπὸ Χριστοῦ, οἵτινες ἐν νόμῳ **δικαιοῦσθε**, τῆς χάριτος ἐξεπέσατε.
5:5   ἡμεῖς γὰρ πνεύματι ἐκ πίστεως ἐλπίδα **δικαιοσύνης** ἀπεκδεχόμεθα.
5:6   ἐν γὰρ Χριστῷ Ἰησοῦ οὔτε **περιτομή** τι ἰσχύει οὔτε ἀκροβυστία ἀλλὰ πίστις δι᾽ ἀγάπης ἐνεργουμένη.

5:2a Pay attention! I Paul say to you **that**
5:2b if you become **circumcised**, the Anointed will be of no benefit to you.
5:3a And I testify again to every man who becomes **circumcised that**
5:3b [he] is obliged to perform **the entire Torah.**
5:4   You have cut yourself off from the Anointed, you who are becoming **justified** in the Torah, you have fallen from grace.
5:5   For by the spirit from faithfulness, we are awaiting the hope of **righteousness.**
5:6   For in the Anointed, Jesus, neither **circumcision** is strong nor foreskin, but faithfulness working through love (is strong).[147]

As in Gal 1:6–9 and 3:1–5, a sense of urgency is especially apparent at the unit's start (Gal 5:2a). The suddenness of Paul's "Pay attention!" (Ἴδε; 5:2a),[148] echoes Gal 1:6 and 3:1a, and as is the case in those earlier opening verses, serves to bring the audience's attention to the situation at hand. Paul's "Pay attention!" is literally a "wake up" call. And as with Gal 1:6 and 3:1a, here too his exclamation is also a form of audience rebuke. Paul reprimands the Galatians for being asleep at the wheel. Once again, Paul deploys a string of short phrases, seen especially at the start of the unit (5:2a, 2b, 3a, 3b). These short cola add movement to the unit and serve to give the sense of a need to take swift immediate action.

Repetition, apparent throughout (marked in bold-faced type above), serves to reinforce two alternative positions Paul develops. We see repetition of the ending syllable of the second-person plural middle-voice Greek verbs σθε (5:2b, 4).[149] In each instance of their use, they signify the negative consequence of following on the advice of the others, of Paul's competitors. Their similar forms and functions reinforce each other. In the first instance, the σθε ending involves becoming circumcised (5:2b), which in turn brings about the negative effect of losing the benefits of the Anointed, and in the second, the σθε-ending verb denotes being made righteous through the Torah, with the negative ramification of being cut off from the Anointed (5:4). The second-person plural (you) endings call the Galatians to themselves, and this made-to-be-dire situation directly applicable to them. His many references to circumcision (5:2b, 3a, 6) are a form of *polyptoton*—the repetition of the same word in different forms—signaling this notion's significance for the unit.[150] In two instances (5:2b, 3a), Paul marks circumcision as carrying negative consequences. Repetition in the form of ending sound ον (*homoioptoton*) in the phrase ὅλον τὸν νόμον ("the entire Torah"; 5:3b) draws attention to one of the negative consequences of becoming circumcised.

Moreover, and with another instance of *polyptoton*, Paul twice repeats the Greek word for righteousness (δικαιοῦσθε, 5:4, and δικαιοσύνης, 5:5). With this term, he engages in the same tactic he employs with the term "good news" (Gal 1:6–7). As we saw above, Paul gives the same name, "good news," to both his own agenda and to that of his competitors. Yet Paul in no way intends any other news but his to be good. Indeed, he invalidates his

competitors' good news, as being no news at all. By employing
the same term—and assessing one positively and the other one
negatively—he facilitates a head-to-head conflict between himself
and others. Similarly, in this unit, Paul employs the term "righteousness" to refer both to his agenda and to that of his competitors. He assesses the righteousness he proposes positively (5:5),
and that of his competition negatively (5:4). He thus creates yet
another[151] face-off and this time between two opposing ways of
becoming righteous. The distinction Paul draws between two
different means of becoming righteousness, however, cannot be
taken at face value.[152] Paul instead uses the term "righteousness"
polemically to win his audience to his side.

While the term "circumcision" occurs with frequency, it is
not the rite itself that is at issue but instead Paul's competition.[153]
Indeed, discussions that pertain to circumcision present themselves with such regularity (Gal 2:3, 7–9, 12; 5:1–3, 6, 11; 6:12–13,
15) that commentators understand it to be Paul's primary issue
of concern.[154] His rhetoric, however, indicates that circumcision
in and of itself is not at issue. Paul does not, for example, detail
physical disadvantages of circumcision;[155] indeed, he appears to
be neutral with regard to the practice itself (Gal 5:6). As is readily
apparent from even a cursory reading of Galatians, it is Paul's opponents or competitors who are urging the Galatians to become
circumcised (Gal 5:7–12, 6:12–13). His comments regarding the
non-adoption of circumcision by Galatian non-Jewish males are
conditioned and strongly determined by his competition.

The unit's strength is in Paul's own and strong rejection of circumcision, a rejection that is itself hyperbolic (see below). Paul
involves himself intimately and comes out heatedly over the issue
of circumcision for the Galatian non-Jews. In Gal 5:2a, he remarks,
"I Paul" (ἐγὼ Παῦλος) "say to you" (λέγω ὑμῖν). In an inflected
language like Greek—in which the subject is supplied within the
verb itself—personal pronouns (such as, ἐγώ, "I") are entirely
unnecessary. Indeed, they are redundant and whenever present
indicate emphasis. In addition to the unneeded-for-meaning pronoun "I," Paul also inserts his own name (Παῦλος, "Paul")—the

entire two-word expression is strong and stronger than what we have seen above in the compositions of Demosthenes and Cicero. Betz rightly notes that the employment of the personal pronoun along with Paul's own name is an emphatic way of mobilizing "his whole authority as an apostle."[156] Indeed, with his expression "I Paul" (ἐγὼ Παῦλος), Paul not only takes a strong and commandingly authoritative position over his audience,[157] but also, and at the same time, over his competitors. It is as though Paul were saying to the Galatians, "Although these other persons are insisting that you must become circumcised, *I Paul*,[158] someone equal to if not more authoritative than they (Gal 1:1), am telling you not to pursue it." Indeed, circumcision functions as a direct point of contention between Paul and his competitors: they say circumcision is necessary and Paul forbids it. Moreover, in 5:5, one finds another extraneous first-person plural pronoun we (ἡμεῖς) at the verse's head. The Greek verb ἀπεκδεχόμεθα ("we are awaiting") already signals the first-person plural designation. By employing and strategically placing the pronoun we (ἡμεῖς) at the start of the phrase, Paul emphasizes the distinction between two opposing sides[159] and clarifies that he resides on the Galatians' side, the "correct" one.

Paul's stated reasons for rejecting circumcision are hyperbolic. Indeed, his exaggerated and negatively construed ramifications of the Galatian adoption of circumcision undermine the sense in which Paul is literally against the rite and indicate instead that he is most interested in the Galatian non-adoption of it. Exaggeration around the subject of circumcision is evident in Paul's expression "to perform the entire Torah," (ὅλον τὸν νόμον ποιῆσαι; 5:3b).[160] With this expression, he not only engages in hyperbole but also in obfuscation, as he leaves to the Galatians' imagination just what that expression means.

In attempting to make sense of the expression ὅλον τὸν νόμον ποιῆσαι ("to perform the entire Torah"; 5:3b), commentators fall into a trap that does not hold up to textual verification. Betz's comments typify the traditional interpretation of this expression. He remarks, "'Doing the whole Torah' means doing every one of the requirements, because the transgression of even one may endanger the whole effort."[161] Betz raises the possibility that Paul is referring to no fewer than 613 commandments.[162] Yet, and as I have argued elsewhere,[163] the first mention of 613 commandments occurs in the sixth century, with the writing of the Babylonian Talmud (*Makkoth*, 23b). Moreover, even when first discussed (*Makkoth*, 23b), there is no universal agreement among the rabbis regarding an obligation to follow all 613 of them. For instance, R. Joshua b. Levi claims there that only three commandments are required: the annual recital of the Scroll of Esther, saluting the divine name, and bringing the Levite tithe to the temple chamber. In the following Talmudic section, *Makkoth*, 24a, David reduces the 613 commandments to eleven. More reductions follow, with Isaiah to six, Micah to three, Isaiah again and now to two, and finally Habakuk to one ("But the righteous shall live by his faith").

While the notion of having to carry out all the requirements of Torah conjures an image of innumerable commandments to follow, no such long immutable list existed to burden Jews with Torah regulations, not at the time of Paul and not in the centuries that followed. The expression "the entire Torah" (ὅλον τὸν νόμον), then, is hyperbolic.[164] With it, Paul creates an aura of anxiety; he worries his audience with a warning that has no basis in fact or in scripture. Just as Demosthenes exaggerates the imminent threat of Philip to Athens (*Phil.* 1.10), so too does Paul embellish and indeed misrepresent this consequence of becoming circumcised.

Paul's first stated negative consequence of becoming circumcised is also problematic (Gal 5:2b). He claims that by becoming circumcised the Galatians will lose the "benefit of the Anointed," yet such a claim is, of course, unverifiable. Given the fact that he engages in hyperbole with his expression "to perform the entire Torah" (Gal 5:3b), one can assume that here too he is equally hyperbolic. Finally, the fact that Paul is literally and vehemently against the circumcision of Galatian non-Jews is problematic given the fact that in Gal 5:6 he claims that both circumcision and its opposite condition, foreskin, are not important in and of themselves (cf. Gal 6:15, 1 Cor 7:19). Paul provides no substantive reason why the Galatian non-Jews should avoid circumcision—such as it being hazardous to health or politically dangerous or illicit—which suggests that circumcision itself is not at issue and is not Paul's primary concern with regard to it. Paul's discussions of the subject of circumcision are instead intimately tied to the notion of a conflict between him and his competitors. Paul makes circumcision into a contentious issue.

Finally, this unit contains several close parallels to Cicero's *Third Philippic* (34–36). Both authors go to extremes to provoke and unsettle their respective audiences. Cicero suggests that by not taking immediate action against Antony, the senators risk losing their wisdom and courage (3.34b) and even the Republic itself (3.35c). And Paul creates an unfounded sense of anxiety over the obligation "to perform the entire Torah" (Gal 5:3b) and becoming righteous by means of Torah observance. Like Cicero (3.35e, 36b), Paul too employs the first-person plural ("we"; 5:5) to promote the sense of an existing agreement between the audience and the speaker/author. Moreover, both Cicero and Paul return to their crises at or near the end of their respective writings.

In sum, taken together these Pauline units contain many of the signs of urgency. Short phrases and repetition occur in all of them and with abundance. Paul also employs words that refer to time (1:6, 9a). To startle the Galatians and draw them to the present and to the developing crisis, Paul starts each unit with an exclamation, with suddenness (1:6, 3:1a, 5:2). Like Demosthenes and Cicero, Paul engages in audience rebuke (1:6, 3:1–5, 5:2a). With it, he adopts a dominant position vis-à-vis his audience and, like Demosthenes, he attempts to gain his audience's attention by pointing out their failures. When taken together, these rhetorical tropes serve to coax the Galatians to make a fast decisive decision in favor of Paul and against his competitors.

Conclusion

Urgency turns a situation that is not necessarily of imminent concern into a crisis demanding immediate attention. Taddeo observed in Demosthenes' *Philippics* a set of rhetorical devices aimed at creating a sense of urgency around the threat of Philip. He grouped these techniques together and labeled them the "καιρός" ("right moment") theme. As Taddeo explains it, Cicero learned of and borrowed this theme from Demosthenes to turn his fight against Antony into a crisis. While we have no indication that Paul knew of a καιρός theme employed by Demosthenes and Cicero, he nevertheless develops a situation in Galatia into a crisis demanding immediate attention using many of the same techniques used by these earlier orators.

Particular rhetorical devices contribute to a sense of urgency and include short clipped phrases, rhetorical questions, and the repetition of key words and expressions. Yet across the compositions of all three rhetoric-of-crisis authors, we also found the use of time words and audience rebuke. Demosthenes, Cicero, and Paul all rebuke their audiences (Demosthenes, *Phil.* 1.10a–b, 10d, 10f–g; Cicero, *Phil.* 3.2a–b, 2f; Paul, Gal 1:6, 3:1–5, 5:2a). With rebuke, these authors "get under the skin" of their hearers to coax them into taking immediate action in the authors' favor. Words referring to time dot all of these units and serve to call attention to the present moment. For Demosthenes, Cicero, and Paul, the developed crisis—the purpose to which the techniques of urgency are put—concerns competitors. At the start of his Philippic-cycle speeches, Demosthenes lets it be known that had his Athenian political opponents given the necessary advice the first time around, he would have no need now to address the senate. Adopting an aggressive campaign against Philip distinguishes Demosthenes from his political rivals. Cicero's crisis concerns the "evils" of his archrival Antony. Consistently depicting Antony and his actions since the Ides of March in negative terms contributes to the notion of his being an imminent threat. While Paul does not name his competitors, the crisis he develops through rhetorical techniques consistent with urgency concerns his competitors just as much and as fully as it does for both Demosthenes and Cicero. Paul's competitors come into view in how he treats issues—the good news, the means of righteousness, and circumcision—topics deemed central for the Christian tradition. As indicated, Paul does not detail the inherent benefits or detriments of these issues in reasoned and neutral language, but instead surrounds them with emotion and hyperbole. Most indicative of the presence of competitors, however, is the fact that with these issues Paul creates two mutually exclusive alternatives for his audience. The Galatians are to choose between the "good" or "correct" alternative, Paul's, and the "bad" or "wrong" one, the position of his competitors.

By reading these units in the pursuit of truth, Pauline readers and interpreters misconstrue these rhetorically constructed units for fact.[165] In truth- and fact-seeking readings, the issues Paul raises—the good news, the means of righteousness, and circumcision—loom large; one can without exaggeration say, "exceedingly large." Paul's good news, righteousness by faith, and the rejection of circumcision for non-Jews become significant issues in and of themselves. Indeed, they come to represent Paul himself. Paul is understood as being literally against righteousness through Torah and the practice of circumcision for non-Jews. The literal importance of these issues not only goes beyond what these units warrant, but also interpreters over the generations—as I discuss in the introduction—attribute reasons for Paul's stance on these issues that have been and continue to be not only anachronistic but often harshly and unfoundedly anti-Jewish.

In contrast to truth- or fact-seeking readings, a rhetoric-of-crisis analysis of these Pauline units begins with the understanding that Paul, like other ancient authors of his time, employs *strategies* to win over an audience.[166] A rhetoric-of-crisis reading aims to uncover those strategies. Thus, we have seen how Paul goes to extremes to make his case, how he creates a sense of drama over issues, and how he develops distinctions when none previously existed: how he, with techniques consistent with promoting urgency, magnifies a situation into a crisis. This reading creates a space for understanding Paul as a strategist and for understanding issues that have come to be known as centrally Pauline—namely, the good news, righteousness by means of faith, and the rejection of circumcision of non-Jews—instrumentally, not magnifying them beyond what the text itself indicates. As seen in the units above, Paul deals with these issues polemically, and thus his statements regarding them cannot be taken at face value.

In the next chapter, I discuss how these three authors employ ethos to win their audiences to their perspectives. Demosthenes, Cicero, and Paul self-fashion loftily and with a strong sense of self-importance to gain adherence for their positions.

2

Persuading through
the Promotion
of Self

> His self-presentation is . . . an exercise in impres-
> sion management, public relations, and self-
> justification — and so needs to be read in the context
> of competing political interests and agendas.
> (Mader, "Foresight, Hindsight," 41)

This leg of the rhetoric of crisis consists of devices aimed to advance the author's own persona or ethos. With regard to the importance of ethos on argumentation, James May writes, "Ethos is
an abiding and essential element in the art of verbal persuasion.
Indeed, every verbal undertaking aimed at producing conviction
involves, implicitly or explicitly, the presentation of character, an
advancement of a persona capable of influencing an audience to
no small degree."[1]

Aristotle knew of and wrote about the persuasive power of
ethos. In his *Art of Rhetoric*, he notes that speakers engage in three
broadly construed methods or proofs to persuade audiences,
ethos, pathos, and logos. Indeed, his first category — and the one
he considers to be the most important for persuasion — is ethos,
the character of the speaker (ἐν τῷ ἤθει τοῦ λέγοντος; *Rhet.*
1.2.3). He remarks:

> The orator persuades by moral character when his speech is
> delivered in such a manner as to render him worthy of con-
> fidence; for we feel confidence in a greater degree and more

readily in persons of worth in regard to everything in general,
but where there is no certainty and there is room for doubt,
our confidence is absolute (παντελῶς). But this confidence
must be due to the speech itself, not to any preconceived idea
of the speaker's character; for it is not the case, as some writers
of rhetorical treatises lay down in their "Art," that the worth
of the orator in no way contributes to his [sic] powers of persuasion; on the contrary, moral character, so to say, constitutes
the most effective means of proof (κυριωτάτων ἔχει πίστιν τὸ
ἦθος). (*Rhet.* 1.2.4–5)[2]

The Greek word Aristotle employs and which Freese translates
as "moral character" is ἦθος ("ethos"). In rhetoric "ethos" means
"delineation of character."[3] With his translation "moral character," Freese paraphrases Aristotle, but in a sense, he has it right.
For, to gain confidence in a speaker and thereby be persuaded an
audience is looking not just for any kind of character but instead
for a "good" or "worthy" one.

Aristotle begins by explaining that an orator persuades by
means of ethos as part of his or her self-presentation in oral delivery.[4] Such a remark ostensibly undermines this type of persuasion
on readers through written compositions. Yet Aristotle appears
to anticipate the later dependency upon written compositions, as
he goes on to speak of the importance of the ability of the speech
itself to persuade. As we shall see below, authors not only make
their own characters discernable through their rhetorical style[5] but
so too do they leave traces of their means of persuasion through
ethos.

Romans in particular placed great value on personal character,
and in that period authors relied heavily on ethos for persuasion.[6]
May remarks, "Character was an extraordinarily important element in the social and political milieu of Republican Rome and
exerted a considerable amount of influence on native Roman
oratory."[7] Romans revered authority and esteemed those who
could exhibit wisdom and expert knowledge and who assumed
a sense of responsibility.[8] To gain authority, however, persons had

to prove themselves worthy of it through their actions.[9] Due to the high level of importance character wielded in Roman society, judicial orators often dwelt more on the litigants' character than on logical arguments or other types of proofs.[10] And in all oratory, "trustworthy"[11] speakers, those of good character, had a much better chance of persuading audiences than those with tarnished reputations.[12]

When it came to directly speaking of the merits of one's own character, social convention dictated against it. Indeed, it was seemingly politically disadvantageous to give the impression of promoting an elevated self-image.[13] Yet despite this social taboo against self-promotion, all the rhetoric-of-crisis authors engage in discussions of self and do so with considerable aplomb. Addressing this obvious inconsistency between acceptable and unacceptable behavior, George Lyons comments, "In antiquity the cultural ideal of the magnanimous man who never discussed himself came inevitably into conflict with the irrepressible impertinence of the lately self-conscious man who found it imperative to do so."[14] Indeed, and as we will see below, through techniques such as the open acknowledgement of the convention against discussions of self, candor with regard to personal faults, rhetorical tropes that showcase expert abilities, and exaggeration of one's abilities and renown, all three authors fully and strategically engage in persuasion through ethos.

Persuasion through ethos also falls into the category of ancient autobiography. And as Lyons explains, there are important distinctions between ancient and modern autobiography.

> The major interest of most ancient biographers and autobiographers was not historical reality but human potentiality and idealization. Thus, exaggeration and/or suppression were considered legitimate devices. Ancient biographers and autobiographers seldom began with personal experiences but from existing ideals and literary forms, whether from consciously imitated model works, philosophical presuppositions as to the constituents of virtue, or generally followed rhetorical rules.

This partnership of rhetoric and philosophy resulted in a dubious mixture of sincerity and posing, fact and fantasy, truth and fiction, actual and ideal.[15]

In order to self-characterize in the best light, rhetoric-of-crisis authors exaggerate their qualities and qualifications, use candor to their best advantage, resort to foresight, and impress their audiences with their style of discourse. As is the case with each leg of the rhetoric-of-crisis model, here too persuasion in and of itself, and not the advancement of truth, is the primary goal.[16]

Here, as is the case in each component of the rhetoric-of-crisis model, the authors' opponents or competitors are in view. Indeed, each author's self-characterization or, better put, self-promotion as trustworthy, competent, and as having the audiences' best interests at heart, occurs within a competitive environment and in response to the challenges of opponents. Thus, at the same time in which these authors present themselves as worthy of belief, they explicitly and implicitly diminish their opponents as less worthy than they and as having characteristics far less admirable than their own.[17]

Ethos Building of Demosthenes

While there are many instances of ethos-building within Demosthenes' Philippic-cycle speeches, an extended passage within his *Second Philippic* is replete with various forms of character augmentation, of persuasion through ethos. The passage under review also provides a clear example of how Demosthenes loftily self-fashions within a context of political competition.[18] As Mader remarks, Demosthenes develops a confident and reliable self-image while simultaneously denying legitimacy to his opponents.[19]

Demosthenes lacked full support for the hardline approach he adopted against Philip.[20] At the same time, his senatorial opponents, Aeschines and Philocrates, were politically established and by some accounts more politically astute than he. Thus, Demosthenes deployed arguments from ethos and indeed developed a near ideal version of himself to gain an edge over his savvy political opponents. The passage from his *Second Philippic* follows:

2.28   It would indeed have been fair, men of Athens, to call
        upon **those** who conveyed to you Philip's promises, on the
        strength of which you were induced to conclude the Peace.

2.29a   For I should never myself have consented to serve on
        the embassy, nor would you, I am sure, have suspended
        military operations, if you had imagined that Philip after
        securing peace would act as he has done; but his words
        at the time were very different from his present actions.

2.29b   Yes, and there are **others** who ought to be called upon.

2.29c   **Whom** do I mean?

2.29d   **The men [τοὺς]** who, when peace was made and when
        I [ἐγὼ], returning from the second embassy — that sent
        to administer the oaths — found [αἰσθόμενος] that
        the state was being imposed upon, and spoke out and
        protested and refused to give up Thermopylae and the
        Phocians —

2.30a   **the men** [designated by the verb λέγοντας that follows],
        I say, who told you [λέγοντας] that I, being a water-
        drinker, was naturally a disagreeable, cross-grained
        fellow, and that Philip, if he got through the Pass, would
        do just what you would pray for, would fortify Thespiae
        and Plataea, and humble the Theban pride, and dig a
        trench across the Chersonese at his own charges, and
        restore to you Euboea and Oropus in lieu of Amphipolis.

2.30b   All this was said from this very platform, as I am sure
        you recollect, although you are not remarkable for keep-
        ing in mind those who injure you.

2.31a   And the crowning disgrace is that your posterity also is
        bound by the same peace which these hopes prompted
        you to conclude; so completely were you led astray.

2.31b   Why do I mention this now and assert that **these men**
        [τούτους] ought to be called upon?

2.31c   I vow that I will boldly tell you the whole truth [τἀληθῆ
        μετὰ παρρησίας ἐρῶ] and keep nothing back.

2.32a   It is not that by descending to abuse I may lay myself
        open to retaliation in your presence, while I give those

who from the first have fallen foul of me an excuse for
making further profit out of Philip.

2.32b Nor do I wish to indulge in idle talk.

2.32c But I think that one day Philip's policy will cause you more
distress than it does now, for I see the plot thickening.

2.33a I hope I may prove a false prophet, but I fear the catas-
trophe is even now only too near.

2.33b So when you can no longer shut your eyes to what is
happening, when you do not need me or someone else
to tell you, but can all see for yourselves and be quite
certain that all this is directed against you, then I expect
you will be angry and exasperated.[21]

Demosthenes impresses his audience with his sophisticated
rhetorical style.[22] Indeed, he is known for this skill. In his *On
Types of Style* (Περὶ ἰδεῶν), Hermogenes notes that Demosthenes
delicately combines seven different stylistic elements: clarity,
grandeur, beauty, rapidity, character, sincerity, and force (Περὶ
ἰδεῶν 218).[23] Demosthenes wove these seven elements together
into one style, "the Demosthenic, the most beautiful" (Περὶ
ἰδεῶν 221).[24] Echoing Hermogenes, Wooten comments that
Demosthenes' speeches contain "vigor, directness and immediacy
that was rarely equaled in ancient oratory."[25] His style is marked
by variety and above all by "firm control."[26] In the passage above,
Demosthenes showcases his vigor, expertise, and firm control to
persuade his Athenian senatorial audience of his own trustworthy and dependable counsel and to demonstrate the unreliability
of his competitors.

Demosthenes structures this unit around the expression "the
men." These unnamed[27] "men" represent his political opponents
in the senate, Aeschines and Philocrates.[28] Demosthenes treats his
opponents first and then develops his own "virtuous" character
by way of contrast to his constructed characterization of them.

He employs a periodic style[29] that includes a mix of long[30]
and short periods. In line 2.29a—an analytic period, in which the
principal thought is stated at the outset and its explanation follows—Demosthenes explains why the Athenians' prior and pas-

sive approach to Philip, the current approach of his opponents, is wrong. Elsewhere in the unit (2.29d, 30a), he creates suspenseful periods—in which subordinate clauses occur at the start and the main clause follows—to build curiosity around the subject of the men. As an example of the latter, Demosthenes drops a reference to the men early in the unit (2.29d), highlighting his intention to discuss something about them, but then he delays the completion of this discussion until much later, to the end of 2.30a. Indeed, twenty-nine words separate the τοὺς (the pronoun that refers to "the men"; 2.29d) from its associated participle λέγοντας ("speaking"; 2.30a).[31] Wooten refers to this long separation between grammatical elements intended to go together as "violent hyperbaton."[32] Yet in the rhetoric of Demosthenes, even this extreme distance between grammatical elements meant to be together does not detract from the sentence's clarity,[33] as all the intervening clauses contain descriptions that are logical and chronological.[34]

Long elaborate suspenseful periods serve to highlight the differences between the actions of Demosthenes and the men. While it begins with an allusion to the men (τοὺς), line 2.29d is essentially a long interruption consisting of Demosthenes' own positive actions on behalf of the Athenians. An internal phrase that begins with "I" (ἐγὼ), which is itself separated from its associated participle "found" (αἰσθόμενος), also creates suspense (2.29d) and continues to emphasize Demosthenes and his positive actions for the Athenians. The second long suspenseful period (2.30a), on the other hand, reprises and resolves the discussion of the men (λέγοντας, "those speaking").[35]

Several short periods (2.29b, 29c, 31b) not only add variety to the unit but also contribute to the suspense Demosthenes seeks to build around the issue of the men. Two short periods (2.29c, 31b) consist of rhetorical questions and function to cause the audience to question the men's motives.

To summarize thus far, the two long suspenseful periods are highly artistic and function to highlight and contrast the actions between Demosthenes and his opponents. Their sophistication showcases Demosthenes' skills, his pizzazz as an orator as well as his skills in assessing political events.[36] Indeed, line 2.30a can be

considered a use of *apheleia*, a style intended to convince an audience of the orator's ability to perceive and explain complex issues
in a simple fashion.[37]

Beyond showcasing his oratorical skills and political know-
how, Demosthenes employs other rhetorical methods to win over
his audience through self-promotion. He accentuates/exaggerates
his good character,[38] and develops both a practical/reasonable and
trustworthy self-image. He calls attention to his trustworthiness
by stating what he will do.[39] Thus, he vows to boldly tell the truth
(τἀληθῆ μετὰ παρρησίας ἐρῶ), to hold nothing back (2.31c), and
he pledges not to engage in idle talk (ἀδολεσχῶ; 2.32b).[40]

Through *parrhesia*, a claim to candor,[41] he enhances his own
credibility. Indeed each of the rhetoric-of-crisis authors engages in
a claim to candor to strengthen their image. In 2.30a Demosthenes
discloses that his opponents, the men, have accused him of being disagreeable and a water drinker.[42] Yet because he makes this
potentially negative incident known, he impresses his audience
with a show of candor. This technique serves to strengthen a sense
of his honesty and reliability with his audience.[43] Furthermore,
he embeds his opponents' negative remarks against him within
a discussion that concerns their untrustworthiness (2.30a). The
strategic placement of their remarks serves to render the remarks
themselves of little or no merit.[44] This too serves, in turn, to enhance his self-image to the detriment of his opponents.

As is common in his Philippic orations, Demosthenes engages
in audience castigation. Here, he accuses the Athenian senators
of being short on memory and easily led astray (2.30b, 31a). Yet
audience castigation, like the high oratorical style he showcases,
is itself a form of authoritative self-fashioning. Demosthenes' reprimands function to legitimate the advice he offers.[45]

Foresight[46] is yet another way in which Demosthenes engages
in positive self-fashioning. Indeed, according to Mader, foresight
is one of three primary ways in which Demosthenes builds an
ideal version of himself.[47] In this unit, Demosthenes predicts that
Philip will cause more harm in the future (2.32c, 33a) and that his
audience will become angry when it happens (2.33b).

Demosthenes' attempts to persuade through ethos are not merely for the purpose of augmenting his self-image, but also concern his desire to outshine his political opponents. Indeed, this entire unit involves his constructed contrast between his own "reliable and proven advice" concerning Philip and the "ill advice" of his unnamed opponents, the men. The issue of his political opponents figures prominently in the passage (2.28, 29b, 29c, 29d, 30a, 30b, 31a, 31b). From the outset, Demosthenes challenges the Athenians to call these men to account for their actions. According to him, these men made promises to the Athenians regarding Philip's actions that were incorrect and have as a result caused harm (2.28, 31a). Demosthenes' vows to tell the truth (2.30a–2.31c) and to refrain from idle talk (2.32b) imply that his opponents cannot be relied upon to do the same. According to Mader, even Demosthenes' recourse to foresight (2.32c, 33a) has as its underlying purpose his self-presentation in a light superior to that of his opponents. [48]

In sum, in this short passage, there are many instances of persuasion through ethos. Demosthenes' sophisticated style showcases his talent as a highly skilled orator. His sophisticated and highly ornamental rhetorical style along with the castigation of his audience indicates his strong control over his language and his audience, and thus gives the impression of an authoritative self. Through rhetorical techniques such as the claim to candor (*parrhesia*) and forethought, Demosthenes gives the impression that he is both trustworthy and wise. By discussing uncomplimentary aspects of his character—which may or may not have been accurate—within the context of his unreliable opponents, he handily minimizes their potentially damaging effects. His appeal from ethos serves not only to self-present in a positive light, as a credible and worthy speaker and politician, but also to contrast his own trustworthy character to the unreliability of his opponents.

Ethos Building of Cicero

One would likely expect to see a degree of self-promotion in Cicero's *Fourteenth Philippic*. Cicero delivered this speech just after his public recognition of his fight against Antony and at the news of a victory over Antony's troops at the Battle at Forum Gallorum (21 April 23). On the day of its delivery, but without Cicero's knowledge,[49] Antony suffered an even more decisive defeat at the Battle of Mutina, one that resulted in his withdrawal from combat. In this final[50] Philippic speech, Cicero discusses the celebrations of the previous day and councilman Publius Servilius' proposal for a public thanksgiving for the recent military heroes of Forum Gallorum. Since, to his knowledge, his enemy Antony had yet to be defeated, Cicero once again, and as is typical of all his Philippic speeches, uses this speech as another chance to have Antony declared a *hostis* (public enemy).[51] To win acceptance for the latter, Cicero makes the legal point that no celebration of victory has ever been decreed over the defeat of a fellow *citizen* (14.6–10).

While in the passage that follows Cicero argues from ethos, any number of passages could have been selected to demonstrate how Cicero builds up a positive portrayal of himself. As May comments, ethos-building is the single constant feature in all of Cicero's fifty speeches covering a forty-year period.[52] Like Demosthenes' arguments seen above, Cicero self-presents with an exaggerated sense of self-importance. He employs the festivities of the previous days—a public honor bestowed on him—to reaffirm and even augment his own favorable public persona. He raises the issue of a false rumor potentially very damaging to his reputation, yet he uses this incident to strengthen his own character and to tarnish the characters of those responsible for circulating it. As with Demosthenes, Cicero too self-fashions within a context of competition.[53] The passage reads as follows:

14.12 For with what honor, rejoicing, and congratulation [*honore, laetitia, gratulatione*] should those liberators [*liberatores*] of this city enter this temple in person, when yesterday on account of their [liberators'] achievements the Roman people bore me from my house [*domo*] to the Capitol and back again to my house [*domum*] in an ovation, almost a triumph [*prope triumphantem*]!

14.13a For to my mind, a true, genuine triumph is only when those who have deserved well of the Republic receive the tributes of a united community [*consensu civitatas*].

14.13b If in the shared joy [*in communi gaudio*] of the Roman people they were congratulating [*gratulabantur*] one [*uni*] individual, that was a great mark of esteem;

14.13c if they were thanking one [*uni*] individual, all the greater;

14.13d if both, no more splendid compliment can be conceived of.

14.13e Someone may say: "Do you, then, indulge in self-applause?"

14.13f It is against my will, to be sure, [*Equidem invitus*] but a sense of injury[54] makes me vainglorious, contrary to my habit.

14.13g Is it not enough[55] that persons [*hominibus*] ignorant [*ignaris*] of the meaning of true worth make no return of gratitude to those who deserve well?

14.13h Will even those who devote all their care to the preservation of the Republic be targets for backbiting and envy?

14.14a You know that during the past few days there was a vast amount of talk that on Shepherds' Day,[56] that is today,

14.14b I would come down to the Forum with the fasces.[57]

14.14c I suppose that such a rumor has been concocted against a gladiator or a bandit or a Catiline, not against a man who has made sure that nothing of that kind can happen in the Republic.

14.14d Was it likely that I [*An (ut) ego*], who hoisted, overthrew, and dashed down Catiline, when he made such an attempt, should suddenly reveal myself a Catiline?

14.14e With what [*Quibus*] auspices was I, an augur, to have accepted those fasces,

14.14f how long [*quatenus*] was I going to keep them,

14.14g to whom [*cui*] should I have handed them over?

14.14h Could anyone [*qui*] have been so wicked as to invent this tale or so mad as to believe it? (14.13–14)[58]

As with Demosthenes, Cicero deploys a sophisticated oratorical style. May notes that a well-designed speech helps to establish

an orator as sensible, virtuous, and trustworthy. It is through
methods such as invention, arrangement, style, and delivery that
an orator demonstrates moral character.[59] In the passage above,
Cicero's strong mastery of language and rhetorical tropes assist
him in his development of a positive self-image or moral character. The passage opens with a long period (14.12), and contains
multi-layered conditional clauses (14.13b, 13c, 13d); internal
dialog (14.13e); a string of rhetorical questions (14.13g, 13h, 14d,
14e, 14f, 14g, 14h); the repetition of terms, often in the form of
anaphora (14.13b, 13c); vivid description (14.14b) and *asyndeton*
(14.12, 14d).

Form and content, as we saw above with Demosthenes, operate together to advance a lofty self-image.[60] In the long and complex period that begins the unit (14.12), Cicero brings himself into
the orbit of the actual liberators of Rome, of the military men.[61] He
does this in two ways. One, he divides the long opening period
into two sections; the first half belongs to a discussion of the liberators (*liberators*), and the entire second half, beginning with the
words "when yesterday," concerns Cicero himself (14.12). With
one long breath, then, he discusses two separate incidents, effectively joining the two together. Two, he employs the same word
for congratulations (*gratulatione*), first for the liberators, that is, for
the military heroes (14.12), and then for the events that concern
himself (*gratulabantur*; 14.13b). Ostensibly, Cicero wishes to honor
the recent heroism on the battlefield of the Republican command-
ers Gaius Pansa and Aulus Hirtius, those who lost their lives for
the cause. Yet by mentioning his own celebration together with
and stylistically similar to the military heroism of these others,
Cicero conflates the two incidents and thereby brings the honor
due the military liberators onto himself.[62]

Moreover, the mere mention of the public affirmation of the
previous day brings the event to the attention of his present audience. Cicero, however, goes beyond a simple passing comment
of the previous day and instead elaborates upon the public acclaim given him. With *enargeia*—the description of a situation
or action as though it were present[63]—Cicero vividly rehearses
and embellishes upon the events of the previous day. Whereas a

crowd escorted him from his home to the capitol and back again
(14.12), Cicero refers to his public escort as a near triumph (*prope
triumphantem*;[64] 14.13a). He informs his audience of the two elements best suited to honor a person dedicated to the betterment of
the republic[65] (14.13a, 13b, 13c, 13d)—shared congratulations and
thanks to one individual—and then claims that the public has just
yesterday accorded both to him![66] Moreover, through repetition
of the notion of a consensus of opinion behind his public congratulations (*consensus*, community, 14.13a, and *in communi gaudio*, 14.13b), he emphasizes the public's appreciation. Yet with this
comment, he likely overstates his case.[67] Finally, by twice remark-
ing that the consensual group addressed themselves to "one individual" (*uni*; 14.13b, 13c), he calls attention to the fact that their
acclaim was for him (*uni*) alone.

In a gesture that appears to tilt in the direction of genuineness
and sincerity (*parrhesia*), Cicero openly acknowledges his engagement in self-aggrandizement (14.13e, 13f).[68] Yet the sophisticated
style by which he acknowledges his act of self-boasting undermines the sincerity of his apology for it. Indeed, Cicero's employment of a rhetorical device called *prosopopoeia*, a sophisticated
technique whereby an author creates a fictitious dialog partner[69]
(14.13e), indicates his full control over his arguments. Given the
steady flow of self-promotion in the unit and his commanding
rhetorical style, the comment that he engages in the practice of
self-acclaim "against his will" (*invitus*; 14.13f) can be seen as at
best only half-genuine.[70]

Like Demosthenes, Cicero lays bare an accusation against him
potentially very damaging to his character, another use of *parrhesia* (a claim to candor that risks the goodwill of the audience),[71]
yet he handily dispatches of it without suffering damage from
it (14.14a, 14b). Cicero's political opponents circulated a rumor
that he was planning to proclaim himself dictator.[72] He adopts
a strongly offensive stance toward the rumor. He attacks his opponents for their ignorance (14.13g), and then bombards his audience with a string of five rhetorical questions that border on
sarcasm,[73] in which he makes a mockery of his opponents' accusation. By introducing each question with a different interrogatory

expression ("was I?," "with what?," "how long?," "to whom?,"
"who?"; 14.14d, 14e, 14f, 14g, 14h), Cicero challenges their malicious rumor from seemingly every possible angle. While intended
to rebuke those circulating the rumor—his opponents—the questions, in the form of a monologue,[74] also function to caution his
listening audience against being swayed by such a rumor and by
the opponents themselves. Through his retaliatory efforts, as seen
especially with the series of rhetorical questions, Cicero maintains
and even enhances his authoritative self-image, despite the damaging accusation.

Like Demosthenes with his "men," Cicero too self-aggran-
dizes by creating contrastive characterizations between himself
and his senatorial political opponents. After developing a highly
favorable ethos in the first half of the unit, exaggerating his public acclaim beyond what was warranted, he turns to his political
opponents (see 14.13g ff). The scathing and nearly satirical image he creates of his opponents in the second half of the unit creates a sharp contrast to his own positive self-fashioning found
in the first half.[75] Like Demosthenes, Cicero does not name his
opponents. Indeed, his "persons" (hominibus; 14.13g) functions
similarly to Demosthenes' "the men," in that with the impersonal
term, he creates audience curiosity and suspense. Cicero compares the malicious rumor presently circulating against him to the
Catiline conspiracy[76] (14.14c, 14d [2x]). In that earlier incident, the
Roman senator Catiline (108–62 BCE) conspired to overthrow the
Republic. Cicero's reference to Catiline is likely an indirect attack
on Antony, whom he elsewhere accuses of being like Catiline.[77]
Finally, and in a passage beyond the one presented here, with
Demosthenic-like foresight, a technique associated with the desire to undermine an opponent, Cicero predicts that "when the
time is right" the source of this false rumor will be uncovered (sed
suo tempore totius huius sceleris fons aperietur; 14.15).[78]

In sum, throughout this passage, Cicero engages in extensive
positive self-fashioning. Like Demosthenes, he shows himself to
be a master of oratorical style and with it he showcases his talent. To bolster his importance and esteem, Cicero aggrandizes his
public acclaim. According to Cicero's reportage of the events of

the previous day, the honors paid to him were similar to those given in a triumph. He conflates the public's praise of him with the acclaim due to military heroes. In his strong challenge against his political opponents, Cicero demonstrates and affirms his strength of character. Employing a string of cleverly designed rhetorical questions, Cicero handily diminishes the intelligence of those who spread the rumor against him. Like Demosthenes, Cicero's own positive self-fashioning performs a dual purpose: it not only magnifies his ethos but also simultaneously establishes a strong contrast to his political opponents in the senate.[79]

Ethos Building of Paul

Paul's recourse to arguments from ethos occurs right at the start of Galatians (1:1–5), in his salutation[80] or epistolary prescript,[81] and recurs in a lengthy section found shortly thereafter (1:10–2:21).[82] Both sections are forms of ancient rather than modern autobiography. The position and length, especially of the second passage, provides a strong indication that Paul is invested in developing his own positive persona for the purpose of persuasion.[83] One of the primary ways in which Paul self-fashions loftily is by describing himself as a man wholly of God.

As was the case with Demosthenes and Cicero, Paul too develops his ethos within a competitive context.[84] Competition is in view in the specific ways in which he self-characterizes and by the fact that each autobiographical section serves as a frame for a short section in which he takes up the topic of his opponents (1:6–9). Through his arguments from ethos, Paul attempts to win the Galatians to his own perspective and from the side of his opponents.

The Divinely Commissioned Apostle

Like Demosthenes and Cicero, Paul constructs a lofty persona. His self-fashioning occurs at the very start of Galatians (Gal 1:1), when he lets it be known that he is a God-commissioned apostle. His tone is strident and combative. His methods of self-fashioning are similar to those employed by Demosthenes and Cicero. The salutation reads as follows.

1:1a Παῦλος ἀπόστολος
　　1:1b οὐκ ἀπ᾽ ἀνθρώπων
　　　1:1c οὐδὲ δι᾽ ἀνθρώπου
　　　1:1d ἀλλὰ διὰ Ἰησοῦ Χριστοῦ
1:1e καὶ θεοῦ πατρὸς τοῦ ἐγείραντος αὐτὸν ἐκ νεκρῶν
1:2a καὶ οἱ σὺν ἐμοὶ πάντες ἀδελφοὶ
1:2b ταῖς ἐκκλησίαις τῆς Γαλατίας
1:3 χάρις ὑμῖν καὶ εἰρήνη ἀπὸ θεοῦ πατρὸς ἡμῶν καὶ
κυρίου Ἰησοῦ Χριστοῦ
　　1:4a τοῦ δόντος ἑαυτὸν ὑπὲρ τῶν ἁμαρτιῶν ἡμῶν,
1:4b ὅπως ἐξέληται ἡμᾶς ἐκ τοῦ αἰῶνος τοῦ ἐνεστῶτος
πονηροῦ κατὰ τὸ θέλημα τοῦ θεοῦ καὶ πατρὸς ἡμῶν,
　　　1:5 ᾧ ἡ δόξα εἰς τοὺς αἰῶνας τῶν αἰώνων, ἀμήν.

1:1a *Paul, apostle*
　　1:1b **not** by **humans**
　　　1:1c **nor** by a **human**
　　　1:1d but by *Jesus, Anointed,*
　　　　1:1e and God, the father, who raised him from the dead,
1:2a and all the brothers with me
1:2b to the assemblies of Galatia,
1:3 Grace to you and peace from God, our father and the
lord Jesus, the Anointed
　　1:4a who gave himself for our sins,
1:4b in order that he might remove us from the present evil
age, according to the will of God and our father,
　　　1:5 to whom be the glory for ever and ever.
Amen.[85]

Like the units in the speeches of Demosthenes and Cicero above, Gal 1:1–5[86] is highly stylized.[87] As such, it functions to showcase rhetorical talent.[88] Using very short cola, Paul strongly asserts his God-commissioned apostleship (1:1c, 1e). He argues from the negative position, by insisting upon what he is not. For this, he deploys double adversatives (words that denote the negative) in parallel clauses (1:1b, 1c). The adversatives οὐκ ("not") and οὐδὲ ("and not")[89] (marked in bold-faced type above) head their respective short clauses (cola), and as such receive more significance than if they were buried within them.[90] His placement of adversatives and their duplication in the form of *polyptoton*,[91] the repetition of a word under a different form, serve as emphasis and add strength to Paul's utterances and to Paul himself.[92] Paul twice repeats that Greek word for human (ἀνθρώπων, ἀνθρώπου) (1:1b, 1c; marked in bold-faced type), another form of *polyptoton*. Taken together, the rhetorical techniques function to display his skills at composition,[93] while they also produce a strong counter-image against which Paul creates his own positive self-characterization.

Paul establishes a forthright and assertive/authoritative[94] ethos in Galatians. A brief comparison to his other extant letters makes this more apparent. In 1 Thessalonians, Philippians, and Philemon, Paul does not mention his apostleship at all. For example, in Phil 1:1, he remarks that he and another named companion, Timothy, are "servants" or "slaves" (δοῦλοι) of Jesus, the Anointed. In Philemon, Paul calls himself a prisoner (δέσμιος) and mentions Timothy as a brother. In 1 Thessalonians, Paul includes himself as a letter sender along with Silvanus and Timothy and applies no additional descriptors. In each of these other salutations, Paul issues a friendly greeting of grace and peace without any harsh or abrasive tone.

In 1 and 2 Corinthians and in Romans, Paul does refer to his apostleship but in ways that differ from Galatians. Paul begins 2 Corinthians with identical wording of Galatians. He employs the expression Παῦλος ἀπόστολος ("Paul, apostle"). But after that initial correspondence, the salutation of 2 Corinthians deviates significantly from Galatians. Only Galatians contains the two adversative phrases, which create friction around the term "apostle."[95] Second Corinthians 1:1 reads, Χριστοῦ Ἰησοῦ διὰ θελήματος θεοῦ καὶ Τιμόθεος ὁ ἀδελφὸς ("Paul, apostle of the Anointed Jesus through the will of God, and Timothy, the brother"). In 2 Corinthians, and as in his other salutations, Paul is simply descriptive; his tone is positive and non-confrontational.[96] First

Corinthians begins with the phrase Παῦλος κλητὸς ἀπόστολος ("Paul called [to be] apostle"). The adjective κλητὸς ("called") separates the name Paul from his title apostle and serves a descriptive and positively construed purpose. Paul's most elaborate salutation is found in Romans.[97] In that letter, Paul seemingly borrows from his other letters, as it is a mash-up of several self-descriptors. He combines the notion of being a servant from Philippians, a called apostle from 1 Corinthians, and the notion of being "set apart for the good news of God" (cf. Gal 1:15; Rom 1:1). Like these other five salutations, there is nothing particularly confrontational about the opening of Romans. While elaborate, Rom 1:1 is otherwise descriptive in nature. By comparison with Galatians, these other six salutations are lame. In Galatians, Paul projects a highly confrontational and authoritative persona.[98]

Furthermore, with the exception of Romans, in his other extant salutations, Paul mentions by name another or other male colleagues as co-senders of the letter. By contrast, in Galatians, no other person is singled out *by name*. Thus, in Galatians, as in Romans, no other named person deflects attention away from Paul himself.

The term "apostle"[99] is not in and of itself lofty, but in Paul's hands and in Galatians it becomes so.[100] In Greek the word means, "messenger,"[101] "ambassador," or "envoy." Indeed, the SV consistently translates ἀπόστολος as "envoy," likely to downplay an otherworldly sense of the term.[102] But in this unit, hearers are meant to understand "apostle" as distinctive, otherworldly and lofty.[103] Indeed, Paul "carefully crafts" himself as an apostle.[104] He employs the same grammatical construction (marked in italics above) for the divine figure Jesus (cf. "Paul, apostle," Παῦλος ἀπόστολος; 1:1a and "Jesus, Anointed,"[105] Ιησοῦ Χριστοῦ; 1:1d) as he does for himself as an apostle. Both expressions include only a first name followed by a title.

Paul describes his apostleship and how it came to be in the highest of terms. Leading with adversatives, he twice remarks that he is not an ordinary or human apostle sent by human beings (1:1b, 1c), but rather one commissioned by no less than two divine figures, Jesus, the raised Anointed one (1:1d),[106] and God (1:1e). *Polyptoton*, and as mentioned above, on the words for "not" and "human," reinforces and emphasizes this point (1:1b, 1c).[107] Furthermore, and as Betz remarks, Paul juxtaposes the phrase "not through a human" (1:1c) with "but through Jesus, the Anointed" (1:1d), and the phrase "not from humans" (1:1b) with "and God, the father, who raised him from the dead" (1:1e),[108] strengthening the connection he seeks to draw between himself and these divine figures as well as the contrast he is developing between himself and other types of commissioned apostles.

As mentioned, Paul employs negative constructions (adversatives), not used in his other salutations, to describe his apostleship. Adversatives are not neutral descriptors. Chaïm Perelman and Lucie Olbrechts-Tyteca remind readers that authors choose how they present their material. By presenting something in the negative, authors do more than simply make a statement; they also make a value judgment.[109] Thus, by defining his apostleship with adversatives, Paul displays an interest in letting it be known not so much that he is an apostle, but instead that his apostleship is different from and indeed superior to another type, or even to any other type of apostleship. Johan Vos remarks, "The only function of the *correctio* [the twofold adversatives] is to accentuate the positive part of the statement," namely, that divine beings commission Paul's apostleship.[110] Furthermore, according to Perelman and Olbrechts-Tyteca, statements expressed in the negative always imply the presence of others.[111] Thus, Paul's self-presentation indicates the influence of competition.

Finally, in 1:4b Paul employs the striking and one-time expression "the present evil age." As he remarks, Jesus the Anointed delivers, removes or lifts (ἐξέληται, from ἐξαιρέω), a person from the "the present evil age" (τοῦ αἰῶνος τοῦ ἐνεστῶτος πονηροῦ; 1:4b). While the phrase has been interpreted theologically, and as an instance of apocalypticism,[112] motivated by Paul's negative assessment of the human condition,[113] the context does not lend itself to such an interpretation. As seen, the adversatives οὐκ and οὐδὲ ("not," "and not"; 1:1b, 1c) characterize Paul's self-presentation as an apostle. These are indicators of competition. It is certainly within the realm of possibility that with the expression "the present evil age" Paul is making a highly negative assessment,[114] verging on the hyperbolic, of his own present situation[115] with his competition.[116] The strident tone apparent in the salutation undermines the sense in which Paul is rendering an impersonal assessment of the state of the world, but indicates instead an impassioned appraisal — whether genuine or feigned — around something specific and of immediate concern. If this interpretation is correct, one can say that already in his salutation, Paul assesses his current situation as a crisis of evil proportions.

In sum, in Gal 1:1–5 Paul is assertive, authoritative, and confrontational. While his salutation is brief, with it he nonetheless showcases his talents in the art of argumentation. By aligning himself with two divine figures, and by creating a hierarchy between types of apostles, Paul carefully crafts his own apostleship to self-present in a lofty fashion so as to outshine others. Over a half-century ago John Knox wrote, "Only a blind reader of Paul's epistles could miss the signs of the egoism and pride that are back of this [Paul's] indignation."[117]

A Trustworthy Man of God

In a second unit (Gal 1:10–17), often mined for "facts" about Paul, the author Paul skillfully attempts to win the Galatians to his perspective largely through ethos.[118] Typical of ancient autobiographies, Paul engages in a discussion of his past and present actions.[119] As was the case with Demosthenes and Cicero, Paul's self-disclosures are selective: he discusses only aspects of his past life necessary for the development of a self-characterization that is strong enough to persuade his audience and gain their agreement for his views. And like Demosthenes and Cicero, competition is highly determinative of what Paul narrates about himself.

While the fuller autobiographical section extends from Gal 1:10–2:21,[120] its length and complexity render it too cumbersome for the present study. The first part of the section (Gal 1:10–17) provides material sufficient for an assessment of the ways in which Paul develops his own strong persona so as to be persuasive.[121]

1:10a Ἄρτι γὰρ **ἀνθρώπους πείθω** ἢ τὸν θεόν;[122]
1:10b ἢ ζητῶ **ἀνθρώποις ἀρέσκειν**;
1:10c εἰ ἔτι **ἀνθρώποις ἤρεσκον**, Χριστοῦ δοῦλος οὐκ ἂν ἤμην.
1:11 Γνωρίζω γὰρ ὑμῖν, ἀδελφοί, τὸ εὐαγγέλιον τὸ εὐαγγελισθὲν ὑπ᾽ ἐμοῦ ὅτι οὐκ ἔστιν κατὰ **ἄνθρωπον·**
1:12a οὐδὲ γὰρ ἐγὼ παρὰ **ἀνθρώπου** παρέλαβον αὐτὸ
1:12b οὔτε ἐδιδάχθην ἀλλὰ δι᾽ ἀποκαλύψεως Ἰησοῦ Χριστοῦ.
1:13a Ἠκούσατε γὰρ τὴν ἐμὴν ἀναστροφήν ποτε ἐν τῷ Ἰουδαϊσμῷ,
1:13b ὅτι καθ᾽ ὑπερβολὴν ἐδίωκον τὴν ἐκκλησίαν τοῦ θεοῦ καὶ ἐπόρθουν αὐτήν,
1:14a καὶ προέκοπτον ἐν τῷ Ἰουδαϊσμῷ ὑπὲρ πολλοὺς συνηλικιώτας ἐν τῷ γένει μου,
1:14b περισσοτέρως ζηλωτὴς ὑπάρχων τῶν πατρικῶν μου παραδόσεων.
1:15a Ὅτε δὲ εὐδόκησεν [ὁ θεὸς] ὁ ἀφορίσας με ἐκ κοιλίας μητρός μου
1:15b καὶ καλέσας διὰ τῆς χάριτος αὐτοῦ ἀποκαλύψαι τὸν υἱὸν αὐτοῦ ἐν ἐμοί, ἵνα εὐαγγελίζωμαι αὐτὸν ἐν τοῖς ἔθνεσιν,
1:16 εὐθέως οὐ προσανεθέμην σαρκὶ καὶ αἵματι
1:17a οὐδὲ ἀνῆλθον εἰς Ἱεροσόλυμα πρὸς τοὺς πρὸ ἐμοῦ ἀποστόλους,
1:17b ἀλλ᾽ ἀπῆλθον εἰς Ἀραβίαν καὶ πάλιν ὑπέστρεψα εἰς Δαμασκόν.

1:10a For am I now **persuading men** or God?
1:10b Or am I seeking to **please men**?
1:10c If I were still **pleasing men**, I would not be the Anointed's slave.
1:11 For I am making known to you, brothers, the good news proclaimed by me is not according to a **man**.
1:12a For I did not receive it from a **man**
1:12b nor was I taught it but [I received it] through a revelation of Jesus, the Anointed.
1:13a For you heard of my former behavior in Judaism,[123]

1:13b that I persecuted to the superlative degree[124] the
        assembly of God and tried to destroy it.
1:14a and [how] I advanced in Judaism beyond many of my
        people of the same age.
1:14b I was extremely zealous for the traditions of the ancestors.
1:15a But when it pleased [God], who separated me from my
        mother's womb
1:15b and called [me] through his grace to reveal his son in me,
        so that I might proclaim him among the non-Jews,
1:16   immediately, I did not consult with flesh and blood
1:17a nor did I go into Jerusalem, to those who were apostles
        before me,
1:17b but I went into Arabia and again I returned to Damascus.[125]

As in the section above, Paul self-fashions around the notion of
his being a man of God. And more so in this section than in the letter's salutation, Paul emphasizes his association with God.[126] The
words he speaks are not his own but instead God's (1:11, cf. 1:1a).
God is the source and even the content of the good news (1:12b)
he proclaims; and God charged him to proclaim it (1:15b). Paul
claims to be a slave or servant (δοῦλος) of Jesus, the Anointed
(1:10c). Conceptually, slaves have no will or agency and instead
act according to the desires of their master. Moreover, Paul states
that God was the active agent in his life even before his birth
(1:15a). With his expression ὁ ἀφορίσας με ἐκ κοιλίας μητρός
μου ("[God] who separated me from my mother's womb"; 1:15a),
likely borrowed from Hebrew scriptures,[127] Paul self-depicts as an
ancient judge or prophet of Israel, those who by definition act on
God's orders. Paul thus self-fashions as an agent of God set apart
for God's mission (1:10c, 11, 12a, 12b, 15a, 15b, cf. 1:1).
    As in his salutation, here too Paul develops an authoritative
ethos. However, in contrast to the earlier section, in this unit he
employs irony[128] and rebuke[129] to develop it. Irony presupposes
an attitude of superiority with regard to its target audience. With
his ironic rhetorical questions, Paul, like Cicero in the passage
above (14.14d, 14e, 14f, 14g), rebukes his audience for their breach

of faith in him. This form of assertiveness[130] undermines the very common interpretation that Paul is apologetic.[131] Beverly Gaventa comments, "Virtually all commentators on Galatians agree that the single purpose of Galatians 1 and 2 is apologetic."[132] Paul's arguments indicate that he is creating an offensive and authoritative/assertive self-presentation, not an apologetic one.

With his first rhetorical question, Paul denies both[133] that he is in the business of persuasion and that he is persuading God.[134] The first part of his question is hyperbolic and self-contradictory: Paul claims to be out of the business of persuasion while he simultaneously engages in the act itself (1:10a).[135] With this rhetorical question, Paul appears to be suggesting that as a man of God, as God's mouthpiece, his words supersede rhetoric. The idea of denying the attempt to persuade God—the second part of the question—is intuitively easier to understand than the first (1:10a). To persuade God is to take up a position of equality with God, while Paul claims instead to be something else: to be God's agent (1:1a, 1d, 1e, 11, 15b), God's prophet (1:15a), and God's slave (1:10c).[136] His double question strengthens his accusation against his audience. At the same time, however, the two questions serve to impress them as someone who is bold and authoritative, as someone who is beyond reproach and therefore a reliable mouthpiece of God.

With his second full rhetorical question (1:10b), Paul reinforces the notion that he can be relied upon to act appropriately. His discussion in the form of a question is fully at home with how Demosthenes self-fashions. Paul participates in ironic rebuke—indirectly accusing his audience of any suggestion that he is in business of pleasing people. He repeats the Greek verb that denotes pleasing but with a different form (*polyptoton*; see ἀρέσκειν, 1:10b; ἤρεσκον 1:10c), thereby emphasizing his denial of it. With the notion of pleasing people, Paul engages in a common form of ancient polemics.[137] To criticize their opponents, ancient rhetors would accuse them of being "people pleasers" and thus insincere. For instance, Demosthenes writes that unlike his opponents, he tells the truth, even when it is unpleasant or uncomfortable.

For my own part, I have never yet chosen to court your favor
by saying anything that I was not quite convinced would be
to your advantage; and today, keeping nothing back, I have
given free utterance to my plain sentiments. (Demosthenes,
Phil. 1.51)[138]

I vow that I will boldly tell you the whole truth and keep
nothing back. (Demosthenes, *Phil.* 2.32)[139]

I am afraid it is an ominous thing to say, but yet the truth . . .
I do not think they [our state of affairs] have been in a worse
condition than they are today. Perhaps, indeed, this condition
of our affairs may be attributed to many causes and not just to
one or two, but a careful examination will convince you that it
is above all due to those who study to win your favour rather
than to give you the best advice. (Demosthenes, *Phil.* 3.1–2)[140]

In Gal 1:13–14 Paul raises aspects of his character potentially
damaging[141] to the highly favorable self-portrayal he presents to
his Galatian audience. Yet as was the case with Demosthenes and
Cicero, his self-disclosures do not harm the ethos he builds. Like
Demosthenes and Cicero, Paul puts potentially damaging aspects
of his past life to use, to bring about an overall positive evaluation
of himself and one that ultimately enhances rather than detracts
from his favorable persona.

Like Demosthenes and Cicero, Paul too is highly selective with
regard to what he divulges about himself[142] and thus demonstrates full control of his self-disclosures.[143] He discusses his own
persecution[144] of Jesus followers ("the assembly of God"; 1:13b)
and amplifies the harm he caused. Rather than remark that he
fought against Jesus followers, he instead states that he strongly
persecuted them (καθ᾽ ὑπερβολὴν ἐδίωκον), even attempting
to destroy (ἐπόρθουν) them (1:13b).[145] The verb ἐπόρθουν is an
imperfect, implying continual past action, of the verb πορθέω,
which means "to destroy, ravage, waste, or plunder."[146] The Greek
word ὑπερβολὴν ("exceedingly," or "to the superlative degree")
is strong and emotionally invocative (1:13b). As a standalone adverb ὑπερ in Greek means "over-much, above measure,"[147] just

as today, the word "hyper," a transliteration of the Greek word, means excessive. Paul repeats the word ὑπὲρ in 1.14b. While in the second instance, ὑπὲρ is a preposition meaning "more than," by repeating the lexime ὑπὲρ, Paul creates a reference back to the ὑπερβολὴν ("to the superlative degree") in 1:13b. Why paint his past actions in such strongly negative terms, when he could easily have minimized them?

Similarly, when Paul discusses his early education (1:14a, 14b), he hyperbolically self-portrays as someone not just interested in the traditions of the fathers but very zealous (περισσοτέρως ζηλωτὴς) for them. According to Scott, when Paul claims to be zealous, he is claiming that he "is a standout example of what it means to be a Jew."[148] The Greek comparative adverb περισσοτέρως, translated above as "extremely" (1:14b), means "even more so." The adverb heads its phrase and is thus emphasized. The object of Paul's zeal—the traditions of the ancestors— receives special emphasis through the repetition of the ending ων and ῶν sounds (consonance, seen above in bold-faced type; 1:14b). Pauline scholars and commentators tend to see a cause and effect relationship between Paul's zeal for his ancestral traditions and his strong persecution of Jesus followers.[149] Paul's zeal for the traditions reflects back on his self-description of strongly persecuting assemblies of Jesus people and functions to build a composite image of someone who was fiery and fervent. Paul self-portrays as a type of religious fanatic.

Yet Paul does not allow his negative self-disclosures to have the last word but instead employs them to his own advantage and to enhance his ethos. He juxtaposes his "bad" and human-driven past with his "good" present and attributes the change to God. Paul's ardently defined past life falls on the human side of the contrast he builds (Gal 1:13–14), while his seemingly more reasonable and divine-driven side occurs when God reveals his son and mission to him (Gal 1:15–16). According to Paul Koptak, Paul structures the entire unit (Gal 1:1–24) by his created opposition between human and divine.[150] Verse 1:15a marks the transition point between his former and present self. The expression, Ὅτε δὲ ("but when") signals both a temporal and circumstantial change.

The adversative conjunction δὲ ("but") indicates a changed situation and the adverb Ὅτε ("when") denotes a change in time. On
the temporal plane, Paul relegates his excessive and damaging
actions to his past, to a prior time. Based on this factor alone, he
argues that his past self is different from who he is now. On the
situational plane, Paul credits God as the responsible "agent" of
his new and changed life (1:15a, 15b). As mentioned above, Paul
overwhelmingly self-fashions as a man of God. In these verses,
too, he attributes the positive change from his past behavior—
most notably, a halt in his harmful persecuting activities—to God.
The sharp contrast he draws between his former and present behaviors serves as a confirmation of God's presence in his present
life.[151]

In the remaining verses of the unit, Paul continues to self-
present as someone who now operates under divine direction
(1:16–17). He twice notes that he does not consult with others
(1:16, 1:17a), but instead goes alone to Arabia[152] and Damascus. By
implication, then, Paul is untarnished by the influence of others,
and thus remains solely under the guidance of God.[153]

Finally, like Demosthenes and Cicero, Paul develops his self-
presentation within the context of competition.[154] Indeed his oppositional rhetoric within the unit—which parallels that of his
salutation[155]—is the clearest indication that competition is in
view. As seen in Gal 1:1, Paul here too employs adversatives, οὐδὲ
("and not"; 1:12a) and οὔτε ("neither"; 1:12b), when describing
his good news. As with his apostleship (1:1), rather than elaborate
upon his good news,[156] he instead privileges the fact that his good
news is distinct from some other kind of news. He emphasizes
not the substance but instead the contrast between his good news
and another form of good news. This type of argumentation signals the presence of others.[157] The contrast he draws concerns the
constructed difference between a divine orientation, by which he
self-characterizes, and a human one (1:12a, 12b, cf 1:16, 17a, 17b),
which is by implication characteristic of his opponents. Indeed,
in five consecutive phrases, and with a further instance of *polyptoton*, Paul repeats the Greek word for human (ἄνθρωπος; 1:10a,
10b, 10c, 11, 12a) (marked in bold-faced type above), and in each

occurrence assesses it negatively.[158] Moreover, Paul's two auto-biographical narratives, his arguments from ethos (Gal 1:1–5, 10–2:21), frame 1:6–9, in which he makes direct and harsh statements against his competitors.[159] Inside the frame, he denies the validity of any other good news (1:7, cf. 1:8, 9), and harshly and forcefully denigrates his competitors. Thus, in like manner to Demosthenes and Cicero, Paul self-fashions with his competitors in view.[160]

By contrast, in many and especially in traditional readings of Paul, such as in the Augustinian-Lutheran view,[161] Gal 1:13–16 is read in a historical-positivist[162] fashion for the purpose of es-tablishing historical facts and as an apology. Indeed, over large swaths of the history of the scholarship on Paul, these verses have been understood as evidence of Paul's conversion from Judaism to Christianity.[163] An apologetic and historical-positivist interpreter reasons that since Paul abandoned his native religion, he was obviously dissatisfied by it. Yet Paul's presumed rejection of his ancestral traditions results in a confusing and inherently inconsis-tent portrait of him. Such a reading struggles, and in my opinion never succeeds, to reconcile how Paul can speak "unfavorably" of his ancestral traditions and then at the same time rely heavily upon these same traditions for his arguments. Even when conver-sion itself has not been in view, interpreters focused on extracting "facts"[164] from his "autobiography,"[165] often consider these verses as centrally important for understanding Paul.[166] Yet by taking these verses at face value and by raising their significance over what is warranted by the context—a form of decontextualiza-tion—Paul is turned into a standout figure, someone unique on account of his revelation. However, as noted above, ancient au-thors did not write factual reports or "true" confessions. Instead, they stretched and manipulated the "truth"[167] to make persuasive arguments. These verses cannot be taken at face value, nor can they be considered on an order different from or "higher" than rhetoric.[168]

In sum, Paul's persuasion from ethos plays a significant role in Galatians as a whole. His fuller self-presentation extends to Gal 2:21, indicating that approximately one-third of the letter pertains to Pauline self-fashioning. Paul self-presents loftily as a man of God, someone whom God chose and called on a mission. Rhetorical techniques such as adversatives, rhetorical questions, hyperbole, and ironic rebuke indicate firm control over his discourse and careful craftsmanship. The techniques themselves effuse a sense of authority. Typical of ancient autobiographers, Paul is highly selective regarding his self-disclosures. His candor with regard to his earlier zeal for his ancestral traditions and his violent attacks on Jesus followers does not tarnish the lofty character he develops, but serves instead as additional evidence of his trustworthiness. The firm control over his rhetoric and his high selectivity with regard to his self-disclosures undermines the view that in 1:13–16 Paul is apologetic.

As is the case with Demosthenes and Cicero, Paul develops his persona within a context of competition. His use of adversatives is one of the strongest confirmations that others are in view. Paul self-portrays by way of contrast to others: his good news is *not* a human message but divine; his message stems *not* from human but from divine origin. His qualifications and his divinely commissioned mission and message are superior to that of others.

Conclusion

Demosthenes, Cicero, and Paul similarly self-fashion and similarly argue from character or ethos. Their technical skills in the art of argumentation play a role in their development of a strong authoritative self. Each author demonstrates full control over his arguments and thus exudes an authoritative self. Demosthenes employs an elaborate periodic style that includes both analytical and suspenseful periods. He takes the rhetorical trope *hyperbaton* to an extreme. Cicero engages in multi-layered conditional clauses, internal dialog, a lengthy string of ironic rhetorical questions, and repetition. While the two sections from Paul's letter are shorter than the cited passages from the speeches of Demosthenes and Cicero,[169] they nevertheless exhibit many signs of sophistication and careful craftsmanship. Paul employs repetition to his advantage, repeating the Greek word for human seven times in twelve short verses, ironic rhetorical questions, multiple adversatives and hyperbole. By comparison with the passages from

Demosthenes and Cicero, Paul's statements are sharper and more to the point. Concerning Demosthenes' self-presentation, Wooten aptly remarks "He controls the style; the style does not control him."[170] This statement applies to not just Demosthenes, but to Cicero and Paul as well.

Each author's heavy-handed approach to his audience provides additional evidence of authoritative self-fashioning. Demosthenes explicitly chastises his audience, accusing them of having a poor memory and of being easily led astray (2.30b, 31a). While less directly critical of their audiences, both Cicero and Paul nevertheless indicate their command over them. Cicero's lengthy string of rhetorical questions that concerns a rumor against him borders on sarcasm. While they are principally meant to demean his political opponents, their presence in the discourse serves to demonstrate his ability to outwit and out-argue his competition and to caution his audience against engaging in such tactics. Paul reprimands his audience for the suggestion that he would consider being engaged in mere persuasion or that he aims to please people at the expense of dealing in the truth (Gal 1:10). He, like Cicero, reserves his harsher remarks for his opponents (Gal 1:7–9). Yet by expressing his animosity for and indignation of his opponents in the hearing of those he tries to persuade, he bolsters his own authoritative self-image.

Demosthenes', Cicero's, and Paul's authoritative self-fashionings extend to the highly selective nature of their self-disclosures. Each author carefully controls what he divulges and how he does so. Negative self-disclosures enhance rather than detract from their own positive self-fashioning. By embedding "damaging" remarks within his negative characterization of unreliable men, Demosthenes raises but then handily discounts their negative criticisms. With high rhetorical flourish, Cicero squelches the rumor that he would have himself proclaimed supreme ruler; his ironic rhetorical questions serve to humiliate those who circulate it. Like Demosthenes and Cicero, Paul too is highly selective and strategic with regard to what and to how he discloses behaviors potentially damaging to his character. Paul uses negative self-characteristics more purposefully than the other two authors, building his positive self-portrait by way of contrast to a negative one. His embellishment of his past—as a zealous follower of the Torah and as an ardent persecutor of Jesus followers—serves as evidence for his present and positively construed trustworthy self.

All three authors exaggerate their credentials so as to persuade. Demosthenes claims that unlike the men, he spoke out about Philip's abuses (2.29d); he vows to tell only the truth and not to waste his audience's time with idle talk. Although claiming not to be in the habit of self-congratulation, Cicero not only speaks about the honors paid to him on the previous day but also embellishes upon them, comparing his own public congratulations to a military triumph. As such, he puts himself on the same level as the recent military heroes, conflating their military heroism with his political legacy. By claiming united Roman support of his senatorial actions, Cicero exaggerates the public acclaim and simultaneously augments his own stature. From the opening verse of Galatians and through the first part of his longer-section autobiography, Paul claims and maintains a strong association with God. He is not just any apostle but is instead commissioned by two divine beings. God set him apart from the womb—making him a favored one from before his birth—and called him on a special mission. Interestingly, all three authors claim to have "extra" sight. Demosthenes (2.32c, 33a, 33b) and Cicero (14.15) claim to have foresight and Paul speaks of his insight/revelation (Gal 1:7).

Finally, each author self-characterizes within a context of competition. Demosthenes' episode of self-fashioning is embedded within a discussion of the men, his opponents (*Phil*. 2.28–33b). He self-promotes by first creating a negative portrayal of these men, those whom he characterizes as leading the Athenians astray. In the context of these unnamed political opponents, who have misjudged Philip's true intentions, Demosthenes self-presents as someone who can be counted on to tell the truth and who does not waste the audience's time with idle talk. It is by way of contrast to the men that Demosthenes presents himself as the reliable one and the "obvious" choice between the two alternatives. Cicero also integrates his lofty self-presentation in the context of his political opponents, those who have spread a false rumor about him. Only after his lofty self-presentation that deals with his public celebration does he chastise his opponents for the false rumor they spread concerning him. The public's praise for him undermines his engagement in deception. While Paul's opponents are less easily apparent than those of Demosthenes and Cicero, his method of self-presentation, especially with his use of adversatives in describing both his apostleship and his good news, provide a clear indication that others influence his narration. In other words, Paul does not supply a neutral description of himself, nor is he interested in letting his audience know that he is an apostle or that he has good news to tell. Instead, Paul's self-description focuses on his claim that he is unlike another, or any other, type of apostle and that he proclaims good news different from and superior to another's.

In a quest to find the social situation and facts that inform these sections of Paul's letter to the Galatians, interpreters often make the assumption that Paul's statements regarding his apostleship and his good news are targeted responses to criticisms his opponents made against him. Through a process known as mirror reading, Paul's self-descriptions are thought to reflect back certain details of his opponents' accusations. In this interpretation, Paul defends his apostleship from the charge that he is not an apostle and the validity of his good news from the insinuation that he has no news worthy to tell. In this defensive reading, Paul is less of an agenda setter than a respondent. While a defensive reading fits well with the notion that Paul is supplying an open and honest report of his life, it comports poorly with his otherwise fully strategic and fully authoritative/assertive arguments found elsewhere in Galatians. Such an understanding also does not comport well with how ancient autobiographers self-disclose. As we have seen in the units of Galatians 1 above, Paul does not merely list his credentials as an apostle, so as to level the playing field between himself and his competitors, but instead portrays himself as an apostle of the loftiest type. That is to say, Paul is engaged in persuading his audience that he is superior to other apostles who claim that role. He is on the offensive not the defensive. His self-descriptions indicate that he, like Demosthenes and Cicero, employs ethos to win the Galatians to his side.

The apologetic or defensive reading of Paul began as early as the fourth century and with the interpretations of the Christian Bishop Chrysostom. This view was more recently reconfirmed and strengthened with Betz's highly influential 1979 commentary on Galatians. Yet this reading creates an extreme, while unacknowledged, and enigmatic understanding of Paul. Paul is understood as having been literally a religious fanatic in his past. He is a puzzling character because he seemingly leaves his ancestral traditions behind, while at the same time, continues to rely heavily upon them. The apologetic and face-value reading of Gal 1:13–16 has contributed to the long-held belief that Paul converted from Judaism to Christianity. This view is indefensible on historical grounds and has caused inestimable damage to Jews and Judaism from ancient to modern times. Even the ameliorated apologetic reading—that denies Paul's conversion and claims instead that he was set apart and called by God on a mission to non-Jews only— does not sufficiently resolve the conundrum for understanding Paul. In the latter or "non-conversion" interpretation of Paul, the difficulty remains with reconciling Paul's lassiez-faire (Gal 5:6, 6:15; 1 Cor 7:19) and pro-Torah statements for all (Rom 2:13) with a strict policy of non-observance for non-Jews. Moreover, the latter interpretation often continues to distinguish between a former Paul, bound by his traditions, and a new Paul, who is freed from them. The new Paul easily slips into being an enlightened Paul, which carries by default deleterious consequences for Jews and Judaism. Unlike modern biographers and autobiographers, ancients did not tell their own stories for the purpose of revealing inner truths but instead to persuade. As shown above, Paul self-characterizes with much control, with a targeted use of rhetorical tropes, and with exaggeration, indicators of ancient and not modern autobiography. His style conforms to that of Demosthenes and Cicero. All three of these ancient rhetoric-of-crisis authors employed ethos for the purpose of persuasion. By interpreting otherwise, are we to say that Paul was someone other than an ancient author and that he thereby requires special criteria of evaluation?

In the next chapter, I take up and elaborate upon emotive language, and indicate how authors employ it to diminish their opponents and/or their points of view. In addition, I return to several of the topics raised here in the subsequent chapters.

3

Persuading through Emotive Language

Proofs, it is true, may induce the judges to regard
our case as superior to that of our opponent, but the
appeal to the emotions will do more, for it will make
them wish our case to be the better. And what they
wish, they will also believe. (Quintilian, *Inst.* 6.2.5)[1]

Arousing emotions is another component of the rhetoric of crisis.
By employing and appealing to emotions, authors seek to engage
more than just the intellect.[2] Emotions increase personal involve-
ment—on the part of the author, the audience, and even the interpreter[3]—in the situation at hand and are strong contributing
factors in persuasion.

For the purposes of persuasion and from the perspective of
authors, there are two basic methods for arousing emotions in audiences, with overlap between them. Authors can make known
their own emotions to their audiences. Aristotle argued that hearers are drawn to and sympathize with those who speak emotionally even when what is being argued is false (*Rhet.* 3.7.4). Cicero
too remarked that listeners will not be emotionally moved to act
without the help of an emotive speaker (*De or.* 2.189). While in
written compositions authorial emotions are not as readily perceived, readers nevertheless sense them through the stylistic features of discourses. Whether actual or feigned, authors charge an
atmosphere with their emotions.

Another way in which authors arouse emotions within oral
and written discourse—and the means often found in the discussions that follow—is through the treatment of their subject matter.

Indeed, ancient authors developed forms of argumentation and common tropes to bring about specific emotive responses in audiences. Thus, by detailing socially deplorable and vile characteristics, they bring about hatred and the accompanying desire to dissociate from the person discussed. According to Cicero, to generate hatred the orator must demonstrate the person "doing something destructive or unprofitable."[4] To arouse fear, authors were to discuss the "perils" of the individual.[5]

To turn their audiences against their enemies/competitors, Demosthenes, Cicero, and Paul employ a range of rhetorical techniques. And integral in all the rhetorical techniques employed is the authors' reliance upon socially recognized values of acceptable and unacceptable behaviors. Rhetorical techniques typically employed to arouse audience emotions—exaggerated claims, graphic images and, extended narratives—reify and then also reinforce shared cultural values in order to elicit hatred, disgust, and aversion for opponents. As seen in the previous chapter, here too the employment of rhetorical techniques aimed to elicit emotions can result in the development of two mutually exclusive alternatives.

Of further note, unlike with urgency, in which authors rebuke their audiences, at times shaming them into action, with emotive argumentation, Demosthenes, Cicero, and Paul attempt instead to build agreement or harmony with their audiences. Thus, it appears as though author-audience unity-building is the best method for persuading of the evils of an opponent.

Demosthenes against Philip

Demosthenes makes plentiful use of emotions for persuasion. He lays bear his own fiery emotions against Philip and against his enemies/opponents, and then also stirs up audience hatred through his depictions of them. Demosthenes deploys both of these methods of eliciting audience emotion in his *Third Philippic*,[6] considered by several modern classicists to be stylistically among his finest orations.[7] Indeed, Wooten finds an "undercurrent of emotion, either negative or positive, that runs through much of the speech, like blood in the body."[8] While in his earlier speeches, and especially in his *Olynthiac First–Third*, Demosthenes experiments with bringing about an effective balance between persuasion through logic and emotions, he does not achieve it until his *Third Philippic*.[9] He brings about the necessary balance through the frequent repetition of key ideas—approaching the same theme multiple times but from different directions, which in turn gives the impression of offering much information when in fact it does not—and ring composition,[10] yet another method that enables the return to the same idea.

Demosthenes' *Third Philippic* was likely delivered in early summer 341[11] and just after his *On the Chersonesus*.[12] Each oration addresses the same situation. With these two speeches Demosthenes takes advantage of anti-Macedonian sentiments already brewing among the Athenians.[13] At this time, Philip was in Thrace, in the north of Macedon, and menacing the Chersonesus and Byzantium (far northeast Thrace).[14] Athens had sent colonists to ensure the flow of grains in Thracian Chersonesus and Diopeithes with troops to support them, but the colonists had come into conflict with those allied with Philip. Demosthenes' *Third Philippic* is in part to argue in favor of Diopeithes' appeal for additional money and aid,[15] and for direct support of the Chersonesus and Byzantium (3.73). Yet Demosthenes also takes advantage of this situation,[16] the adverse conditions in Thrace, to further his hardline approach against Philip. Demosthenes argues that Athens should prepare itself for war (3.70) and summon and gather as many Greeks as possible to form an alliance against Philip (3.73).

Demosthenes faced an uphill battle to gain Athenian support for his hardline approach to Philip. His credibility with the Athenian senators was low, due in part to his own inconsistent position with regard to Philip.[17] In 348 and again in 346, Demosthenes along with nine other delegates met with Philip in Pella to work out a peace agreement—the Peace of Philocrates—with him.[18] Later, however, Demosthenes changed course. In the years that followed, and even as early as 346, Demosthenes lost confidence in the peace process[19] and adopted instead a hawk-like approach to Philip. John Buckler questions whether or not Demosthenes, despite his presence during both sessions with Philip, fully understood the various agreements forged during the two meetings the delegates had with him. According to Buckler, Demosthenes' archrival Aeschines appears to have had a clearer and more commonsense approach to Philip than did Demosthenes.[20]

Demosthenes' newer hostile approach to Philip, however, served to distinguish him from his two main political rivals, Philocrates and Aeschines. The latter became his arch political enemy from 346 until the end of his life. Indeed, with his *Third Philippic*, in addition to riding the tide of anti-Macedonian sentiments, Demosthenes was also capitalizing on negative sentiments growing around these two Athenian senators. In 344 Philocrates was charged with corruption and deception of the Athenian people for the role he played as author of the peace treaty and sentenced to death. He survived by fleeing Athens before his sentence was announced.[21] At the same time, Demosthenes himself renewed charges of corruption, treason, and complicity with Philocrates against Aeschines[22] for the role he, Aeschines, played in the peace negotiations.[23]

Indeed, in his *Third Philippic* Demosthenes makes Philip the scapegoat for his fundamental animosity against Aeschines. Through the ample use of multiple forms of repetition, he exaggerates the immediacy of Philip's threat and plays loose with the facts of the Peace of Philocrates. He uses the threat of Philip for his own political advantage, not only to augment his own prestige, but also to build support for his hardline approach over and against the conciliatory stance of his arch political rival Aeschines.[24]

By comparison with his earlier Philippic speeches, there is a noticeable shift in the attitude Demosthenes takes toward his audience. Instead of harshly reprimanding his auditors,[25] in his *Third Philippic* Demosthenes eases up considerably on audience criticism and instead reserves his harshest criticisms for Philip. The shift suggests that to instill or reinforce vehemence[26] against an opponent, an author courts the audience. The *proemium*[27] (opening) of Demosthenes' *Third Philippic* offers a good illustration of his changed and now more favorable disposition toward his audience. Demosthenes attacks Philip rather than his audience (3.1), provokes animosity for his Athenian political rivals (3.2), and makes a plea for the goodwill of his audience (3.3–4).[28]

Turning Philip into a Global Threat

A primary way in which Demosthenes builds his case against Philip is by claiming that he is a menace who threatens the entire Greek world,[29] a characterization that begins from the first line of his *Third Philippic*. Demosthenes remarks that Philip's unjust acts are aimed not just (οὐ μόνον, "not only") at Athens (ὑμᾶς, "you"), but also to all other nations (τοὺς ἄλλους, "all besides"), (οὐ μόνον ὑμᾶς, ἀλλὰ καὶ τοὺς ἄλλους[30] ἀδικεῖ; 3.1).[31] To develop this portrayal of Philip, Demosthenes greatly exaggerates Philip's treachery and plays loose with the facts. Section 17 from his *Third Philippic* follows.

3.17a ὥστε καὶ **Μεγάρων** ἁπτόμενον
3.17b καὶ ἐν **Εὐβοίᾳ** τυραννίδα κατασκευάζοντα
3.17c καὶ νῦν ἐπὶ **Θρᾴκην** παριόντα
3.17d καὶ τὰ ἐν **Πελοποννήσῳ** σκευωρούμενον
3.17e καὶ πάνθ᾽ ὅσα πράττει μετὰ τῆς δυνάμεως ποιοῦντα,
3.17f λύειν φημὶ τὴν εἰρήνην καὶ πολεμεῖν ὑμῖν,

3.17a I assert that when he lays hands on **Megara**,
3.17b sets up tyrannies in **Euboea**
3.17c makes his way as now into [against] **Thrace**
3.17d hatches plots in the **Peloponnese**
3.17e and carries out all of these operations with his armed forces
3.17f he is breaking the peace and making war upon *you*.[32]

To bring about a treacherous characterization of Philip, Demosthenes makes ample use of geographical locations/place names (marked in bold-faced type above) and then accentuates them through their near parallel placement within similarly styled short successive phrases.[33] Three of the four phrases contain a preposition (ἐν, "in" or ἐπὶ, best translated as "against") that emphasizes its associated geographical location. The repetition of the preposition "in" (ἐv) in alternating phrases (17b and 17d) also contributes a sense of rhythm, and thereby makes all four phrases more memorable.

That each of the first four lines is structurally very similar (3.17a–d) adds to their ability to make an impression on hearers. All the cola are short and contain nearly the same number of syllables (*isocolon*). The repetition of the Greek conjunction "and" (καὶ) (3.17a–d)—not readily apparent in Vince's translation nor in modern Greek editions—is an instance of *polysyndeton* (the repetitive use of coordinating conjunctions) and *anaphora* (the repetition of the first word or word group in parallel clauses).[34] Each phrase ends with an indicative[35] participle denoting Philip's unjust actions, although the name "Philip" is absent. The ending sounds of the first five phrases repeat and create a rhythmic ABBA pattern. Vince's English translation loses the sense in which Philip's acts of aggressions all rhyme. The rhyming functions to connect and reinforce the various aggressive acts; rhyming ending sounds (*homoioteleuton*) create emphasis.[36] Demosthenes, then, effectively and strategically creates a similarly structured and similarly sounding list[37] of Philip's aggressive and unjust actions against various places.

Ronnet notes that Demosthenes is a master list-maker.[38] Lists make their impression by the mere presence of an abundance of like elements. They surprise (*étonner*) hearers. They are intended to overwhelm auditors, who are not meant to contemplate each individual word or lexime.[39] With his list of similarly structured phrases, Demosthenes creates rhythmic steps of impending doom.

The fifth phrase of the unit (3.17e) functions to sum up the aggression outlined in the structured list. In harmony with the phrases in the structured list, it too ends in a present active participle that rhymes with the B patterned phrases above it (17b, 17c), and, like those other phrases, it too refers to the abusive actions of Philip. With this fifth phrase, Demosthenes creates one subjugated group of nations, all of whom (πάνθ᾽ ὅσα), are victims of Philip's tyranny.

The final phrase of the unit (3.17f) differs from the previous five, and thus stikes an auditor because it interrupts a customary pattern.[40] The verb λύειν ("to unbind" or "to break") begins the phrase. Its placement at the head indicates its importance in Demosthenes' argument. Indeed, Demosthenes intends to worry the Athenians that Philip has already broken (λύειν) the Peace of Philocrates. The facts, however, speak otherwise. While Philip was threatening all the named territories (Euboea, Megara, the Peloponnese and Thrace), none of these regions were included in this peace treaty.[41] Furthermore, by employing the Greek words "the peace" (τὴν εἰρήνην; 3.17f), which is a direct reference to the Peace of Philocrates, Demosthenes also indirectly refers to his political rival Aeschines, who not only supports the treaty but whom Demosthenes accuses as being responsible for the present threat of Philip (cf. 3.1).

Moreover, Demosthenes seeks to induce fear in his audience with a second present infinitive verb (πολεμεῖν) ("to make war"; 3.17f). Taken together, the two infinitive verbs (λύειν and πολεμεῖν) indicate Philip's current and ongoing actions. And with his use of the emphatic second-person plural pronoun "you" (ὑμῖν) in the last position of its phrase (3.17f),[42] Demosthenes emphasizes Philip's direct threat to the Athenians themselves. Demosthenes, however, is once again stretching the truth. Philip is not, at least not as yet, at war with Athens.[43] Facts are not of significance to Demosthenes. His goal of bringing his auditors to the conclusion he wishes them to draw,[44] that Philip has already broken the peace and is presently waging war on them, trumps the facts of the situation. Buckler remarks that more important to Demosthenes than the truth were "a half-truth, a plausible lie, or a mere malicious personal insult."[45] "Pure rules of evidence, as idealized in a modern court, are often lacking in their [Demosthenes' and Aeschines'] speeches. Instead, their primary aim was to persuade their audience at any given time of the wisdom of their policies and the purity of their motives."[46]

Elaborating on the Global Threat of Philip

Prior to focusing a second time on Philip's tyranny, Demosthenes turns briefly to the subject of his audience to build rapport with them (*Phil.* 3.21–26). As in this speech's opening, it is once again apparent that here too he avoids harsh criticism of the Athenians' present lack of action against Philip. He begins with the stated observation—with some implied criticism—that the Athenians have allowed Philip to operate without controls. Philip does what he wants (τὸ ποιεῖν ὅ τι βούλεται); he cuts down[47] (περικόπτειν) and plunders (λωποδυτεῖν) city after city and reduces them all to slavery (καταδουλοῦσθαι; *Phil.* 3.22). Yet rather than draw the logical conclusion and criticize his audience for their failure to obstruct Philip's incursions—an accusation he does not hesitate to make in his earlier speeches—Demosthenes shifts his argument and speaks instead of his audience's heroic past.[48] He remarks that Athens reigned for seventy-three[49] years and prior to that Sparta for twenty-nine[50] years (*Phil.* 3.23). During that entire hundred-year period, nations put controls on excessive aggression against neighboring states and abided by a shared sense of duty to help others in the case of abuses in warfare (*Phil.* 3.21–25). Rather than admonish the Athenians for not living up to the standards of their ancestors, he instead uses this "historical" narrative to encourage them to hold themselves to their own former high standard (*Phil.* 3.23–24). And in an act of self-criticism, Demosthenes admits that all nations, including the Athenians, can be accused of past abuses of power, but he avoids associating Athens' past abuses with present-day Athenians (*Phil.* 3.23).[51]

As mentioned, Demosthenes' change in attitude toward his audience is striking. Unlike his earlier speeches, here he courts the Athenians. His changed attitude may be due in part to the fact that Demosthenes' own position with regard to Philip, as Yunis and Buckler remark, is not well accepted.[52] Indeed, Demosthenes ends this section with a strong criticism not of his Athenian audience, but of Philip:

κaίτοι πάνθ' ὅσ' ἐξημάρτηται καὶ Λακεδαιμονίοις ἐν τοῖς τριάκοντ' ἐκείνοις ἔτεσιν καὶ τοῖς ἡμετέροις προγόνοις ἐν τοῖς ἑβδομήκοντα, ἐλάττον' ἐστίν, ὦ ἄνδρες Ἀθηναῖοι, ὧν Φίλιππος ἐν τρισὶ καὶ δέκ' οὐχ ὅλοις ἔτεσιν, οἷς ἐπιπολάζει, ἠδίκηκε τοὺς Ἕλληνας, μᾶλλον δ' οὐδὲ μέρος τούτων ἐκεῖνα.

Yet all the faults committed by the Lacedaemonians in those thirty years, and by our ancestors in their seventy years of supremacy, are fewer, men of Athens, than the wrongs which Philip has done to the Greeks in the thirteen incomplete years in which he has been coming to the top—or rather, they are not a fraction of them. (3.25)[53]

In 3.26–27, a unit that resembles section 17 above, Demosthenes continues his direct attack against Philip. Through repetition and hyperbole Demosthenes reinforces the notion that Philip is a growing and global threat.

3.26a Ὄλυνθον μὲν δὴ **καὶ Μεθώνην καὶ Ἀπολλωνίαν καὶ** δύο **καὶ** τριάκοντα πόλεις ἐπὶ **Θρᾴκης** ἐῶ,

3.26b **ἃς ἁπάσας οὕτως ὠμῶς** ἀνῄρηκεν ὥστε μηδ᾽ εἰ πώποτ᾽ ᾠκήθησαν προσελθόντ᾽ εἶναι ῥᾴδιον εἰπεῖν:

3.26c **καὶ** τὸ **Φωκέων** ἔθνος τοσοῦτον ἀνῃρημένον σιωπῶ.

3.26d ἀλλὰ **Θετταλία** πῶς ἔχει;

3.26e οὐχὶ τὰς **πολιτείας** καὶ τὰς **πόλεις** αὐτῶν παρῄρηται καὶ τετραρχίας κατέστησεν, ἵνα μὴ μόνον κατὰ **πόλεις** ἀλλὰ καὶ κατ᾽ ἔθνη δουλεύωσιν;

3.27a αἱ δ᾽ ἐν **Εὐβοίᾳ** πόλεις οὐκ ἤδη τυραννοῦνται,

3.27b καὶ ταῦτ᾽ ἐν νήσῳ πλησίον **Θηβῶν** καὶ **Ἀθηνῶν**;

3.27c οὐ διαρρήδην εἰς τὰς ἐπιστολὰς γράφει "ἐμοὶ δ᾽ ἐστὶν εἰρήνη πρὸς τοὺς ἀκούειν ἐμοῦ βουλομένους";

3.27d καὶ οὐ γράφει μὲν ταῦτα, τοῖς δ᾽ ἔργοις οὐ ποιεῖ,

3.27e ἀλλ᾽ ἐφ᾽ **Ἑλλήσποντον** οἴχεται,

3.27f πρότερον ἧκεν ἐπ᾽ **Ἀμβρακίαν**,

3.27g **Ἦλιν** ἔχει τηλικαύτην πόλιν ἐν **Πελοποννήσῳ**,

3.27h **Μεγάροις** ἐπεβούλευσεν πρώην,

3.27i οὔθ᾽ ἡ Ἑλλὰς οὔθ᾽ ἡ βάρβαρος τὴν πλεονεξίαν χωρεῖ τἀνθρώπου.

3.26a I pass over **Olynthus** and **Methone** and **Apollonia** and the two and thirty cities in or near **Thrace**,

3.26b all of which Philip has destroyed so ruthlessly that a traveler would find it hard to say whether they had ever been inhabited.

3.26c I say nothing of the destruction of the important nation
       of the **Phocians**.

3.26d But how stands the case of the **Thessalians**?

3.26e Has he not robbed them of their free constitutions and
       of their very cities, setting up tetrarchies in order to
       enslave them, not city by city, but tribe by tribe?

3.27a Are not tyrannies already established in **Euboea**,

3.27b an island, remember, not far from **Thebes** and **Athens**?

3.27c Does he not write explicitly in his letters, "I am at peace
       with those who are willing to obey me"?

3.27d And he does not merely write this without putting it
       into practice;

3.27e but he is off to the **Hellespont**,

3.27f just as before he hurried to **Ambracia**;

3.27g in the **Peloponnese** he occupies the important city of
       Elis;

3.27h only the other day he intrigued against the **Megarians**.

3.27i Neither the Greek nor the barbarian world is big
       enough for the fellow's ambition.[54]

As seen in section 17, city and nation names appear here too, in
high frequency and often near the head of phrases (3.26a, 26c, 26d,
27a, 27e, 27g, 27h). While Demosthenes explicitly names fourteen
different locations including Athens (marked in bold-faced type
above) in danger from the threat of Philip, some of these places
are those he has mentioned previously. He harks back to Thrace,
Euboea, Peloponnesse, and Megara (Megarians), four places mentioned in section 17. With regard to his reference to Euboea, by
employing the Greek term for "tyrannies" when referring to it
(τυραννοῦνται, 3.27a, cf. τυραννίδα, 3.17b),[55] he repeats his own
earlier phrase using nearly identical words. Thus, by repeating
the same geographical places in nearly identical phraseology,
Demosthenes gives the impression that the threat of Philip is
greater than it is.

Demosthenes employs a double *paraleipsis* (ἐῶ, σιωπῶ, "I pass
over," "I say nothing"; 3.26a, 26c)[56] to seemingly sneak in the enu-

meration of additional places Philip invades. *Paraleipsis* is a technique whereby an author mentions a subject, while at the same time feigning not to mention it. The effect of *paraleipsis* calls attention to the subject rather than suppress it. In this passage, Demosthenes mentions five territories by name—adding that Philip has utterly destroyed each one—all the while saying he does not want to mention them (3.26a, 26c). Furthermore, the presence of *polysyndeton* (the repetitive use of the conjunction καὶ ["and"]) within the same phrases in which one finds *paraleipsis* serves to emphasize and intensify rather than dismiss Philip's geographical reach. Indeed, Demosthenes has already mentioned Philip's forays into Olynthus (3.11)[57] and Thrace (3.17). Clearly, then, Demosthenes does *not* want to pass over the mention of these places: by contrast, he intends to imprint them on the minds of his hearers. He seeks to create angst and fear, to magnify the reach and the threat of Philip. Wooten aptly remarks, "Demosthenes . . . seems to be offering many arguments and much information to back them up but, in fact, treats a fairly small number of ideas, proved with information already adduced, which he presents fully enough and *often enough* to give them sufficient weight to make them memorable."[58]

In addition to repetition of place names and the use of *paraleipsis*, Demosthenes employs other rhetorical devices to exacerbate Philip's aggressions and hence increase the unit's emotional impact. The opening phrase (3.26b) is striking for its use of repetitive beginning and ending sounds. It reads, ἃς ἁπάσας οὕτως ὠμῶς ἀνῄρηκεν (literally, "who altogether so savagely destroyed"). There is alliteration of the leading vowel ἁ at the start of the line and repetition of the ending consonant (*homoioteleuton*), with his expression οὕτως ὠμῶς ("so savagely") in the central part. With alliteration, Demosthenes emphasizes "all" ἁπάσας the territories Philip has destroyed. The Greek word ἁπάσας is an intensified form of the much more common word for "all," πᾶς. The four leading words lead up to and announce the verb ἀνῄρηκεν ("he took away" or "he destroyed"), whose tense designates completed past action. The subject of the verb is the unnamed perpetrator (Philip), who has savagely destroyed[59] the three named cities Olynthus, Methone, and Apollonia and then thirty-two[60] more near Thrace. Demosthenes again emphasizes Philip's brutality by repeating the Greek verb "to destroy" as a perfect participle (ἀνῃρημένον; 3.26c). In its second use, the verb refers to Philip's destruction of the Phocians.[61]

While line 3.26e does not contain a particular place name, by emphasizing the Greek word for cities, Demosthenes reinforces the pervasiveness of Philip's reach. Indeed, the line is replete in various types of repetition all working to highlight the notion of cities: *anaphora*, repetition of the definite article τὰς in two succeeding phrases; repetition of the word "cities" (πόλεις) (2x), with the line beginning with a close cousin of this word, πολιτείας ("constitutions");[62] and alliteration of the κα in the long final phrase κατὰ πόλεις ἀλλὰ καὶ κατ᾽, a phrase that refers to the enslavement of cities.

To add to the emotional impact of the unit, Demosthenes asks a series of four rhetorical questions (3.26d, 26e, 27a, 27c)[63] intended to point out the abuses of Philip. The questions come across as matters of fact. Coming as they do as a group, they function to overwhelm an audience, giving auditors little chance to assess each one individually. In 3.27c Demosthenes again alludes to the peace treaty and then accuses Philip of not abiding by it. Philip, however and as mentioned, does not actually break the terms of the treaty.[64]

Demosthenes ends the unit with a highly exaggerated nonsensical negative characterization of Philip. At the end of section 31, which concludes a major section of the speech,[65] Demosthenes claims that Philip cannot be categorized as either a Greek or a barbarian.[66] Philip is not only not a Greek and not related to Greeks but not even a barbarian, but instead a pestilent knave from Macedon, from where it was never yet possible to buy a decent slave[67] (οὐ μόνον οὐχ Ἕλληνος ὄντος οὐδὲ προσήκοντος οὐδὲν τοῖς Ἕλλησιν, ἀλλ᾽ οὐδὲ Βαρβάρου . . . , ἀλλ᾽ ὀλέθρου Μακεδόνος, ὅθεν οὐδ᾽ ἀνδράποδον σπουδαῖον οὐδὲν ἦν πρότερον πρίασθαι; 3.31). Technically this is nonsense, as Philip was Greek; Macedonians considered themselves part of the Greek world.[68] Facts are of secondary importance to authorial purpose, and as we shall see below, Cicero resorts to similar tactics in his disparagement of Antony.

In sum, largely through the abundant use of place names and the plentiful and creative employment of repetition, Demosthenes turns Philip into an ever-present and looming threat not just to Athens but also to the larger world. Demosthenes amplifies the threat of Philip; his lengthy lists of cities and peoples touched by Philip's military might function to magnify Philip's reach and to induce fear and a need for action against him. Even Ryder, who tends to take Demosthenes more or less at his word, readily admits that Demosthenes exaggerates in his discussions of Philip's incursions. By avoiding the overuse of Philip's name, Demosthenes portrays Philip's threat as an evil with no associated agent and hence less controllable, in turn inducing more fear. And by categorizing Philip as not belonging to any known race of humans, neither Greek nor barbarian, Demosthenes turns Philip into someone who is totally other, into an alien being, and hence into someone whom the Athenians can more easily hate. Kennedy's comment is apt: Demosthenes "so focuses Athenian interests that the question seems not one of advantage but of necessity, not the choice of a course of action, but the pursuit of the only possibility."[69]

To reiterate, while Philip was campaigning in the areas Demosthenes enumerates, he was technically not moving into territories deemed off limits by the peace treaty. Many of the areas of Philip's present intrigues were far to the north of Athens. Demosthenes twice alludes to the peace treaty and gives the impression that Philip has already broken it. Yet Philip never technically did. Raising the issue of the Peace of Philocrates served a political purpose, as through an allusion to it, Demosthenes positions himself against his chief political foe Aeschines, who continued to believe that Philip would uphold it.

By comparison with his previous Philippic-cycle speeches, in his *Third Philippic* Demosthenes backs away from audience condemnation. His changed attitude may in part be due to his insecurity with regard to his own newly adopted position toward

Philip. Yet it also suggests that to gain a strong negative audience response against Philip, he must court his audience.

Cicero's Demeaning
of Antony

Cicero's *Third Philippic* marks the beginning of his official speeches against Antony.[70] As mentioned, Cicero had not initially intended to participate in this December 20, 44 BCE meeting of the senate, but recent developments in the province of Cisalpine Gaul necessitated his attendance. Yet as Van der Blom explains, factors other than Brutus' retention of the governorship of Cisalpine Gaul account for Cicero's re-emergence into the political realm.[71] Like Demosthenes, Cicero too was riding the tide of growing animosity among the senators against his political opponent. In his own explanation for why he reentered the political arena, Cicero remarks that he was haunted by Antony. He comments, "I have been away, on route to Greece; and ever since the voice of the commonwealth called me home halfway through my journey, Mark Antony has not left me a quiet moment" (*Fam.* 10.1.1).[72]

As Van der Blom explains, after the murder of Julius Caesar, Cicero was content to leave the political realm. He had confidence that Gaius Cassius Longinus and Marcus Junius Brutus, the conspirators of the plot against Caesar, would take charge of the Republic. But in the days and months subsequent to Caesar's murder, Antony instead grew in power. Brutus' rebellious actions signaled that the time was ripe for an all-out attack against Antony.[73] In all likelihood, Cicero did not require much external prompting to wage a concerted attack against Antony: there was a deep personal and philosophical divide between the two.[74] Cicero did not trust Antony.[75] Indeed, at the assassination of Caesar, Cicero remarked that Antony should have been murdered along with him.[76] Van der Blom notes that Cicero's "antagonism was based on a combined disagreement with Antony's policies, personality, and the values he represented."[77] According to her, Cicero reentered politics to defend his dignity and to respond to Antony's challenge.[78] His gamble, however, cost him his life.[79]

In reentering the political arena, Cicero's main goal was to obtain legal sanction for a war against Antony. That is, Cicero had to have Antony declared an enemy of the state, a *hostis*, a subject I take up more directly and in greater detail in the next chapter. To accomplish his goal, Cicero employs exaggerated claims, graphic descriptions, as well as evocative language to arouse fear and disgust for Antony. He paints Antony as a tyrant and as a beast.

Turning Antony into a Tyrant

Cicero often resorts to depicting Antony as a tyrant. Such an invective was commonplace in antiquity. One finds its use in ancient Greeks such as Herodotus (*Hist.* 1.59, 3.80.5, 5.91–92), Euripides' *Supplices* (426–55), Aeschylus' *Promethus Bound* and *Agamemnon*, and other ancient authors.[80] Tom Stevenson notes that in antiquity a tyrant had certain stock characteristics.

> The conventional tyrant was fundamentally a figure of vice rather than virtue. His personal faults gave rise to his political ones, and thereby implied them. He was in general paranoid, cruel and unstable, both psychologically and emotionally; he ruled through violence and fear, employing an armed body guard to suppress civic freedoms; unlike the good king, he killed citizens; he was dominated by evil advisers and women, refusing to listen to the best men; he was a creature of lust who was often associated with rape; he was given to public displays of fury and excess; his court was a libidinous raucous place; he disregarded the state laws and institutions, ruling in arbitrary, repressive fashion according to his moods.[81]

For his depiction of Antony, Cicero makes use of many of the stock characteristics Stevenson enumerates. In the following short passage,[82] he highlights and exaggerates Antony's brutality. He characterizes Antony as a cruel and unfeeling ruler, who even slaughtered Roman soldiers.[83] Through the creation of a gruesome graphic image, and by drawing connections between Antony's willful slaughter of Roman soldiers and the Roman

senators he addresses, Cicero elicits fear[84] and hatred for Antony.
A short passage from his *Third Philippic* follows:

3.4a Quippe qui in hospitis tectis Brundisi fortissimos viros
    optimosque civis **iugulari** iusserit;
3.4b quorum ante pedes eius morientium sanguine os uxoris
    respersum esse constabat.
3.4c Hac ille crudelitate imbutus, cum multo nobis omnibus
    veniret iratior quam illis fuerat quos **trucidarat**, cui tan-
    dem nostrum aut cui omnino bono pepercisset?

3.4a He, who ordered very brave men and exemplary
    citizens **to be murdered** under his host's roof at Brundi-
    sium!
3.4b It was commonly reported that as they lay dying at his
    feet, their blood splashed into his wife's face.
3.4c Stained by such cruelty, and far more angry with all
    of us than he had been with the **slaughtered** victims,
    would he have spared any of us, or any honest man, in
    the end?[85]

In the passage above, Cicero forges a connection between
Antony's brutal treatment of soldiers in the strategic port city
Brundisium (located on the southeastern coast of present-day
Italy; 3.4a) and the actions he would take against Roman senators (3.4c). He creates this connection through ring composition,
a feature common in oral delivery that reprises a topic or theme
touched on earlier. When used in tightly knit passages—which
enable a more easily recognizable recurrence of an earlier topic—
ring composition creates emphasis and heightens a passage's emotional impact.[86] In the passage above, Cicero begins this theme
with the verb *iugulari* ("to cut the throat," to "kill," or "to slay";
3.4a), and then repeats this notion with the verb *trucidarat* ("to cut
to pieces," "to slaughter"; 3.4c). In 3.4a, Antony's target is Roman
soldiers at Brundisium, while in 3.4c his object is Roman senators.

Beyond ring composition, Cicero employs other rhetorical
tropes, such as *epitheton* and a rhetorical question, to draw connections between Antony's brutal killing of the soldiers in Brundisium

and the cruelty he would inflict upon Roman senators. With *epitheton* — "an attributive addition to a substantive"[87] — Cicero creates an additional cognitive link between those killed in Brundisium (3.4a) and the Roman senatorial audience he addresses (3.4c). When referring to the slaughter at Brundisium, Cicero employs the expression *fortissimos viros optimosque civis* ("very brave men and exemplary citizens"; 3.4a), a phrase that leaves unspecified to whom it pertains, to soldiers, to citizens, or to both. The ambiguity serves to extend the notion of Antony's cruelty beyond that of rebellious soldiers to a "bloody killing against Roman citizens."[88] In case there is any doubt that Cicero is attempting to draw a connection between Antony's slaughter at Brundisium and the type of cruelty he would inflict upon the senators, he makes explicit such a connection with his rhetorical question (3.4c).[89] Antony would not spare Roman senators with whom he is far angrier than the soldiers in Brundisium (3.4c, cf 5.22). Indeed, Cicero's rhetorical question invites his senatorial audience to imagine how Antony would treat them (3.4c). As Wooten remarks, imagining a scenario is more emotionally compelling than describing it.[90]

In addition, to bring his hearers around to the belief in Antony's mercilessness, Cicero creates a graphic image of the scene. Although the details of the slaughter are few and small (3.4b),[91] they are nevertheless emotionally provocative.[92] He describes blood splashing up and onto Antony's wife's[93] face (3.4b). With the detail that Antony wounded men as they lay dying at his feet (*ante pedes eius morientium*), Cicero depicts his foe as lacking in human sympathy and cruel to the extreme (3.4b).[94] Only newly inflicted wounds would create enough force to cause an upward gush of blood. Both Antony and his wife are implicated in this crime; both have "blood on their hands." Antony is said to be "stained by such cruelty" (*hac ille crudelitate imbutus*; 3.4c), and his unnamed wife has blood (*sanguine*) on her face (3.4b). Of further note, the insertion of Antony's wife into the scene is yet another way in which Cicero draws on stock characteristics to depict Antony as a tyrant. Here, Antony falls victim to listening to the voice of a woman, that is, involving a woman in the affairs of men. Her presence — since women were not ordinarily on military campaigns—marks Antony as someone who flaunts social conventions.[95]

As a rhetorical trope, a graphic description is meant to make the scene it describes "present" to its audience.[96] Indeed, a graphic description is a form of *enargeia*, "the description of a situation or action as though it were present."[97] According to Perelman and Olbrechts-Tyteca, "presence acts directly on our sensibility."[98] That on which the eye dwells becomes "overestimated."[99] One of the goals of a speaker is to make present by "verbal magic alone" what is actually absent but what the speaker deems important to make known.[100]

While a slaughter did take place in Brundisium in October 44, Cicero was not an eyewitness to it.[101] More important to Cicero than the actual facts of the slaughter is the visceral response of fear, disgust, and outrage[102] he desires to engender by his vivid and exaggerated depiction of it. Cicero portrays Antony's killing of Romans as entirely gratuitous: he provides no context by which to understand why the killing would have taken place.[103]

Elsewhere in his *Third Philippic* Cicero participates in fanciful comparisons to other rulers, both present and past, to amplify Antony's brutality and to defame his character more generally. By comparison with Antony, who sold off the wealth of the realm to individuals (3.10), Octavian invested in the military out of his own resources (3.3). While Antony wreaked havoc by killing Romans citizens, Octavian, although only a youth, displayed "an incredible and divine spirit and energy"[104] (*incredibili ac divina quadam mente atque virtute*) to save the Republic (3.3). And by contrast to Antony, often depicted as a beast (see below), Octavian exhibits "godlike greatness of heart, mind and judgment"[105] (*divina animi, ingeni, consili magnitudine*; 5.23).

In comparing Antony to Rome's former king Tarquin, Cicero comes close to turning Tarquin, one of Rome's cruelest rulers, into a hero.[106] According to the historical record, Tarquin was the last of Rome's kings (534–510 BCE), and during his tyrannical reign, he put many senators to death. He is alleged to have killed his father-in-law Servius Tullius and proclaimed himself absolute ruler. His son's rape of the noblewoman Lucretia initiated a senatorial revolt

and resulted in Tarquin's expulsion from Rome and the abolition
of the monarchy.[107] In one of his own treatises, Cicero himself refers to Tarquin as a most savage beast (*De republica* 2.48). Yet in
this speech against his enemy Antony, Cicero cleans up considerably the story of Tarquin—playing loose with history—and omits
the gruesome details surrounding his despotic rule.[108]

> What did Tarquin ever do to compare with countless deeds
> both past and present of Antonius? The kings too had a sen-
> ate: but armed barbarians did not figure in the royal council
> chamber as they do when Antonius holds a senate. . . . We are
> not told that Tarquin ever executed Roman citizens: whereas
> *he* murdered those whom he had thrown into custody at
> Suessa, and at Brundisium he slaughtered some three hun-
> dred very brave men and most loyal citizens. (*Phil.* 3.9–10)[109]

Cicero turns Tarquin into a respectable ancestor simply to
strengthen his case against Antony.[110] As Wooten remarks with
regard to Demosthenes, harking back to a shared ancestry evokes
sympathy in one's audience.[111]

In sum, to create fear, hatred, and disgust for Antony, Cicero
deploys the conventional term of vilification, "tyrant." In his
hands, however, its conventionality does not diminish or detract
from its emotional impact. As shown, Cicero worked strategically
with this familiar polemical term to demonize Antony. Through
the use of ring composition and rhetorical questioning, he worries the senators into believing that Antony's slaughter of the
soldiers in Brundisium is similar to what he would do to them.
With graphic imagery, *enargeia*, he brings to life, makes present,
Antony's cruelty. Finally, by playing loose with history, Cicero
strengthens the communal bonds with his audience, which in
turn reinforces a shared animosity for Antony.

Turning Antony into a Beast

Cicero depicts Antony as not only a tyrant but also as a beast.
Indeed, over the course of his *Third Philippic*, he goes from depicting Antony as "un" Roman, meaning that he has an array of
uncivil-like characteristics,[112] to "no" Roman, denoting an enemy

of the Republic, and by the end, as a "non human," no more than a beast (*belua*).[113]

While Cicero refers to other enemies as beasts,[114] his depiction of Antony as a beast is sustained and developed.[115] In his *Second Philippic*—his longest and most virulent attack against Antony[116] and thought to have been a template[117] for his delivered speeches[118]—Cicero compares Antony to the mythical Charybdis, the monster that has the form of a whirlpool and devours huge quantities of water. Like Charybdis, Antony is said to have devoured and squandered entire storehouses of goods (*Phil.* 2.66–67).[119] While depicting an opponent as overly self-indulgent was common in ancient Greek polemics,[120] Cicero's comparison of Antony to Charybdis takes a common political invective to new heights.

Cicero's first explicit declaration of Antony as a beast (*belua*)[121] occurs in his *Third Philippic* at section 28.[122]

3.28a Hanc vero taeterrimam beluam quis ferre potest aut quo modo?

3.28b Quid est in Antonio praeter libidinem, crudelitatem, petulantiam, audaciam?

3.28c Ex his totus vitiis congluinatus est.

3.28d Nihil apparet in eo ingenuum, nihil moderatum, nihil pudens, nihil pudicum.

3.28a But this most hideous monster,[123] who can endure him or how?

3.28b What is there in Antonius, save lust, cruelty, insolence, audacity?

3.28c He is entirely made up of these vices glued together.

3.28d No trace in him of gentlemanly feeling, of moderation, of self-respect, of modesty.[124]

The passage creates two contrasting images, one of a beast Antony (3.28a), and the other of an upstanding Roman citizen, Antony's antithesis (3.28d). In doing so, Cicero creates a chasm between the two that not only fosters abhorrence for the beast but also implicitly challenges his fellow Roman senators to moral rectitude, that is, to live up to the image he paints of them. The sharp contrast Cicero draws makes siding with Antony synonymous with social ostracism and shame and brings the senators down to the level of a beast.

According to Cicero, Antony is a most horrid beast. Using another superlative adjective and *epitheton* for emphasis, he calls Antony a *taeterrimam beluam* ("most hideous monster"; 3.28a).[125] Other synonyms for the Latin adjective *taeter* include hideous, repulsive, shameful, disgraceful, and abominable. The phrase *quis ferre potest aut quo modo* ("who can endure him or how"; 3.28a) harkens back to the image of an uncontainable whirlwind Charybdis,[126] a metaphor for Antony with which Cicero experimented in his *Second Philippic*, a treatise completed only two months prior to his *Third Philippic*. In addition, by not immediately identifying the "beast" by name (3.28a), Cicero allows the image of a beast itself to linger in the imagination of his audience. Delaying mention of the enemy's name is a technique also found in Demosthenes (*Phil.* 3.26–27).

Cicero's beast, Antony, is socially[127] and politically[128] lethal. Antony completely disregards social conventions and values. Conforming to social conventions and especially the ability to be honored was—if one takes to heart what Cicero writes in his philosophical treatises—of utmost importance to him. In his *De Officiis*, Cicero writes that a crisis of the republic was due not to a failure in the system itself but only to "immoral and degenerate leaders."[129] According to Cicero, there are "natural principles" (*naturae principia*) that constitute human community. These principles consist in the combined use of reason and speech,[130] and rely upon teaching, learning, communicating, debating and making judgments. These principles and behaviors are what separate men from beasts (*De officiis* 1.52). Thus, Antony fails to live up to standards of moral rectitude Cicero has a hand in developing.

Cicero methodically lays out Antony's socially unacceptable traits—many of which pertain to a lack of self-control.[131] In carefully crafted asyndetic[132] sequences consisting of four elements each, Cicero describes the various ways in which Antony is a beast (3.28b) and unlike an upright citizen (3.28d). Cicero then

makes a one-for-one contrast between the elements in each phrase
(3.28b, 28d). Taken together, the two lines make for, in the words
of Manuwald, a "vivid and persuasive" portrayal.[133] Lines 3.28b
and 3.28d are also another instance of ring composition and now
with an intervening graphic image (3.28c).

Antony's first beastly trait is *libido* (3.28b), which pertains to
inordinate desire or lust and is opposed to *ingenuum* (3.28d), a
term that refers to someone befitting of a noble birth. Indeed, elsewhere[134] Cicero exploits this negative notion of inordinate desire,
which here heads the list of Antony's defects. The second trait is
crudelitatem (3.28b), which is translated as "cruelty" or "barbar-
ity" and is contrasted with *moderatum* (3.28d), the ability to exhibit
restraint. This beastly characteristic pertains more generally to a
tyrant,[135] as Stevenson explains. *Petulantiam* (3.28b) is impudence
and its antithesis is *pudens*, which pertains to modesty and chastity (3.28d). The final trait Cicero mentions is *audaciam* (overconfi-
dence, presumption) with *pudicum* (modesty, chastity, and virtue)
being denied to Antony. The intervening line (3.28c) contains a
graphic image of Antony imagined as nothing but the negative
characteristics *libidinem, crudelitatem, petulantiam, audaciam* all
glued together.

In sum, Cicero's beast, Antony, lacks self-control in all areas
of life. Cicero likens him to a whirlwind, as out of control and as
leaving a path of destruction in his wake. By specifying the characteristics of a beast antithetically to those of an upright Roman
citizen, Cicero not only draws a stark contrast between the two
but also creates an aversion and accompanying need to distance
onself from Antony.

Paul: Creating Fear and Dishonoring Opponents

Like Demosthenes and Cicero, Paul also aims—through the use of
exaggerated claims, graphic images, and extended narratives—to
provoke the emotions[136] of his audience against his opponents.[137]
Unlike Demosthenes and Cicero, however, Paul disparages his
opponents with highly charged invectives belonging to the realm
of malevolent spiritual forces. Yet like the earlier orators, he too
works to distance his audience from his opponents by alluding to

values and beliefs that he and his audience but not his opponents share. While Paul does not and indeed cannot allude to a shared history as a means of creating a common bond with his non-Jewish audience, he instead develops an extended narrative or allegory to bring about a sense of commonality with them. Through allegory Paul rewrites narratives of his own people so as to draw the Galatians over to his point of view.

Conjuring the Demonic to Provoke Fear

Curses (1:8–9) and bewitchment (3:1) are among the techniques Paul employs to arouse his audience's fear of and loathing for his opponents. Due to their inherent ability to frighten, the references to malevolent spirits serve more generally to heighten the overall emotional impact of his letter. Paul's first evocation of curses occurs early in his letter body, just subsequent to the salutation and in a unit previously discussed. The verses are as follows:

1:8a ἀλλὰ καὶ ἐὰν ἡμεῖς ἢ ἄγγελος ἐξ οὐρανοῦ
  εὐαγγελίζηται [ὑμῖν] παρ᾽ ὃ εὐηγγελισάμεθα ὑμῖν,
1:8b **ἀνάθεμα ἔστω.**
1:9a ὡς προειρήκαμεν καὶ ἄρτι πάλιν λέγω·
1:9b εἴ τις ὑμᾶς εὐαγγελίζεται παρ᾽ ὃ παρελάβετε,
1:9c **ἀνάθεμα ἔστω.**

1:8a but even if we or an angel from heaven should proclaim good news [to you] contrary to what we proclaimed to you,
1:8b **let that one be accursed!**
1:9a as we have said before and yet I say again:
1:9b if someone proclaims to you a gospel contrary to what you received,
1:9c **let that one be accursed!**[138]

In this short section, Paul twice curses (marked in bold-faced type above) his opponents.[139] Paul's curses are identically formed (*anaphora*; 1:8b, 9c) and hence emphasized. With them, he creates a highly charged emotional, malevolent, and otherworldly atmosphere around his opponents.[140]

By evoking curses, Paul is very likely borrowing on references to curses in Deuteronomy.[141] Indeed, as we shall see in the section discussed below, in Gal 3:10 and 3:12 Paul pulls directly from Deut 27:26 and 21:23 for further discussions that also concern the notion of a curse. The invocation of a curse does not mean, as some have argued, that Paul is somehow departing from the realm of rhetoric.[142] While the use of curse language is relatively rare among Greco-Roman authors,[143] cursing functions in argumentation similarly to other terms that make evil present; these types of terms are intended to persuade by engendering fear and hatred. While Paul's use of curse language provides an indication of his conceptual world and of his confidence in the effectiveness of this concept to arouse the desired emotions in his audience, it does not remove his discourse from the realm of rhetoric.[144]

Curses had a fearsome reputation among some ancient peoples. According to Michael D. Swartz, curses suggested harmful effects that extended beyond mental harm to the fear of physical pain.[145] Regardless of whether or not Paul meant actual harm to his opponents,[146] his discourse intended to conjure images of it. Moreover, with his evocation of curses, Paul strongly prejudiced his Galatian audience against his opponents.[147]

Once Paul starts on the motif of curses, he remains with it, keeping this concept alive and active (3:1, 10, 12). Each further repetition of the notion of a curse strengthens the concept itself and serves to recall its first association with his opponents (1:8–9). As in Gal 1:8–9, in Gal 3:1[148] Paul makes his anger apparent.[149] His angry tone, evident elsewhere as well (Gal 1:6–9; 2:14; 3:2–5, 21; 4:21; 5:1–12), adds to the emotional impact of structural units and to the letter as a whole. Following is Gal 3:1 displayed as it would have been heard.

3:1a Ὦ ἀνόητοι Γαλάται,
3:1b τίς ὑμᾶς ἐβάσκανεν,
3:1c οἷς κατ᾽ ὀφθαλμοὺς Ἰησοῦς Χριστὸς προεγράφη ἐσταυρωμένος;

3:1a Oh foolish Galatians!
3:1b Who has **bewitched** you?

3:1c [It was] before your eyes Jesus the Anointed was portrayed as crucified![150]

In this verse Paul refers to the practice of bewitchment
(ἐβάσκανεν; 3:1b)[151] and indirectly accuses his opponents[152] of
bewitching the Galatians. For this concept, Paul likely once again
draws from Deuteronomy.[153] Bewitchment[154] itself, however, regards the practice of evil eye, a belief that continues to this day.[155]
At base, evil eye concerns envy. According to Nanos, "Envy is
manifested when one seeks to prevent another from obtaining
some good, or begrudges the occasion of this good fortune."[156]
Envy operates independently of its object, as it may be expressed
even when the one envying the good already possesses it or when
the envier does not care to have the good. Practioners of evil eye
target those within their own social circle[157] and/or those they
consider to be competitors.[158] Paul, then, is inferring that his opponents have cast the evil eye on the Galatians out of envy.[159]

Evil eye practices, however, also have a sinister side. Like the
performative function of curses, the evil eye intends harm to its
recipients. Persons bewitching another with the evil eye desire to
severely diminish the health and livelihood of their recipient(s).
Its effects were considered as potentially deadly.[160] Ancient authors, such as Philostratus, Pliny, and Plutarch describe the material harm caused by the evil eye.[161] John H. Elliott explains:

> Basic to this belief [evil eye] is the conviction that certain indi-
> viduals, animals, demons, or gods have the power of casting
> an evil spirit or causing some malignant effect upon every
> object, animate or inanimate, upon which their eye or glance
> may fall. Through the power of their eye, which may operate
> involuntarily as well as intentionally, such Evil Eye possessors
> were thought capable of injuring or destroying the life and
> health of others, their means of sustenance and livelihood,
> their honor and personal fortune. As the eye was considered
> the window to and of the heart and the physical channel of
> one's innermost attitudes, desires, and intentions, an Evil Eye
> was linked with the negative moral attitudes of envy and

greed, stinginess and covetousness, and was considered directed against objects of the possessor's displeasure or envy.[162]

Paul's suggestion that his opponents participate in evil eye practices is highly derogatory of his opponents and intends to agitate in a worrisome way his audience. By alluding to this practice, Paul charges the atmosphere. Paul's audience should not only ignore these others, but also consider them in some way associated with this malevolent practice.[163] With his curses and allusion to bewitchment, he effectively turns these unnamed others into persons to be feared[164] and, like Demosthenes and Cicero, effects simplicity of audience decision-making.

Having conjured the demonic realm around his opponents, Paul's subsequent references to curses (Gal 3:10 [2x], 13 [3x]) function to re-awaken that realm and the accompanying fear and apprehension that surround it.[165] In 3:10 and 3:13, Paul associates curses with works of Torah, that is, with that for which his opponents advocate. In these later verses, Paul quotes from passages in Deuteronomy (LXX; shown in italics below). Verse 3:10 reads:

3:10a Οσοι γὰρ ἐξ ἔργων **νόμου** εἰσίν, ὑπὸ **κατάραν** εἰσίν·
3:10b γέγραπται γὰρ ὅτι *ἐπικατάρατος* πᾶς ὃς οὐκ ἐμμένει *πᾶσιν τοῖς γεγραμμένοις ἐν τῷ βιβλίῳ τοῦ* **νόμου** *τοῦ ποιῆσαι αὐτά.*

3:10a For whosoever is from works of **Torah**, is under a **curse**;
3:10b for it is written: ***Yet more accursed*** *is everyone who does not remain in all that is written in the scroll of the* **Torah** *to do it.*[166]

As we have seen in previous passages, here too, repetition creates emphasis.[167] Unlike in Gal 1:8–9, however, in which we find the exact repetition of words and phrases, with κατάραν, a noun (3:10a), and ἐπικατάρατος, an adjective (3:10b; marked in bold-faced type above), we have an instance of *adnominatio* (repetition of the same word, but with a different form). Yet with the Greek for Torah (νόμου), Paul engages again in *anaphora* (the repetition of the same word and form). Furthermore, by creating a chiastic pattern (ABBA) with them, Paul calls attention to terms for curse and Torah and strengthens the connection he seeks to draw between them (3:10a, 10b).

In Gal 3:10b, Paul borrows from Deut 27:26 (LXX) but alters his source text[168] in such a way as to strengthen the connection he seeks to establish between Torah and curse. While Paul's changes may at first glance appear to be slight, they significantly alter the sense of his source text. Indeed, with his modification of the Deuteronomic verse, he handily turns a concluding scriptural command (Deut 27:26)—which functions logically within its own context—into an exaggerated, opaque, and generalized[169] injunction against Torah itself.[170] Moreover, his use and modification of scripture indicates considerable sophistication: he does not merely mimic his source, but instead molds it for his own purpose. His use of scripture in Gal 3:10 and Gal 3:13 (see below) provides a clear indication of his in-depth knowledge of his source materials and of his own facility with Greek grammar. A comparison of Deut 27:26 and Gal 3:10 follows.

> Deut 27:26 Ἐπικατάρατος πᾶς **ἄνθρωπος**, ὃς οὐκ ἐμμενεῖ **ἐν πᾶσιν τοῖς λόγοις τοῦ νόμου τούτου** τοῦ ποιῆσαι αὐτούς.
>
> Deut 27:26 Yet more accursed is every **man** who does not remain **in all the words of this Torah** to enact them.
>
> Gal 3:10 Ἐπικατάρατος πᾶς **ὃς** οὐκ ἐμμένει[171] **πᾶσιν τοῖς γεγραμμένοις ἐν τῷ βιβλίῳ τοῦ νόμου** τοῦ ποιῆσαι **αὐτά.**
>
> Gal 3:10 Yet more accursed is everyone **who** does not remain **in all that is written in the scroll of the Torah** to enact them.[172]

In borrowing from Deut 27:26, Paul actually makes multiple yet only slightly perceptible changes to it (marked in bold-faced type above). First, he drops from Deut 27:26 the word ἄνθρωπος ("person"), normally translated as "man." In Deut 27:26, we find the longer phrase πᾶς ἄνθρωπος ("every man"). In dropping the ἄνθρωπος and retaining only the πᾶς ("all"), Paul changes from

the more specific case ("every man") to the more general and impersonal designation ("everyone"). Second, Paul alters the phrase
ἐν πᾶσιν τοῖς λόγοις τοῦ νόμου τούτου ("in all the words of this
Torah"; Deut 27:26) and replaces it with the longer phrase πᾶσιν
τοῖς γεγραμμένοις ἐν τῷ βιβλίῳ τοῦ νόμου ("all that is written in the scroll of the Torah"). The inserted dative phrase τοῖς
γεγραμμένοις ἐν τῷ βιβλίῳ ("written in the scroll of the Torah")
greatly extends that to which the curse applies. The perfect participle γεγραμμένοις ("written"), a verbal form that indicates completed past actions, adds weight or authority to the words of the
Torah and a sense of fixity not apparent in the Deuteronomic text.
Paul also omits the definite article τούτου ("this") of Deut 27:26
that serves in the source text to limit the scope of the curse to a
specific list of laws (see the discussion below). Its removal turns
a command intended to refer to certain socially abhorrent behaviors into one that applies more generally to the entire Torah. To
restate, Deut 27:26 reports that every man who does not remain in
all the words of *this* Torah is cursed, whereas Paul states that everyone who does not follow and observe all that is written in the
entire Torah is cursed (Gal 3:10b). Paul's modification, not on the
surface so readily apparent, is significant. Indeed, both Betz and
Martyn remark that Paul has Gal 3:10 say the opposite of Deut
27:26.[173]

Deuteronomy 27:26 is the last of twelve explicit curses
Moses advances to warn the Israelites against conduct contrary
to God's commandments, actions that would violate the Ten
Commandments (see Exod 20:1–17, Deut 5:6–21). These actions
include the making of idols; dishonoring father or mother; de-
priving the alien, orphan, or widow; committing incest; as well
as other prohibitions (Deut 27:15–25). Deuteronomy 27:26 does
not refer to every commandment of Torah, whether they be ritual,
moral, or both, but only to *these particular commandments* listed
(Deut 27:15–25). The injunctions listed in Deut 27:15–25 refer to
behaviors Paul himself elsewhere cautions against: idolatry (Gal
5:20, 1 Cor 5:9, Rom 1:23), rebellion against parents (Rom 1:30),
and incest (1 Cor 5:1–2). Thus, it is not that Paul is fundamentally
at odds with the spirit of Deut 27:15–25. Rather Paul's interest in

this text is seemingly due to the fact that it references a curse. The fact that the scope of its curse is limited gets in Paul's way. Thus, he alters the phrase. Paul's goal is to extend the applicability of the curse.

In making the specific changes outlined above, Paul leaves behind the original sense of Deut 27:15–25, in which a curse occurs for particular and socially abhorrent practices—that it is reserved for those who practice idolatry, incest, or murder—and instead, he has scripture remark that a curse applies to everyone who fails to practice all commandments of Torah (the entire scroll). His reason for making Torah particularly difficult, if not impossible, to follow without being cursed is to worry his Galatian audience. Gal 3:10 functions to caution his audience against adopting Torah. Martyn remarks that Paul's interpretation of Deut 27:26 leads to the sense that "by pronouncing a curse, the Law [Torah] establishes a sphere of inimical power that is universal."[174] Paul greatly strengthens[175] over that of his source text the notion of the curse and its effects. Like Demosthenes and Cicero, he plays loose with his source—removing parts and adding others—so as to bring about his desired objective of persuasion.

Paul employs the term κατάρα ("curse") one final time in verse Gal 3:13,[176] in which he once again associates it with the Torah. With his expression ἐκ τῆς κατάρας τοῦ νόμου ("from the curse of the Torah"; 3:13a), he adds the sense in which the Torah itself is cursed.

3:13a Χριστὸς ἡμᾶς ἐξηγόρασεν ἐκ τῆς **κατάρας** τοῦ νόμου γενόμενος ὑπὲρ ἡμῶν **κατάρα**,
3:13b ὅτι γέγραπται· **ἐπικατάρατος** πᾶς ὁ κρεμάμενος ἐπὶ ξύλου,

3:13a The Anointed redeemed us from the **curse** of the Torah by becoming a **curse** for us,
3:13b for it is written: ***yet more accursed*** *is everyone who hangs on a tree,*[177]

The Greek word for curse (κατάρα) is prominent (3:13a [2x], 13b; marked in bold-faced type above). With each new iteration,

Paul employs a slightly different form (*adnominatio*). He first refers to a curse as an inherent part of the Torah, and in the other
two uses of this word, he remarks that the curse refers to a person.

The association of the Torah with the curse (3:13a) has caused
exegetes sensitive to the perception of anti-Judaism in Paul to find
work-arounds to lessen the anti-Torah connotation implied by this
verse. Betz, for example, comments that Paul *comes close* to associating the Torah with a curse.[178] In his attempt to weaken the sense
that Paul is anti-Torah, Richard Hays writes, "When Paul's allusion to Deuteronomy is taken fully into account, one time-worn
issue of Pauline exegesis solves itself: 'the curse of the Law' from
which Christ redeems us (Gal 3:13) is not the Law itself regarded
as a curse, but the curse that the Law *pronounces* in Deuteronomy
27."[179] While a pronouncement may be present in Deuteronomy,
Paul is employing the notion of the curse of the Torah not as a
literal indicator, but instead rhetorically. Moreover, in a rhetorical reading, limiting the force of the statement undermines the
meaning. The Jewish Paul is here and elsewhere engaged in a series of polemical arguments with other Jews. He depicts the Torah
as being cursed to demean his opponents, those who push the
Galatians for Torah adoption.

Paul offers the Anointed as a replacement for the Torah (3:13a).
Susan Eastman remarks that just as amulets "absorb" the harmful
effects of the evil eye (3:1), so too does Christ on the cross.[180] While
Eastman rightly sees the connections between Paul's various em-
ployments of curses and evil eye bewitchment, her comparison
of the crucified Anointed and an amulet weakens the intended
effect of Paul's statement (3:13a). Amulets protect from harm. Like
a shield, they ward off evil;[181] they do not absorb the harm, as Paul
posits the Anointed did.

Paul's statement that the Anointed takes on the curse—he ab-
sorbs it—provides a solution to the problem of the curse of the
Torah that he has himself created. In other words, having indicated that the curse comes about when any of the Torah is dis-
obeyed (3:10)—something his audience would not have known
prior to his articulation of it—Paul now offers the Anointed as a
way out of this now difficult situation he produced. To avoid a

curse, his audience is to side with the Anointed and not with the Torah.

The second phrase in the above passage (Gal 3:13b) is, like 3:10b above, borrowed from scripture and from Deuteronomy (Deut 21:23). As is the case in 3:10, here too Paul repurposes a scriptural verse to make an entirely different point. And as before, he modifies the wording of his source text.[182]

Deut 21:23 **κεκατηραμένος ὑπὸ θεοῦ** πᾶς κρεμάμενος ἐπὶ ξύλου
Deut 21:23 **Cursed by God** is everyone hung on a tree

Gal 3:13b Ἐπικατάρατος [. . .] πᾶς ὁ κρεμάμενος ἐπὶ ξύλου
Gal 3:13b **Yet more accursed** is everyone who is hung on a tree[183]

The changes to Deut 21:23 are subtle but nevertheless meaningful. The κεκατηραμένος of Deut 21:23 is a perfect middle participle and denotes "being accursed," while the ἐπικατάρατος of Gal 3:13b is an intensified adjective meaning "yet more accursed," yielding only a slight difference in meaning.[184] With this change, Paul makes the notion of a curse stronger than his source text grants.

More significantly, however, Paul omits the phrase "by God" (ὑπὸ θεοῦ) present in his source text. In Deut 21:23, it is disobedience to God that warrants the curse. According to Deut 21:23, the person hanging on a tree has broken a specific divine commandment that according to the legal code warrants death. As Betz remarks, "Deut 21:22–23 contains a *legal regulation* for the hanging of criminals: when someone is convicted of a capital crime and is put to death, you shall hang him on a gibbet; his body shall not remain on the gibbet overnight, but you shall bury him on the same day, for 'cursed by God is everyone who hangs on the gibbet.'"[185] With the omission of the phrase "by God," the divine injunction falls away with the result that no reason is known or given for the curse. Shorn of the divine legislation, the curse applies automatically and universally, and as a result becomes more frightful. In Galatians, no human can prevent the curse. Paul writes that anyone (or everyone) who hangs on a tree is cursed. Furthermore, by omitting the phrase "by God," Paul alienates the Galatians not from God but only from Torah. While in the context of Galatians Paul has the curse apply to the Anointed, the notion of a curse in and of itself nevertheless looms large and threatening. Paul, then, creates an aura of malevolency around Torah but not God. Martyn comments, "In a highly significant move Paul omits the phrase 'by God,' thus dissociating the curse from God, linking it solely to the Law, and causing the quoted text to conform to his prefixed exegesis."[186]

In sum, Paul conjures the demonic realm to stir his audience's emotions, to create a charged and fearful atmosphere around his opponents and around the Torah they promote. Starting in Gal 1:8, he twice curses those who advance a message different from his own. With his curses, he locates his opponents on the side of malevolent forces. In Galatians 3, he refers to the evil eye bewitchment and again to curses, effectively reawakening the demonic realm. He associates curses with the Torah itself and with those who practice it. The notion of curses and bewitchment would have engendered fear, as Paul's ancient hearers would likely have associated curses and the evil eye practices with activities that cause physical harm. Paul draws upon scripture for its authority and to undergird his arguments, but he uses his source texts selectively and then makes strategic alterations to them that change their original sense. As such, he indicates more interest in specific words that serve his rhetorical purposes than in the source texts' original meaning and intent. In Gal 3:10b, Paul associates a curse with the disobedience of any part of Torah, the entire scroll, and in Gal 3:13b he makes the act of hanging on a tree, originally intended to indicate a violation of a divine injunction, an act that in and of itself implies a curse. Both modifications to scripture broaden the extent of the applicability of the curse and thereby strengthen the notion of a curse. Paul sought to provoke fear and aversion for his opponents and for the Torah practices they advocated. As Eastman comments, Paul's purpose in employing bewitchment and curses is to contrast the "death-dealing effects" of those promoting the Torah with his own "life-giving" message.[187]

Those of Torah are as those having sex with a slave woman

In Gal 4:21–27, Paul provokes his audience's emotions against his opponents through an extended narrative or allegory, one that, among other things, alludes to the sexual availability of slaves. The *Oxford English Dictionary* defines a modern allegory as, "a story, picture, etc. which uses symbols to convey a hidden or ulterior meaning, typically a moral or political one."[188] The etymology of the English term "allegory" is based on two Greek words, *allos* ("other") and *agoreuein* ("to speak in the agora" or "to speak publically").[189] The Greek word ἀλληγορία means to "say something other than what one seems to say."[190] Like the modern understanding, ancient allegories were also recognized as story, having a beginning, middle, and end and including events and characters along with their interactions.[191] Stories function like graphic images in that they too arouse emotions.

Like a story, allegory establishes an unspoken agreement between its author and hearers/readers for a new interpretation of a text. Thus, when Paul signals that what follows is an allegory (ἅτινά ἐστιν ἀλληγορούμενα; 4:24), he begins what he hopes will be an agreement with his Galatian auditors for his new reading/story. Elizabeth Castelli assesses that Paul's allegory serves as a "consensus-building trope."[192]

Just as allegory seeks to establish an agreement for a new interpretation, it also has another dimension: it denies the original meaning of the text on which it is based. David Dawson explains that allegory "implies an antithetical stance toward a previous saying."[193] According to Dawson, allegory functions to "reinterpret the world intratextually."[194] In doing so, authors create new scriptural understandings. Putting the issue more sharply, because she fills in the negative implications of Paul's allegory, Castelli remarks that allegory does violence to the traditional text.[195]

Dawson is interested in the intended purpose of allegory. According to him, allegory served to challenge prior or contemporaneous cultural and religious worldviews and to advance alternative ones.[196] Allegory served to defeat or invalidate competitive understandings or readings.[197] Ancient authors, such as Philo (ca. 20 BCE–ca. 50 CE), Valentinus (ca. 100–ca. 175 CE) and Clement of Alexandria (ca. 150–ca. 215 CE), employed allegory to "endorse, revise, and subvert competing world views and forms of life."[198] As I indicate below, through his allegory Paul creates a new and emotionally charged story that overturns prior readings.[199] His allegory springs from his own competitive environment. With his allegory, Paul challenges the views of his competitors, those who promote Torah adoption (4:21).[200]

Paul's allegory (Gal 4:21–27) stands as the concluding proof in a section that already contains several arguments against Torah adoption (Gal 3:1–5:1). As last in a series of arguments, it carries significant weight in his overall argument.[201] While drawn from the Genesis narratives of Abram/Abraham, Sarai/Sarah and Hagar (Genesis 16, 17 and 21), Paul takes these source texts into a new direction.[202] Through his reshaping of the Genesis narratives, he severely diminishes the character Hagar in particular. She represents those associated with Torah.[203] Through the allusions he makes, Paul likens Hagar to an object for sexual pleasure. The passage appears below only in English translation.

4:21 Tell me, you who desire to be subject to the law, will you not listen to the law?

4:22 For it is written that Abraham had two sons, one by a **slave** woman and the other by a free woman.

4:23 One, the child of the **slave**, was born **according to the flesh** [κατὰ σάρκα]; the other, the child of the free woman [ἐλευθέρας], was born through the promise [δι᾿ ἐπαγγελίας].

4:24 Now this is an allegory [ἅτινά ἐστιν ἀλληγορούμενα]: these women are two covenants. One woman, in fact, is Hagar, from **Mount Sinai**, bearing children for **slavery**.

4:25 Now Hagar is **Mount Sinai** in Arabia and corresponds to the present Jerusalem, for she is in **slavery** with her children.

4:26 But the other woman corresponds to the Jerusalem above [ἄνω Ἰερουσαλήμ]; she is free, and she is our mother.

4:27 For it is written,

"Rejoice, you childless one, you who bear no children, burst into song and shout, you who endure no birthpangs;

for the children of the desolate woman are more numerous than the children of the one who is married."[204]

Female characters form the basis of Paul's allegory and it is through their characterizations that Paul creates two oppositional ways of life[205]—one way under the Torah,[206] associated with the slave woman, Hagar, and the other that is Torah-free, and associated with an unnamed woman (known as Sarai/Sarah from Genesis).[207] Differences between the two women abound. As Castelli writes, "Categories of difference are here not rendered immaterial and meaningless, but rather come to stand for the radical differences between those who are born into slavery (life under the Torah) and those who are born into freedom (life under the promise)."[208]

While verses 22 and 23 are not technically part of the allegory, they provide the backdrop for it. They, like the allegory that follows, are highly interpretive and highly selective in their use of scripture. Paul sets up the allegory with a distinction between flesh and promise. Whereas Hagar bore a son to Abraham[209] "through the flesh" (κατὰ σάρκα), the unnamed and free (ἐλευθέρας) woman bore a son "through the promise" (δι᾽ ἐπαγγελίας; 4:22–23).[210] In Paul's source text, however, there is no indication that Abram's/Abraham's freeborn wife bore him a son in any way other than by the flesh (Gen 17:15–16; 21:1–7).[211] By distinguishing that Hagar's son, and *only her son*, was born according to the flesh, Paul signals a new element of significance and then with it advances the notion that Abraham's relationship with his slave woman was bodily, that is fleshly, as in sexual.[212]

Furthermore, and again in contrast to his source text, through repetition (*exergasia*)[213] Paul emphasizes that Hagar is a slave

(4:22, 23, cf. 4:24, 25; marked in bold-faced type above). Repetition reinforces the difference in the social status between these two women, a distinction not made in his source text. Indeed, the Genesis narratives of Sarai and Hagar read as a criticism of slavery. In Genesis, after the slave Hagar conceives a child with Abram, Abram's freeborn wife, Sarai, begins to see Hagar as an equal. To maintain the power dynamic between free and slave, Sarai sends Hagar away (Gen 16:1–6). After Hagar's departure, the narrative focuses sympathetically on her (Gen 16:7–16),[214] the slave woman, and not on Sarai, the freeborn woman, who is portrayed as abrupt and harsh. By contrast, through the repetition of the Greek word for slave, Paul marks as highly significant the distinction in class between slave and free. Unlike the author of the Genesis narrative, Paul does nothing to win his audience's affection or sympathy for Hagar; indeed, he works to strengthen an abhorrence of her. There is no question that the freeborn woman is superior to the slave Hagar.

Differences between material and spiritual, and sexual[215] and asexual also serve to distinguish these two women for Paul's hearers.[216] In the allegory, the two women reside in two distinct locations. Hagar, the woman who receives more attention, comes from a physical/actual and recognizable geographic location, Mount Sinai.[217] Indeed, using *repotia*,[218] Paul repeats the reference to Mount Sinai (4:24, 25). He also appends the recognizable— but freighted with problems of historical verifiability—name Arabia[219] to Hagar, as well as the expresssion "present Jerusalem" (4:25). These place names reinforce the sense of her physicality of "place." By contrast, the other woman is not identified with any physical location whatsoever but instead with a non-material and non-fleshly place (ἄνω Ἰερουσαλήμ, "Jerusalem above"; 4:26).[220] Hagar is named, while the freeborn woman is not. Without a name, there is much less focus on the woman herself, as an embodied or sexualized being, than on what she is meant to represent, the ethereal Jerusalem.[221] In the allegory, both women have children (4:25, 27), but the unnamed woman's offspring derive from other-than-natural means (asexually; 4:27), even while she has "more children" than does Hagar. Finally, only the unnamed woman is related to the Galatian community and to Paul as their "mother." As a mother, the freeborn woman is intimately and personally related to the community, while at the same time, her relationship to them is asexual. On the other hand, the slave woman, while named, has no defined familial and thereby favorably construed relationship to the Galatians. In the allegory, Hagar always remains a slave, commonly understood as an object or tool.

Unlike the characterization of the free woman, the characterization of Hagar suggests sexual relations.[222] As mentioned, from the outset the slave woman is distinguished as having physical relations with Abraham, "by the flesh" (4:23). Hagar's physicality is accentuated by the fact that she has a name and an earthly position as a slave woman (4:22, 23, 24, 25). In contrast to the free woman, the slave Hagar is associated with physical places.

Regardless of race (Greek, Roman, or Jew), all slave owners exploited their slaves for sexual purposes.[223] Yet as Kyle Harper remarks, sex and one's sexual partners in particular also had social implications. In the ancient world, these relationships served a legitimating function for males. Ancient Greeks were "fixated on the issue of legitimacy" and made the regulation of sexuality a determining factor of it.[224] To define legitimacy, ancients distinguished between "free women" (ἐλεύθεραι), those who could be esteemed as sexually honorable, and another class of women comprised of slaves, prostitutes, and courtesans who could not.[225] While in ancient society the sexual exploitation of slaves was licit and occurred with regularity, no legitimizing benefit would or could accrue from these types of relationships. Thus, by associating the slave Hagar with "those of the Torah" (4:21), Paul links "those of Torah" with a woman from whom no legitimating benefit could obtain. Making such a connection belittles "those of Torah."

In sum, in Gal 4:21–27, Paul provides one final "proof" for why the Galatian non-Jews should not adopt Torah practices.[226] Through allegory, he adopts an antithetical stance to his source text and thereby challenges its worldview. Women dominate the narrative. The Galatian males line up behind one of two distinct female types. More attention is given to the negatively construed slave woman Hagar, who is meant to represent Torah and those who adopt it.

With his allegory, Paul significantly overturns prior scriptural readings. In Genesis both Hagar the slave and Sarai/Sarah the free woman have sexual or fleshly relations and sons by Abram/Abraham. Indeed, in Genesis, unable to conceive a child, Sarai/Sarah encourages Abram to have sexual relations with Hagar, her slave, using the latter as a surrogate. Due to these sexual relations—brought about by the suggestion of Sarai/Sarah and carried out by Abraham out of obedience to her—the free/slave status distinction between these two women becomes blurred (see Genesis 16, 21). In his rewritten allegory, however, Paul omits how Abram comes to have relations with Hagar the slave. Paul assesses Hagar clearly, repeatedly, and only as a slave with no relationship whatsoever with Sarai. Absent the knowledge of Sarai/Sarah's role in legitimating the relations between Abram and Hagar, Abram is understood as simply taking Hagar sexually, just as any ancient slaveholding man would. By assessing relations with the slave, and only with her, as "by the flesh," Paul makes clear that no legitimacy or honor accrues from relations with Hagar, meant to represent those of Torah. In making this type of association, Paul slanders those associated with Torah in ways not unlike how Cicero perjures and creates disgust for Antony.

Conclusion

All three rhetoric-of-crisis authors appeal to their audiences' emotions to convince them of the various negative traits of their enemies/opponents. Through the use of exaggerated claims, graphic images, and extended narratives, these authors provoke both fear and aversion for them and for what they advocate.

All three authors work to bring about author-audience shared sentiments. Indeed, the audience is meant to "catch" the author's own sentiment in support of the characterization the author seeks to draw. This technique is apparent when Paul in Galatians curses his opponents (Gal 1:8–9). His auditors are meant to feel his vehemence, whether heartfelt or not. In his efforts to engender fear and animosity for Philip, Demosthenes departs from his customary adversarial approach to his audience and instead compliments them. As such, Demosthenes' audience can better catch hold of his animosity for Philip.

All the rhetoric-of-crisis authors depict their enemies/opponents at the extreme end of bad/evil. Demosthenes actually eliminates, most likely inadvertently, all possible human categories for Philip. According to him, Philip is so lacking in social qualities that he is neither a Greek nor a barbarian. Historically, however, Philip was a Greek like Demosthenes. By depicting him with characteristics that disqualify him from being Greek, Demosthenes renders Philip unacceptable to a Greek audience. And by characterizing Philip as gobbling up territory after territory, he turns Philip into a frightening global threat. Similarly, Cicero accuses Antony of being the worst sort of tyrant. According to him, nothing stops Antony from brutally killing the Roman senators, just as he killed the soldiers in Brundisium. Likely in imitation of Demosthenes, Cicero casts Antony as a non-human, as a beast. With his multiple references to curses and to the practice of the evil eye, Paul positions his opponents in a malevolent realm. In doing so, he, like Demosthenes and Cicero, strongly prejudices his audience against his opponents and creates a sense of fear of them.

In their effort to demean their opponents, all three authors play loose with their commonly shared histories. All reconfigure their own history, the shared narratives of their people, so as to repurpose it to accentuate the evils or the wrongheadedness of their opponents. Demosthenes and Cicero compare their present enemies, Philip and Antony respectively, unfavorably to former rulers. In doing so, they retell their past much more positively than is historically warranted. Demosthenes argues that Philip's aggressions are far worse than anything before seen. For his part, Cicero remarks that Antony's cruel exploits are worse than those of King Tarquin, one of Rome's most brutal tyrants.

Like Demosthenes and Cicero, Paul pulls from scripture—the narratives of his people—to diminish his opponents and the Torah for which they advocate. Through high selectivity, decontextualization, and the alteration of words and phrases, Paul rewrites his native myths. Nowhere in scripture does it say that those who fail to practice all of Torah are cursed. And according to scripture, the mere fact of hanging on a tree does not warrant a curse. Paul also employs allegory to overturn prior readings. In making these types of allusions, Paul diminishes those of Torah and thereby prejudices his audience against them.

The rhetoric of crisis' employment of emotions for argumentation surfaces underexplored aspects of Paul's letter to the Galatians and changes our understanding of him. Explorations of tropes that arouse emotion surface a concentration of elements that pertain to the malevolent realm. Indeed, references to curses occur with enough frequency to argue that the development of a malevolent realm is a subtheme of Galatians. Within the body of scholarship devoted to Paul's use of curses, however, rarely are all the curses seen together as a theme and relatively little attention has been devoted to their rhetorical effect on the Galatian listeners. The rhetoric-of-crisis model understands that Paul employs curses and the evil eye to scare his audience away from his competitors. Curses function as polemical tools. By contrast, exegetes who engage in fact-seeking readings work to find palatable and reasonable work-arounds to explain Paul's association of Torah with a curse. Yet these work-arounds can and do end in logical inconsistencies. Betz, for instance, writes that for Paul the Torah is a curse but it is not "contrary to the promise made to Abraham."[227] That is, on the one hand, Paul deems the Torah worthless, nothing but a curse, while on the other hand, he has Abraham depending upon it to realize its promises. Logical consistency is not, however, a requirement of polemics.

By contrast to readings concerned with finding historical facts, the rhetoric-of-crisis reading allows room for the full rhetorical effects of Paul's statements, even when they appear unreasonably harsh. A rhetorical analysis does not look for nor does it expect truth claims, so there is no compulsion to soften statements. A rhetorical analysis looks instead for the means of persuasion in order to understand an author's purposes.

In the next chapter, I take up the disjunctive arguments rhetoric-of-crisis authors employ to bring about distance between their enemies/opponents and the audiences they address. In this type of argumentation, authors create and/or employ two diametrically opposite conditions and then establish hierarchical relationships between them.

4

Persuading through Disjuncture

> No other writer . . . is led to such radical and negative conclusions with respect to the law as Paul. . . . All these negative statements are made problematic because other *Pauline* statements contradict them. *Paul's most radical conclusions about the law are thus strangely ambiguous.* There is something strained and artificial in his negativity — artificial from his *own* point of view. He seems at times to argue further in the negative direction than he really intends. (Räisänen, *Paul and the Law*, 201; italics are the author's)

In this final leg of the rhetoric-of-crisis model, authors offer their audiences clear-cut choices between two mutually exclusive alternatives. This type of argumentation has been called "disjunctive mode."[1] With disjunctive argumentation, authors either employ pairs of terms in which the positive or negative valence of each element is common knowledge (examples are pairs such as freedom/slavery or honored councilman/public enemy) or authors engage in a subset of disjunctive argumentation called dissociation. In this latter type of argumentation, authors also offer their audiences mutually exclusive clear-cut alternatives but between notions for which there are no necessary predetermined and commonly known positive or negative valences. Here, the authors' circumstances or situation dictate both the terms and the hierarchy between them. Furthermore, unlike the commonly known and often employed antithetical pair freedom/slavery, with dissociation authors employ pairs of oppositional terms that are not otherwise contrastive. Thus, with dissociation, authors not only create oppositional pairs—where none previously existed—but also establish their arrangement hierarchically to suit their own rhetorical purposes.

As Kathryn Olson notes, dissociation is "an ingenious rhetorical process differentiating and hierarchically arranging usually two elements of a single concept; the rhetor portrays one element as positive and more highly valued, simultaneously devaluing another element by assigning to it the negative qualities of the formerly unified concept."[2] An example of a unified concept is personality. Dissociation breaks this unified notion into two elements, such as social and personal (see below), and assesses one more highly than the other. Demosthenes, for example, breaks the concept of quantity into one and many, privileging the first over the second. In his allegory (Gal 4:23), Paul divides the concept of conception into promise and flesh, prioritizing the first over the second.

Perelman and Olbrechts-Tyteca describe dissociation by means of a term I/term II model. They emphasize the terms' values. As they explain it, the "original status" (i.e., the positive or negative valence) of term I and of term II is often unspecified. Indeed, the terms often have a neutral status or valence. It is through the dissociation of these terms in argumentation that authors assign positive or negative valences to the terms.[3] Perelman and Olbrechts-Tyteca remark that term I often pertains to appearance and is assessed negatively, while term II refers to reality and obtains a positive value.[4] Term II establishes a criterion or a norm by which to distinguish the negative valence of term I. It is important to realize, however, that term II is not fact but instead a *"construction, which . . . establishes a rule that makes it possible to classify the multiple aspects of term I in a hierarchy."*[5] As opposed to term I, term II is coherent, normative, and explanatory. Using the pair social/personal as an example, they remark that term II, personal, indicates what is "innate and natural, sincere and authentic, while every social participation is only superficial and artificial, a 'mask' and an 'armor' behind which we have to rediscover the true person."[6] Ordinarily, social and personal are not antithetical, nor are personal relations in and of themselves superior to social ones. It is instead through these terms' use in dissociative argumentation that authors construct differences between them and determine their values hierarchically.

With disjunctive argumentation, we enter, more so than in the other legs of the rhetoric-of-crisis model, into a category of argumentation that Aristotle referred to as logical proofs. Logical proofs (*logos*) allow authors to demonstrate the "real or apparent truth" of their case (*Rhet.* 1.2.3)[7] and thus these proofs appeal to reason. Logical proofs also fall under a larger category of argumentation Aristotle calls "artistic" or "intrinsic" (ἔντεχνοι) proofs. Unlike unskilled or extrinsic proofs (ἄτεχνοί)—items such as laws, witnesses, or oaths, elements that persuade through elements external to the present discourse—intrinsic/artistic proofs (ἔντεχνοι) depend upon the rhetor's skills in invention (*Rhet.* 1.2.2).

Disjunctive arguments, however, do not appeal exclusively to reason. In as much as they rely upon shared values, that is, the likes and dislikes of their audiences, they also depend upon emotions. Indeed, not only does disjunctive rhetoric rely upon and assume the "correct" tastes (positive or negative) of its audience, but it also employs emotive rhetoric as part of the argumentative process itself. That is, in disjunctive argumentation, we find elements that arouse the emotions, such as exclamations, rhetorical questions, repetition, and the like. Thus, and as we have seen with the other legs of the rhetoric-of-crisis model, aspects of one component permeate into others as well.

Demosthenes, Cicero, and Paul employ disjunctive arguments not only to steer their audience to the "right" course of action—that is, to their preferred choice—but also, and equally important, away from the perspective of their enemies or opponents. Indeed, it is often the negative element within contrasting pairs—the side from which the authors wish to distance their audiences—that receives the most attention. The incorrect/wrong/evil/harmful issues and those persons associated with them drive these disjunctive arguments.

Disjunctive Mode in Demosthenes

After his second embassy to Philip in the summer of 344, Demosthenes went to the smaller states of Argos and Messene in the Peloponnesus to warn them of the dangers of asking Philip for his support.[8] Sparta had begun to threaten these states and Demosthenes urged them not to turn to Philip for aid but instead to Athens.[9] Demosthenes' *Second Philippic* comes on the heels of his embassy to Argos and Messene.[10] In contrast to his senatorial political opponents,[11] Aeschines, in particular, Demosthenes was of the opinion that Philip violated the Peace of Philocrates and could not be trusted and must be stopped. Philip had recently gained control of Thermopylae and could now easily get from there into Phocis and then move through the Gulf of Corinth and into the Peloponnese.[12] Aeschines, also a participant on the embassy to Argos and Messene, trusted Philip and in contrast to Demosthenes held to the view that Philip had not violated the peace treaty.[13] Thus, Demosthenes is dealing with an external threat (Philip) as well as an internal[14] one (Aeschines).[15] He deals with these two threats as though they were one.[16] Mader comments—reiterating an observable theme found in nearly all the units surveyed to this point—that the speech served more generally to distinguish Demosthenes' hardline position against Philip from the more conciliatory approach taken by others among the peace party.[17]

The unit that follows is a portion of a speech Demosthenes claims to have delivered to the Messenians while on envoy to them. Within his *Second Philippic*, the speech to the Messenians functions as a dramatic monologue and a cautionary tale for Demosthenes' Athenian audience. With it, Demosthenes makes the point that whereas the Messenians did not take to heart his warnings against Philip (*Phil.* 2.27), surely the Athenians—who are "wiser" than they—will.[18] Several of its rhetorical elements, such as questions followed by their answers and short exclamatory phrases, stir the emotions. As such, the speech-within-a-speech functions rhetorically to enhance the overall interest[19] and persuasive power of his *Second Philippic*. The passage follows.

2.23a–b "ὑμεῖς δ᾿," ἔφην ἐγώ, "διδόντα μὲν καὶ
ὑπισχνούμενον **θεωρεῖτε** Φίλιππον, ἐξηπατηκότα δ᾿
ἤδη καὶ παρακεκρουμένον ἀπεύχεσθε, εἰ σωφρονεῖτε
δή, **ἰδεῖν.**
2.23c ἔστι τοίνυν νὴ Δί᾿," ἔφην ἐγώ,
2.23d "**παντοδαπὰ** εὑρημένα ταῖς πόλεσιν πρὸς φυλακὴν
καὶ σωτηρίαν,
2.23e οἷον χαρακώματα καὶ τείχη καὶ τάφροι καὶ τἄλλ᾿ ὅσα
τοιαῦτα.
2.24a καὶ ταῦτα μέν ἐστιν ἅπαντα χειροποίητα καὶ
δαπάνης προσδεῖται·
2.24b **ἓν** δέ τι κοινὸν ἡ φύσις τῶν εὖ φρονούντων ἐν αὑτῇ
κέκτηται φυλακτήριον, ὃ πᾶσι μέν ἐστ᾿ ἀγαθὸν
καὶ σωτήριον, μάλιστα δὲ τοῖς πλήθεσι πρὸς τοὺς
τυράννους.
2.24c τί οὖν ἐστι τοῦτο;
2.24d **ἀπιστία.**
2.24e **ταύτην** φυλάττετε, **ταύτης** ἀντέχεσθε·
2.24f ἂν **ταύτην** σῴζητε, οὐδὲν μὴ δεινὸν πάθητε.
2.24g τί ζητεῖτ᾿;" ἔφην.
2.25a "**ἐλευθερίαν.**
2.25b εἶτ᾿ οὐχ ὁρᾶτε Φίλιππον ἀλλοτριωτάτας ταύτῃ καὶ
τὰς προσηγορίας ἔχοντα;
2.25c βασιλεὺς γὰρ καὶ τύραννος ἅπας ἐχθρὸς **ἐλευθερίᾳ**
καὶ νόμοις ἐναντίος.
2.25d οὐ φυλάξεσθ᾿ ὅπως," ἔφην, "μὴ πολέμου ζητοῦντες
ἀπαλλαγῆναι **δεσπότην** εὕρητε;"

2.23a–b "You," I said, "**gaze with wonder** at Philip as he gives
away this and promises that, but if you are truly wise,
pray that you may never **find** that he has deceived and
cozened you,
2.23c Verily [by Zeus]," I said,
2.23d "there are **manifold** means devised by states for protec-
tion and safety
2.23e —stockades, ramparts, fosses and the like.
2.24a And all these are wrought by hand and entail expense.

2.24b But there is **one** common bulwark which the instinct of sensible men possesses within itself, a good and safe one for all, but invaluable for democracies against tyrants.

2.24c And what is that bulwark?

2.24d It is **mistrust**.

2.24e Guard **that**; hold fast to **that**.

2.24f If you preserve it, no harm can touch you.

2.24g What is your object?" I said.

2.25a "**Freedom**.

2.25b Then do you not see that Philip's very titles are utterly irreconcilable with that?

2.25c For every king, every despot is the sworn foe of **freedom** and of law.

2.25d Beware," said I, "lest, seeking to be rid of war, you find a **master**."[20]

Trust vs. Mistrust (πίστις [implied] vs. ἀπιστία)

Multiple instances of disjunctive argumentation mark this dramatic monologue or speech-within-a-speech. Demosthenes breaks the concept of attitude into two parts, trust and mistrust, and then associates other antithetical pairs around it. He construes mistrust positively, and trust, a term that is absent but implied, negatively. The unit builds to the notion of mistrust (ἀπιστία; marked in boldfaced type above), which occurs at the unit's midpoint (2.24d).

Demosthenes steers his audience to the side of mistrust. Not only does the word "mistrust" occur at the unit's highpoint but it also receives considerable emphasis in the unit. It comes in answer to a self-posed question and stands alone in a phrase (2.24d). He reinforces the notion of mistrust through *polyptoton* (the repetition of the same word but in different forms) of the demonstrative pronoun ταύτην,[21] which refers to it (2.24e–f). As mentioned, the antithetical element, trust, is implied. Its presence is assumed, as Demosthenes accuses his audience of trusting Philip (2.23a–b).

In terms of their significance, however, mistrust and trust regard positions and not life attitudes, as is seen by the positional language Demosthenes employs when he refers to them.

Demosthenes insists that his audience be on the side of mistrust. For instance, with two imperative[22] verbs, he implores his audiences "to guard" (φυλάττετε) and to "hold fast" or "cling to" (ἀντέχεσθε)[23] mistrust (2.24e). By contrast, he does not develop a style of life based on mistrust.

While mistrust is an attitude Demosthenes strongly endorses for the Messenians and for his Athenian audience, those "overhearing" his earlier speech, mistrust's significance is limited. An audience attitude of mistrust applies to the current situation,[24] to issues and actions that pertain to Philip and also, by implication, to how they are to regard Demosthenes' political opponents. Indeed, Demosthenes' choice of the oppositional pair mistrust/ trust strongly suggests his opponents' influence. The terms are provocative. In his hands and through dissociation Demosthenes has a tool by which he can easily, distinctly, and directly differentiate his own approach to Philip (mistrust), from that of his political rivals (trust). Aeschines and Philocrates accept or trust[25] that Philip will abide by the peace process. As he mentions, the current "miserable" state of affairs is due to the fact that his political rivals with whom he traveled to Messene *trusted* Philip to uphold the peace treaty (2.35–36). With the term "mistrust," Demosthenes signals to his Messenian and Athenian audiences that they are to stand with him, on the side of mistrust, and not on the side of his rivals.

Gaze with Wonder vs. See and Understand (θεωρεῖτε vs. ἰδεῖν)

Demosthenes develops and deploys a second antithetical pair that is thematically related to the primary trust/mistrust duality. Here, he partitions the notion of seeing into two types, "gaze with wonder" and "see and understand." He privileges the second type over the first. His arrangement of these notions becomes clear when he chastises the Messenians for their complicit attitude. They passively regard ("gaze with wonder"; θεωρεῖτε, marked in bold-faced type above)[26] what transpires in their midst, while Philip is campaigning against them (2.23a).

Two different Greek verbs for seeing, θεωρεῖτε and ἰδεῖν, make possible this dissociation. In contrast to θεωρεῖτε,[27] ἰδεῖν has the more active sense of "look at" or "pay heed to" (2.23b).[28] Metaphorically, ἰδεῖν pertains to mental sight, as in perceiving. Vince translates ἰδεῖν metaphorically as "find." To perceive implies taking a close look, not a superficial and less-self-involving one, a look that could lead to the attitude of mistrust, which Demosthenes is after. The θεωρεῖτε/ἰδεῖν ("gaze with wonder"/"see and understand") pair is complimentary to the trust/mistrust duality already established. The term I and II elements of each pair reinforce each other.

Demosthenes contrasts the audience's trusting and laid-back attitude associated with the sense of θεωρεῖτε with four action-oriented and active participles (διδόντα, "give"; ὑπισχνούμενον, "promise"; ἐξηπατηκότα, "deceive"; παρακεκρουμένον, "mislead"), all of which concern Philip's present or future actions (2.23a). In doing so, he emphasizes that gazing with wonder is the incorrect form of seeing. Moreover, his sharp "you" (ὑμεῖς) that begins the internal monologue functions to gain his audience's attention to his point (2.23a).

Like the contrast Demosthenes builds between trust and mistrust, the opposition between "gazing with wonder" and "seeing and understanding" is limited and situational. Demosthenes chooses the terms θεωρεῖτε and ἰδεῖν for their ability to speak to the specific situation of alternative approaches to Philip. There is no necessary or essential difference between these two terms. Gazing is not always and of necessity of less value than concentrated looking. Demosthenes dissociates the notion of seeing to create a distinction and to force a choice between two positions.

These two different forms of seeing also correspond to a common theme Demosthenes employs to spur his audience to action. Mader names this theme the "knowing-doing gap." According to him, between 350 and 340 BCE Demosthenes repeatedly characterized the Athenian senators as being trapped in this gap. That is, Demosthenes often accuses the Athenians of procrastination and of passing decrees but then not acting upon them.[29] Yet as Madder explains, Demosthenes' employment of the knowing-doing gap has as much, if not more, to do with his fight with his political opponents as it does with the situation of Philip.[30] Indeed, and as we have seen, Demosthenes' use of dissociative argumentation also functions as a mechanism to distinguish himself from his opponents.

Manifold vs. One (παντοδαπὰ vs. ἓν)

Demosthenes divides the concept of quantity into many things and one thing. The manifold/one oppositional pair is yet a third instance of dissociative rhetoric within this short passage. The individual elements of this dichotomous pair correspond to the parallel elements within the other created pairs and serve to strengthen them. In this instance, Demosthenes privileges the term "one" over "manifold"; the former directly pertains to the term around which this unit turns, "mistrust."[31] Moreover, and as we have seen previously, there is nothing inherently positive about "one" or inherently negative about many/manifold; it is instead that Demosthenes arranges the two hierarchically to suit his situation and his overall argument.

He assigns the contrasting terms "many" παντοδαπὰ, ("of every kind," "of all sorts"), and translated above as "manifold" (2.23d), and "one" (ἓν; 2.24b) places of prominence, as heads of their respective phrases. As such, they stand in parallel position to each other (see above marked in bold-faced type), reinforcing the contrast between them. Manifold refers to the many material defenses every large ancient Mediterranean city has and employs. These defenses include stockades, ramparts, fosses, and other things. Demosthenes employs alliteration (the leading τ) and *polysyndeton*[32] (χαρακώματα καὶ τείχη καὶ τάφροι καὶ τἄλλ᾽ ὅσα τοιαῦτα) to emphasize these items, as such marking them as all the more present and obvious to his audiences (2.23e).[33]

According to Demosthenes, the one thing is more important than manifold things (2.24b). Indeed, because he associates φύσις ("by nature"; 2.24b) with the notion of one, this notion falls in line with a classic term II element. One is natural, normative, whereas manifold is not;[34] the latter (term I) involves items that are "made by hand" (χειροποίητα; 2.24a).[35] In addition, to emphasize the differences he seeks to draw between the notions of manifold and one, Demosthenes creates a play[36] on two Greek words containing the same root φυλα. Rather than guarding their territories (the noun φυλακὴν; 2.23d) with multiple material barriers, the audience should instead guard or preserve (the verb φυλάττετε; 2.24e) the one "correct" mental attitude and mistrust Philip.

Demosthenes builds to the notion of one, the "correct" alternative choice, in multiple ways. He introduces the concept with an interjection νὴ Δί᾽ ("by Zeus!")[37] (2.23c). He creates suspense by holding off naming what the one thing signifies:[38] he mentions the notion of one in 2.24b but does not reveal its identity until 2.24d. When he finally reveals that the one thing is mistrust (2.24d), it comes in dramatic form, as an answer to a self-posed and self-evident question (2.24c).

Finally, with his contrast between manifold and one, there is the sense in which Demosthenes himself represents the one, the one right solution. Indeed, Demosthenes is intimately involved in his audience's decision, as seen by the expression "I said" (ἔφην) used four times within this short passage (2.23a, 23c, 24g, 25d).[39] Thus, the audience should heed his (the "one") advice and not that of the manifold rivals[40] who oppose him.

Slavery (Implied) vs. Freedom (δεσπότης vs. ἐλευθερία)

The disjunctive pair slavery/freedom is yet another duality Demosthenes employs to offer clear-cut mutually exclusive alternatives to his audience. Given that each element of the pair would resonate on account of its culturally determined valence, there is no need for Demosthenes or any author, for that matter, employing these opposing terms to assess them; the audiences' preference between them is a given.

While Demosthenes mentions freedom and does so in a dramatic fashion (2.25a), he never actually discusses the concept itself. Instead he defines freedom by way of contrast to a life of misery under the master, or slavemaster (δεσπότης) Philip (2.25d,

2.25b). As a tyrant (τύραννος),[41] Philip is by definition an enemy of freedom (2.25c). Indeed, phrase 2.25c is well known. Brougham remarks upon Demosthenes' "beautiful passage of the mistrust of tyrants being the bulwark of freedom."[42]

The notion of freedom functions to reinforce Demosthenes' insistence for the need to mistrust Philip. Like his term "mistrust" (ἀπιστία; 2.24d), Demosthenes similarly emphasizes the term "freedom" (2.25b). Freedom, like mistrust, stands alone in a phrase (2.25a). Demosthenes also introduces freedom dramatically, as the answer to a rhetorical question he poses. Thus, for Demosthenes, to mistrust Philip is to have freedom or be free. The meaning of freedom, then, is determined by its context. Because freedom and slavery resonated for ancient audiences, Demosthenes employs these notions to strengthen the distinction he is developing between his position and that of his opponents, giving, in turn, a boost to his own position while at the same time diminishing his opponents.

The table below (Table 1) summarizes the various antitheses Demosthenes employs in this unit (*Phil.* 2.23–25).

Table 1

trusting (Aeschines and Philocrates)	mistrustful (Demosthenes)
gaze with wonder (passive approach)	see and understand (active approach)
manifold manual defenses	one intellectual but proactive stance
tyrant/king/Philip/Master (slavery)	freedom/law

In sum, Demosthenes deploys an array of dissociative arguments to distinguish between two fundamentally different approaches to Philip. He employs terms that fit his situation with his political rivals, terms that make very apparent the differences between the two. He narrows down two mutually exclusive alternatives to create ease of decision-making for his audience but also to force a choice.

With disjunctive rhetoric, the individual terms are far less significant in and of themselves than their function and purpose within the argument. Mistrust, for example, is not in and of itself a recommended attitude for a way of life, but is significant instead to designate the "best" attitude to take toward Philip. Similarly, the notion of one is not in and of itself a good, but serves as the desired option when contrasted to manifold within a dissociative argument. The dissociative pairs trust/mistrust, gaze with wonder/see and understand, manifold/one, reify and create difference when none existed before, and cause an audience to take the side assessed to be positive. In other words, with disjunctive argumentation *function*—position-making on the part of the authors—and *purpose*—position-taking on the part of audiences—outweighs the significance of any individual element within contrasting pairs.[43] Furthermore, because these terms reflect opposing positions between Demosthenes and his opponents, rivalry very likely influences their use in disjunctive arguments.

The pair slavery (implied)/freedom is disjunctive but functions identically to those that are dissociative. It differs only in so far as each element has a known valence. Indeed, authors employ this disjunctive pair to exploit it for the powerfully suggestive connotations—and not for the inherent meanings—its terms readily evoke. Demosthenes uses the well-known and highly evocative mutually exclusive alternatives between slavery and freedom to reinforce, to sum up, and to interpret his other and primary dissociative arguments.

Disjunctive Arguments in Cicero

Like Demosthenes, who aimed to distance his audience from his political rivals Aeschines and Philocrates, Cicero, with his disjunctive arguments, aims to distance his audience from his political enemy Antony. Cicero employs the oppositional pairs slavery/freedom and public enemy/councilman and with them contrasts the ignoble Antony to noble and upstanding Roman senators[44] and their values, persons like himself. Indeed, by exaggerating the praiseworthy characteristics of his senatorial audience and the blameworthy and despicable traits of his enemy Antony, he enhances his senatorial audience's honor and respectability and at the same time diminishes nearly to nothing Antony's social standing and honor. To gain his audience's agreement for his negative view of Antony, Cicero exploits values his senatorial audience hold most dear.

Slavery vs. Freedom (*Servitus* vs. *Libertas*)

One of Cicero's most forceful disjunctive arguments is between slavery and freedom and occurs at the conclusion of his *Third Philippic* (3.28–36). The unit itself provokes audience emotions. As in the *exordium* of this speech, here too Cicero makes direct and urgent appeals[45] to his audience. Cicero's *Third Philippic*, as mentioned, is his first-delivered speech against Antony and, as such, it sets the agenda and tone for all the rest of the *Philippics*.[46] With it, Cicero relies heavily on the notion of *libertas* ("freedom").[47] Yet a life that is free is never actually discussed or elaborated upon. In other words, Cicero does not engage in political or philosophical discussions that regard the importance of freedom, nor does he discuss the evils of the institution of slavery, its natural antithesis. Instead, he borrows on and indeed depends upon the common connotations of these terms for his arguments against Antony.[48] As commonly known concepts, *libertas* ("freedom") and *servitus* ("slavery") resonated with ancient audiences; they were, and still are, emotionally charged concepts.

Rather than discuss the notion of freedom, Cicero instead associates freedom with honor and with the Roman senators themselves.[49] At the same time, he fills the opposing concept of slavery with dishonorable traits that characterize Antony. He then offers his free and elite senatorial audience an easy choice of options:[50] freedom, understood as the continuation of the honorable life, or slavery, understood as rule under the tyrant Antony. Excerpts of a larger unit follow:

3.28 hodierno die primum, patres conscripti, longo intervallo in possessionem libertatis pedem *ponimus*: cuius quidem ego quoad potui non modo defensor sed etiam conservator fui.

3.29 per deos immortalis, patres conscripti, patrium animum virtutemque **capiamus**, ut aut libertatem propriam

Romani et generis et nominis **recuperemus** aut mortem servituti **anteponamus.**

3.34 hanc igitur occasionem oblatam tenete, per deos immortalis, patres conscripti, et amplissimi orbis terrae consili principes vos esse aliquando recordamini.

3.35 **faciamus** nos, principes orbis terrarum gentiumque omnium, ut cum dignitate potius cadamus quam cum ignominia serviamus

3.36 ad decus et ad libertatem nati *sumus*: aut haec **teneamus** aut cum dignitate moriamur.

3.28 Today for the first time, Members of the Senate, after a long interval *we took* [*take*] *a step* on the path to freedom: the freedom which, while I could, I not only defended but preserved,

3.29 by the Immortal Gods!, Members of the Senate, **let us** at last **take** our fathers' heart and courage, resolving to **regain** the freedom that belongs to the Roman race and name or else to **prefer** death to slavery.

3.34 Therefore, seize this proffered opportunity, by the Immortal Gods!, Members of the Senate, and at long last remember that you are leaders of the most august council in the world.

3.35 **let us**, who **stand** foremost in the world and all nations, see to it that we fall with dignity rather than serve with ignominy.

3.36 *We were* [*are*] born for honour and freedom: **let us** either **retain** them or die with dignity.[51]

Rather than define freedom, Cicero instead refers to it as a metaphorical place on which the senators are to stand and to which to make a claim.[52] As such, freedom functions as a position, as seen above in Demosthenes' use of disjunctive arguments. The notion of place is apparent in the opening line, in a phrase Manuwald refers to as a "vivid and graphic metaphor."[53] The phrase *in pos-*

sessionem libertatis pedem ponimus ("we took a step on the path to freedom"; 3.28) sets the direction for the unit. A literal translation is "we are setting down (our) feet in possession of freedom." The preposition "in" with the accusative case noun *possessionem* is uncommon; as it is employed here, it indicates a process[54] rather than a result.[55] Both the active present-tense indicative verb *ponimus* ("we are setting down") and the entire phrase suggest movement. The senators, then, are to "take a stand" on "freedom." That is, they are to locate themselves there.

As this unit progresses, Cicero continues to employ the notion of freedom in the same way, as a place. Rather than explain and detail freedom, using a series of subjunctive[56] verbs (marked in bold-faced type above), Cicero instead simply exhorts the senators to it.[57] These verbs are *capiamus*, "seize" (3.29); *anteponamus*, "prefer" (3.29); *recuperemus*, "regain" (3.29); *faciamus*, "stand" (3.35); and *teneamus*, "retain" (3.36). Two verbs in the present active indicative mood (marked in italics above)—*ponimus*, "we put down" or "we set down" (3.28); and *sumus*, "we are" (3.36)—bookend the unit. They too refer to freedom and, like the exhortations in the subjunctive mood, concern a position or metaphorical location.

Other elements in the unit also indicate that Cicero simply implores the senators to freedom. In 3.34 he urges the senators to seize (*tenete*) this opportunity for freedom. The "we are" (3.36) serves to remind his audience of where they belong as well as to urge them to the place where Cicero would have them reside. To further encourage the senators to take the side of freedom, Cicero assures them that everyone is united with them there:[58] generals, the troops, the Roman people as a group (3.32), other wise and courageous councilmen (3.36), Cicero himself (3.32–34)[59] and even the gods (3.34, 36).[60] As will be seen below, by choosing freedom—and not its alternative, slavery—the senators necessarily and by default adopt a position opposite that of Antony.

Cicero strengthens his developing case for freedom by associating himself on that side.[61] At the very start of the unit (3.28), he claims to be a defender of freedom.[62] His audience is made to believe that they can count on him. Indeed, throughout the section, Cicero employs first-person plural imperatives ("let us"), verbal forms that also contribute to a general sense of urgency.[63] The first-person plural imperatives provide the sense in which the senators and Cicero all move together into freedom.

Finally, to win the senators to his position, Cicero compliments them. Four times within the unit (3.28, 29, 33, 34), he refers to his senatorial audience as *patres conscripti* ("Members of the Senate" or "Fathers of the Senate"). While formulaic, the expression nevertheless serves to remind his audience of their privileged place within Roman society. His flattery of his senatorial audience is also apparent in his statement that freedom belongs (*propriam*) to the Roman race and name (*generis et nominis*; 3.29).[64] The adjective *proprius* means "peculiar to them," "fitting," or "proper." His compliments extend to his characterization of the senators as being born (*nati*) for honor (*decus*)[65] and freedom (*libertas*; 3.36). With the expression *amplissimi orbis terrae consili principes* ("leading members of the most august council of the world"; 3.34), Cicero not only honors the senators but he also raises the bar for their standard of behavior.[66] The adjective *amplissimi* is a superlative meaning "great," "glorious," or "splendid." The presence of *homoioteleuton* (similar ending sounds) in *conscripti amplissimi consili recordamini* reinforces the point that the senators (*conscripti*) are to think of themselves (*recordamini*) as such (i.e., as great and glorious). Toward the end of the unit (3.35), Cicero calls the senators "champion gladiators" (*gladiatores nobiles*). While he normally employs the term *gladiator* for Antony, as a metaphor for cutthroat/assassin/ruffian,[67] in 3.35 he breaks from his custom and employs the term in a positive sense, as a metaphor for courage and strength. As Eleanor Cowan remarks, Cicero's presentation of *libertas* was "calculated to appeal to traditional optimate values and to associate, in particular, *libertas* and *dignitas* (dignity)."[68]

In failing to define freedom, Cicero follows the conventional rhetorical use of this notion. Freedom, as Matthew Roller explains, had no inherent meaning; in ancient usage, it was always understood in relationship to slavery. For ancients, freedom was simply the flipside of slavery, an institution that existed and the understanding of which had a conceptual core.[69] While slavery was well known and discussed, freedom was not.[70] Without a conceptual core, ancients defined freedom contextually and to suit their own rhetorical purposes. Roller explains:

> For Roman aristocrats, then, the word *servitus* and its cognates carried powerful negative connotations. These derived from the slave's stereotyped liability to moral and physical degradation, coercion by the threat and application of force, and circumscription of personal volition. Meanwhile *libertas* and its cognates, marking the absence of the undesirable conditions associated with slavery, could carry strongly positive connotations.[71]

As an institution, slavery was an integral part of ancient society and the life of a slave was indeed grim.[72] As early as the fourth century BCE, Aristotle discussed slavery and defined it as a subordinate condition; according to him, a slave was no more than a tool.[73] In the first century BCE, ancient Italy could be characterized as a slave society,[74] with 20–30 percent of the population enslaved.[75]

Roman jurists defined slavery as a state of "absolute subjection."[76] Slaves were refused citizen status along with its accompanying rights. A slave had no legal kin and could not assume the rights or responsibilities of marriage;[77] a master would have imposed his or her identity onto the slave. As Aristotle remarked, slaves were considered mere bodies,[78] subject on multiple fronts to the authority of their master. Their clothes were sparse and poor; slaves often had inadequate food and shelter. They feared being sold and thereby separated from their families.[79] Slaves were beaten over seemingly minor incidences,[80] such as a poorly prepared meal,[81] and no laws prohibited the torture of slaves for evidence in a trial.[82] Foreign invaders, including and especially Rome, either killed its captives or else turned them into slaves. Furthermore, in ancient cities such as Rome, slaves were domestic servants and added to the wealth and elite status of their masters.

According to Roller, the physical and legal degradation of slaves had corresponding negative effects on their moral assessment. The negative moral assessment in turn spilled over into negative stereotypes of slaves as criminal, lazy, deceitful, and hostile toward their masters.[83] These stereotypical representations reveal a widespread bias against slaves among the elites.[84]

Sandra Joshel and Jennifer Glancy also discuss how terms related to slavery were current within the culture and resonated as metaphors for the control of the body and mind. Roman satirists, poets, philosophers, and historians referred to slavery to denigrate someone or certain acts.[85]

While freedom remains largely undefined—and is instead a metaphorical place on which the senators are to stand, slavery, readily known for its negative connotations, functions as a convenient catchword for Antony's deplorable nature. In a second example shown below, Cicero exploits the term "slavery," on account of its well-known negative valences, and like Demosthenes with his characterization of Philip, employs it to further diminish Antony. The long phrase below (3.28b), printed in italics, fills in a gap between 3.28 and 3.29 listed above:

3.28a Today for the first time, Members of the Senate, after a long interval we took a step on the path to freedom, the freedom which, while I could, I not only defended but preserved. When I could do that no longer, I held my peace and endured those disastrous and grievous times, not abjectly nor quite without dignity.

3.28b *But this most hideous monster, who can endure him or how? What is there in Antonius save lust, cruelty, insolence, audacity? He is entirely made up of these vices glued together. No trace in him of gentlemanly feeling, of moderation, of self-respect, of modesty.*

3.29 Therefore, since it has now come to this critical question, whether he pays his penalty to the *Res publica* or we become slaves, by the Immortal Gods!, Members of the Senate, let us at last take our fathers' heart and courage, resolving to regain the freedom that belongs to the Roman race and name or else to prefer death to slavery.[86]

With the inner phrase (3.28b), Cicero assesses Antony as a monster, and in the upper and lower framing passages (3.28a, 29), repeated from the unit listed earlier, he employs the terms "slavery" and "freedom." As a monster, Antony consists of lust, cruelty, insolence, and audacity (3.28b). In 3.29 Cicero employs the term "slavery," which now becomes associated with life under the monster Antony. Slavery, on account of its negative connotations, functions to intensify the evils of Antony. And by applying this term to Antony, Cicero increases the negative consequence of the audience's failure to rule against him.

In 3.30–31, not listed here, Cicero engages in the same method of argumentation as in 3.28–29. Sandwiched between calls for freedom, as seen above (3.28, 29, 34, 35, 36), is a long passage devoted to the faults and abuses of power of Antony. Cicero details many of Antony's mishandlings: he emptied Caesar's house, plundered his gardens, sold exemptions, removed provinces from the imperial jurisdiction, had false laws and false decrees inscribed in bronze and posted on the capitol walls, set up a market to sell items in Caesar's house, excluded people from the Forum, drowned himself with wine, and gave free-born women and children to the soldiers.[87] Following this lengthy negative portrayal of Antony, Cicero calls the senators thrice more to freedom (3.34, 35, 36). Based on this lengthy assessment as well as Cicero's use of the term "freedom," Antony becomes once again associated with slavery.

In sum, Cicero employs the terms "slavery" and "freedom" in his disjunctive arguments for their known connotations. In the ancient world, slavery always had a point of reference with the grim institution of slavery. When contrasted with slavery, freedom would always be the preferred choice. By choosing these terms, Cicero, like Demosthenes, tips the scales to his advantage. Cicero, however, never discusses the evils of the institution of slavery, but instead defines slavery as a life under the dishonorable and monster-like Antony. Similarly, he never discusses any inherent benefits of freedom but instead exhorts his audience to that place. The states of slavery and freedom are not in view nor are they what are at stake in his arguments. Cicero instead employs slavery and freedom on account of their well-known valences so as to help fashion hard and fast distinctions between himself and

Antony. As shown in summary form in the table below (Table 2), slavery and freedom function together within a larger set of dichotomies to provide obvious and mutually exclusive alternatives for his Roman senatorial audience.

Table 2

slavery (*servitas*)	freedom (*libertas*)
monster (Antony) (3.28)	dignity (Cicero and the senators) (3.28)
Antony plunders (3.30–31)	honest senatorial men (3.29)
ignominy (3.35)	honor (3.36)

Public Enemy vs. Respected Councilman (*Hostis* vs. *Consul*)

A second antithetical pair Cicero employs in his fight against Antony is that between *hostis* ("public enemy")[88] and *consul* ("respected councilman"). Over the course of his *Philippics*, Cicero repeatedly strives to turn Antony into a public enemy (*Phil.* 3.14, 21; 4.1, 6; 5.23, 29; 7.9–10, 13, 15; 12.17; 14.4, 6, 10, 21, 24). He argued this point in December 44 (*Philippic Three* and *Four*), again in January 43 (*Philippic Five* and *Seven*), a month later (*Philippic Eight*) and finally in April 43 (*Philippic Fourteen*). That he repeatedly failed to convince the senators is an indication of the strength of the opposition he faced in the senate.[89] Just as the term *servitus* is a catchword for the abuses of Antony, so too is the term *hostis*.[90] Accordingly, Manuwald remarks that *hostis* "succinctly summarizes Antonius' attitude and paradigmatically describes Antonius as envisaged by Cicero."[91]

In his *Fourth Philippic*, Cicero devotes considerable attention to a discussion of Antony as a public enemy.[92] He raises this topic in the speech's opening (see below) and returns to it at the speech's close (*Phil.* 4.14). His *Fourth Philippic* is a *contio* speech, delivered not before the senate but before the non-voting assembly of Roman people (*Quirites*).[93] He delivered it in the forum on the same day (20 December 44) as his *Third Philippic* on the senate floor. The topics are the same, only the audience and Cicero's style differ.

Roman orators participated in *contiones* to inform the people of major political developments and/or to present problems and proposals to be voted on at a later date by the senate. Along with being a method of communication between the senate and the people, *contiones* were often used as testing grounds for popular opinion.[94] Modern scholarship is divided on the importance of the role popular opinion played in Republican Rome.[95] Formerly, the scholarly consensus was that because the people did not have a vote within the political process, their opinions were of little use. More recently, however, scholars have rethought that former assumption and now find that because political issues were presented and then commented upon at *contiones*, the people did play an important role in the Roman political system.[96] Cicero himself commented on the politicians' use of *contiones*. According to him, senators used the medium of *contio* for their own political purposes, as well as to sway public opinion.[97] According to Manuwald, orators depended upon *contiones* to win popular support for their position[98] and then through this support, they were able to boost their own image in the senate. As I indicate below, with his *Fourth Philippic* Cicero not only informs the people of senatorial actions, but also imposes his own view of the "facts" in order to sway the people's opinion against Antony.[99] It is also clear from the passage below that with his *contio*, Cicero attempts to enhance his own reputation.[100]

   With his speech before the people, Cicero plays loosely with the facts of the situation.[101] He presents the declaration of Antony as a public enemy as a *fait accompli*, when in fact no such declaration took place. Assessing the situation more generously, Manuwald comments that Cicero presented the situation according to his own "interpretation."[102] Cicero not only misrepresents the facts, but he also attempts to persuade the audience by repeatedly complimenting them. The passage reads:

4.1a frequentia vestrum incredibilis, Quirites, contioque
   tanta quantam meminisse non videor et alacritatem
   mihi summam **defendendae rei publicae** adfert et spem
   recuperandae.

4.1b quamquam animus mihi quidem numquam defuit:

4.1c tempora defuerunt,

4.1d quae simul ac primum aliquid lucis ostendere visa sunt,
   princeps **vestrae libertatis** defendendae fui.

4.1e quod si id ante facere conatus essem, nunc facere non possem.

4.1f hodierno enim die, Quirites, ne mediocrem rem actam arbitremini, fundamenta iacta sunt reliquarum actionum.

4.1g nam est **hostis** a senatu nondum verbo appellatus, sed re iam iudicatus Antonius.

4.2a nunc vero multo sum erectior quod vos quoque illum **hostem** esse **tanto consensu tantoque clamore approbavistis**.

4.2b neque enim, Quirites, fieri potest ut non aut ei sint impii qui contra **consulem** exercitus comparaverunt, aut ille **hostis** contra quem iure arma sumpta sunt.

4.2c hanc igitur dubitationem, quamquam nulla erat, tamen ne qua posset esse senatus hodierno die sustulit.

4.1a Your extraordinary numbers, Men of Rome, and the size of this assembly, **larger than any I seem to remember**, fill me with a lively eagerness to defend the *Res publica* and with hope of regaining it.

4.1b True, my courage has never failed me.

4.1c It was the times that failed:

4.1d As soon as they seemed to show a glimmer of light, I took the lead in defending **your freedom**.

4.1e Had I attempted to do this earlier, I should not be able to do it now.

4.1f For today, Men of Rome, in case you think we have been transacting some business of minor importance, the groundwork has been laid for future operations.

4.1g For Antonius has been pronounced a **public enemy** by the Senate, not yet in words, but in effect.

4.2a Now it much emboldens me that you too **confirm by your loud and unanimous voice** that he is a **public enemy**.

4.2b And after all, Men of Rome, there is no way out of it: either those who have raised armies against a **Consul** are treacherous, or he against whom arms have been rightly taken up is an **enemy**.

4.2c This doubt, therefore, the Senate has today eliminated;
not that any doubt existed, but in case there could be.[103]

Cicero wastes no time in getting to the issue of Antony as a
public enemy and, in what is likely an effort to bring such an
event to reality, he simply declares it so. Whereas in his *Third
Philippic*, Cicero works to convince his senatorial audience to
make the "proper" choice with regard to Antony—by citing co-
pious examples of the crimes and hideous behavior of Antony—
with his *contio* speech, he simply declares the people's decision
for them (4.2a). Accordingly, Cicero states that the people (i.e., his
present audience) have already agreed to declare Antony a public
enemy (4.2a).[104] He describes the declaration using the perfect active indicative verb indicating completed past action *approbavistis*
("approved" or "confirmed"; 4.2a). Moreover, he claims that the
people's agreement of Antony's declaration as a public enemy was
unanimous (4.2a).[105] With regard to such strong consensual agreement, Fogel comments, "if it takes the gods to create such a strong
public opinion in Rome, and it does, then we cannot doubt that
the public opinion is the opinion of the gods themselves too."[106]
In further underscoring the people's assent, Cicero states that
the people approved with much fanfare (*tanto consensu tantoque
clamore*, "such a consensus so great a noise"; 4.2a). The repetition
of the word (*tanto*) ("so much") with a different form (*tantoque*)
("of such size") is an instance of *anaphora* and serves here to emphasize and exaggerate the people's agreement.

In making such a declaration, Cicero baldly misrepresents the
facts. Indeed, he takes more liberties with the people—blatantly
changing the facts of the situation—than he does with his senatorial audience. While Cicero's actual goal in his *Third Philippic* was
to have Antony declared a public enemy, he instead played it safe
in the senate and *did not make that motion* before them.[107] Moreover,
even when the senate reconvened in January 43 (*Philippic Five*),
the senators proposed an embassy be sent to Antony, effectively
backing away again from taking actions to have him declared a
public enemy.[108] The senate only officially declared Antony *hostis*

on 26 April 43, after Cicero delivered his final Philippic speech. With the people, however, Cicero simply relates the situation as he wishes it to be. He tells the people that they (the people) approved of a senatorial action that never actually took place.

Although Cicero already declares a victory against Antony, he nevertheless works at the same time to persuade the people of "their" position. He does this on the one hand by praising them and on the other hand by portraying himself in a favorable light. He compliments the people on their high numbers in attendance. Large assemblies were a source of honor not just for the orator but also for those gathered.[109] Yet it is doubtful that a large number was actually in attendance that day. The phrase *tanta quantam meminisse non videor* ("larger than any I seem to remember"; 4.1a) suggests that the large size of the crowd is Cicero's own and subjective interpretation and thus most likely an exaggeration.[110] It was to Cicero's advantage to claim a large attendance, as it serves to confirm "their" decision and make it all the more popular and "correct." Furthermore, with the often-repeated title *Quirites* ("Men of Rome";[111] 4.1a, 1f, 2b), although the common form of address for the people in *contio* speeches,[112] Cicero nonetheless acknowledges his audience with a term of honor. Indeed, according to Karl-J. Hölkeskamp, to address the assembled public *in contione* as *Quirites* is a "highly suggestive rhetorical signal" that recreates and reaffirms Roman identity, along with the accompanying roles and privileges of being a Roman citizen.[113] Furthermore, with his use of the possessive pronoun *vestrae* ("your"; 4.1d), Cicero involves the people emotionally,[114] and claims he is working on their behalf for their *libertas* ("freedom"; 4.1d).

The contrast between public enemy (*hostis*) and respected councilman (*consul*) is evident throughout the opening (4.1a–2c), and sets the agenda for the entire speech. The terms help to structure the opening, with each one representing one of two opposing sides, Antony and Cicero respectively. The first segment of the opening (4.1a–1f) is devoted to a highly positive self-evaluation of the councilman Cicero, and the second pertains to the declaration of Antony as a public enemy (4.1g–2c).

As we saw with *servitus* and *libertas*, whereby the concept of freedom (*libertas*) took on a meaning as life not under the slave-like rule of Antony, here too *hostis*, in this case the negative concept, receives its sense from its antithetical term *consul*, the positive one.

Cicero himself assumes the position of the respected model councilman (*consul*) and then fills the notion with a surplus of positive value. He claims to be eager and ready to defend the *Res publica*, the Republic (*defendendae rei publicae*; 4.1a). He lets it be known that his courage (*animus*) never fails him (4.1b) and that he has been working to defend freedom (*libertatis defendendae*; 4.1d). He indicates that he did not delay acting on behalf of the Republic. With the metaphorical expression *aliquid lucis ostendere visa sunt* ("showing a glimmer of light"; 4.1d), he claims to have acted as soon as the opportunity presented itself.[115] Not only did Cicero not delay speaking out against Antony, but he also ruled against him before anyone else did (*princeps vestrae libertatis defendendae fui*, "I took the lead in defending your freedom"; 4.1d).[116] These rulings against Antony are those that allegedly took place earlier that day in the senate, but never in fact did (4.1f). Finally, Cicero represents his actions as being of utmost importance ("foundational," *fundamenta*).[117] Such a lofty self-description serves not only to greatly enhance Cicero's standing in the eyes of the people,[118] but it also simultaneously serves to create a gulf between himself (*consul*) and Antony (*hostis*). Manuwald comments that while Cicero assesses Antony as a "public enemy," he characterizes himself as "savior of the *res* publica."[119]

Indeed, Cicero does not define or characterize the notion of *hostis* at all, he simply and abruptly contends that Antony is a public enemy (*hostis*; 4.1g, 2a, 2b). *Hostis* comes to represent everything that is not *consul*. That is, Antony (*hostis*) is not the defender of the Republic, he is not courageous, and he does not work for the freedom of the people. When in 4.2b Cicero offers the people two mutually exclusive alternatives, their choice is self-evident.[120]

In sum, in the example above, Cicero's disjunctive argument between *hostis* and *consul* occurs at the start of *Philippic Four*, a *contio* speech. As such the argument sets the tone for the entire speech. He adopts a heavy-handed approach, one that is reminiscent of how Demosthenes customarily deals with his senatorial audience. With the people, there is less a sense in which Cicero is aiming to persuade, than the bold declaration of how "things are." Cicero is also not concerned about misrepresenting the facts. While he informs the people of the senate's ruling on this matter (4.2c), in point of fact, the senate never ruled Antony as public enemy on that day. Cicero's lofty self-descriptions suggest that he took the opportunity of this speech to enhance his overall reputation so as to advance his cause. With his disjunctive argument, Cicero does not amplify on just how Antony is a public enemy (*hostis*) but instead fills the notion of *hostis* with significations that are antithetical to Cicero's own highly embellished and strongly positive self-portrayal as a defender/savior of the Republic.

Disjunctive Rhetoric in Paul

Paul makes abundant use of oppositional pairs in Galatians. Indeed, in their recent book *The Authentic Letters of Paul*, Arthur Dewey et al. cite twenty-one distinct oppositions[121] in Galatians. And Elizabeth Castelli remarks that in Galatians Paul is "relentlessly dualistic and oppositional."[122] She writes:

> Paul presents a series of binary oppositions whose repetition and amplification work rhetorically to persuade his readers to adopt his view of things and to reject alternative views. Slave and free, law and promise, flesh and spirit echo as irreconcilably separate in Paul's argument against the adequacy of the law for providing a framework for life in the new Christian creation.[123]

Castelli rightly observes that Paul's oppositions function rhetorically to persuade of his own point of view and against that of others. Indeed, I argue that just as is the case for both Demosthenes and Cicero, Paul's employment of disjunctive arguments serves to steer his audience away from his opponents. Indeed, his abundant use of oppositions evinces that his dispute with his opponents is of considerable significance.[124]

Paul participates not just in disjunctive but also, like Demosthenes, in dissociative argumentation. That is, he wholly creates many of his oppositions. For example, Paul establishes and maintains a contrast between "works of Torah" and "trust," and hierarchically arranges the first under the second. He establishes another dissociative pair between the terms "flesh" and "promise." In and of themselves, these four terms do not have any necessary or inherent positive or negative valence. That is, Paul could have just as easily assessed "works of Torah" positively and "trust" negatively,[125] rather than the reverse. As mentioned above, in dissociative rhetoric authors create oppositions and then also assign values, arranging them, according to their own schemes, to fit their own situations. As we saw in his *Second Philippic*, Demosthenes chose the term "mistrust" to directly distinguish himself from his opponents, those who trusted Philip. Paul creates and employs dissociative arguments similarly and for the same purpose.

Returning for the moment to Castelli's quote above, while she rightly observes both the abundance of binary oppositions and their purpose in persuasion, she, and in line with many other Pauline interpreters, finds that the reason for Paul's abundant use of oppositions is that he finds Torah to be an inadequate "framework for life in the new Christian creation." That is, she understands Paul to be persuading against Torah itself.

Authors, however, as we have already seen in the speech units of Demosthenes and Cicero, do not deploy disjunctive and dissociative arguments in order to detail and evaluate the individual terms of their oppositional pairs. Rather, they choose terms creatively to fit their particular situations and then use them to distinguish two opposing positions. They are less interested in the individual terms' semantic range of meanings than in their ability to differentiate between two positions or two sides. Indeed, the individual terms have only a limited contextual range of meaning. For instance, for Demosthenes mistrust is not a prescription for how one should lead one's life, but instead represents the "proper" approach for the senators to take to Philip. The contrasting notion of trust serves not as a bound duty, and in this case something to avoid, but instead is the "wrong" approach to Philip. The two notions function together as convenient identifiers, as catchwords, and thus as aids to differentiate between two opposing positions with regard to Philip. By employing them, Demosthenes enables his audience to line up behind one side or the other. In other words, he forces a choice.

This same situation applies for Paul. In his dissociative arguments in which he employs the term "works of Torah," Paul is not concerned one way or another with the advantages or disadvantages of Torah observances themselves. Like Demosthenes and his use of the notion of trust, works of Torah functions primarily as an identifier of his opponents. Furthermore, it is highly unlikely that Paul considered Torah inadequate as a way of life, as many of his own arguments, and as seen in the previous chapters, indicate significant dependence upon Torah. In addition, and apart from his dissociative arguments that employ the term "works of Torah," Paul speaks favorably of Torah (see Gal 3:21; Rom 2:12–16, 3:1–2, 7:1–20). Moreover, Paul does not articulate any uniform problematic with regard to it.[126]

As is the case with Demosthenes and Cicero, Paul's many disjunctive arguments employ terms that function primarily as identifiers or catchwords representative of two opposing positions. Like Demosthenes and Cicero, his disjunctive arguments are for the purpose of persuading his audience to his side rather than that of his opponents or competitors. Like the other rhetoric-of-crisis authors, Paul selects disjunctive terms and arranges them hierarchically to fit his present situation and rhetorical purposes.

Works of Torah (Law) vs. Trust (ἔργων νόμου vs. πίστις)

A principal antithesis Paul employs and to which he often returns is between works of Torah (ἔργων νόμου),[127] often translated as "works of law" and "trust" (πίστις), often translated as "faith." With this constructed oppositional pair, Paul participates in dissociative rhetoric, whereby "works of Torah" becomes a term I (negative) and "trust" becomes a term II (positive). There are various passages that pertain to this distinction (Gal 2:15–16; 3:2–5, 6–10, 11–12, 5:1–6, cf 3:18, 22, 25), yet Gal 3:6–10, in which one finds Paul's use of Abraham, offers a good example of how he hierarchically arranges these two terms, building positive value around the notion of trust, making that notion normative, and negative value around the notion of works of Torah.[128] Paul remarks:

3:6 Καθὼς Ἀβραὰμ *ἐπίστευσεν* τῷ θεῷ, καὶ ἐλογίσθη αὐτῷ εἰς δικαιοσύνην[129]

3:7 γινώσκετε ἄρα ὅτι οἱ ἐκ **πίστεως**, οὗτοι υἱοί εἰσιν Ἀβραάμ

3:8a προϊδοῦσα δὲ ἡ γραφὴ ὅτι ἐκ **πίστεως** δικαιοῖ τὰ ἔθνη ὁ θεός,

3:8b προευηγγελίσατο τῷ Ἀβραὰμ ὅτι ἐνευλογηθήσονται ἐν σοὶ πάντα τὰ ἔθνη·

3:9 ὥστε **οἱ ἐκ πίστεως** εὐλογοῦνται σὺν τῷ **πιστῷ** Ἀβραάμ.

3:10a Ὅσοι γὰρ ἐξ **ἔργων νόμου** εἰσίν, ὑπὸ κατάραν εἰσίν·

3:10b γέγραπται γὰρ ὅτι ἐπικατάρατος πᾶς ὃς οὐκ ἐμμένει πᾶσιν τοῖς γεγραμμένοις ἐν τῷ βιβλίῳ τοῦ νόμου τοῦ ποιῆσαι αὐτά.

3:6 Just as Abraham *"trusted in God, and it was reckoned to him as righteousness,"*

3:7 Recognize, therefore, that those of **trust**, these are the sons of Abraham.

3:8a And scripture foreseeing that God justifies non-Jews from **trust**

3:8b proclaimed the good news beforehand to Abraham: *"In you shall all the non-Jews be blessed."*

3:9 Thus, **those of trust** are blessed with Abraham, who **trusted**.

3:10a For [by contrast][130] **those who are from works of Torah** are under a curse.

3:10b For it is written: *"Yet more accursed is everyone who does not remain in all that in the scroll of the Torah to do it."*[131]

In his dissociative argument, Paul does not detail or evaluate the significance of either the term "trust" or the expression "works of Torah." While Paul makes trust normative and construes it positively in his opposition between it and works of Torah, Paul does not emphasize the inherent good of trusting. Indeed, his justification for trust being superior to works of Torah is weak and appears to be forced.[132] And like Cicero's term *hostis*, works of Torah takes on a negative signification in large measure because it is antithetical to trust in a dissociative argument.

Paul assesses trust more highly than works of Torah but in ways that do not regard the inherent good of trust itself. He justifies his argument for the benefit of trust over works of Torah through the employment of Gen 15:6 (shown above in italics; Gal 3:6), a verse that concerns Abraham and his trust in God. Yet Paul says very little about Abraham[133]—a character who had a lengthy trusting relationship with God—for him to serve as a strong role model of a figure who trusted God.[134]

Galatians 3:6 is nearly a direct quote from Gen 15:6,[135] but it represents only a microcosm of the Abrahamic narrative in the book of Genesis, which spans twelve full chapters (Genesis 12–24). Perhaps the most well-known and moving/heroic account concerning Abraham occurs in Genesis 22, when in trusting obedience to God Abraham agrees to sacrifice his son Isaac. But in that narrative, Abraham is not said to "trust" God, although according to the narrative sense of the passage, he does, but instead to "fear" (φοβῇ) God (Gen 22:12). In yet another passage from Genesis, Abraham becomes the father of the Israelite nation by becoming circumcised, when, and again in trustful obedience to God's command, he performed a work of Torah (Genesis 17). This latter aspect of Abraham's history, however, is especially damaging to Paul's argument in Galatians, as Abraham performed the precise work of Torah Paul dissuades his Galatian audience from performing (Gal 5:2–6).[136] Indeed, just as a full and accurate history of Tarquin weakens Cicero's case, Abraham's full history severely undermines Paul's.[137] While these are only two among many memorable events in the life of Abraham, they provide some evidence of Abraham's trusting life and thus of Paul's omissions in dealing with trust, as well as proof of his high selectivity in the use of this verse. Paul's choice of Gen 15:6 appears to be dictated more by the presence of the verb "trusted" (ἐπίστευσεν)[138] than about being a person of trust. Trust, however, is significant as a position opposed to works of Torah.

Beyond the lack of a strong and complete scriptural support for trusting, Paul otherwise insufficiently argues for the benefits of trusting. For instance, he begins with its benefit of righteousness (δικαιοσύνην; Gal 3:6, Gen 15:6) but concludes his argument concerning trust and its association with non-Jews not with the benefit of righteousness but instead with the benefit of God's blessing (ἐνευλογηθήσονται, εὐλογοῦνται;[139] 3:8b, 9). Paul likely substituted the benefit of righteousness with that of blessing to introduce and construct the subsequent contrast he draws between it (blessing) and a curse. But this seemingly free and easy substitution of the benefits of trusting undermines trust's inherent worth and instead lends support to the notion that these terms' primary function is for the purpose of making distinctions between opposing positions.

While Paul's arguments concerning the basic worth or good of trusting are weak,[140] Paul emphasizes this term. Words for "trust" (ἐπίστευσεν, 3:6; πίστεως, 3:7, 8a, 9; and πιστῷ, 3:9) dominate the passage and pertain either to Abraham or to non-Jewish Galatians or to both. Yet rather than elaborate on the notion of trust, Paul instead employs the term as a position or location. With it, he creates a people of trust, "those of trust" (οἱ ἐκ πίστεως; 3:7, 9). He then locates the Galatian non-Jews, his audience, there, on the side of trust (3:8a). Indeed, by calling the Galatians "sons of Abraham"[141] (3:7), Paul, like Cicero with his complimentary titles for his audiences, encourages the Galatian non-Jews to be on the side of trust.

As with his employment of the normative term II word "trust," Paul does not detail or explain the detriments of works of Torah (term I). The expression instead, like trust, represents a group of people, "those of works of Torah" (Ὅσοι ἐξ ἔργων νόμου; 3:10a), and a position to avoid adopting. According to Paul, "those of trust" are blessed (3:9) and "those of works of Torah" are under a curse (3:10a). Paul builds the terms/expressions "trust" and "works of Torah" into two longer expressions, "those of trust" and "those of works of Torah," and into locations, their primary significations. These contrastive positions serve to distinguish two groups of persons. Paul locates his Galatian audience on one side, on the side of trust, and dissociates them from the other, the side of works of Torah.

In sum, Paul creates two peoples, "those of trust" (οἱ ἐκ πίστεως) and "those of works of Torah" (3:10a–b). These new monikers appear to be the unit's aim. With the terms "trust" and "works of Torah" Paul creates an opposition between two notions where none previously existed. There is no essential or evaluative difference between works of Torah and trust—as I indicate in the discussion on Abraham, works of Torah themselves concern trust. Like other dissociative pairs seen above, Paul constructs this pair in order to create a sense of difference. He arranges these notions hierarchically to suit his own rhetorical purpose. His lack of detail and explanation and his weak justification for the importance of trust and for the reasons to avoid works of Torah—typical of dissociative argumentation—indicate that the concepts of trust and works of Torah are not in and of themselves significant.[142] By contrast, the terms "trust" and "works of Torah" have a positive rhetorical function in that they operate together to distinguish not two fundamentally different ways of life, as neither term is exploited for its individual semantic range of meaning, but instead two mutually exclusive positions, Paul's and that of his opponents.[143]

Flesh vs. Promise (and Spirit) (σάρξ vs. ἐπαγγελία [and πνεῦμα])
Yoke of Slavery vs. Freedom (ζυγῷ δουλείας vs. ἐλευθέρα)

A second short passage (Gal 4:28–5:1) contains several antithetical pairs out of which Paul constructs additional dissociative arguments. Unlike the other passages discussed to this point, this one does not break at the standard chapter division, as seen in most translations. Betz follows the customary division between chapters four and five, seeing a natural break at Gal 4:31. According to him, Gal 4:31 concludes the *probatio* or proof section of the letter[144] and 5:1 begins the *exhortatio*[145] (exhortation). Other scholars, however, assess that the break between chapters four and five falls more naturally after Gal 5:1.[146] Indeed, the unit defined by 4:28–5:1 functions as a summation of Gal 4:21–27, Paul's allegory.[147]

Paul fills the entire larger structural unit (4:21–5:1) with so many hard and fast oppositions that one scholar comments, "Dichotomies undoubtedly are the structuring principle of Gal 4:21–31."[148] Paul contrasts "child of the slave," and "child of the free" (4:23); "born according to the flesh," and "born through the promise" (4:23); Hagar and the "free woman" (4:24–26); "slave woman" and "free woman" (4:22–26); "present-day Jerusalem" and "Jerusalem above" (4:25–26); and "slavery" and "freedom" (5:1).[149]

As we saw above with Paul's use of the dichotomy between works of Torah and trust, with the antitheses he creates in 4:28–5:1, he aims to steer his audience to the "proper" choice between two opposing options he offers. The two opposing options correspond to, represent, and reinforce two distinct groups of persons, "those of the Torah" and "those of trust." The terms Paul employs in the summary section (4:28–5:1) also correspond to the oppositions he develops in his allegory (4:21–27). Thus, the Torah side (4:21) is associated with Hagar,[150] slavery, and flesh. The trust side corresponds with the free woman, freedom, promise, and spirit.

As we saw above with the concepts of works of Torah and trust, the dissociations between flesh and promise (4:28) and flesh and spirit (4:29) are not necessarily oppositional, like cold is to hot. Moreover, each term is not in itself either inherently positive or negative. Paul also arranges these notions hierarchically to suit his own purposes. Flesh, for instance, is not of necessity a negative notion. Indeed, in Gal 4:13 Paul refers to the notion of flesh with no negative implications.[151] Yet in this unit, Paul turns flesh into a negative notion through its repeated association with the known-negative slavery (Gal 4:23, 29–30).[152] In the same regard, spirit does not necessarily have a positive connotation that makes it superior to flesh. Yet by associating it, along with its companion

notion of promise, with the well-recognized and positively construed concept of freedom, spirit takes on positive connotations
(4:23, 29–30). A table below (Table 3) lists many of these dichotomous terms.

Table 3

those of the Torah	those not of the Torah (trust)
son, born of the slave woman	son, born of the free woman
son, born of the flesh	son, born according to the promise
Hagar, a slave woman	free woman
present-day Jerusalem	Jerusalem above
child, according to the flesh	child, according to the spirit
"yoke of slavery"	"freedom"

The passage reads as follows:

4:28 **Ὑμεῖς** δέ, ἀδελφοί, κατὰ Ἰσαὰκ **ἐπαγγελίας** τέκνα
ἐστέ.

4:29a ἀλλ᾽ ὥσπερ τότε ὁ κατὰ **σάρκα** γεννηθεὶς ἐδίωκεν
τὸν κατὰ **πνεῦμα**,

4:29b οὕτως καὶ νῦν.

4:30a ἀλλὰ τί λέγει ἡ γραφή;

4:30b ἔκβαλε τὴν **παιδίσκην** καὶ τὸν υἱὸν αὐτῆς·

4:30c οὐ γὰρ μὴ κληρονομήσει ὁ υἱὸς τῆς **παιδίσκης** μετὰ τοῦ
υἱοῦ τῆς **ἐλευθέρας**.

4:31 διό, ἀδελφοί, **οὐκ ἐσμὲν παιδίσκης** τέκνα ἀλλὰ **τῆς**
ἐλευθέρας.

5:1a Τῇ **ἐλευθερίᾳ**[153] ἡμᾶς Χριστὸς **ἠλευθέρωσεν**·

5:1b **στήκετε** οὖν καὶ μὴ πάλιν ζυγῷ δουλείας ἐνέχεσθε.

4:28 Now **YOU**, brothers, **are** children of the **promise**, like
Isaac.

4:29a But just as then the one born according to the **flesh**
persecuted the one according to the **spirit**,

4:29b so also now.

4:30a Yet what does scripture say?

4:30b *Cast out the **slave woman** and her son.*

4:30c *For the son of the **slave woman** will not share the inheri-
tance with the son of the **free woman**.*

4:31 Therefore, brothers, **we are not children of the slave woman** but of the **free woman.**
5:1a For **freedom** the Anointed has **freed** us.
5:1b Thus, **stand firm** and do not again **hold yourself in** a **yoke of slavery.**[154]

Position-establishing language dominates this unit (4:28, 31; 5:1a, 1b), and Paul emphasizes position over any inherent significations of the antithetical terms he employs. In verses 4:28,[155] 4:31, and 5:1 Paul issues clear directives indicating how the Galatians are to self-locate. Indeed, his authoritative stance throughout this unit is reminiscent of the position Cicero adopts with his *Quirites*. Verse 4:28 begins with the pronoun you (Ὑμεῖς), which in an inflected language is unneeded, and here represents an emphatic command. The "you" also serves to capture the audience's attention. Paul states, "Now, YOU are children of the promise." In 4:31 he reiterates that the Galatians are "children of the free woman." He clarifies that they do not belong to the other side, to the "children of the slave woman" (4:31). Moreover, Paul's choice of verbs bears out his emphasis on the importance of position-taking. With his use of the present active indicative verb ἐστέ ("you are"; 4:28) and ἐσμέν[156] ("we are"; 4:31), Paul clearly indicates where his audience is to self-locate. In 5:1, with στήκετε ("stand firm"; 5:1b) and ἐνέχεσθε ("become entangled in"; 5:1b), he switches to the imperative mood and thereby becomes more forceful with regard to the Galatians' location. The verb ἐνέχεσθε is from ἐνέχω and can be read as a passive imperative, as in the sense "become entangled in," as Betz understands it,[157] or as a middle imperative, as in "hold yourself in." Both senses are similar and refer to, like στήκετε ("stand firm"), a position. While insistent with regard to how the Galatians are to self-locate, Paul, with his use of family terminology, with words such as "brothers" (ἀδελφοί) and "children" (τέκνα; 4:28, 31), also reveals, again like Cicero with his *Quirites*, his desire/need to gain his audience's agreement.

In 5:1, Paul switches to the language of freedom and slavery and hence to a disjunctive argument. Galatians 5:1 is important because it serves to summarize[158] both the smaller unit under

review (4:28–5:1) as well as the larger one begun at 4:21.[159] With regard to the notions of freedom (5:1a) and of yoke of slavery (ζυγῷ
δουλείας; 5:1b), Paul, like Cicero, supplies no discussion regarding
either a state of freedom or a condition of slavery. Paul instead
simply states that the Anointed has "freed" (ἠλευθέρωσεν) "us"
(ἡμᾶς) for "freedom"[160] (Τῇ ἐλευθερίᾳ), therefore, the Galatians
are not to return to slavery (a "yoke of slavery"). While Paul does
not elaborate upon the notion of freedom, the term has associa-
tions with the free woman (4:30, 31, cf. 4:22, 26) and with a location as defined by the expression "children of the promise," (4:28)
and "children of the free woman" (4:31).

The expression "yoke of slavery" is also very likely a metaphor for circumcision.[161] Paul explicitly counsels against the circumcision of non-Jewish Galatians in the next verse (5:2). While
Paul and other ancient authors discuss circumcision's significance
variously,[162] it is generally understood as an act and mark that
signifies a Jew.[163] Nanos well articulates this basic and common
understanding of circumcision. As he puts it, circumcision "sym-
bolizes a public social act of transfer for a non-Jewish person into
the Jewish community and thus places him in subordination to its
norms."[164] Yet to understand that Paul is arguing that circumcision or becoming a circumcised Jew in some way or other literally
or metaphorically enslaves[165] is to misinterpret yoke of slavery—overly emphasizing the significance of one term—in Paul's
disjunctive argument (Gal 5:1). The notion of yoke of slavery/
slavery serves, like its opposition freedom, first and foremost as
a location. As with freedom, Paul does not define slavery or yoke
of slavery, but instead associates slavery with the slave woman
Hagar (4:30b, 30c, 31, cf. 4:22, 23, 24, 25) and with a location as
defined by the expression "children of the slave woman" (4:31).
Each woman, the free one and the slave, represents one of two
alternative positions or locations. As mentioned above, authors
employ terms such as freedom and slavery not for their inherent
significations but instead as aids in authorial distinction-making
and audience decision-making. Paul attaches a negative valence
to circumcision[166] to persuade the Galatians not to side with his
opponents.

Making the "proper" choice or self-location is the issue here. Three times within this (4:28, 31 and 5:1b) Paul states—at times more gently than at others—how the Galatians are to position themselves within the various mutually exclusive alternatives he offers. His authoritative exhortations are reminiscent of the approach Cicero adopts with the people, the *Quirites*. As with other rhetoric-of-crisis authors, Paul exploits the notions of slavery and freedom for their known negative and positive connotations. He then carries these known connotations into the other dissociative pairs he constructs, such as flesh/promise and flesh/spirit. While Paul leaves his opponents unnamed and in the background, he foregrounds concepts or issues, especially those that concern the Torah, issues representative of them—to steer his audience away from them and to his own position.

To reiterate, like Demosthenes and Cicero, Paul employs the notions of freedom and slavery/yoke of slavery for their commonly known connotations. In disjunctive argumentation, however, the literal concepts of freedom and slavery[167] are not in and of themselves what is at issue. All of these authors employ these terms to help clarify mutually exclusive alternative positions for their audiences. They do not discuss the good of freedom or the evils of slavery, but instead borrow the terms as aids in their audiences' decision-making. Paul associates slavery and "yoke of slavery" with Torah and circumcision, which represent the position of his opponents. The notion of slavery functions well and conveniently for its negative connotations to dissuade an audience from a particular option or point of view. Circumcision is caught up, an innocent victim so to speak, in the polemics between Paul and his opponents. As a side note, that Paul counsels so strongly against the circumcision of non-Jewish Galatians indicates that he was not bound by "fixed" requirements of ancient Judaism.[168]

Other interpreters of Paul, however, believe that the notions of freedom and slavery have their own inherent and even high signification in Paul's letter to the Galatians. Betz, for example, places much emphasis on freedom as an existential state. According to him, freedom underlies the entire argument of Galatians.[169] Freedom is the "central theological concept which sums up the

Christian's situation before God as well as the world."[170] Paul's call to freedom concerns a "primordial potential" for freedom,[171] which was lost when Adam introduced sin into the world. In liberating people from sin, Christ makes possible a sin-free existence.[172] Betz, however, imports these understandings of freedom into Paul's text. In verse 5:1a Paul provides no indication whatsoever regarding the type of freedom for which Christ freed,[173] nor does he there or elsewhere discuss how Christian salvation pertains to it. The concept of freedom does not appear to dominate the entire argument of Galatians, but instead the word "freedom" (ἐλευθερία) occurs only in Gal 2:4; 5:1, 13. Moreover, the notion of Christ freeing from sin is absent from Gal 5:1, from this unit, and from the letter as a whole. The second half of Gal 5:1 (5:1b) concerns not sin but, as indicated, slavery ("yoke of slavery").

Similarly, Betz understands Paul's reference to the yoke of slavery to imply something inherently negative, slave-like, about Torah observance. According to him, a yoke of slavery means "taking up of the yoke of Jewish Torah" (5:2–12; i.e., circumcision) and "the corruption of the flesh" (5:13–24).[174] Yet as we saw, yoke of slavery instead plays a rhetorical role as the flip side of freedom. It, like freedom, functions in a disjunctive argument as an option between two mutually exclusive alternatives. Paul's purpose in using the term "yoke of slavery" is to distance his Galatian audience from his opponents, those advocating circumcision. Ironically, Betz himself comes around to this view, albeit expressing it in anachronistic language. He remarks, "Paul's intention is clear; he wants to create a dualistic polarity between 'Judaism' and 'Christianity,' in order to discredit his Jewish-Christian opposition."[175] Nearly thirty-five years later, it is more historically accurate to say, "Paul's intention is clear; he wants to create a dualistic polarity between his Jewish group and another Jewish group with which he is in dispute in order to discredit them."

In sum, Paul, like Demosthenes and Cicero, constructs disjunctive arguments in order to offer his audience choices between two mutually exclusive alternative positions. The primary signification of the various terms of the oppositional pairs Paul creates is not in their literal signification. At issue are not states of promise, spirit, flesh, slavery, and freedom, but instead that these notions distinguish positions. They function to provoke a "proper" choice between two mutually exclusive alternatives. Similarly, the term "yoke of slavery" does not indicate that circumcision is somehow literally enslaving, nor does the term "freedom" signal some kind of liberation (religious, political, sociological, or otherwise), but instead the two terms function rhetorically and together to provide clear cut alternatives for the audience. All the oppositional terms Paul employs are powerful rhetorically for their ability to distinguish between two mutually exclusive options and for the purpose of providing audience ease in decision-making rather than for any inherent or literal meaning.

Conclusion

As we have seen, these ancient authors employ disjunctive argumentation to distance their audiences from their opponents and at the same time to win support for their own perspectives. That these authors are seeking to persuade their audience to their own point of view is also apparent in the ways in which they employ language aimed to appeal and to please. Cicero, for example, tells his senatorial audience that they were born for honor and freedom. Paul employs familial terms, predominately masculine, such as "brothers," and "sons" to win the Galatians to his side.

Demosthenes, Cicero, and Paul select terms for their dissociative arguments and then arrange them hierarchically to fit their own rhetorical situations.[176] Demosthenes, for example, chose the term "mistrust" because it served to diametrically distinguish himself from his senatorial political rivals, those who trusted Philip. Paul, by contrast, employs the opposite term "trust" to represent his position and then contrasts it to "works of Torah," a term representative of his opponents. The term "trust" serves as a necessary alternative option in a dissociative argument to specify a position on which Paul and his Galatians can self-locate. The terms authors employ as dissociative pairs provide a window into their situation and purposes. Furthermore, because dissociative terms are situationally determined, any real, essential, common, or universal sense of these terms employed, or of the actual evaluative differences between, them is severely undermined.

The individual terms of dichotomous pairs, rather than being rich in semantic meaning, instead represent a location offered and an audience choice. For Paul, the act of trusting is not at issue or of concern. Instead the notion of trusting becomes "those who trust," and as such represents a position or the place at which the audience is to self-locate. The authors' use of the terms indicates that audience position-taking is at issue. Demosthenes, for example, commands his audience to "hold fast" to mistrust; and Cicero urges his audience to take a "step on the path of freedom." Similarly, Paul exhorts his audience to "stand firm" in a "place" of freedom. Authors create contrasting pairs of terms and deploy them in dissociative arguments for the purpose of providing two mutually exclusive alternatives for their audiences. This overriding rhetorical purpose trumps any inherent or essential meaning of the individual elements within the various contrasting pairs.

In disjunctive arguments, authors also exploit common oppositions for the negative and positive valences they confer. In particular, the concept of slavery, widely known for its negative connotations, in disjunctive argumentation does not regard the institution of slavery but instead negative characteristics of the author's opponents or that which his opponents endorse. According to Demosthenes, slavery is life under the tyrannical king Philip. By contrast, for Cicero, slavery means life under the tyrant Antony. Paul associates slavery with Hagar, who in the allegory is meant to represent "those of Torah," and he links the complimentary expression "yoke of slavery" (likely an allusion to circumcision) to Torah, the position of his opponents. The meaning of slavery is thus variable and determined by its context. None of these authors detail the evils of the actual state of slavery. Rather they use slavery for its negative connotations to prejudice their audiences against their opponents.

This leg of the rhetoric-of-crisis model assesses Paul's binary oppositions differently from other Pauline interpreters. Pauline scholars often treat the individual terms of Paul's dissociative and disjunctive pairs as significant in and of themselves rather than for how they function together and rhetorically. I highlight Betz's interpretation of the dichotomous pair slavery/yoke of slavery and freedom as an example of this more common interpretive method. Betz's interpretation of slavery and freedom is problematic in and of itself in that he overstates his case for the inherent significance of the states of slavery and freedom for Paul. Were these terms significant in Paul's discourse, he would have detailed the merits of one and the disadvantages of the other, yet such discussions are absent. Betz, like other interpreters, also incorrectly places significance on the inherent meanings of the terms when they are meant to represent positions, as they occur in a disjunctive argument. Paul uses the very-commonly-employed-in-polemical-arguments terms "slavery" (or here, "yoke of slavery") and "freedom" together and in opposition to each other as locator words to exaggerate the difference between his position and that of his opponents. Similarly, Paul employs his own newly minted dichotomous pair "works of Torah/trust" in the same way and for the same purpose. With regard to the highly-potent-for-the-tradition dichotomy between works of Torah and trust, interpreters who hold to the inherent value of the individual terms of this pair rarely if ever resolve the inconsistency between Paul's negative statements against Torah and his fundamental dependency upon it. In those readings, that Paul strongly counsels against works of Torah and circumcision often serves as an indication of his own negative assessment of Jews or Judaism. By contrast, in the rhetoric-of-crisis reading, works of Torah and circumcision are in and of themselves *unproblematic* for Paul. Paul assigns these notions a negative valence as part of a process of establishing and offering two mutually exclusive alternatives to his audience. For Paul, it is a question of position-establishing, his own and that of his opponents. With disjunctive argumentation, function trumps any inherent signification of the individual terms employed.

Conclusion

As we have seen, the rhetoric of crisis magnifies a present situation and brings into existence an imminent crisis where none exists. With the tools of the rhetoric-of-crisis model—urgency, character-building (*ethos*), appeals to the emotions (*pathos*), and disjunctive argumentation (*logos*)—Demosthenes, Cicero, and Paul exacerbate an existing situation to gain ascendancy over their opponents for their own political or social/religious agendas. Paul functions no differently than these other two ancient authors.

All three rhetoric-of-crisis authors take an existing situation and build it into a crisis demanding attention. Demosthenes builds the threat of Philip into a crisis demanding immediate attention. Similarly, and following on Demosthenes' model, Cicero employs the situation of Antony's rise to power, in Cicero's estimation Antony's usurpation of power, and exacerbates the dangers of it. In similar fashion, Paul turns his opponents' insistence upon circumcision and works of Torah into a serious problem demanding an immediate response. The crises themselves—those that are self-developed into matters of urgent concern—take a back seat to the authors' desire to gain supremacy over their competition. Indeed, competition with rivals dictates the unfolding of every component of the model.

Demosthenes and Aeschines were known archrivals. Their opposing views of Philip divided Athenian politics. Demosthenes' criticisms of Philip were at base about gaining supremacy over Aeschines, his political rival. As is well known, Cicero and Antony were also strong competitors. Their rivalry divided Roman politics, and is thought to be a strong contributing factor in the demise of the Republic itself.[1] While not explicitly naming his competition, Paul nevertheless combats his rivals by negatively assessing the issues on which they stand. Competition governs and conditions his negative assessment of these rites.[2] He, like Demosthenes and Cicero, is principally engaged in a battle, largely of his own making, with his competitors over issues of authority, legitimacy, and supremacy.

The rhetoric-of-crisis model is flexible, not fixed, and at times the lines between the four dominant components are blurred. As indicated, authors appeal to the emotions when developing a sense of urgency, and employ disjunctive argumentation when building their own lofty self-characterizations. Demosthenes, Cicero, and Paul employ repetition in abundance as seen in all four components of the model. Moreover, these authors do not necessarily employ all the so-called dominant rhetorical techniques in their development of a particular component of the model. While operating within a basic set of criteria, each author builds his crisis uniquely and creatively to fit his own particular situation. The model serves as a heuristic tool for the investigation of the means of persuasion within compositional units of these three ancient authors.

Denigrating competition is one of the prime objectives of the rhetoric of crisis. Two components of the model—emotive argumentation and disjunctive mode—directly address this goal. To bring down their competitors, Demosthenes, Cicero, and Paul engage in negative stereotyping. To tarnish Antony's reputation, Cicero characterizes him as a tyrant, a beast, and as lustful and impudent. With his references to curses and evil eye practices, Paul locates his competitors in a malevolent realm, to a location directly antithetical to his own developed self-characterization as a man of God. With the use of allegory, Paul paints a grim picture of a life lived under the conditions of the Torah observances of his competitors. To equate Torah and those who practice it with a fleshly slave woman evokes uncontrolled human passions and significantly degrades those of Torah.

Rhetorical techniques that promote urgency serve to awaken and make pressing the situation at hand. Cicero, in particular, employs urgency to his rhetorical advantage. Yet his choice to borrow from Demosthenes' καιρός theme in his development of it indicates that Demosthenes before him recognized its effectiveness for persuasion. Short clipped sentences, rhetorical questions, and the repetition of key words and expressions are the dominant techniques for the promotion of urgency. Through these rhetorical devices, authors create swift movement and drum their ideas into their audiences. Audience rebuke, another common technique to promote a sense of urgency, serves to jolt an audience into responding; Demosthenes, Cicero, and Paul do not hesitate to shame their audiences into action.

Demosthenes, Cicero, and Paul all engage in lofty self-fashioning or argumentation through ethos to persuade of their own skill, worthiness, and credibility. They impress their audiences through their compositional and oratorical skills. These ancient authors do not provide straightforward accounts of their lives but instead exaggerate their qualifications. Demosthenes claims to always tell the truth; Cicero depicts himself as savior of the Republic; and Paul claims that two divine beings sanction his apostleship. Demosthenes, Cicero, and Paul also skillfully select what and how they reveal aspects of themselves. Each author raises an issue—a slanderous remark, a malicious rumor, or a shameful history—potentially damaging to his character, but then cleverly weaves his self-disclosures into a larger argument that ultimately serve to advance his own positive self-image. Demosthenes mentions his opponents' accusations that he is disagreeable and a water-drinker. In raising them within the context of his opponents' unreliability, he renders their uncomplimentary remarks harmless. Demosthenes' extensive positive self-fashioning positions him well above the foolhardy remarks and "incompetence" of his opponents. Cicero raises the issue of the malicious rumor that he would have himself declared ruler. With biting sarcasm, firm rhetorical control, and highly sophisticated argumentation, he squelches the rumor and at the same time squarely diminishes those who promulgated it. By exaggerating incidents of his past, making them all the more negative, Paul fashions a distinct contrast between his past and present self. His self-developed contrast serves as further confirmation of his transformation into a man of God. In the case of all three authors, the mere act of raising a seemingly uncomplimentary self-characterization gestures toward honest self-disclosure and hence helps to promote a sense of trustworthiness.

With disjunctive mode Demosthenes, Cicero, and Paul employ oppositional pairs to create stark contrasts between their position and that of their competition. The objective of this type of argumentation is to persuade the audience to take a stand on the positive side of two mutually exclusive alternative positions. To simplify the audiences' choice, authors assess the individual elements of the dichotomous pairs at the extreme ends of their respective scales. These authors either employ terms that are well known and which thereby resonate for their readily known positive or negative connotations, such as "slavery" and "freedom," or else they take hold of two terms not otherwise contrastive but that fit their situations and then rank them hierarchically. As indicated, to criticize his political opponents, Demosthenes creates a dissociative argument around the notions of mistrust and trust. He adopts the term "mistrust" for himself in opposition to his trusting opponents. In doing so, he provides two clear and mutually exclusive options for his Athenian audience. In the case of well-known dichotomies, such as slavery/freedom, the actual or existential states of slavery and freedom are not in view. Rather authors employ these terms for their connotations and then use them as catchwords into which they insert content that fits their own situations, such as Philip's deceit and aggression, Antony's tyranny and social deviant behaviors, or the burdensome requirements of works of Torah. With disjunctive mode, function, the authors' position-making, and purpose, the audiences' position-taking, trump any inherent significance of the individual elements of the antithetical pairs.

In Galatians, Paul creates a multitude of antitheses, and he, like Demosthenes and Cicero, employs them to persuade his audience to avoid going over to the side of his competitors. Paul is perhaps best known for the contrast he draws between works of Torah and trust. Paul is less—or even not—interested in the notion of leading a trusting life, as he never fully develops the notion of trusting. Similarly, works of Torah and circumcision do not in and of themselves represent incorrect ways of living. Rather, Paul opposes works of Torah and trust to establish two alternative positions for the purpose of position-taking. The same holds true for the other oppositional pairs Paul deploys. His term "yoke of slavery," a metaphor for circumcision, also a work of Torah, is simply a negative epithet reflective of his competitors. When paired antithetically with freedom in disjunctive argumentation, yoke of slavery is the obvious choice to avoid. Interestingly, each rhetoric-of-crisis author employs the contrastive pair slavery/freedom to sum up the differences between their competitors and themselves.

The rhetoric of crisis can be categorized as a systematic form of ancient polemics. In polemical writings, authors are far less concerned with facts than they are with winning their arguments. Exaggeration replaces facts. Urgency is itself a form of exaggeration. In characterizing their opponents as sub-human or as dabbling in evil practices, Demosthenes, Cicero, and Paul greatly exaggerate their opponents' wickedness. Stretching the truth is particularly evident in the ways in which each author treats current events, history, and their own traditions. Demosthenes repeatedly gives the impression that Philip has already broken the peace accord, when indeed he had not. If anything, having wavered with regard to his support of the Peace of Philocrates, it was Demosthenes himself who was less reliable than Philip. On 20 December 44, the Roman senate never took up the question of whether or not Antony should be ruled a public enemy (*hostis*), yet that same afternoon and in his speech before the people, Cicero characterized the situation as more or less a done deal. In characterizing Antony's brutality as knowing no bounds, Cicero rewrites the narrative of Rome's most tyrannical king Tarquin, depicting the latter as far less cruel than he was. Like Demosthenes and Cicero, Paul manipulates and rewrites scripture (his tradition) to his own advantage. Nowhere does scripture state that a person must follow every word of Torah or risk being cursed. Scripture does not condemn the unqualified act of hanging on a tree. With his allegory, Paul engages in a reinterpretation of scriptural readings and essentially rewrites parts of the Genesis narrative to make it serve his own rhetorical purposes of denigrating the agenda of his competitors.

A rhetoric-of-crisis reading of Paul's letter to the Galatians challenges several dominant interpretations and unearths a portrait of Paul that differs from the more common understandings of him. As Penner and Lopez remark, "Most scholars of Pauline literature . . . are invested in constructing 'real' history and belief systems in and behind the texts we possess."[3] In a history-oriented approach, Paul is understood to supply a trustworthy account of his divine commissioning for a mission to non-Jews. He finds that Torah and its practices themselves, notably, circumcision, are actually harmful[4] or jeopardizing in some way or another to his God-given mission.[5] In these readings, those with whom Paul argues—known by various names, such as, opponents, teachers, influencers, or agitators—are significant not as active agents, who provide a context, function as the implied audience, and inform the construction of Paul's arguments more generally throughout Galatians—but more so as a source of clues for unearthing "facts" about Paul and his mission.

By contrast, in the rhetoric-of-crisis reading, Paul is understood not as a standout figure but instead as an ancient author not unlike others of his time. His self-characterizations of being divinely commissioned and as having been set apart by God to proclaim the good news are read as strategies, as exaggerated self-fashionings told for the specific purpose of winning the Galatians to his side and away from his competition. In Paul's case, he develops the adoption of works of Torah and circumcision into a crisis, not for theological, sociological, or political reasons, but simply because they reflect the position of his competitors. He advances hyperbolic reasons why the Galatians should not adopt circumcision. These rites are caught up in the middle—innocent victims—of his polemical fight with his competitors.

The rhetoric-of-crisis reading makes sense of Paul's numerous—even overabundant—use of dichotomies. Creating a sense a difference brings about the need to make distinct choices between two alternative positions. The rhetoric-of crisis-reading does not attempt to minimize the various dichotomies, especially that between works of Torah and trust, but instead unmasks them as rhetorical tools for polemics. A rhetorical reading obviates the need to make excuses for or logical sense of Paul's various statements concerning Torah that can strain comprehension. This reading understands Paul's targeted remarks against his opponents as exaggerations.

According to Heidi Wendt, the social landscape of the early imperial period was one of intellectual experimentation with accompanying competition for followers.[6] During that time, freelance experts—"self-authorized purveyor[s] of specialized skills, teachings, and related services"[7]—came onto the scene and employed and developed their skills in order to garner prestige and gain followers. Wendt remarks that "Statements about the law, Israelites, and Judaizing are best understood . . . not as evidence of Paul negotiating a complex relationship to Judaism or Judean ancestry but as position-takings among freelance experts competing for followers."[8] A social landscape of freelance experts competing for followers provides an on-the-ground social context that dovetails with my rhetorical reading of Paul's letter to the Galatians.

Interestingly, in the generation that follows Paul, the author of the canonical book of Acts depicts him giving a speech to Athenians (Acts 17:22–31), thus mimicking Demosthenes. And this same author names Paul's birthplace—a detail not indicated in Paul's letters—as Tarsus in Cilicia, the place in which Cicero held a governorship.[9] These later and albeit limited details in Acts provide at least the suggestion that an ancient author also sensed Paul's arguments aimed at persuasion in ways that paralleled those of Demosthenes and Cicero.

Notes

Introduction

1. In his letter to the Galatians, Paul employs the Greek ἔθνη to refer to those to whom he considers himself called (Gal 1:16; 2:2, 8–9). According to Paul, ἔθνη are non-Jews or the uncircumcised (Gal 2:8–9; 3:8, 14). Paul also distinguishes Jews from ἔθνη (Gal 2:14, 15), and his Galatian audience is non-Jewish (ἔθνη). In the scholarship on Paul and in modern English translations (NRSV, ASV, NAB, NIV) of Paul's letter to the Galatians, ἔθνη is often translated as "gentiles" or "Gentiles." Caroline Johnson Hodge, for example, writes, "Paul is a *Ioudaios* (the Greek term for 'Jew' or 'Judean') who has come to believe that Jesus of Nazareth is a messianic agent of God and Paul claims to have been called to bring his gospel to non-Jews, to gentiles" (*If Sons, Then Heirs*, 5). As Christopher Stanley correctly notes, however, the term "Gentiles" is a "social construction of reality developed by a particular people-group (Jews) in a concrete historical situation. Those whom the Jews lumped together as Gentiles defined themselves as Greeks, Romans, Phrygians, Galatians, Cappadocians, and members of various other ethnic populations." See "'Neither Jew nor Greek,'" 105. See also Scott, *The Real Paul*, 57–60; Elliott, *The Arrogance of Nations*, 46–47. While the term "gentiles" is prominent in the scholarship on Paul, the English translation for ἔθνη that avoids being anachronistic is "nations."

2. For this understanding of circumcision, see Schiffman, *Who Was a Jew? Rabbinic and Halakhic Perspectives on the Jewish-Christian Schism*, 25, 39; Nolland, "Uncircumcised Proselytes?"; Fredriksen, "Judaism, the Circumcision of Gentiles, and Apocalyptic Hope," 239. See also Shaye Cohen who writes, "The Greek-speaking Jews of the second temple period and the Hebrew- (and Aramaic-) speaking Jews after 70 CE debated the meaning of circumcision and the ritual's exact place in the conversion process, but as far as is known no (non-Christian) Jewish community in antiquity accepted male proselytes who were not circumcised. Perhaps the god of the Jews would be pleased with gentiles who venerated him and practiced some of the laws, and perhaps in the coming eschaton gentiles would not need to be circumcised to be part of god's holy people; but if those gentiles wanted to join the Jewish community in the here and now, they had to accept circumcision" ("Crossing the Boundary and Becoming a Jew," 27). In addition, according to Cohen, for Josephus "the essence of 'conversion'" is circumcision. See his "Respect for Judaism by Gentiles According to Josephus," 421.

3. See, for example, Räisänen, *Paul and the Law*, 190.

4. For more on the new approach to Paul, see Zetterholm, *Approaches to Paul*, 95–163. See also Eisenbaum, *Paul Was Not a Christian*, 172–95; Scott, *The Real Paul*.

5. In the mid-twentieth century, Krister Stendahl argued convincingly that Paul never converted to another religion but instead was called by God on a mission to the gentiles. See "Paul Among Jews and Gentiles," 8. On this, see also Stowers, *A Rereading of Romans*, 156. Daniel Boyarin writes that Paul "lived and died convinced that he was a Jew living out Judaism" (*A Radical Jew*, 2). In his book *Paul and the Stoics*, Troels Engberg-Pedersen writes, "Paul did not in any way see his own form of Christ faith as constituting a break with Judaism. On the contrary,

in the best sectarian manner he conceived of it as the true apogee of Judaism" (*Paul and the Stoics*, 15). Arthur Dewey writes that modern views regarding the notion that Paul converted have been influenced by the work of William James, A. D. Nock, and Alan Segal. According to Dewey, these writers rely on modern categories such as emotional experience and are as such inadequate for defining Paul's first-century context and rhetorical situation. See his "The Masks of Paul," 159–68. In her 2009 monograph *Paul Was Not a Christian*, Pamela Eisenbaum, a former student of Stendahl, summarizes much of the recent scholarship and clearly outlines several important implications for understanding Paul as a Jew. See also, Michael White, who writes that Paul "clearly saw himself as a pious Jew who had been called on by God, through Jesus, to take this message to non-Jews" (*From Jesus to Christianity*, 145).

Mark Nanos is at present one of the—if not the strongest—proponents of this position. Nanos pushes beyond Stendahl's and many of these other more general evaluations of Paul as a Jew and argues that Paul was Torah-observant throughout his life. Furthermore, Nanos argues that Paul wanted non-Jews to observe certain aspects of the Torah. See his *The Mystery of Romans*, 3–9 passim; *Irony of Galatians*, 2–9 passim. For a brief summary of Nanos' position see Zetterholm, *Approaches to Paul*, 147–55.

6. Eisenbaum, *Paul Was Not a Christian*, 172–95.

7. This is a common understanding of what Paul is about. For example, see Scott, *The Real Paul*, 60. See also Eisenbaum who writes, "I assert that the most important theological force motivating Paul's mission was a thoroughgoing commitment to Jewish monotheism and how to bring the nations of the world to that realization as history draws to a close" (*Paul Was Not a Christian*, 173).

8. Richard Horsley's edited volume is dedicated to Krister Stendahl. The introduction to his volume includes a very good summary of Stendahl's contribution to the field of Pauline studies. See "Krister Stendahl's Challenge to Pauline Studies," 2–5.

9. By reference to what Paul says of himself in Gal 1:15–16, Stendahl presses the fact that Paul was "called" by God (as a Jew) on a mission to gentiles. He writes, "Serving the one and the same God, Paul receives a new and special calling in God's service. God's Messiah asks him as a Jew to bring God's message to the Gentiles. The emphasis in the accounts is always on this assignment, not on the conversion" ("Paul Among Jews and Gentiles," 7).

10. Daniel Boyarin, for example, remarks that Christianity and Judaism did not become distinct from each other until late antiquity. See *Border Lines*, 21. Moreover, both terms connote the idea of a formed and conceptually unified religion, yet such an idea about religion belongs more to the modern era than to the ancient world. Judith Lieu comments, "The conceptual baggage these terms [Judaism and Christianity] carry belong rather more to our contemporary agenda" (*Christian Identity in the Jewish and Graeco-Roman World*, 306). See also Scott, *The Real Paul*, 68.

11. See especially Stendahl, "The Apostle Paul and the Introspective Conscience of the West," 78–96.

12. Luther, *Lectures on Galatians 1535: Chapters 1–4*, 126.

13. Eisenbaum remarks, "The 'doctrine' of justification by faith is a product of the Reformation; it is not inherent in Paul's letters, even if Reformation theologians are indebted to Paul for the idea" (*Paul Was Not a Christian*, 205).

14. Stendahl, "Paul Among Jews and Gentiles," 13.

15. Sanders, *Paul and Palestinian Judaism*, 544.

16. Sanders, *Paul and Palestinian Judaism*, 75.

17. Sanders, *Paul and Palestinian Judaism*, 421–22.

18. Stendahl, "The Apostle Paul and the Introspective Conscience of the West," 81.

19. Pauline scholars have misinterpreted Stendahl to affirm a two-covenant philosophy, whereby God would justify the gentiles through Christ and the Jews through the Torah. Stendhal, however, did not adopt a two-covenant view of Paul. On this issue, see his *Final Account*, x.

20. Stendahl writes, "The only *metanoia* (repentance/conversion) and the only grace which counts is the one now available in Messiah Jesus. Once this has been seen, it appears that Paul's references to the impossibility of fulfilling the Law [Torah] is part of a theological and theoretical scriptural argument about the relation between Jews and Gentiles" (*Paul Among Jews and Gentiles*, 81; italics are the author's).

21. Sanders, *Paul, the Law, and the Jewish People*, 1–5, 20–27.

22. Sanders, *Paul, the Law, and the Jewish People*, 27.

23. See, for example, his recent edited volume with Magnus Zetterholm, *Paul within Judaism: Restoring the First-Century Context to the Apostle*.

24. Nanos, *Mystery of Romans*, 9. See also the good summary of the views of Mark Nanos in Zetterholm, *Approaches to Paul*, 147–55.

25. Nanos, *Mystery of Romans*, 9–10. Unlike F. C. Baur (1792–1860), Nanos does not posit an anti-Jewish understanding of Paul. As mentioned, according to Nanos, Paul is thoroughly Jewish and continued throughout his lifetime to practice Judaism. Yet Nanos' understanding that Paul considered God's oneness to be compromised should non-Jews become circumcised Jews requires a type of global religious agenda that is not evident from Paul's letters.

26. The universalistic approach to Paul began with F. C. Baur (1792–1860). According to Baur, Paul's aim was to refute Jewish exclusiveness. See *Paul the Apostle of Jesus Christ*, 356–57. There is an anti-Jewishness to Baur's theory: Baur claimed Jews believed that they had a "theocratic supremacy" (theokratische Primat der jüdischen Nation) and an absolute claim on God. See his *Paulus, der Apostel Jesu Christi sein Leben und Wirken, seine Briefe und seine Lehre*, 2.1189. Baur writes, "The main idea running through its entire extent [Romans] is the absolute nothingness of all claims founded on Jewish exclusiveness. The aim of the Apostle is to confute the Jewish exclusiveness so thoroughly and radically that he fairly stands in advance of the consciousness of the time" (*Paul the Apostle of Jesus Christ*, 1.356–57).

A universalistic view of Paul pervades much of the present scholarship on Paul. This is not to say that modern scholars who hold to this view of Paul are anti-Jewish, but instead that this view is very prevalent. Boyarin, for example, speaks of Baur's influence on his own understanding of Paul. See *Radical Jew*, 11 passim. According to Boyarin, Paul is a cultural critic of Judaism troubled by the ethnocentrism of both biblical and post-biblical religion. See ibid., 52. A review of this literature would likely require another monograph, and much of that work has been done. Magnus Zetterholm provides a very good review of the recent scholarship on Paul. See *Approaches to Paul*.

27. Expressing the views of many Pauline scholars, Victor Furnish writes, "His [Paul's] aim in writing was to address the particular needs of specific Christian [sic] congregations, in specific locations, involved in specific situations, at specific times" (*The Moral Teachings of Paul*, 15).

28. There are numerous recent approaches to Paul. Bernard Scott, for example, argues that according to Paul, the circumcision of non-Jews means their subjection

to the powers not of Judaism but of Rome. See *The Real Paul*, 180. For a similar view to Scott, see Kahl, *Galatians Re-Imagined*, 274 passim. For an excellent summary of the traditional and newer approaches to Paul, see Zetterholm, *Approaches to Paul*.

29. Eisenbaum, *Paul Was Not a Christian*, 173.

30. Eisenbaum, *Paul Was Not a Christian*, 96–98.

31. I have dealt with that subject in an earlier work, and indicate that there was considerable variety in the understanding of the ancient rite of circumcision. See Livesey, *Circumcision as a Malleable Symbol*.

32. With the publication of Hans Dieter Betz's commentary on Galatians, rhetorical analysis of scripture was rediscovered in America. Prior to Betz, English professors of the pre-WWI era dabbled in ancient rhetorical theory, and shortly thereafter Composition professors took up the discipline. Along with Betz, biblical scholars in North America, such as Wilhelm Wuellner, Burton Mack, James Hester, Stanley Porter, Jeffrey Reed, Ronald Hock and Thomas Olbricht, were early adopters of rhetorical analysis. For a brief history, see Thomas Olbricht's preface in Porter and Olbricht, *Rhetoric and the New Testament*, 9.

Recent scholarship on Paul and rhetoric include: Sampley and Lampe, *Paul and Rhetoric*; Wire, *The Corinthian Women Prophets*; Anderson, *Ancient Rhetorical Theory and Paul*; Callan, "The Style of Galatians," 495–516; Classen, "Paul and Ancient Greek and Roman Rhetoric," 265–91; Elliott, *The Rhetoric of Romans*; Fairweather, "The Epistle to the Galatians and Classical Rhetoric: Parts 1 & 2," 1–38; Hall, "Rhetorical Outline for Galatians," 29–38; Kennedy, *New Testament Interpretation through Rhetorical Criticism*; Kern, *Rhetoric and Galatians*; Lyons, *Pauline Biography*; Schüssler Fiorenza, *Rhetoric and Ethics*; Smit, "Deliberative Speech," 39–59; Mack, *Rhetoric and the New Testament*; Thurén, *Derhetorizing Paul*.

Although many scholars have taken up the study of Paul from a rhetorical perspective, generally speaking, they seem reluctant to subject Paul's letter to the Galatians to a full rhetorical analysis. The remarks of J. Louis Martyn get at the heart of their hesitation. In his 1997 commentary on Galatians, Martyn remarks that rhetoric can "serve the gospel" but that "the gospel itself is not fundamentally a matter of rhetorical persuasion" (*Galatians*, 22). Martyn adds that while there are rhetorical elements found in Galatians, the letter itself does not conform to any of the ancient rhetorical categories (ibid., 20–23). According to him, Galatians is a "highly situational sermon." See ibid., 23.

33. Indeed, for Todd Penner and Davina Lopez, that Paul is rhetorical is a given. They comment, "There is no place outside of rhetoric in Paul's letters. Every word links with other words, forming series of statements that play a role in making arguments that Paul, presumably, finds important to share with his recipients" (Penner and Lopez, "Rhetorical Approaches," 37).

34. See also Phil 3:3, 5; 1 Cor 7:18–19; Rom 2:25–29; 3:1, 30; 4:9–12; 15:8.

35. Heikki Räisänen comments, "Through the pressure of events he was led to search for arguments for a global rejection of the law. . . . He thus came upon several *ad hoc* arguments for the termination of the law (the analogies of marriage and will; the legislation through angels) and its allegedly sin-engendering and sin-enhancing nature etc. The numerous problems and self-contradictions in his statements expose the overall theory as more or less artificial" (*Paul and the Law*, 261–62).

36. There is considerable scholarship on Paul's opponents and their identity. See Georgi, *The Opponents of Paul in Second Corinthians*. See also recent articles in Porter, *Paul and His Opponents*. For surveys on the history of this issue, see Sumney, "Studying Paul's Opponents: Advantages and Challenges," 7–58; Jewett,

"The Agitators and the Galatian Congregation," 198–212; Eckert, *Die urchristliche Verkündigung im Streit zwischen Paulus und seinen Gegnern nach dem Galaterbrief*; Gunther, *St. Paul's Opponents and Their Backgrounds*; Schütz, *Paul and the Anatomy of Apostolic Authority*; Ellis, "Paul and His Opponents," 264–98; Robinson and Koester, *Trajectories Through Early Christianity*, 12–23; Nanos, *Irony of Galatians*, 115–92.

37. Paul employs many of the classical forms of vilification against his opponents. On this, see Thurén, "Was Paul Angry?" 312. Thurén remarks that Paul's purpose was to "reveal them as 'bad guys.'" See ibid., 313.

38. Thurén remarks, "By creating an urgent, black-and-white situation the apostle invites the addressees to take a stand" ("Was Paul Angry?" 319).

39. Cohen's writings include, *From the Maccabees to the Mishnah*; *Beginnings of Jewishness*; *Why Aren't Jewish Women Circumcised?*

40. Cohen, "The Letter of Paul to the Galatians," 332.

41. In discussing the scholarship on the identity and mission of the opponents, Nanos finds four different and dominant views. According to him, those troubling Paul have been called Judaizers, opponents or rivals, agitators or troublemakers, and teachers. See *Irony of Galatians*, 115. Betz uses the term "opponents" for Paul's rivals. According to him, the opponents are "Jewish-Christian missionaries rivaling Paul." They desired to make converts from among Paul's churches. See his *Galatians*, 58. Robert Jewett employs the term "agitators." According to Jewett, the agitators were Jews by birth and Christians by belief. They were trying to persuade the Galatians to become circumcised to avoid persecution from Jewish Zealots. The Zealots were themselves pressing for the circumcision of those in Judea and the surrounding countryside. See "Agitators," 203–5. By contrast, J. Louis Martyn adopts the term "teachers" for this group. According to him, the teachers are "messianic Jews," who are preaching another gospel, one that has the law as its foundation. See *Galatians*, 118–21.

In contrast to any of these views and names, Mark Nanos argues that the group should be called "influencers." They are not Jewish believers in Christ (Jewish Christians, Christian Jews or *Judaizers*), who believe that all Christ believers must also, and like them, become circumcised, but are instead non-Christ-believing Jews, who aim to make the Galatians full members of Judaism through the ritual of circumcision. See *Irony of Galatians*, 6, 13, 205.

42. Wooten specializes in ancient Greek rhetoric and oratory. He has written extensively on the influence of Demosthenes on Cicero. See *Cicero's* Philippics *and their Demosthenic Model: The Rhetoric of Crisis*. I rely on his recent commentary on Demosthenes' first three Philippic orations for this present study. See *Demosthenes' Philippic I*.

43. For discussion of this method of argumentation see Wooten, *Rhetoric of Crisis*. See also Manuwald, *Introduction and Texts*, 123. According to her, "the overall rhetorical character of Cicero's *Philippics*" can be understood by the term "rhetoric of crisis." See ibid.

44. Marcus Tullius Cicero, *Philippics 1–6*, xxxi. See also Manuwald, *Introduction and Texts*, 123.

45. Cicero, *Philippics 1–6*, xxxi. See also Hall, "The *Philippics*," 283–94.

46. Wooten, *Rhetoric of Crisis*, 58.

47. Manuwald remarks, "[The] description of the opponent (which contrasts with that of the representatives of the other party) functions as a decisive argument for taking action against him. In both Demosthenes and Cicero the enemy and the consequences of his victory are contrasted with the advantages of the type

of political system defended by the orators" (*Introduction and Texts*, 133). See also Wooten, *Rhetoric of Crisis*, 65.

48. Wooten, *Rhetoric of Crisis*, 58. Wooten uses male pronouns, but he is referring to two males (Demosthenes and Cicero). Paul, too, is male. Maleness, competition between males, is likely what in part explains this type of rhetoric.

49. To make clear, these four steps are not explicit in Wooten's rhetoric-of-crisis model, but instead spring from it. The four components derive from my reading of Wooten's analysis of the speeches of Demosthenes and Cicero and from my own analysis of the compositions of all three ancient authors (Demosthenes, Cicero, and Paul).

50. For biographical information on Demosthenes, see also Worthington, *Demosthenes of Athens and the Fall of Classical Greece*; Trevett, *Demosthenes, Speeches 1–17*, 1–5; Wooten, *Demosthenes' Philippic I*, 6–16; Badian, "The Road to Prominence," 9–36; Worthington, *Demosthenes: Statesman and Orator*; Carlier, *Démosthène*; Demosthenes, *Olynthiacs, Philippics*, xi–xii; Jaeger, *Demosthenes: The Origin and Growth of His Policy*.

51. This speech also marks a turning point in Demosthenes' career, as all the surviving speeches from this date forward concern the danger to Athens from the growth of Macedonian forces. See Trevett, *Demosthenes, Speeches 1–17*, 68.

52. Demosthenes, *Olynthiacs, Philippics*, 67.

53. Commentaries on Demosthenes' *Philippics* include Heslop, *Demosthenis Orationes Publicae*; Weil, *Les Harangues de Démosthène*; Sandys, *Demosthenes: Texts and Notes*; Wooten, *Demosthenes' Philippic I*.

54. These include three *Olynthiac* speeches, four Philippic speeches, *On the Peace*, and *On the Chersonese*. Some modern critics have considered Demosthenes' *Fourth Philippic* not genuine, yet that view has recently been overturned. The speech raises questions concerning its authenticity because it contains two long passages from other speeches. J. H. Vince, for example, calls it "spurious" (Demosthenes, *Olynthiacs, Philippics*, 268–69). See also Sandys, *Demosthenes: Texts and Notes*, v. By contrast, Jeremy Trevett argues convincingly that the speech is genuine. According to him, scholars in antiquity considered it genuine. While two long passages are similar to other speeches, especially to his *On the Chersonese*, Trevett argues that Demosthenes could have delivered both speeches regardless of the overlap in content or that he simply might have delivered only the *Fourth Philippic* and not *On the Chersonese*. See *Demosthenes, Speeches 1–17*, 177–79.

55. In many ways, Philip paved the way for the successes of his son, Alexander the Great. During his reign, he greatly expanded the territory of Macedon and doubled its population. He created a first-rate and professional military, built roads and towns, and effectively exploited Macedon's natural resources, improving trade and its economy. For more on Philip, see Worthington, *Philip II of Macedonia*, 196–98.

56. Wooten, *Demosthenes' Philippic I*, 5.

57. Wooten provides some background information on the situation in Thrace. See *Demosthenes' Philippic I*, 5.

58. Trevett, *Demosthenes, Speeches 1–17*, 70.

59. Wooten, *Demosthenes' Philippic I*, 10.

60. Wooten, *Demosthenes' Philippic I*, 10.

61. Yunis, *Taming Democracy*, 248.

62. For the historical background of Cicero's *Philippics*, see Frisch, *Cicero's Fight for the Republic*, 10–118; Manuwald, *Introduction and Texts*, 9–47; Cicero, *Philippics 1–6*, xxv–xxviii; Hall, "The *Philippics*" 273–80; Harries, *Cicero and the Jurists: From*

Citizens' Law to the Lawful State, 204–29; Van der Blom, "*Officium* and *Res publica*," 287–320.

63. Cicero, *Philippics 1–6*, xxv–xxvi.

64. Kathryn Tempest writes that Cicero was obsessed with his own sense of importance. He had a desire for "fame, praise and recognition for his achievements" (Tempest, *Cicero: Politics and Persuasion in Ancient Rome*, 3). According to Elizabeth Rawson, Cicero had a passion for glory, which drove him. See her *Cicero: A Portrait*, 9.

65. I rely heavily on Manuwald's 2007 two-volume work on Cicero's *Philippics* for this study. See her *Commentary; Introduction and Texts*.

66. Manuwald, *Introduction and Texts*, 130. See also ibid., 47.

67. Donat Taddeo remarks, "The model for Antony in Demosthenes is obviously Philip of Macedon" ("Signs of Demosthenes in Cicero's *Philippics*," 12). See also Wooten who claims that Cicero had been studying Demosthenes intensely and with Antony, Cicero considered he was in a situation similar to that of Demosthenes and Philip. See *Rhetoric of Crisis*, 59.

68. Manuwald, *Introduction and Texts*, 121; Hall, "The *Philippics*," 300–301. D. R. Shackleton Bailey remarks, "The choice of the name *Philippics* indicates that Cicero was inviting comparison between himself and the great Athenian orator Demosthenes, and thereby aspiring to be viewed as Demosthenes' Roman counterpart" (Cicero, *Philippics 1–6*, xxii). See also, Quintilian, *Institutio oratoria* 10.1.105 and Plutarch's pairing of the two orators in his parallel lives in *Comparatio Demosthenis et Ciceronis*. For the similarities in the styles between Demosthenes and Cicero, see Wooten, *Rhetoric of Crisis*; Taddeo, "Signs of Demosthenes in Cicero's *Philippics*."

69. While the *Philippics* in their current form comprise a total of fourteen speeches, the first two are later additions, written by Cicero but never actually delivered. See Cicero, *Philippics 1–6*, xx–xxi. Of the twelve written and delivered speeches, the first two speeches (*Third and Fourth Philippic*) deal more directly with Antony and a characterization of him. The subsequent five speeches concern the first embassy to Antony and the second group of again five speeches regards events in the east and the military struggle with Antony. Cicero delivered the final speech, the *Fourteenth Philippic*, on 21 April 43, on the day of a significant military defeat of Antony's troops near Mutina, and only in this final speech does he succeed in having Antony declared a public enemy (*hostis*). See ibid., xxi.

70. Manuwald, "Cicero Versus Antonius," 39. As Jürgen von Ungern-Sternberg remarks, it is now common to understand the rivalry between Antony and Cicero as a clash between aristocrats or *optimates* (Cicero's group) and the democrats or *populares* (Antony's group). See "The Crisis of the Republic," 95–96.

71. The declaration of Antony as a public enemy was the way in which he could bring his enemy down through legislation (licitly). Yet getting the legislation passed was very difficult and Cicero faced an uphill battle: Antony was acting proconsular governor and as such possessed the imperium granted by the Roman legislation. Thus, Cicero had to convince the Roman senate to oust their fellow councilman (Cicero, *Philippics 1–6*, xxv). On this point see also Jal, "'Hostis (Publicus),'" 207.

72. Commentaries on Cicero's *Philippics* include King, *The Philippic Orations of M. Tullius Cicero*; Long, *M. Tullii Ciceronis Orationes*; Manuwald, *Commentary*; Ramsey, *Cicero, Marcus Tullius: Philippics I–II*; Lacey, *Cicero: Second Philippic Oration*; Cristofoli, *Cicerone e la II Filippica*.

73. Manuwald, *Introduction and Texts*, 112–13.

74. For a fuller explanation, see Frisch, *Cicero's Fight for the Republic*, 42–56. Frisch also mentions that in the days after Caesar's assassination, Antony and Lepidus broke into Caesar's house and had all of his papers and his cash transferred over to Antony. See ibid., 49–50.

75. Van der Blom, "*Officium* and *Res publica*," 291–92.

76. Cicero, *Att.* 14.9.2. Quoted in Frisch, *Cicero's Fight for the Republic*, 119. Frisch notes, however, that there was a friendly exchange of letters between Cicero and Antony even after the Ides of March. See ibid., 82. James May remarks that with the rise of Antony, Cicero felt they had merely replaced one tyrant for another. See his "Cicero: His Life and Career," 15.

77. Cicero turned the conflict "into a defense of the traditional political system and the whole *res publica* against one person who endangered it." See Manuwald, *Introduction and Texts*, 130.

78. Van der Blom, "*Officium* and *Res publica*," 296. See also Tempest, *Cicero: Politics and Persuasion in Ancient Rome*, 193. Hartvig Frisch notes, "This [Cicero's] hatred against Antony is gradually becoming a passion, which assumes a downright pathological character" (*Cicero's Fight for the Republic*, 121).

79. Van der Blom, "*Officium* and *Res publica*," 298.

80. Harries, *Cicero and the Jurists*, 221–22; Van der Blom, "*Officium* and *Res publica*," 298.

81. It is well known that Cicero was considered a "new man" or novus homo. On this, see Tempest, *Cicero: Politics and Persuasion in Ancient Rome*, 20; Rawson, *Cicero: A Portrait*, 12; Mitchell, *Cicero, the Senior Statesman*, 4. Thomas Habinek remarks that because Cicero was a new man, his authority as a *consul* was relatively weak (Habinek, *Ancient Rhetoric and Oratory*, 26). John Dugan fashions an entire monograph around this theme. See his *Making a New Man*.

82. Bailey explains, "Still, even a 'new man,' whose forebears had never sat in the Senate, might reasonably hope to get as far as the Praetorship, provided he had money, connections, and ability. Even noblemen did not climb the ladder without effort—there were not enough offices to go round. The 'new man' naturally had to work harder to establish himself as a political prospect and collect votes" (*Cicero*, 9). Cicero says of himself, "But I am not permitted the same privileges as men of noble birth, who, even while sleeping, still see all the honors of the Roman people laid at their feet; in this state I must live under far different conditions and according to a very different law" (*In Verrem* 2.5.180; cited in May, "Cicero: His Life and Career," 7).

83. In his private letters, Cicero voices his concerns about Octavian. See Cicero, *Att.* 15.12.12; 16.9; 16.14.1.

Taddeo remarks that Cicero exploits the sudden appearance of Octavian as Rome's savior so that he can increase the pressure on the senate to oust Antony. According to Taddeo, the presence of Octavian allows Cicero to present the situation at hand as ripe for change, as a *kairos* moment. See "Signs of Demosthenes in Cicero's *Philippics*," 7. Similarly, Bailey writes, "As a practical counterweight to Antony's considerable military might, Cicero backed Octavian." It was Cicero's hope to be able to influence this young man. See Cicero, *Philippics 1–6*, xxvi–xxvii. See also Manuwald, *Introduction and Texts*, 93–96. Henrietta van der Blom also explores the relationship between Cicero and Octavian. She too remarks that when Cicero first met Octavian in 44 he was not terribly impressed by him. She comments that Cicero recognized his talents but was wary of Octavian because of his family connections. It was Octavian who encouraged Cicero to enter into the political fight against Antony. For more details on this, see "*Officium and Res publica*," 294, 307–8, 308 n. 92.

84. Plutarch, *Cic.* 49.1–6. For more on the death of Cicero at the hands of Antony's men, see Harries, *Cicero and the Jurists*, 204, 206; Hall, "The *Philippics*," 302; Tempest, *Cicero: Politics and Persuasion in Ancient Rome*, 204–5; Manuwald, *Introduction and Texts*, 140. That Cicero knew the risk he was taking by siding with Octavian over Antony, see Van der Blom, "*Officium* and *Res publica*," 308 n. 92. One might also mention that Demosthenes also paid dearly for his views. Having been condemned by pro-Macedonian forces, he took his own life. On this see Trevett, *Demosthenes, Speeches 1–17*, 3.

85. When thinking rhetorically, this statement is not as scandalous as it may at first seem to be. As Penner and Lopez remark, in the ancient world, "Facts" and "Truth" are contingent upon the authors' rhetorical aims. "Truth" is not fixed but instead malleable. See their "Rhetorical Approaches," 40.

86. That view, however, has been advanced. For the view that Galatians conforms to the genre of deliberative rhetoric and is similar to a deliberative speech, see Kennedy, *New Testament Interpretation through Rhetorical Criticism*, 144–46; Smit, "Deliberative Speech," 1–26; Hall, "Rhetorical Outline for Galatians," 29–38.

I find that because Paul's arguments regard an admonition against future action on the part of the Galatians, the letter as a whole conforms more closely to the deliberative species of rhetoric than to judicial or to epideictic. For a good explanation of the three species of rhetoric, judicial, deliberative, and epideictic, see Kennedy, *New Testament Interpretation through Rhetorical Criticism*, 19. In deliberative rhetoric, the author seeks to persuade an audience to take some action in the future. Deliberative rhetoric can take a positive form (as in exhortation) or a negative one (dissuasion). See ibid., 20. In Galatians, Paul works to dissuade his audience from taking a certain course of action.

87. Tod Penner and Davina Lopez remark, "At one level, it matters little whether Paul had formal rhetorical training. His writings that we have, those designated as either 'authentic' or 'deutero-Pauline,' evidence what we might expect: Paul performs the 'art of persuasion,' regardless of whether his 'art' would be judged as 'adequate' or 'superior' by, say, Quintilian or Stanley Fish" ("Rhetorical Approaches," 36–37). And Kennedy comments, "It is not a necessary premise of this study that the evangelists or Saint Paul had formally studied Greek rhetoric. In the case of Paul the evidence is somewhat ambivalent. . . . Even if he had not studied in a Greek school, there were many handbooks of rhetoric in common circulation, which he could have seen. He and the evangelists as well would indeed have been hard put to escape an awareness of rhetoric as practiced in the culture around them, for the rhetorical theory of the schools found its immediate application in almost every form of oral and written communication: in official documents and public letters, in private correspondence, in the law courts and assemblies, in speeches at festivals and commemorations, and in literary composition in both prose and verse" (*New Testament Interpretation through Rhetorical Criticism*, 9–10). For the view that Paul used rhetoric but was not schooled in it, see Classen, "Paul's Epistles and Ancient Rhetoric," 98; Elmer, "Setting the Record Straight," 32; Fairweather, "Galatians and Classical Rhetoric: Part 3," 242.

88. Unless otherwise indicated, I rely on the Loeb Classical Library translator J. H. Vince for Demosthenes' *Philippics*. See Demosthenes, *Olynthiacs, Philippics*. Gesine Manuwald and D. R. Shackleton Bailey are the translators on which I depend for Cicero's *Philippics*. See Manuwald, *Introduction and Texts*; Bailey's Cicero, *Philippics 1–6* and Cicero, *Philippics 7–14*. The translations of units of Paul's letter to the Galatians are my own.

89. Wooten, *Rhetoric of Crisis*, 58.

90. Scholars have recognized polemics in Paul. See Räisänen who writes, "The numerous problems and self-contradictions in his statements expose the overall theory as more or less artificial. It would seem that the difficulties can best be explained if the whole theory owes its origin to a polemical situation" (*Paul and the Law*, 262).

See also Mack, *Rhetoric and the New Testament*, 66; Schütz, *Paul and the Anatomy of Apostolic Authority*, 128.

1

Creating a Sense of Urgency

1. Bailey notes that for Cicero the need for timely action is conveyed by "short, clipped sentences, rhetorical questions, and the repetition of important key words" (Cicero, *Philippics 1–6*, xxxi).

2. Margaret Lee and Bernard Scott write, "A silent reader accepts a printed composition's surface structure as given and so has no need to construct it. The meaning-making project of silent readers focuses on insight into the significations of various words and phrases. Successful interpretation depends on a silent reader's ability to discern relationships among abstract concepts at the level of semantics. . . . In memorial cultures dependent on speech, the dynamics of comprehension differ because they depend on sound. Auditory signals organize a spoken composition's surface instead of visual marks that interpret print" (*Sound Mapping*, 135). See also Ong, *Orality and Literacy*, 56–57.

3. In his monograph *Immanent Art*, John Foley discusses the importance of repetition for oral performance and for the transmission of meaning. Foley remarks that with oral-derived texts, the term "repetition" is really a misnomer and that a better term is "recreation." Each occurrence of a word or expression suggests a re-signification of meaning. See his *Immanent Art*, 56–57. Walter Ong too finds that redundancy is a feature of oral delivery. See *Orality and Literacy*, 40.

4. Lee and Scott describe repetition as "sound's structuring device" (*Sound Mapping*, 135–65).

5. Wooten, *Demosthenes' Philippic I*, 12.

6. See *First Philippic* 34.15–16. I discuss violent *hyperbaton* in detail in chapter two on self-fashioning.

7. Wooten, *Demosthenes' Philippic I*, 13–14.

8. Taddeo, "Signs of Demosthenes in Cicero's *Philippics*," 1–2.

9. Taddeo, "Signs of Demosthenes in Cicero's *Philippics*," 3.

10. Taddeo, "Signs of Demosthenes in Cicero's *Philippics*," 1–2, 3, 6. Taddeo develops the comparison throughout his first chapter. That Cicero borrowed this theme from Demosthenes, see also Wooten, *Rhetoric of Crisis*, 61, 72.

11. Yunis, *Taming Democracy*, 255.

12. Yunis, *Taming Democracy*, 248. See also Buckler, "Demosthenes and Aeschines," 114–58.

13. Yunis, *Taming Democracy*, 260. See also Buckler, "Demosthenes and Aeschines," 114–58.

14. The assembly made up the heart of the democratic system in Athens and consisted of adult males. Six thousand men attended these meetings. Such a size meant that between one- and two-fifths of the citizens came together in one place during those events. Theoretically any one could address the assembly. For more about the constitution of the assembly, see Yunis, *Taming Democracy*, 7–12.

15. Wooten, *Demosthenes' Philippic I*, 41. An orator, who wished to appeal to

the widest possible audience, had to somehow master the ability of combining the complex and the simple. Indeed, according to Lee and Scott, the classical manuals of style advocated a mixture of styles to create interest. Demetrius of Phalerum commented, "Discourse should neither . . . consist wholly of a string of periods, nor be wholly disconnected, but should rather combine the two methods. It will then be elaborate and simple at the same time, and draw charm from both sources, being neither too untutored nor too artificial" (*Eloc.* 15). See *Sound Mapping*, 119.

16. Wooten, *Demosthenes' Philippic I*, 41.

17. Wooten diagrams the first six phrases. See *Demosthenes' Philippic I*, 39.

18. The text and its versification is from Wooten, *Demosthenes' Philippic I*, 19.

19. Translation by Jeremy Trevett in *Demosthenes, Speeches 1–17*, 71.

20. Wooten, *Demosthenes' Philippic I*, 40.

21. For a discussion on how literary compositions created different kinds of music, see Lee and Scott, *Sound Mapping*, 119–20.

22. Wooten, *Demosthenes' Philippic I*, 41.

23. Wooten, *Demosthenes' Philippic I*, 40.

24. According to Galen Rowe, *chiasmus* is "a feature of *isocolon* in which the second of two coordinate clauses reverses the order of the first." *Isocolon* regards two or more successive coordinate clauses that have approximately the same length and form. See "Style," 137.

25. With regard to the important role opponents play in Demosthenes' Philippic orations, see especially Buckler, "Demosthenes and Aeschines," 114–58.

26. Rowe defines *paronomasia* as "a play on words which sound nearly the same but have distinctly different meanings" ("Style," 132).

27. While repetitive sounds shape meaning for hearers, distinctive sounds, especially those found at the start or end of a phrase, draw listeners' attention; they too create emphasis. See Lee and Scott, *Sound Mapping*, 151–55.

28. Demosthenes engages here in *paronomasia*, about which, see n. 26.

29. Wooten, *Demosthenes' Philippic I*, 44.

30. According to Bailey, these are common signs of urgency as found in Cicero. See Cicero, *Philippics 1–6*, xxxi.

31. The writer of the treatise *On the Method of Force* remarked that when a question involves a supposition that cannot be denied, it has one of three different objectives dependent upon its intended audience. If the question is addressed to the listening audience, it implies a rebuke. If the question is addressed to the orator's opponents, it takes the form of a refutation. If, however, the question is addressed to the orator him or herself, then it functions to attract the audience's attention and demonstrate the confidence of the orator. See Wooten, *Demosthenes' Philippic I*, 64.

32. Indeed, Harvey Yunis comments that Demosthenes made his messages purposefully unpleasant for his audience. They were often seen as a bitter pill to swallow. Yet this was the way in which Demosthenes made the situation at hand into one of dire urgency. See *Taming Democracy*, 261.

33. Ronnet, *Étude sur le style de Démosthène*, 21. On this, see also Plutarch, *Demosthenes* 14.3.

34. Mader, "Foresight, Hindsight," 353. According to Wooten, Demosthenes' rebukes are an indication of his anger. Demosthenes frequently resorts to "strong criticism, conveyed by means of provocative comparisons, impatient rhetorical questions, and clauses that are short and choppy . . . the sort of language that angry people use" ("On the Road to *Philippic* III," 17).

35. As Wooten remarks, Demosthenes "praises Philip as a means of reproaching the Athenians for not doing what he has done" (*Demosthenes' Philippic I*, 54).

36. Wooten, *Demosthenes' Philippic I*, 61–62.
37. The text and versification numbering follows Wooten, *Demosthenes' Philippic I*, 22.
38. Translation is by Jeremy Trevett in *Demosthenes, Speeches 1–17*, 73. Quotation marks seen above are found in the Greek text of the Loeb edition of Demosthenes, *Olynthiacs, Philippics*, 74.
39. Wooten, *Demosthenes' Philippic I*, 14.
40. On this point, see Wooten, *Demosthenes' Philippic I*, 65. Wooten is following Dilts's work on the *scholia* in the writings of Demosthenes.
41. Wooten cites M. R. Dilts's *Scholia Demosthenica*, vol. 1. in *Demosthenes' Philippic I*, 64.
42. The expression suggests spontaneity rather than premeditated thought and, as such, it heightens the emotional impact. See Wooten, *Demosthenes' Philippic I*, 64.
43. In his book *Shame and Necessity*, Bernard Williams also draws a connection between these two terms for ancient Greeks. According to Williams, the concept of necessity was not based in a duty itself derived from the notion of morality but rather in a shared cultural experience around the notion of shame. Shame is at base connected with nakedness and the desire to cover it up. Regarding a shame culture, he writes, "The basic experience connected with shame is that of being seen, inappropriately, by the wrong people, in the wrong condition." A basic need of ancients was the avoidance of shame. They feared what people would say about their shameful actions. See *Shame and Necessity*, 75–79.
44. As Cecil Wooten points out, the patterned response to Demosthenes' question, which regards the definition of the present developments, consists of subject and predicate phrases with two nearly identical numbers of syllables (ten and eleven) in each. The phrases are τὴν ὑπὲρ τῶν πραγμάτων αἰσχύνην (subject) and τοῖς ἐλευθέροις μεγίστην ἀνάγκην (predicate; 1.10e). Each of these phrases terminates in a three-syllable word that rhymes (αἰσχύνην, ἀνάγκην). See *Demosthenes' Philippic I*, 64.
45. With regard to the way in which Demosthenes introduces his "villain," Wooten states, there is a "striking juxtaposition of a noun [ἀνήρ, man] and the participles [Μακεδὼν, καταπολεμῶν/Macedonian, waging war] that describe it" (*Demosthenes' Philippic I*, 65).
46. Cicero delivered this speech and the next one, *Philippic Four*, on the same day, 20 December 44. See Bailey in Cicero, *Philippics 1–6*, xxi.
47. Wilfried Stroh called Cicero's *Third Philippic*, "the most important and fateful speech of his life" ("wichtigste und verhängnisvollste Rede seines Lebens"; as quoted in Manuwald, *Commentary*, 295).
48. According to Manuwald, tribunes of the *plebs* could convene meetings of the senate for exceptional purposes. In this instance, some scholars have suspected that those senators hostile to Antony were behind calling this special meeting. Manuwald, however, doubts that Cicero himself was responsible for calling the meeting, as Cicero reported that he was not planning on attending it. See Manuwald, *Commentary*, 297.
49. See Bailey in Cicero, *Philippics 1–6*, 174.
50. For more on this situation, see Manuwald, *Introduction and Texts*, 13. In Cicero's view, Antony's newer legislation was "passed illegally" (ibid.).
51. Manuwald, *Introduction and Texts*, 15.
52. See Bailey in Cicero, *Philippics 1–6*, 174–75. See also Manuwald, *Commentary*, 298–300; Van der Blom, "*Officium* and *Res publica*," 306, 309. D. Brutus was actually

breaking the law but Cicero supported his actions, stating that the situation warranted such measures. In cases such as these, natural law could trump man-made legislation. In explaining Cicero's position, Van der Blom writes, "The statesman works as interpreter of written law and has the insight to fill the gaps in it and even dismiss it when necessary with the help of natural law. In fact, the statesman is obliged to dismiss the written law if the safety of the country and its citizens is threatened, because the duty towards the state is imperative to the statesman" ("*Officium* and *Res publica*," 314).

53. See Manuwald, *Commentary*, 300–301. Cicero makes the case that Antony's allotment of provinces had not been carried out properly. Thus, based on this technicality, he nullifies the prior legislation (see *Phil.* 3.24–26). See ibid., 304. See also Van der Blom, "*Officium* and *Res publica*," 297.

54. On this point, see Wooten, *Rhetoric of Crisis*, 60.

55. Taddeo discusses Cicero's indebtedness to Demosthenes. See "Signs of Demosthenes in Cicero's *Philippics*," 1–31. However, and as Taddeo explains, Cicero does not use the Greek word καιρός (or any Latin equivalent term) but instead borrows on the elements that Demosthenes employed to recreate the same effect (ibid., 4).

56. Manuwald describes Cicero's introductory section (*Phil.* 3.1–2) as a plea for urgency. See *Commentary*, 309.

57. See Manuwald, *Commentary*, 315.

58. Cicero, *Philippics 1–6*, 175–76.

59. The translation is by Manuwald in *Introduction and Texts*, 165.

60. According to Wooten, urgency is especially apparent in the *exordium*. See *Rhetoric of Crisis*, 60.

61. Indeed, Taddeo remarks, "There is hardly a sentence bereft of the idea that the time is critical, that the time for action is now" ("Signs of Demosthenes in Cicero's *Philippics*," 4).

62. Wooten, *Rhetoric of Crisis*, 60.

63. That short phrases are a sign of urgency, see Hall, "The *Philippics*," 299.

64. On this, see Hall, "The *Philippics*," 298. Hall remarks upon the increased use of rhetorical questions over Cicero's other orations. According to Hall, these questions are a sign of the promotion of urgency.

65. Achard, *Pratique Rhétorique et Idéologie Politique dans les Discours "Optimates" de Cicéron*, 504.

66. On this, see Wooten, *Rhetoric of Crisis*, 60.

67. Manuwald, *Commentary*, 319.

68. Julius Caesar reformed the calendar and brought it from 355 to 365 days per year. *Kalends* refers to the first day of the month. Interest was due on the *Kalends*, and birthdays celebrated on the nearest *Kalends* or *Ides* (the middle of the month). The senate often met on the *Kalends* or on the *Ides*. See Rüpke, "Communicating with the Gods," 224.

69. Beginning in 153 BCE, the new consuls began their term of service on this date. This particular January 1 (43) is important because it was the date on which Antony's term of office came to an end. See Manuwald, *Commentary*, 319.

70. On the use of foresight for self-fashioning see Mader, "Foresight, Hindsight," 359–60. While Mader looks at foresight within the *Philippics* of Demosthenes, his insights also apply to Cicero. According to Mader, foresight can only be explained in the context of "competing political agendas of rival groupings" (ibid., 359).

71. On this point, see Manuwald, *Commentary*, 314.

72. Manuwald, *Commentary*, 316.

73. The Republic does, of course, come to an end. Catherine Steel argues that there were signs of its demise already in 146 BCE. She marks the Ides of March (15 March 44 BCE) as the time at which it fell. See *The End of the Roman Republic 146 to 44 BC*, 140–210. And, according to her, the conspirators assassinated Julius Caesar because he intended to establish himself as sole ruler. See ibid., 209. By contrast, von Urgern-Sternberg argues that Augustus finally put an end to the Republic with his military dictatorship, while couching his regime as the "restoration of the traditional Republican political order (*res publica*)" ("The Crisis of the Republic," 95).

Yet it is clear from Cicero's *Third Philippic*, dated to Dec 44, thus after the Ides of March, that he was unaware that the Republic had already fallen, following on Steel's assessment. Cicero did not have the perspective of history. While he argued that the Republic would fall, he still had faith that it would continue and saw Antony as the obstacle for its continuation. Henrietta van der Blom, for example, remarks, "It is obvious that he [Cicero] never lost faith in the republican system, it was only the wickedness of Caesar and afterwards Antony, which prevented politics from working normally. This explains how on the one hand Cicero could exclaim that the *res publica* was non-existent, while on the other that he had put his hopes for the restoration of the *res publica* in Brutus and Cassius" ("*Officium and Res publica*," 299). Thus, Cicero's warning can be understood as an over dramatization of the situation at hand.

74. Donat Taddeo points out that these are the same two alternatives Demosthenes employs with his audience in his fight against Philip. See "Signs of Demosthenes in Cicero's *Philippics*," 17. For more on the common trope, see my chapter four on disjunctive argumentation.

75. For a good interpretation of these sections in Cicero's *Third Philippic*, see Taddeo, "Signs of Demosthenes in Cicero's *Philippics*," 3–26. Taddeo's emphasis is on Cicero's adoption from Demosthenes of a καιρός theme. In his review of Cicero's *Third Philippic*, Taddeo highlights areas in which Cicero is borrowing on the work of Demosthenes.

76. Manuwald refers to the concluding section (*Phil.* 3.28–36) as an appeal to the senate to take immediate action against Antony. See *Commentary*, 309.

77. Translated by Manuwald in *Introduction and Texts*, 185.

78. Manuwald remarks that the use of this phrase suggests a καιρός theme (the right time for action). See *Commentary*, 446.

79. Taddeo sees a parallel to Demosthenes' *Second Olynthiac* (2.2). See his "Signs of Demosthenes in Cicero's *Philippics*," 24–25.

80. Cicero's hatred of Antony was exaggerated and had a lot to do with Cicero himself. I discuss the differences between Cicero and Antony in the Introduction. In my chapter on emotive argumentation, I detail Cicero's use of exaggerated and pejorative epithets for Antony. Henrietta van der Blom summarizes the differences between Antony and Cicero. The two had opposing personalities, values, and political views. Cicero's antagonism against Antony was based on these basic differences. See "*Officium and Res publica*," 295–98. She remarks, "Cicero's contempt for Antony was obvious" (ibid., 301). "His [Cicero's] self-esteem was as much of a factor as his much criticized vanity" (ibid., 316–17). According to her, what spurred Cicero to speak out so boldly against Antony was his direct challenge as well as a changed military situation. See ibid., 295–98. Tom Stevenson discusses the personal stake Cicero had in depicting Antony as a tyrant. He writes, "The *Philippics* . . . can then be read as an ongoing contribution to this discourse between Cicero and his enemies, each accusing the other of being a tyrant" ("Antony as 'Tyrant' in Cicero's First Philippic," 178). And as Robin Seager argues, by turn-

ing Antony into an enemy, he, Cicero, facilitates his own position as "savior" of the republic. See "Ciceronian Invective: Themes and Variations," 33.

81. Cicero, himself, is in part responsible for the Republic's demise. For more on this evaluation, see Tatum, "The Final Crisis (69–44)," 209; Ungern-Sternberg, "The Crisis of the Republic," 95; Steel, *End of the Roman Republic 146 to 44 bc*, 226–53.

82. Henrietta van der Blom remarks, "It is obvious that he [Cicero] never lost faith in the republican system, it was only the wickedness of Caesar and afterwards Antony, which prevented politics from working normally. This explains how on the one hand Cicero could exclaim that the *res publica* was non-existent, while on the other that he had put his hopes for the restoration of the *res publica* in Brutus and Cassius" ("*Officium and Res publica*," 299).

83. Taddeo, "Signs of Demosthenes in Cicero's *Philippics*," 23.

84. The theme of the contrast between freedom (*libertas*) and slavery (*servitute*) is a frequent one within the *Philippics*. See *Phil.* 2.113; 3.19, 29, 32–36; 4.4, 11; 5.6, 21, 42; 6.19; 7.11, 14; 8.12, 29; 10.18–20; 11.3, 21, 24; 12.2, 15; 13.1, 6–7, 15, 47; 14.37. See Manuwald, *Commentary*, 428.

85. Braun, "Stabilisierung und Destabilisierung sozialer Werte in Ciceros Reden," 72. For more on the use of words such as "slavery" and "freedom," see my chapter four on disjunctive argumentation.

86. In his *Second Olynthiac*, Demosthenes leads off by stating how it is clear that the gods have been beneficent to Athens. That men have been found willing to fight against Philip is also seen as work of the gods (1.1). See Taddeo, "Signs of Demosthenes in Cicero's *Philippics*," 22.

87. According to Werner Jaeger, by evoking the gods, Demosthenes is calling his audience to a higher purpose. Jaeger remarked upon the importance of the gods in Demosthenes' arguments that concern urgency or καιρός. He notes, "Any statesman who wishes to guide the Athenians at such a moment . . . is always confronted with one primary task: to impregnate these human beings with their own deeper discernment and to evoke such a unity of purpose as will transform a congeries of aimless, vacillating individuals into a united body of followers. . . . This is what gives rise to Demosthenes' almost surprisingly extensive observations on the gods and the part they play in the present situation. . . . The καιρός too is a religious reality. It is preeminently the sway of a higher power" (*Demosthenes: The Origin and Growth of His Policy*, 129–31).

88. Jörg Rüpke notes that this form of communication with the gods occurred in daily speech, in oratory, or in letters but would not have worked in rituals, as the latter required the invocation of a specific deity. See "Communicating with the Gods," 226.

89. Manuwald, *Commentary*, 429, 446, 448. The expression *per deo immortalis!* occurs frequently within the *Philippics* (*Phil.* 1.20, 29, 38; 2.14, 19, 90; 3.34; 4.9; 5.14, 25, 27, 39; 7.25; 8.23, 29; 10.7, 11; 11.10; 12.7, 13; 13.5; 14.10, 25). It is also a frequent refrain in Demosthenes (*Or.* 1.15, 19, 23; 3.17, 32; 6.13, 14, 23, 31; 8.7, 9, 16, 17, 32, 34, 49, 50; 9.15, 43, 54, 65, 70, 76; 10.7, 17, 20, 24, 26, 50, 73). See *Commentary*, 429.

90. Ungern-Sternberg notes that since the nineteenth century and based on the testimony of Cicero and Sallust as well as on modern problems, it has been common to understand the crisis of the Republic as a struggle between the *optimates* and the *populares*. Antony represented the *populares*, those who favor the people, and Cicero the *optimates*, the aristocrats. See "The Crisis of the Republic," 95.

For more on this see also, Steel, *End of the Roman Republic 146 to 44 bc*, 226–53. See also W. Jeffrey Tatum who attributes the downfall of the Republic to "unrestrained sharp practices by the political elite in their contest for individual domination"

("The Final Crisis (69–44)," 209). In this view, Cicero himself, but unknowingly, plays a role in the Republic's demise.

91. Nanos comments, "He [Paul] cannot get to Galatia to set things straight, but the need is urgent" (*Irony of Galatians*, 1). Observing urgency, Betz remarks, "The situation of the Galatian churches, as the apostle had described it in 1:6–7, calls for his immediate reaction" (*Galatians*, 52).

Thurén rightly senses the rhetorical aspect of Paul's "urgency." According to him, while the letter suggests haste, "nothing in the situation actually indicates that Paul was in too much of a hurry to think before writing" ("Was Paul Angry?" 314).

92. That Paul has his competitors in view, see Betz, *Galatians*, 5, 46; Betz, "The Literary Composition and Function of Paul's Letter to the Galatians," 9; Hall, "Rhetorical Outline for Galatians," 35, 38.

93. White, "Introductory Formulae in the Body of the Pauline Letter," 97. Robert Hall refers to this section as the proposition. He writes, "The purpose of the proposition is to make clear what the letter or speech as a whole wants to prove" ("Rhetorical Outline for Galatians," 35). George Kennedy also regards Gal 1:6–9 as the proposition section. See *New Testament Interpretation through Rhetorical Criticism*, 148. According to Hall and others, Gal 1:6–9 is central for the letter as a whole. See "Rhetorical Outline for Galatians," 35. Betz understands the purpose of Galatians in ways that parallel that of Hall. See *Galatians*, 46; "Literary Composition and Function," 9.

94. See Betz, *Galatians*, 44. Betz may have been following on earlier interpreters of Paul. The sixteenth-century theologian and exegete Philipp Melanchthon considered Gal 1:6–2:21 as the *exordium*. According to him, Paul was driven by his passion to pen Galatians. For more on Melanchthon, see Classen, "Paul and Ancient Greek and Roman Rhetoric," 273.

95. Smit, "Deliberative Speech," 39–59.

96. Note that the Scholar's Version (SV) translation of Paul's letters translates the Greek word εὐαγγέλιον as "world transforming message." See Dewey et al., *The Authentic Letters of Paul*, 21, 205–6 passim.

97. The translation is my own.

98. Smit, "Deliberative Speech," 46.

99. Demosthenes employs this expression in several of his Philippic-cycle speeches before the Athenian assembly (*Second Olynthiac* 23, 24, 25; *Third Olynthiac* 19, 32; *First Philippic* 43; *Second Philippic* 6; *Fourth Philippic* 34, 71). See Preuss, *Index Demosthenicus*, 147. This term also appears in Antiphon, Lysias, Plato *Apol.* 17A, 24A; *Crito* 50C and Isocrates *Ep.* 2.19; 9.8. See Betz, *Galatians*, 47 n. 39.

100. As Betz remarks, Martin Luther in his 1535 commentary on Galatians noticed the artificiality of the rebuke. See *Galatians*, 47 n. 38.

101. According to Nanos, Paul is employing "ironic rebuke." He calls vv. 6–7 "intimidating ironic rebuke." In ancient usage irony referred to, among other things, "saying the opposite of what one means." Irony creates and brings to light a tension between what seems to be the case and what is the case. In this passage, Paul is less "surprised" than he is "disappointed" (*Irony of Galatians*, 41, 45). Nanos' assessment of how best to understand θαυμάζω in this passage is in line with the view of Nils Dahl in "Paul's Letter to the Galatians," 117–30.

Troy Martin, however, argues that in Gal 1:6–7 there is neither irony nor rebuke. Following Cornelius Lapide's and Henrich Schott's 1876 commentary on Galatians, Martin claims that the θαυμάζω in Gal 1:6 is the second half or apodosis of the conditional phrase that begins with the εἰ μή in v. 7. This means that θαυμάζω is conditioned by the protasis of v.7, and that Paul would only have been surprised if there were no agitators. As it is, however, there are agitators. According to Martin, Paul is not surprised by the actions of the Galatians but instead shifts the blame to the agitators. See "Syntax of Surprise," 79–98.

102. John White, on the other hand, notes that the use of this verb for astonishment in the letter's opening is formulaic. According to White, with his θαυμάζω, Paul conveys "dissatisfaction and an intimation that communication has broken down" ("Introductory Formulae," 96).

I find that Paul is being intentionally dramatic to get the audience's attention. With θαυμάζω, he is generating urgency.

103. In its present context, μετατίθεσθε is a second-person plural middle indicative verb. Its root sense is to "place differently" (ΛΟΓΕΙΟΝ, "μετατίθημι," accessed April 17, 2015, http://logeion.uchicago.edu/index.html#μετατίθεσθε).

104. Betz, *Galatians*, 44. The NRSV provides the same translation as Betz. Similarly, Nanos translates μετατίθεσθε as "defecting." See *Irony of Galatians*, 32.

105. Paul states, "you are . . . changing from the one who called you in the grace of the Anointed." The "one who called" (καλέσαντος) the Galatians could be either God or Paul himself. Paul was likely referring to God. See Betz, *Galatians*, 48.

106. Sounds that occur at both the beginning and ending of units receive special emphasis. See Lee and Scott, *Sound Mapping*, 151.

107. Interestingly, Betz remarks that the expression οὕτως ταχέως ("so quickly") is "rhetorical in origin." Yet he quickly veers away from this insight. See *Galatians*, 47. The expression is readily understandable in the context of urgency. Yet see Thurén who argues that this expression is rhetorical and indicates a development of a sense of haste. See his *Derhetorizing Paul*, 64–65.

108. As Lee and Scott explain, "Cacophony refers to unpleasant sounds or a displeasing overall auditory effect"; and it makes a "stronger impression than aurally nondescript or unrepeated sounds" (*Sound Mapping*, 178).

109. That Paul's use of time words is rhetorical and serve to give the impression of haste or urgency. See Thurén, *Derhetorizing Paul*, 64–65.

110. The vagueness with which Paul raises the subject of the good news coheres with the rhetoric-of-crisis model. With regard to Cicero's strategy, Manuwald remarks, "the issue is discussed without its difficult aspects being clarified; the decisive points with regard to the orator's argument are neither proved nor refuted" (*Introduction and Texts*, 110).

111. Nanos astutely notes, "Paul ironically undermines the good that is present in the label 'good news,' granting this other message a standing 'as though' equal to that of '*the* good news *of Christ*' when it is, by his reckoning, instead directly opposed to that news and thus should be regarded oppositely. It is *bad* news, worthy of anathema" (*Irony of Galatians*, 53; italics are the author's).

112. With regard to Paul, Thurén remarks that the text "does not indicate that Paul saw any dramatic difference in the practical life between the two versions of Christianity in Galatia" (*Derhetorizing Paul*, 72).

113. Similarly, in his *De corona*, Demosthenes prays to the gods and wishes harm to his enemies with a curse formula. He writes, "I pray to all the gods that they refuse assent to this desire but rather implant in these men a better mind and a better spirit; if they are beyond cure may they, and they alone, be quickly and utterly destroyed (ἐξώλεις καὶ προώλεις), wherever they might be, and may the rest of us be granted swift release and safe security from the terrors which hang over us" (*Cor.* 18.324). Translated by John J. Keaney in Demosthenes, *Demosthenes' On the Crown*, 124.

114. Nanos remarks, "This is the time not for another rational argument, although such an appeal will likely be made as well, but for the emotions to be engaged" (*Irony of Galatians*, 61).

115. They are intended to convey strong emotion. See Rowe, "Style," 143.

116. Classen writes, "the repetition of the curse gives the whole an element of agitation and excitement" ("Paul's Epistles and Ancient Rhetoric," 106).

117. While Paul begins by rebuking his Galatian audience, he reserves his deeper animosity for his opponents, those troubling the Galatians (1:7b). On this point, see Dahl, "Paul's Letter to the Galatians," 128. See also William Walker, who comments that in general Paul's tenor with regard to his opponents is "scathing" ("Does the 'We' Include Paul's Opponents?" 564).

118. Betz, *Galatians*, 45. The first-century BCE work *Rhetorica ad Herennium* defines demagoguery as follows: "From the discussion of the person of our adversaries we shall secure goodwill by bringing them into hatred, unpopularity, or contempt. We shall force hatred upon them by adducing some base, highhanded treacherous, cruel, impudent, malicious, or shameful act of theirs. We shall make our adversaries unpopular by setting forth their violent behaviour, their dominance, factiousness, wealth, lack of self-restraint, high birth, clients, hospitality, club allegiance, or marriage alliances and by making clear that they rely more upon these supports than upon the truth. We shall bring our adversaries into contempt by presenting their idleness, cowardice, sloth, and luxurious habits" (*Rhet. ad Her.* 1.5.8). As translated by Betz in *Galatians*, 45 n. 15.

119. As Lee and Scott remark, the New Testament as well as all other ancient writings originated as speech. "Compositions read aloud are declaimed breath by breath. As composition's basic breath unit, the colon [a breath unit] serves as composition's structural foundation. Displaying compositions in colometric form simulates their breath-by-breath delivery and allows their structural outlines to emerge" (*Sound Mapping*, 136).

120. Betz, *Galatians*, 47.

121. Betz translates ταράσσοντες as those "who disturb." Betz understands this word to be a political one. See *Galatians*, 49. William Walker translates ταράσσοντες as those who are "confusing" the Galatians. See "Does the 'We' Include Paul's Opponents?" 564.

122. The NRSV strengthens the sense of this aorist infinitive verb and gives it the meaning "pervert."

123. For ancients, mixing rhetorical methods, employing some prepared logic, some emotional appeal, and some examples from nature created more credibility and not less. In mixing his methods of persuasion, Paul demonstrates that he is writing to convince. See Cronjé, "Defamiliarization," 226.

124. Smit remarks that Gal 3:1 begins the *confirmatio*, the place in the speech in which the author "supports his position with arguments." See "Deliberative Speech," 49. Betz calls this section the beginning of the *probatio*, the presentation of proofs. While the names differ, their intended purposes are similar (*Galatians*, 137).

125. Classen, too, logically connects Gal 1:6–9 and 3:1–5. According to him, in Gal 1:6–9 Paul establishes the situation of the Galatians, that certain persons have turned them away from the true gospel. Paul readdresses this same subject in 3:1–5. Paul is "emphasizing the immediate relevance for them [the Galatians] of the preceding arguments." See "Paul's Epistles and Ancient Rhetoric," 108. Dahl connects the two units on the basis of rebuke. He argues that Gal 1:6–9 is in the form of ironic rebuke, which in turn is "restated in the form of ironic and rebuking questions" in 3:1–5. See "Paul's Letter to the Galatians," 132.

126. The translation is my own.

127. Rowe, "Style," 145.

128. Paul or his scribe may have been unaware that he was using *metabasis*.

129. Classen, "Paul's Epistles and Ancient Rhetoric," 108. See also Nanos, who finds ironic rebuke in Gal 3:1–5; *Irony of Galatians*, 43–44 passim. So too does Dahl, "Paul's Letter to the Galatians," 126, 132 passim.

130. Betz comments that the unit beginning at 3:1 is no longer friendly but is instead "biting and aggressive" (*Galatians*, 130). According to Nanos, Paul is holding the Galatians accountable for their actions. "Paul expected more of them" (*Irony of Galatians*, 45). I am looking at the role that Paul's anger is intended to play on his audience.

131. The noun ἀνόητος means "not thought on," "unheard of," "senseless," or "silly." In an active sense, which is what we find here, it means "not understanding," "unintelligent" (ΛΟΓΕΙΟΝ, "ἀνόητοι," accessed April 18, 2015, http://logeion.uchicago.edu/index.html#ἀνόητοι).

The NRSV and Betz translate the word as "foolish." Nils Dahl finds that with this term, Paul is calling the Galatians "barbarians" ("Paul's Letter to the Galatians," 123). Aristotle (*Rhet.* 1.10.4/1368b) defines such a person as having "mistaken ideas of right and wrong (δίκαιον καὶ ἄδικον)."

132. Paul asks each question so as to elicit his intended response. On this, see Cronjé, "Defamiliarization," 218–19.

133. According to Dahl each question also carries a note of irony. Paul engages here in ironic rebuke ("Paul's Letter to the Galatians," 126–27). For instances of ironic rebuke in Galatians, see especially Nanos, *Irony of Galatians*, 32–61. Nanos finds irony in Gal 1:13–16, 23–24; 2:2, 6–9, 14–18; 3:1–5, 10–14; 4:8–20, 21–31; 5:1–4, 11–12, 23; 6:3–5, 7–10, 11, 12–13, 14. See ibid., 38.

134. Many Pauline interpreters comment on the presence of anger in Galatians. To name just a few, see Harris, *The New Testament*, 339. J. Louis Martyn remarks, "To read this letter is to be involved in high drama, for one senses between Paul and the Galatians both deep affection and angry tension" (*Galatians*, 13). In her recent book *Revelations*, Elaine Pagels writes, "Paul had sent a blunt and angry letter about a dispute with Peter to believers in the city of Galatia, in Asia Minor" (*Revelations*, 56). See also Scott, *The Real Paul*, 19.

By contrast, Thurén reads Paul's passionate statements with suspicion. As he comments, one cannot know with certainty whether or not Paul was actually angry. See "Was Paul Angry?" 317.

I am interested here in the role Paul's anger is intended to play on his audience. I find that he employs anger as an additional means of persuasion to gain acceptance for his views over and against those of his competitors.

135. Cronjé, "Defamiliarization," 219.

136. That Paul dramatizes his current situation to force the Galatians to choose between alternative positions, see Thurén, "Was Paul Angry?" 317. Paul sets up oppositions with these questions and then returns to those same topics later on. Abraham, for example, is a witness to the faith/trust and what is heard (3:2b, 5), as seen in Gal 3:6–14. Paul reprises the larger topic of the qualitative difference between works of Torah and faithfulness/trust (3:2b, 5) elsewhere (see 3:15–18, 23–26; 4:1–7, 21–5:1; 5:2–6). On this point, see also Classen, "Paul's Epistles and Ancient Rhetoric," 108.

137. There is controversy over how best to interpret this phrase. The SV translators write, "Surely it meant something!" (Dewey et al., *The Authentic Letters of Paul*, 55). Betz remarks that the verse has been read either as an encouragement, as the SV translators take it, or as a threat. See *Galatians*, 135 n. 69.

138. Betz writes, "Paul acts as if he is at the end of his wits" (*Galatians*, 134). Galen Rowe sees in this phrase a form of *dubitatio*, a type of *aporia*, in which the author feigns uncertainty. See "Style," 140.

139. Lee and Scott, *Sound Mapping*, 118.

140. Regarding the negative influence of the opponents, Nanos interprets, "Paul attributes this 'affect' [of the evil eye] to their having had their own eyes wrongly aimed; instead of looking to the crucified Christ for their identification, they have looked to the influencers instead" (*Irony of Galatians*, 54).

141. See Walker, "Does the 'We' Include Paul's Opponents?" 564.

142. On this, see Thurén, "Was Paul Angry?" 317.

143. According to Betz, the section is marked by exhortation and *parenesis* (*Galatians*, 253). Martyn also calls Gal 5:2–12 an exhortation. See his *Galatians*, 468. Nanos remarks that Gal 5:2–18 functions simply as *parenesis*. See *Irony of Galatians*, 72.

144. Smit raises the question of whether or not Gal 5:13–6:10 is a later addition to the letter. According to him, the structure and line of thought are clearer without this section. See "Deliberative Speech," 58–59.

145. Smit views Gal 5:1 as the first summing up of the section defined by 4:21–31 and Gal 5:2–6 as the second summing up. See "Deliberative Speech," 52–53.

146. In Gal 5:2–12 Paul declares the consequences of the Galatians' actions should they take up the recommendation of these others. Martyn notes a logical break at 5:2 and not 5:1, as does Betz. See Martyn, *Galatians*, 478. According to Nanos, a new section begins with Gal 5:2. See *Irony of Galatians*, 72.

147. The translation is my own.

148. From the verb for seeing εἶδον, "I see."

149. According to Lee and Scott, sounds that occur at the beginning or end or a sound group receive special attention. They receive attention because their placement helps to define the sound group itself, its structure. The structure is what orients the listener to the speech. When the sound is repeated, as it is in the case of σθε, it cues the audience to what to listen for. In other words, the repeated sounds are where the author intends emphasis and attention. See their *Sound Mapping*, 151–52.

150. Martyn comments that in the section defined by Gal 5:2–12, circumcision occurs five times, which indicates to him (Martyn) that Paul is thinking very "concretely" about the present situation of the Galatians. See *Galatians*, 469.

151. On the construction of difference, see Räisänen, *Paul and the Law*, 200.

152. In *Paul and Palestinian Judaism*, Sanders made indefensible the notion that Jews employed the Torah to become righteous. See also Räisänen, *Paul and the Law*, 178.

153. Martyn remarks that Paul's comment that circumcision obligates one "to perform the entire Torah" (5:3b) makes sense in the context of a polemical statement against Paul's opponents. See *Galatians*, 470–71.

154. Brigitte Kahl remarks that the issue of circumcision is central to the letter as a whole. She comments, "Nobody would question that circumcision is the most burning problem of Galatians" ("No Longer Male," 40).

155. Paul's discussion of circumcision is very unlike that of his contemporary Jew Philo of Alexandria. Philo was genuinely interested in the physical practice of circumcision and encouraged it among Jews. Unlike Paul, who appears to be unconcerned about the physicality of circumcision itself, Philo details a list of circumcision's benefits. See *On the Special Laws* 1.4–10, *Questions and Answers on Genesis* 3.46–52, and *On the Migration of Abraham* 89–93.

156. Betz, *Galatians*, 258.

157. J. Louis Martyn writes, "Paul compels the Galatians to turn their attention from the voice of scripture in 4:21–5:1 (emphatically in 4:30) to his own voice, that of an apostle" (*Galatians*, 469).

158. In contrast to how I am arguing here, Martyn notes that with his "I, Paul," Paul is using language of "testifying." Paul is functioning as a "pedagogical witness." He is supplying the Galatians with information that has been denied to them by the teachers. See Martyn, *Galatians*, 469.

159. "By means of the emphatic pronoun 'we,' Paul draws a strong contrast between those Galatians who, undergoing circumcision, are leaving the gracious realm of Christ (v. 4), and those who, with himself, remain in Christ (vv. 5–6), thus being linked with the Spirit, with faith, and with hope" (Martyn, *Galatians*, 472).

160. There is a large body of secondary literature on this term. Several Pauline scholars understand it as shorthand for being fully Jewish, converted to Judaism. See Nanos, *Irony of Galatians*, 95; Williams, *Galatians*, 136–37; Tyson, "'Works of Law' in Galatians," 428.

161. Betz, *Galatians*, 261.

162. Betz, *Galatians*, 260. In his commentary on Galatians, J. Louis Martyn remarks that Paul is referring to the "plural law" and likely to the obligation that gentiles would have, once they embark on Torah observance. See *Galatians*, 470.

163. Livesey, *Circumcision as a Malleable Symbol*, 89–90 n. 37.

164. By contrast, Betz posits that the Galatians knew just what they would be getting into by observing the whole Torah (*Galatians*, 261).

165. See Tod Penner and Davina Lopez, who remark, "Most scholars of Pauline literature, for example, are invested in constructing 'real' history and belief systems in and behind the texts we possess" ("Rhetorical Approaches," 41). Yet, as they explain, "The character of 'facts' and 'truth' is always inherently rhetorical, and, while they are useful within various social-historical contexts to differing persuasive ends, 'facts' and 'truth' are ultimately tropes that have to be contextualized within wider systems of meaning-making in order to be more fully understood" (ibid., 40). They go on to explain, "In the ancient world, 'truth' and 'facts' were contingent upon the argumentative aims to be achieved, which may be difficult to accept in a culture like ours that is ostensibly committed to 'truth' and 'facts,' as essential elements in determining what kind of rhetoric is 'good.' 'Truth' was a malleable concept for the ancients."

166. Penner and Lopez remark, "There is no place outside of rhetoric in Paul's letters" ("Rhetorical Approaches," 37).

2

Persuading through the Promotion of Self

1. May, *Trials of Character*, 1.

2. Translation is by Freese in Aristotle, *The 'Art' of Rhetoric*, 17.

3. LSJ 766. Kennedy remarks, "Ethos means 'character' and may be defined as the credibility that the author or speaker is able to establish in his work" (*New Testament Interpretation through Rhetorical Criticism*, 15).

4. There is no getting around the importance of the influence of what moderns call "performance" for rhetorical strategy. Manuwald appears to accord it a category unto itself. She writes, "A convincing and engaging delivery, which relies on all available informational, text linguistic, stylistic, aesthetic and paralinguistic

phenomena, is obviously another essential element of an effective rhetorical strategy" (*Introduction and Texts*, 113).

5. The eighteenth-century French naturalist Georges-Louis LeClerc Buffon writes, "le style est l'homme même" ("the style is the man [sic] himself"; as quoted in Wooten, *Rhetoric of Crisis*, 20).

6. For this same view, see Lyons, *Pauline Biography*, 27.

7. May, *Trials of Character*, 6. See also Rosenstein, "Aristocratic Values," 365–82, especially 369.

8. May, *Trials of Character*, 6–9.

9. May, *Trials of Character*, 6–10. See also Rosenstein, "Aristocratic Values," 370–71.

10. May, *Trials of Character*, 9–10.

11. In his *Pauline Biography*, Lyons comments, "To be persuasive the speaker must first persuade his audience to trust him" (*Pauline Biography*, 27).

12. I write this chapter in the midst of the recent suspension of NBC Nightly News anchorman Brian Williams. Why was he suspended? He lied about his experience in Iraq and the network feared that the public would no longer trust what he said. See Steel and Somaiya, "Brian Williams Suspended for 6 Months without Pay," *New York Times* (2/11/2015): nytimes.com/2015/02/11/business/media/brian-williams-suspended-by-nbc-news-for-six-months.html.

13. Carlier, "Démosthène par lui-même," 47. And Lyons remarks that it would have been common sense to render an autobiography as inoffensive as possible. See his *Pauline Biography*, 7.

14. Lyons, *Pauline Biography*, 68.

15. Lyons, *Pauline Biography*, 30.

16. Lyons, *Pauline Biography*, 29.

17. Stevenson argues that the main reason Cicero depicts Antony as a tyrant is to present himself as the good or worthy alternative, as the "father of the country." He writes, "They [the *Philippics*] condemn Antony as a tyrant in terms which highlight Cicero's claim to the position of *Pater* (*Parens*) *Patriae*" ("Tyrants, Kings and Fathers in the *Philippics*," 110).

18. Mader, "Foresight, Hindsight," 341. Demosthenes engages in considerable self-fashioning in his most well known speech, *De Corona* (On the Crown). In that speech, he engages in self-promotion and at the same time demeans his primary political opponent Aeschines. He issues invectives against Aeschines (18.122–31), and depicts Aeschines as treacherous (18.132–59), before providing a positive assessment of his own leadership (18.227–51, 297–305) and trustworthiness (18.276–96). Just prior to the speech's close, Demosthenes recaps a comparison between the two leaders (18.306–23). For an outline of the entire speech, see Yunis, *Demosthenes, Speeches 18 and 19*, 30–31.

19. Mader remarks that the creation of his ideal self-image was for "maximum public and political effect" ("Foresight, Hindsight," 343).

20. Yunis writes, "The Athenians only reluctantly embraced Demosthenes' harsh view of Philip and only gradually decided to adopt his advice. Though no longer new to the speaker's platform, when he delivered the earliest (published) speech on Philip (Dem. 4 in 351), he was still a young politician and had little effect on Athenian policy" (*Taming Democracy*, 258).

21. The translation is by Vince in Demosthenes, *Olynthiacs, Philippics*, 139, 141.

22. Rowe notes that ornamentation, aspects such as "strength, polish, acuity, abundance, gaiety, delight, precision, variety, and clarity" function to "please the listeners, thus making them attentive and disposed to believe the speaker" ("Style," 124).

23. Cited from Hermogenes, *Hermogenes' On Types of Style*, 3.

24. Cited from Hermogenes, *Hermogenes' On Types of Style*, 5.

25. Wooten, *Rhetoric of Crisis*, 22.

26. Wooten comments, "He [Demosthenes] controls the style; the style does not control him" (*Rhetoric of Crisis*, 29).

27. In his polemical writings, Demosthenes does not divulge the identity of those he attacks. See Weil, *Les Harangues de Démosthène*, 233 n. 3.

28. Demosthenes is alluding to Aeschines and Philocrates. See Demosthenes, *Olynthiacs, Philippics*, 140 n. a. On this, see also Sandys, *Demosthenes: Texts and Notes*, xxxii.

29. Regarding periodic style, Wooten remarks that they combine several thoughts into one independent sentence and that their hallmark is subordination. "The period is so constructed that the various ideas that make up the sentence are 'rounded off' at the end into a complete thought" (*Rhetoric of Crisis*, 33). For more on periodic style, see Lee and Scott, *Sound Mapping*, 171.

30. There are three different types of long periods. The first is an analytic type in which the main point is stated at the start and the ramifications of it follow. The second is just the reverse: subordinate clauses come at the start and the main clause comes at the end. This type builds suspense. The third kind is called a "logical" period. Here, clauses that set the stage for the main idea or principal clause come first, followed by the main clause, and actions and/or ideas that logically proceed from the main clause come at the end. See Wooten, *Rhetoric of Crisis*, 34–36.

31. Wooten, *Demosthenes' Philippic I*, 135. See also Sandys, *Demosthenes: Texts and Notes*, 135.

32. Wooten, *Demosthenes' Philippic I*, 135.

33. Elsewhere, Wooten remarks that Demosthenes seeks to be clear but not trite or commonplace. See *Rhetoric of Crisis*, 25.

34. Wooten, *Demosthenes' Philippic I*, 135.

35. The λέγοντας resolves the τοὺς (2.29d). See Weil, *Les Harangues de Démosthène*, 232 n. 12.

36. Yunis writes, "Demosthenes speaks as any competent *rhētōr* must, as an expert in foreign affairs" (*Taming Democracy*, 259).

37. Wooten, *Rhetoric of Crisis*, 38.

38. Lyons delineates four primary *topoi* of ancient autobiographers: 1) a treatment of the author's ancestry, 2) a discussion of the author's upbringing including education and profession, 3) a presentation of actions to demonstrate moral character, and 4) a comparison between the author and other exemplary persons often for the purpose of imitation. See *Pauline Biography*, 28, 61.

39. "Démosthène utilise fréquemment le première personne, mais pour dire ce qu'il voit, ce qu'il sait, ce qu'il craint, ce qu'il propose, non pour raconter sa vie." ("Demosthenes often employs the first person, but to say what he sees, what he knows, what he fears, what he proposes, not to recount his life.") See Carlier, "Démosthène par lui-même," 50. Rhetorically, this is an instance of *sermocinatio*, defined as "the creation (not quotation) of statements, conversations, soliloquies, or unexpressed thoughts attributed to normal persons, real or imagined." On this see Rowe, "Style," 144.

40. Taddeo remarks, "Demosthenes' purpose is to associate himself with the interests of the citizens in general." This is one of the ways in which Demosthenes self-fashions. See "Signs of Demosthenes in Cicero's *Philippics*," 50.

41. Rowe, "Style," 139.

42. Sandys comments that Demosthenes employs the exact wording Aeschines employed to describe him. See *Demosthenes: Texts and Notes*, 135.

43. This is the rhetorical payoff of *parrhesia*. See Rowe, "Style," 139.

44. Demosthenes' admission is also a form of *synchoresis*, described as "an admission of the truth of an opponent's argument, which is subsequently shown to have no damaging effect" (Rowe, "Style," 147). Indeed, John Buckler infers that there may have been truth to the original accusation. He remarks that both Demosthenes and Aeschines were "mean, meretricious and scurrilous" ("Demosthenes and Aeschines," 115).

45. Mader, "Foresight, Hindsight," 353.

46. Mader, "Foresight, Hindsight," 359.

47. In addition to foresight (*pronoia*), he employs *parrhesia* (frank or candid speech), and *agathos polites* (being a good citizen). See Mader, "Foresight, Hindsight," 359.

48. Mader remarks, "Demosthenes' . . . emphasis on foresight can be explained only in the context of the competing political agendas of rival groupings" ("Foresight, Hindsight," 359).

49. As Bailey remarks, the speech ends with a "note of expectation, rather than on a celebration of a great victory." The great victory only became known in Rome a week after this speech was delivered. The sense of expectation agrees in character with how Demosthenes ends his Philippic-cycle of speeches. See Cicero, *Philippics 1–6*, xxi.

50. According to Wooten and King, there is evidence that Cicero wrote other Philippic speeches. King writes that Arusianus quotes two small fragments of what looks to be a *Sixteenth Philippic* of Cicero. See King, *Cicero: Philippic Orations*, 319. See also Wooten, *Rhetoric of Crisis*, 164.

51. Once the news of Antony's defeat at Mutina reached Rome, the senate declared him a public enemy, yet prior to that time, the senate had hesitated to do so. See Cicero, *Philippics 1–6*, lxvii; King, *Cicero: Philippic Orations*, 323, n. 3–4.

52. May, *Trials of Character*, 11.

53. King explains that once Pansa left on his campaign against Antony, Cicero was left alone and practically in charge of the affairs in Rome. It was at this point that his political opponents in the senate spread a rumor that he (Cicero) planned to take over as dictator. See *Cicero: Philippic Orations*, 317.

54. The injury is the false rumor that Cicero planned to seize power.

55. Bailey remarks that the statement means to say, "Is it not 'bad enough' that he was denied a recognition of his worth" (Cicero, *Philippics 7–14*, 305 n. 11).

56. This was Rome's birthday, celebrated on 21 April. See Bailey in Cicero, *Philippics 7–14*, 306 n. 12.

57. The symbol of Roman imperial power; by carrying this, Cicero would have effectively declared himself dictator. See Bailey in Cicero, *Philippics 7–14*, 306 n. 13.

58. Translated by Bailey in Cicero, *Philippics 7–14*, 305, 307.

59. May, *Trials of Character*, 2.

60. As May comments, "ethical narrative" would often function as the speech's proof. See *Trials of Character*, 9.

61. According to Taddeo, like Demosthenes, in his self-fashioning Cicero too presents himself as working for the best interest of the nation. See "Signs of Demosthenes in Cicero's *Philippics*," 50–52.

62. On this point, see King in Cicero, *The Fourteen Philippic Orations of Marcus Tullius Cicero*, 326 n. 7.

63. For the definition of *enargeia*, see Rowe, "Style," 143.

64. Bailey remarks that Cicero compares the rejoicing to an *ovatio*, which is a triumphal procession of lesser importance than a triumph. See Cicero, *Philippics 7–14*, 304, n. 10. However, with the expression *prope triumphantem*, Cicero makes

explicit his desire to draw a comparison between the events that honored him and a true military triumph. For the triumph's important role in establishing Roman imperial values, see Karl-J. Hölkeskamp. He remarks, "The most spectacular procession . . . was of course the triumph—the venerable entry of the victorious general and his army into the city. . . . At its center stood, on the one hand, the victorious magistrate and general himself, who could personally lay claim to the victory as the holder of imperium and the power to take the auspices . . . , and on the other, the deed itself—a deed for the *res publica*, its greatness (*maiestas*) and imperial power" ("History and Collective Memory," 483). For more on the significance of the triumph, see also Rosenstein, "Aristocratic Values," 370.

65. Here, Cicero engages in a form of *sermocinatio*. See my note 39 above.

66. John Patterson remarks that the "quest for glory" was played out in the public; it required a public setting. See Patterson, *Political Life in the City of Rome*, 52.

67. Jill Harries comments, "The emphasis on the size of the meeting and the unanimity of the opinions expressed by its applause in this, the published version of the speech, is designed to reinforce the legitimacy of Cicero's stance" (*Cicero and the Jurists*, 220).

68. "Cicero thinks he may hear the word 'self-praise' from his audience, and replies that generally he is not boastful, but in political life one may come across such want of judgment that it is necessary to clear up things" (Frisch, *Cicero's Fight for the Republic*, 284).

69. See Rowe, "Style," 144. For a fuller discussion of *prosopopoeia* or speech-in-character including Paul's use of it, see Stowers, *Rereading of Romans*, 16–21.

70. This is a prime example of Lyons's comment cited above and repeated here. "In antiquity the cultural ideal of the magnanimous man who never discussed himself came inevitably into conflict with the irrepressible impertinence of the lately self-conscious man who found it imperative to do so" (*Pauline Biography*, 68).

71. Rowe, "Style," 139.

72. Bailey posits that the main source of the false rumor is Calenus, Antony's agent and procurator in Rome. See Cicero, *Philippics 7–14*, 308 n. 17. In a subsequent section of this speech, Cicero provides more details surrounding this rumor circulating against him. He claims there that it is based on a faulty report from Mutina, "traitorous fellow citizens" (*impii cives*) gathered and hatched a plot to murder him and take control themselves. These others would create public hate and distrust of Cicero by stating that Cicero himself planned to assume the role of dictator. His trusted friend and a tribune of the plebs, Publius Apuleius, let Cicero in on this plot against him (*Phil.* 14.15–16).

73. Cicero is sharply focused and his confrontational style includes sarcasm. See Hall, "The *Philippics*," 299.

74. The string of questions is a form of *aitiologia*, an imaginary dialogue in the form of questions. For this definition, see Rowe, "Style," 140.

75. See Stevenson, who observes a similar tactic in Cicero's depiction of Antony as a tyrant. According to him, Cicero's condemnation of Antony as a tyrant also functioned to highlight himself (Cicero) as Antony's polar opposite. See his "Tyrants, Kings and Fathers," 96.

76. For a brief history of Catiline and the Catiline conspiracy, see Steel, *The End of the Roman Republic 146 to 44 BC*, 150–58. See also W. Jeffrey Tatum, who explains that Catiline turned to conspiracy after his second defeat for consulship. See "The Final Crisis (69–44)," 193–97.

77. Cicero fashioned Antony as the "new Catiline." See Harries, *Cicero and the Jurists*, 204. Cicero was very much against Catiline, whom he considered to be a "revolutionary villain." Cicero referred to Antony as a Catiline at the beginning

of his sustained attack against him (*Phil.* 2.1, 118) and then returned to this theme both here (4.14) and elsewhere (*Phil.* 8.15; 13.22; 14.14). See also Van der Blom, "*Officium* and *Res publica*," 303.

78. While in the present passage Cicero does not engage in foresight, in his exploration of the influence of Demosthenes on Cicero's *Philippics*, Donat Taddeo comments that Cicero borrows the technique from Demosthenes and that it is prevalent in his writings, and especially in his *Second Philippic*. Both orators use it to advance their own self-image. See "Signs of Demosthenes in Cicero's *Philippics*," 57–58.

79. Both Demosthenes and Cicero align their own "good" policies and principles with those of the state. Their opponents are by default against the betterment of the state. "This," writes Taddeo, "is the ultimate justification for the policies which each has advocated in his public life; implicitly, it is the most damning of indictments against their opponents. For in opposing Demosthenes and Cicero, they are opposing the very life-spirit of Athens and Rome" ("Signs of Demosthenes in Cicero's *Philippics*," 57).

80. The SV lays out two possible rhetorical outlines for Galatians, one for judicial and the other for deliberative rhetoric. See Dewey et al., *The Authentic Letters of Paul*, 161–62. While I am not strictly following one outline or the other, if asked to choose between the two, I would categorize Galatians as deliberative rhetoric. These two categories, however, are not terribly significant for my arguments, as I am dealing with specific units and not making an argument about the overall category of rhetoric Paul employs in Galatians. For the view that Galatians is a form of deliberative rhetoric, see Hall, "Rhetorical Outline for Galatians," 38.

81. Betz calls the salutation in Galatians an "epistolary prescript" (*Galatians*, 37).

82. For the view that Gal 1:10–2:21 is an autobiographical section, see Lyons, *Pauline Biography*, 130. Section Gal 1:10–6:10 has also been considered as the "proof" section of the letter, with the shorter section (1:10–2:21) called the "narration." For this view, see Kennedy, *New Testament Interpretation through Rhetorical Criticism*, 150. See also Dewey et al., *The Authentic Letters of Paul*, 162, under the heading "Deliberative."

83. "Paul thus projects the image of himself that is deemed appropriate to the argumentative ends he seeks to achieve" (Penner and Lopez, "Rhetorical Approaches," 41). Lyons puts Paul's purpose in his autobiographical sections as follows: "He [Paul] is establishing his ethos as a means of promoting confidence in himself and the gospel he represents to dispose his readers favorably toward his argumentation, and to present himself as a model for them to imitate" (*Pauline Biography*, 173). While I agree with Lyons regarding Paul's argumentation from ethos as a means of promoting confidence in himself, I disagree that Paul is also about urging his audience to imitate him. Beverly Gaventa follows on Lyons and also argues that in Galatians Paul is coaxing the Galatians to imitate him. See her "Autobiography as Paradigm," 313, 319.

84. Some Pauline scholars adopt the view that Paul responds to specific allegations against him made by his opponents. Lyons reviews the scholarship on this issue. See Lyons, *Pauline Biography*, 78–112. In his Galatians commentary, J. Louis Martyn, for example, lays out a point-by-point summary of the opponents' positions. See *Galatians*, 120–26. I do not hold to this view. I understand Paul to be controlling his arguments and guiding the Galatians in the direction in which he wishes them to go. Paul is not defensive but instead offensive. See Johan Vos, who comments, "Paul's self-presentation in Gal 1:1 is the starting point not of

a defensive but of an offensive sort of argument: he first strengthened his position as an envoy of God before he launched his attack on the opponents" ("Paul's Argumentation in Galatians 1–2," 71).

85. The translation is my own.

86. Although Lyons discusses Gal 1:1–5 as though it were an ancient autobiographical section, he does not name it as such. See *Pauline Biography*, 124–25.

87. Paul is employing the tools of the language in "the most effective manner possible." See Classen, "Paul and Ancient Greek and Roman Rhetoric," 281.

88. Ian J. Elmer notes that there is "no doubt that Paul is a skillful rhetorician who could twist a story to his own ends" ("Setting the Record Straight," 32). Classen finds that Paul gives the impression that God is speaking and not him. He comments, "Attentive reading reveals that by means of several additions, carefully constructed sentences and equally well-chosen words the apostle most impressively conveys what he wants his readers to feel: that they are being addressed not so much by him, but in the name of God and together with him of Jesus Christ" ("Paul and Ancient Greek and Roman Rhetoric," 281).

89. Lyons notes that the "negative and antithetic elaboration" on the notion of apostle is found nowhere else in Paul's extant letters. See *Pauline Biography*, 124. On this see Nanos, who writes that Paul begins "the letter with a polemic sharply contrasting God's authority with that of human agents or agencies" (*Irony of Galatians*, 39).

90. On this point, see Lee and Scott, *Sound Mapping*, 156.

91. Rowe, "Style," 132.

92. See Johan S. Vos, who argues that the two adversatives in Gal 1:1 are in the form of a twofold "*correctio*," which underscores Paul's "claim to authority" ("Paul's Argumentation in Galatians 1–2," 71).

93. Robert Berchman finds that in Gal 1:1–5 Paul "argues from authority, opposites, relations, and difference" ("Galatians (1:1–5): Paul and Greco-Roman Rhetoric," 71). According to him, Paul employs a syllogistic structure in this unit, which includes *lysis* (statement), *ergasia* (the working out of the statement) and *pardeigma* (example). See ibid., 64.

94. Hall remarks, "Paul asserts a powerful ethos as the one chosen by God" ("Rhetorical Outline for Galatians," 34). Berchman notes, Gal 1:1 "establishes Paul's view that he is a true apostle. Paul amplifies this fact topically and syllogistically. His rhetorical argument leaves little room for either his opponents in Galatia, or the Galatians themselves, to reject his claims, or as Paul will argue later, to ignore the course of conduct he advocates" ("Galatians (1:1–5): Paul and Greco-Roman Rhetoric," 65). Similarly, Troy Martin comments, "Beginning with the prescript and continuing throughout the letter, Paul establishes as a matter of record that he is the authorized representative of the deity . . ." ("Apostasy to Paganism," 80).

95. See also Gaventa, who notes that within his other salutations Paul's description of his vocation is "couched in positive terms" ("Autobiography as Paradigm," 309).

96. 2 Cor 1:1 corresponds to a thought that clings to reality. Such thoughts can only be expressed in the positive. See Perelman and Olbrechts-Tyteca, *Traité de l'argumentation*, 208. No opposition is present in this description.

97. The SV translators write of the opening of Romans, "From the very beginning of the letter we can detect a change in length and elegance from the other letter openings of Paul" (Dewey et al., *The Authentic Letters of Paul*, 201). According to these scholars, in Romans "Paul is establishing himself as an envoy in grandiloquent terms" (ibid.). In his remarks on Paul's salutations, Calvin Roetzel finds that

Romans is Paul's "most original adaptation of the conventional letter opening" (*The Letters of Paul*, 55).

98. In agreement, see Vos, "Paul's Argumentation in Galatians 1–2," 171.

99. In the last quarter of the twentieth century Betz remarked, "At present the question as to the origin and the idea of the apostolate is one of the most intricate and difficult problems of New Testament scholarship" (*Galatians*, 74).

100. Berchman remarks that Paul establishes himself as the "true apostle" ("Galatians (1:1–5): Paul and Greco-Roman Rhetoric," 65).

101. ΛΟΓΕΙΟΝ, "ἀπόστολος," accessed January 17, 2015, http://logeion.uchicago.edu/index.html#ἀπόστολος.

102. See Dewey et al., *The Authentic Letters of Paul*, 51 and passim.

103. In his monograph *Chapters in the Life of Paul*, John Knox remarks that for Paul "apostle" meant one who had seen the lord and was commissioned directly by God. See *Chapters in the Life of Paul*, 117.

104. Lyons comments that the definition of apostle in Galatians is characteristically Pauline and carefully crafted. See *Pauline Biography*, 125, 133.

105. I follow the SV and translate Χριστοῦ as "the Anointed." See Dewey et al., *The Authentic Letters of Paul*, 51 passim.

106. Betz remarks that two "authorities" approve Paul's apostleship (*Galatians*, 39). Apparently, however, Marcion's copy of Galatians does not include the phrase "and God the Father" (ibid., 39, n. 26). On this see also BeDuhn, *The First New Testament*, 229. Burton Mack comments more generally that issues of authority "overwhelm" readers of the New Testament. One finds an appeal to external authorities, such as Jesus, the Holy Spirit or God, as "guarantors." See *Rhetoric and the New Testament*, 96.

107. On this point see Classen, "Paul and Ancient Greek and Roman Rhetoric," 282–83.

108. Betz, *Galatians*, 39.

109. Perelman and Olbrechts-Tyteca, *Traité de l'argumentation*, 207–8.

110. Vos, "Paul's Argumentation in Galatians 1–2," 171.

111. Perelman and Olbrechts-Tyteca write, "la négation est une réaction à une affirmation réele ou virtuelle d'autrui." ("the negation is a reaction to a real or virtual affirmation of others"). See Perelman and Olbrechts-Tyteca, *Traité de l'argumentation*, 208.

112. According to Betz, the phrase comes from Jewish apocalypticism. He also sees parallels of this expression in Paul's other writings at Rom 12:2; 1 Cor 1:20; 2:6, 8; 3:18–19; 2 Cor 4:4, yet none of these verses mention that exact expression. See *Galatians*, 42 n. 58. Similarly, Alan Segal writes, "Paul's conversion brings an apocalyptic warrant to a new community, which is stated in Gal 1:4: "our Lord Jesus Christ, who gave himself for our sins, in order to delivers us from the present evil age" (*Paul the Convert*, 160).

113. According to Betz, Paul believed in the "demonic power of sin, by which mankind is 'enslaved'" (*Galatians*, 42). J. Louis Martyn comments, "The human plight consists fundamentally of enslavement to supra-human powers; and God's redemptive act is his deed of liberation" (*Galatians*, 97). N. T. Wright follows on the thoughts of both Betz and Martyn: Jews are awaiting redemption and Paul echoes the concerns of Second-Temple Jews of his time. See his two-volume work *Paul and the Faithfulness of God*, 1.550, 2.749.

114. J. Louis Martyn notes that in 1:4b Paul is "composing relatively freely" (*Galatians*, 96).

115. According to Martyn, the verb Paul employs in 1:4b, ἐξαιρέω, is "highly situational" (*Galatians*, 96).

116. By contrast, Hall remarks that the expression the "present evil age" antici-pates "freedom from slavery to the *stoicheia* in 4:1–11 and as being free children of the heavenly Jerusalem in the Hagar-Sarah allegory (Gal 4:21–5:1)" ("Rhetorical Outline for Galatians," 34). Yet neither of those two passages Hall cites from Galatians chapter four refers to the "present evil age." The SV translators find that the expression is significant for Paul's purpose in writing, yet for them Paul is ideologically motivated. They write, "For Paul what is at stake is quite clear: a life of freedom lived out of confidence in God or an existence still subject to the confining forces that dominate the present age" (Dewey et al., *The Authentic Letters of Paul*, 41).

117. Knox, *Chapters in the Life of Paul*, 99. According to Knox, Paul's indignation was aroused by two things, 1) efforts to bring his converts under the Jewish law, and 2) any effort to undermine his own position. While I disagree with point one, as I indicate in my chapter on disjunctive rhetoric, Knox's second reason for Paul's indignation is spot on. See ibid., 98.

118. According to Lyons, through ethos building Paul is attempting to per-suade his audience to imitate him. See *Pauline Biography*, 137 passim. In contrast to Lyons, I do not find that Paul is urging his audience to imitate him.

119. For a list of *topoi* typical of ancient autobiographies, see Lyons, *Pauline Biography*, 28, 61.

120. While categorizing Gal 1:10–2:21 as an ancient autobiography, Lyons finds that Gal 1:13 is the stronger beginning to the autobiographical section than is Gal 1:10. See *Pauline Biography*, 130.

121. Lyons, *Pauline Biography*, 30.

122. Hall refers to Gal 1:10 as the start of the proof section of Galatians and he terms the section defined by Gal 1:10–2:21 the narration section. See his "Rhetorical Outline for Galatians," 38. For this same outline, see the SV under the heading "Deliberative" in Dewey et al., *The Authentic Letters of Paul*, 162. While Gal 1:10 marks an abrupt transition from the previous verse (Gal 1:9), Betz does not make a section break at this point. Instead he views Gal 1:6–11 as a unit and refers to it as the *exordium* or opening. He reasons that Gal 1:10–11 are transitional verses. See *Galatians*, 54. Betz also finds that Gal 1:12–2:14 designates the *narration*. See ibid., 44–57. See also Kennedy, who remarks that Gal 1:6–10 is the letter's opening. According to Kennedy, the proof section of Galatians runs from Gal 1:11–5:1. See *New Testament Interpretation through Rhetorical Criticism*, 148–50.

123. In the entire NT, the word "Judaism" appears only here and in Gal 1:14. According to Shaye Cohen, the Greek term refers to the "distinctive ways and manners, customs and beliefs of the Judean people" ("The Letter of Paul to the Galatians," 333). On the uniqueness of the term "Judaism," see also Betz, *Galatians*, 67 n. 105. Outside the NT, the term is next found in the letters of Ignatius (*Magn.* 8.1; 10.3; *Phld.* 6.1).

124. For this translation of καθ᾽ ὑπερβολὴν, see ΛΟΓΕΙΟΝ, "ὑπερβολὴν," accessed February 10, 2015, http://logeion.uchicago.edu/index.html#ὑπερβολὴν. Bernard Scott translates καθ᾽ ὑπερβολὴν as "to the full measure" (*The Real Paul*, 22).

125. The translation is my own.

126. Paul E. Koptak remarks that in this autobiographical section, "every ac-tion and motive" is "measured against" Paul's basic notion of being from God. He relates to "every person as friend or foe for that same reason" ("Rhetorical Identification," 162).

127. Bernard Scott explains that Paul is likely comparing himself to prophets such as Isaiah (Isa 49:1) and Jeremiah (Jer 1:4–5). See *The Real Paul*, 25. Betz simply

calls the expression ἐκ κοιλίας μητρός a "septuagintism." See *Galatians*, 70 n. 136.
One might also cite Samson (Judg 13:5) and 1 Samuel (1 Sam 11), two well-known
judges of Hebrew scriptures, whose births an angel or the Lord predict and who
are called "nazirites." The term "nazirite" stems from a Hebrew verb transliter-
ated as "nazir" and means "consecrated" or "separated." See *BDB* 634. The birth
narratives of Samson and Samuel are nearly identical; one is very likely borrowed
from the other.

128. Paul's questions should be taken with irony. On this see Betz, *Galatians*, 55.

129. Nanos finds in 1:10 an instance of ironic rebuke. See his *Irony of Galatians*,
67, 39.

130. According to John Schütz, Paul is involved here (and in the first two chapters of Galatians) in a "Pauline polemic." They are "aggressive explication rather
than defensive response" (*Paul and the Anatomy of Apostolic Authority*, 128).

131. For the ubiquitousness of the notion that Paul is defending his apostleship,
see Jerry Sumney, "Studying Paul's Opponents," 18. According to Sumney, various
studies have made Paul's defensive posture difficult to sustain. See ibid.

Lyons insists that in the autobiographical sections of Galatians Paul is not apologetic and is not responding to specific charges against him. See *Pauline Biography*,
8, 79–96, 125, 133. According to him, Paul employs "pleonastic tautology" (repetition of the same idea but with different words) to provide clarity and does not
reply to charges against him. See ibid., 110. That Paul is not acting defensively, see
also Schütz, *Paul and the Anatomy of Apostolic Authority*, 127.

132. Gaventa, "Autobiography as Paradigm," 309–10.

133. By contrast, reading the Greek verb πείθω as "striving to please," Debbie
Hunn comments that in Gal 1:10 Paul states that he is not striving to please men,
but that he *is* striving to please God. See her "Pleasing God or Pleasing People?"
35, n. 36 passim. This is an unusual reading of the verse and an unusual translation
of πείθω, whose first denotation is persuasion. See ΛΟΓΕΙΟΝ, "πείθω," accessed
May 12, 2015, http://logeion.uchicago.edu/index.html#πείθω.

134. Debbie Hunn devotes an entire article to whether Paul is pleasing men or
God. According to her, Paul's purpose is to defend his gospel and he does so by
expressing the fact that he is now in the business of "pleasing God" rather than
"pleasing people." However, because she understands the Greek word πείθω as
meaning "seeking to please" rather than as "seeking to persuade," the common
meaning of that Greek word, her argument is not well founded. Paul employs a
different Greek word to denote pleasing (ἀρέσκειν, 1:10b; and ἤρεσκον, 1:10c). In
v. 10a, Paul is talking about persuasion.

Furthermore, Hunn understands the conjunction ἤ ("or") as disjunctive. See
her "Pleasing God or Pleasing People?," 24 n. 1. For a similar reading to Hunn,
see Lyons, *Pauline Biography*, 141–43. Lyons, however, translates πείθω (1:10a) as
"obeying" rather than "pleasing." See ibid., 144. On the other hand, Betz understands πείθω as denoting a sense of persuasion. Paul refers to the notion of "pleasing" in 1:10b (twice). Why repeat the idea of pleasing, and with a different verb, in
1:10a? See his *Galatians*, 44.

135. On this point, see Betz, *Galatians*, 54.

136. According to Betz, the expression "persuade God" is "a polemical definition of magic and religious quackery" (*Galatians*, 55).

137. Betz writes, "Persuading men by pleasing them is of course one of the no-
torious strategies of political rhetoric and demagoguery" (*Galatians*, 55).

138. Translation is by Vince in Demosthenes, *Olynthiacs, Philippics*, 99.

139. Translation is by Vince in Demosthenes, *Olynthiacs, Philippics*, 141.

140. Translation is by Vince in Demosthenes, *Olynthiacs, Philippics*, 225.

141. Lyons remarks that discussions of one's past are typical within ancient autobiographies (*Pauline Biography*, 28, 61).

142. According to Lyons, Paul is "fully at home in antiquity to the extent that they [his autobiographical statements] are not purely informative personal histories but serve other motives" (*Pauline Biography*, 66).

143. On this point, see Lyons, *Pauline Biography*, 30. With regard to Gal 1:15, Betz writes, "It is extremely difficult—if not altogether impossible—to extract from Paul's words the facts as they really happened" (*Galatians*, 69). See also Bernard Scott, who writes that Paul's is not a neutral telling of his own story. "He tells his story to prove a point to win a debate" (*The Real Paul*, 20).

144. The subject of why Paul persecuted groups of Jesus followers has been much discussed in the scholarship on Paul. In his recent work, Scott surmises that Paul persecuted Jesus followers because what they claimed about Jesus being God's messiah was a lie. Jesus could not have been God's messiah because he was crucified by Rome. That Rome crucified him meant that Rome won, not Jesus. See *The Real Paul*, 23. On the other hand, Paula Fredriksen has argued that Paul persecuted groups of Jesus followers because the message they preached to both Jews and gentiles would have been dangerous, especially in a diaspora setting. The proclamation of a crucified Messiah and of a coming Messianic kingdom risked alienating the larger and unaffiliated Roman colonial government on whom the early Jesus communities depended. See "Judaism, the Circumcision of Gentiles," 248–55.

145. In his recent book on Paul, Scott provides five different translations of this verse. The SV translates, "how aggressively I harassed God's new community, trying to wipe it out" (*The Real Paul*, 22).

146. ΛΟΓΕΙΟΝ, "πορθέω," accessed February 27, 2015, http://logeion.uchicago.edu/index.html#πορθέω.

147. ΛΟΓΕΙΟΝ, "ὑπερ," accessed February 27, 2015, http://logeion.uchicago.edu/index.html#ὑπερ.

148. Scott, *The Real Paul*, 20. Similarly, according to Betz, Paul was saying that he was "an ardent observer of Torah" (*Galatians*, 68). For a similar view regarding how to understand the meaning of being zealous, see Reumann, *Philippians*, 514.

149. For example, Betz remarks that Paul's "anti-Christian" activity is explained by his "deep devotion and commitment to the Jewish religion" (*Galatians*, 67–68). See also Bernard Scott, who notes the connection between Paul's recounting of his zeal and his persecution of groups of Jesus followers. Indeed, Scott remarks that this pattern repeats in Paul's account of himself in Phil 3:5–6. See *The Real Paul*, 26.

150. See Koptak, "Rhetorical Identification," 161–62.

151. D. F. Tolmie remarks that Paul's hyperbolic remarks regarding his past activities serve to confirm that he could not have changed were it not for God (*Persuading the Galatians*, 56).

152. According to Betz, the reference to Arabia likely refers to the Kingdom of Nabataea, which was called "*provincia Arabia*." The central cities were Petra and Bostra. See *Galatians*, 73–74.

153. Tolmie, *Persuading the Galatians*, 55. Koptak remarks, "His move away from the apostles to Arabia . . . signified his break from a bondage to human tradition and authority" ("Rhetorical Identification," 162).

154. Ian Elmer notes, "Paul's autobiographical material is press-ganged into the service of his rhetoric, and especially into his campaign against others who seemed to have been spreading counter versions of the same story" ("Setting the

Record Straight," 32). I agree with the first part of Elmer's remark but add that it is impossible to know whether or not Paul's competition was "spreading counter versions of the same story."

155. On this point see Lyons who comments, "Galatians 1:11–12 obviously continues and reinforces the man/men-Christ/God contrast introduced in Paul's self-description in 1:1" (*Pauline Biography*, 152).

156. Burton Mack notes that Paul's arguments assume an understanding of his proclamation of the good news, but that Paul offers no explication for it (*Rhetoric and the New Testament*, 68).

157. Perelman and Olbrechts-Tyteca, *Traité de l'argumentation*, 208. This is not a neutral telling. Paul is making an argument and an argument signals the presence of others.

158. Koptak notes that from Gal 1:1–12, Paul repeats the Greek word for human (ἄνθρωπος) seven times. As mentioned, according to him, Paul structures the entire unit from Gal 1:1–24 around the human-divine contrast. See his "Rhetorical Identification," 162.

159. Note Hall also views Gal 1:6–9, a passage we review elsewhere and in greater detail, as giving a "mighty boost" to Paul's ethos. See "Rhetorical Outline for Galatians," 35.

160. Ian Elmer comments, that there was a "long-standing conflict between two factions within the early church, divided not simply along ethnic lines, but ideological ones as well" ("Setting the Record Straight," 37).

161. In his sixteenth-century commentary on Galatians, Martin Luther finds that in Gal 1:13–14 Paul is discussing his former life as a defender of the righteousness of the law. Paul violently persecuted the church of God and even killed persons associated with it. While Paul deserved God's punishment, he instead received God's grace and God called Paul to be an apostle. Luther goes on to state the Gospel is vastly different from the Law. The Gospel reveals the Son of God; Moses (the lawgiver) reveals the Law and also "sin, the conscience, death, the wrath and judgment of God, and hell" (*Lectures on Galatians*, 68–73).

162. For more on this type of misreading and its negative influence, see Schüssler Fiorenza, "Response to John R. Lanci," 177–83 passim.

163. In 1979 Betz employed the term "enormous" in describing the amount of scholarship pertaining to Paul's conversion (*Galatians*, 64 n. 82). The secondary literature on this issue has grown since that time.

While understanding that there is a sense of conversion here, Betz is not in the "hard core" conversion camp. See his *Galatians*, 66–69. Like Krister Stendahl, Betz finds that Paul was called on a mission to gentiles. On this, see Stendahl, "The Apostle Paul and the Introspective Conscience of the West," 84–85. On the issue that Paul did not convert, see especially the work of Pamela Eisenbaum, who follows on the earlier thoughts of Stendahl. See her *Paul Was Not a Christian*.

The book of Acts picks up on the notion of Paul's conversion and embellishes upon it, creating three full-blown conversion narratives. See Acts 9:3–22; 22:6–16; 26:12–18. For the influence of Galatians on the accounts in Acts, see Pervo, *Dating Acts*.

164. Beverly Gaventa astutely remarks that Galatians 1 and 2 is very often gleaned for historical facts. With this approach, commentators lose sight of issues within the text. See her "Autobiography as Paradigm," 312.

165. Understood in the modern rather than in the ancient sense of the term.

166. Even while explaining the fundamental differences between an ancient and modern autobiography, Lyons appears to read Gal 1:10–2:21 at face value.

He writes, "His [Paul's] autobiographical remarks in Gal 1:10–2:21 are shaped throughout by the contrast between his past and present. . . . The decisive event dividing Paul's 'formerly' and 'now' is God's revelation to him of Jesus Christ and his call to preach him among the Gentiles (1:12, 15–16)" (*Pauline Biography*, 150, 171).

167. "'Truth' was a malleable concept for the ancients" (Penner and Lopez, "Rhetorical Approaches," 40).

168. "There is no place outside of rhetoric in Paul's letters" (Penner and Lopez, "Rhetorical Approaches," 37).

169. I am reminded of the SV translators' comment, "Certainly Paul is no Cicero, no Demosthenes." See Dewey et al., *The Authentic Letters of Paul*, 4. Yet they *also* write, "Not to be overlooked is the fact that the letters of Paul display the marks of rhetorical finesse" (ibid).

170. Wooten, *Rhetoric of Crisis*, 29.

3
Persuading through Emotive Language

1. Quintilian, *The Institutio Oratoria of Quintilian*, 419.

2. According to Valentina Arena, Cicero argued that one cannot fully divorce the emotions from reason. See her "The Orator and His Audience," 203–4.

3. Modern discourse theorists argue that interpreters cannot help but bring their own "personal experiences, social locations, and culturally-shaped horizons" to their interpretations. These personal aspects also play a role in interpretation more generally and thus affect not just this leg of the model but all of them. See Schüssler Fiorenza, "Response to John R. Lanci," 180. See also Kotrosits, *Rethinking Early Christian Identity*.

4. See Arena's discussion of Cicero in "The Orator and His Audience," 199.

5. Arena, "The Orator and His Audience," 199.

6. The earliest versions of Demosthenes' *Third Philippic* are in two forms, with one shorter than the other. John Sandys argues that Demosthenes himself added to his own original speech when he edited it. See *Demosthenes*, lix–lxvii.

7. Vince calls it a "consummate work of art" (Demosthenes, *Olynthiacs, Philippics*, 222, 223). Wooten writes that Demosthenes' *Philippic Three* is the "finest deliberative speech from the ancient world" ("On the Road to *Philippic* III," 22). Jaegar remarks that with his third Philippic speech Demosthenes reached "the high-water mark of Greek oratory" (*Demosthenes: The Origin and Growth of His Policy*, 173). See also Sandys, *Demosthenes: Texts and Notes*, vii. By contrast, Stephen Usher notes, "For someone seeking novelty of thought, this speech begins disappointingly, even reverting to sentiments expressed in the *First Philippic*" (*Greek Oratory: Tradition and Originality*, 239).

8. Wooten, "On the Road to *Philippic* III," 14.

9. Wooten, "On the Road to *Philippic* III," 2 passim. As Wooten comments, in his *Third Philippic*, Demosthenes finds his rhythm, "the proper balance in the management of arguments and the modulation of emotion" (ibid.).

10. Wooten, "On the Road to *Philippic* III," 2–3 passim. Ring composition is also a form of chiastic structure. See ibid., 4. In ring composition, authors present a theme, build it to a high point, and then retrace the same steps in reverse direction to the original starting point. For more on ring composition, see the section on Cicero in this chapter.

11. Demosthenes, *Olynthiacs, Philippics*, 222; Wooten, "On the Road to *Philippic* III," 2; Sandys, *Demosthenes: Texts and Notes*, xlix.

12. Wooten remarks that this speech reads like a rough draft of Demosthenes'
Third Philippic. See "On the Road to *Philippic* III," 21.

13. Wooten, *Demosthenes'* Philippic *I,* 137. See also Buckler who comments that
by 343 the Athenians "increasingly saw the peace as a betrayal of their interests"
("Demosthenes and Aeschines," 134).

14. Sandys, *Demosthenes: Texts and Notes,* l.

15. T. T. B. Ryder remarks that Demosthenes' arguments in favor of support for
Diopheithes were likely successful, as the latter was not recalled to Athens. See his
"Demosthenes and Philip II," 78.

16. As Sandys comments, "The Speech is far less concerned with the immediate demand for succors for the Chersonesus than with the general question of
Hellenic policy. As compared with the immediately preceding Speech, the horizon
is enlarged, and the outlook now includes the prospect of forming an alliance to
oppose Philip with the aid of other states of Greece" (*Demosthenes: Texts and Notes,*
lv). See also Ryder who comments that with this speech Demosthenes is concerned
about the position of the Chersonese and with Philip's encroachment into Thrace
("Demosthenes and Philip II," 77).

17. According to Badian, Demosthenes was viewed as lacking real conviction.
See his "The Road to Prominence," 36. Demosthenes had earlier also exaggerated
claims about an impending revival of Spartan hegemony and he claimed that Athens
was in a position to defeat them. Similarly, Yunis comments that the Athenians
only reluctantly embraced Demosthenes' harsh views of Philip. Demosthenes
was not a welcome sight to the Athenians. See his *Taming Democracy,* 258.

18. Wooten, *Demosthenes'* Philippic *I,* 123–24. For more details on the events
leading up to the peace treaty, see Buckler, "Demosthenes and Aeschines," 117–23;
Ryder, "Demosthenes and Philip II," 58–72.

19. Wooten, *Demosthenes'* Philippic *I,* 123. Buckler explains that it is very difficult to get at the precise details of the various conferences with Philip concerning
the peace treaty (the Peace of Philocrates). Nevertheless, according to him, it seems
clear that, for one reason or another, Demosthenes lost confidence in the peace
process in or around 346, at the time of the second embassy in Pella. Aeschines
adopted a position opposite to that of Demosthenes and he (Aeschines) later described the event quite differently than Demosthenes. For further explanation of
these events, see Buckler, "Demosthenes and Aeschines," 121–33. See also Ryder
who details Demosthenes' role in the peace process itself in his "Demosthenes and
Philip II," 58–72.

20. Buckler, "Demosthenes and Aeschines," 115–32.

21. Buckler, "Demosthenes and Aeschines," 134.

22. Three of Aeschines' speeches against Demosthenes are extant (*Against
Timarchus, On the Embassy,* and *Against Ctesiphon*). Despite the tremendous animosity between Demosthenes and Aeschines, apparent in their speeches, John Buckler
cautions against taking their remarks at face value. He comments, "Demosthenes
and Aeschines were both patriots, and none of their allegations of treason and
perfidy should be taken seriously. Only their interpretation of Philip's real aims
divided them. It is still impossible securely to determine whether either of them
accurately gauged the king's ambitions for the simple reason that Philip did not
leave a record of them" ("Demosthenes and Aeschines," 148).

23. Wooten, *Demosthenes'* Philippic *I,* 137. Buckler notes that in 343 Demosthenes was unsuccessful in his charge of treason against Aeschines. In that trial,
Aeschines made the stronger case and was acquitted. See "Demosthenes and
Aeschines," 134–40. Demosthenes remounted a case against Aeschines in 341 and
at that time he successfully argued his charges of duplicity and of deceiving the

Athenian people against him. See ibid., 141–42. According to Ryder, neither the
condemnation of Philocrates nor the subsequent indictment of Aeschines (343 BCE)
would have come to pass had the Athenians not lost heart in the peace process
with Philip. See "Demosthenes and Philip II," 76.

24. In the opening of his *Third Philippic*, Demosthenes attributes the bad state of
affairs in which Athens finds itself to his political opponents (*Phil.* 3.2).

25. According to Wooten, and as we have already discussed with regard to
his *First Philippic*, Demosthenes could be quite harsh with his Athenian audience.
Indeed, a majority of Demosthenes' *First Philippic* involves audience criticism. In
his *Third Philippic*, however, only 25 percent is devoted to a criticism of his audience and within those sections Demosthenes is much less harsh than in his earlier
speech. See Wooten, *Demosthenes' Philippic I*, 138.

26. Hermogenes cites section 31 of this speech as an example of vehemence, the
strongest form of criticism. See *On Types of Style*, 30.

27. As Wooten remarks, the length and nature of the *proemium* suggest "how
intent Demosthenes was to engage the audience's attention before the body of the
speech" (*Demosthenes' Philippic I*, 142).

28. According to Yunis, Demosthenes' preambles are less about laying out the
logic of his arguments than they are about self-promotion at the expense of other
opposing speakers and about characterizing the events of the day as highly important. See *Taming Democracy*, 248.

29. Demosthenes, *Olynthiacs, Philippics*, 222; Wooten, *Demosthenes' Philippic I*,
137; Sandys, *Demosthenes: Texts and Notes*, lii; Ryder, "Demosthenes and Philip II," 78.

30. This Greek adjective that translates as "other" or "another," when used with
an article, as it is here, means "the rest" or "all besides." See ΛΟΓΕΙΟΝ, "ἄλλους,"
accessed September 24, 2015, http://logeion.uchicago.edu/index.html#ἄλλους.

31. Wooten, *Demosthenes' Philippic I*, 138.

32. The translation is by Vince in Demosthenes, *Olynthiacs, Philippics*, 235.
Vince does not translate the Greek conjunction καὶ ("and") and hence loses some
of the power of the rhetoric. In his translation, Stephen Usher italicizes the "you,"
as I have done. See *Greek Oratory: Tradition and Originality*, 240.

33. Stephen Usher remarks, "Demosthenes brings the most urgent rhetoric to bear on these incursions, real or threatened" (*Greek Oratory: Tradition and
Originality*, 239).

34. According to Gilberte Ronnet, *anaphora* was used only rarely in writers
prior to Demosthenes. Demosthenes has the honor of reintroducing this figure of
speech. See *Étude sur le style de Démosthène*, 66.

35. The indicative mood is animated and adds a sense of emotion. See Ronnet,
Étude sur le style de Démosthène, 76.

36. Repetition itself works by guiding the hearers' interpretation; and ending sounds in particular are designed to be emphatic. See Lee and Scott, *Sound
Mapping*, 147–51.

37. With lists orators force their convictions and work to make a striking effect
on their audience. See Ronnet, *Étude sur le style de Démosthène*, 76–77.

38. Ronnet, *Étude sur le style de Démosthène*, 76.

39. Ronnet, *Étude sur le style de Démosthène*, 76.

40. Difference is another way of creating emphasis. On the special function of
distinctive sounds, see Lee and Scott, *Sound Mapping*, 155.

41. Euboea, Megara, and the Peloponnese were not included within the Peace
of Philocrates. On this see Buckler, "Demosthenes and Aeschines," 134. At the start
of his reign (359 BCE), one of Philip's primary goals was to subdue Trace (a land to
the north of Macedon) and by 347 he had nearly accomplished it. Trace too was *not*

part of the peace treaty. See ibid., 120. Viewing the situation a bit differently from Buckler, T. T. B. Ryder remarks that Philip was a concern, particularly in Euboea. See Ryder, "Demosthenes and Philip II," 76.

42. In his analysis of this unit, Usher notes that the final Greek pronoun ὑμῖν (you) is emphatic (17f above). Following Usher's lead, I have italicized it. See Usher, *Greek Oratory: Tradition and Originality*, 240.

43. Philip does not attack Athens and is murdered in 336. Several years prior to that time, Athens signed another accord with Philip. See Ryder, "Demosthenes and Philip II," 82–84.

44. Usher remarks that Demosthenes "brings the most urgent rhetoric to bear on these incursions, real or threatened" (*Greek Oratory: Tradition and Originality*, 239).

45. Buckler, "Demosthenes and Aeschines," 114.

46. Buckler, "Demosthenes and Aeschines," 114.

47. Sandys translates περικόπτειν as "to mutilate." See *Demosthenes: On the Peace*, 207.

48. For the view that Demosthenes associates his audience with heroic attitudes and former "glorious accomplishments." See Wooten, "On the Road to *Philippic* III," 14.

49. Sandys notes that the larger number (seventy-three years), which reflects the years 476–404 BCE, is placed first in order to draw attention to the long duration. See Sandys, *Demosthenes: Texts and Notes*, 208.

50. This refers to the years 404–376 BCE. See Sandys, *Demosthenes: Texts and Notes*, 208.

51. There is "no occasion for making the audience partners in the unpopularity of their ancestors." See Sandys, *Demosthenes: Texts and Notes*, 208.

52. See Yunis, *Taming Democracy*, 258; Buckler, "Demosthenes and Aeschines," 115–32.

53. Translation is by Vince in Demosthenes, *Olynthiacs, Philippics*, 239.

54. Translation is by Vince in Demosthenes, *Olynthiacs, Philippics*, 239, 241. Quotation marks seen above are found in the Greek text of the Loeb edition (ibid., 238).

55. This is an example of the use of ring composition to which Wooten refers. See "On the Road to *Philippic* III," 2.

56. Wooten, *Demosthenes' Philippic I*, 139.

57. Demosthenes speaks of Olynthus in his *First Philippic* and in his *Olynthiacs*. On this, see Sandys, *Demosthenes: Texts and Notes*, 210.

58. Wooten, "On the Road to *Philippic* III," 4. (Emphasis is my own.)

59. Ryder comments, "Demosthenes was surely exaggerating when . . . in the *Third Philippic* he listed the wrongs done by Philip against the Greeks and spoke of 'Olynthus and Methone and Apollonia and the thirty-two cities of Chalcidice, all of which Philip had destroyed so ruthlessly that it would not be easy for someone coming to them to say whether or not they had ever been inhabited.'" According to Ryder, and based on the report in Diodorus (16.53.3), Philip was primarily interested in material gain. He earned money from selling slaves and land and aimed to intimidate cities that opposed him. See "Demosthenes and Philip II," 57–58.

60. These thirty-two cities refer to those of the Olynthian League. See Wooten, *Demosthenes' Philippic I*, 155 n. 13.

61. As late as 343 Demosthenes himself was ready to conclude a new peace treaty with Philip that excluded the Phocians, Athens's ally. For a discussion of this, see Ryder, "Demosthenes and Philip II," 63–66. See also Buckler, who comments that the peace treaty that Demosthenes and Aeschines signed with Philip

did not include Phocis, even though Demosthenes claimed to have argued up to the very end that Phocis be included in it. Buckler finds this latter claim of Demosthenes hard to reconcile with other available evidence. See "Demosthenes and Aeschines," 122–29.

62. Sandys notes the emphatic position of the word "πολιτείας." With the word, Demosthenes signifies that Philip has "even deprived the cities of their constitutions." See *Demosthenes: Texts and Notes*, 210.

63. Wooten comments, "This constant variation in the presentation of Philip's aggressions reflects how energetic and unexpected his activity is" (*Demosthenes' Philippic I*, 156).

64. Buckler, "Demosthenes and Aeschines," 120, 134. Ryder remarks, "But he [Philip] had done nothing against the letter of his treaty with Athens and Demosthenes' allegation that he had violated the Peace and was plotting against all Greeks (6.2) was justified only by the argument that any attempt to extend his influence in southern Greece was a breach of its spirit" ("Demosthenes and Philip II," 72).

65. That we have a summary statement, see Wooten, *Demosthenes' Philippic I*, 155.

66. Demosthenes is "heaping up charges against Philip" (Wooten, *Demosthenes' Philippic I*, 155). The statement is clearly an exaggeration. Yet the thoughts of John Buckler are perhaps worth repeating: "Historical accuracy meant nothing to them [Demosthenes and Aeschines]" ("Demosthenes and Aeschines," 148).

67. There is an inconsistency in Demosthenes' argument: in stating that one cannot purchase a slave from Macedonia, he admits that the Macedonians were not slaves. He "overreaches himself" (Sandys, *Demosthenes: Texts and Notes*, 214). Wooten comments on the presence of strong negative emotion. See "On the Road to *Philippic III*," 14.

68. See Hammond, *Philip of Macedon*, 1; Worthington, *Philip II of Macedonia*, 8. Wooten remarks that Demosthenes hammers away at the fact that Philip is not unlike the Greek people. See his *Rhetoric of Crisis*, 65.

69. As quoted in Yunis, *Taming Democracy*, 260.

70. Already in September of 44 in his *Second Philippi* Cicero was working out his arguments against Antony, a writing he considered too nasty to deliver. He sent it to his friend Atticus for comments. It was in his *Second Philippi* that Cicero first referred to Antony as a Catiline. For further details regarding the beginning of Cicero's verbal fight against Antony, see Van der Blom, "*Officium* and *Res publica*," 302–3. For more on Catiline and the Catiline conspiracy, see Steel, *The End of the Roman Republic 146 to 44 BC*, 150–58.

71. Antony was gathering troops together and Cicero was becoming convinced that he would be targeting Rome; Octavian had acquired troops of his own and had a growing popularity with them; and D. Brutus was successfully resisting Antony's attempt to take over his province of Cisalpine Gaul. See Van der Blom, "*Officium* and *Res publica*," 306.

72. As quoted in Van der Blom, "*Officium* and *Res publica*," 301–2 n. 63.

73. Van der Blom, "*Officium* and *Res publica*," 291, 306.

74. Harries, *Cicero and the Jurists*, 221. Cicero feared Antony. See ibid., 221.

75. Van der Blom, "*Officium* and *Res publica*," 288, 290–92.

76. *Att.* 14.12.1, 14.13.6.

77. Van der Blom, "*Officium* and *Res publica*," 298.

78. Van der Blom, "*Officium* and *Res publica*," 315–16.

79. Harries, *Cicero and the Jurists*, 204. See also Van der Blom, "*Officium* and *Res publica*," 308.

80. Stevenson, "Antony as 'Tyrant' in Cicero's First Philippic," 177.

81. Stevenson, "Antony as 'Tyrant' in Cicero's First Philippic," 177–78.

82. Section 3.4 forms part of the main section or body of the speech, which begins at 3.3 and continues to 3.27. The main section is divided into two logical sections (3.3–14 and 3.15–27). The first section discusses various initiatives against Antony, and the second describes his un-Roman-like behavior. Both sections work together to justify actions the senators are to take against Antony. See Manuwald, *Commentary*, 324.

83. For his portrayal of Antony at Brundisium, Cicero relied on Demosthenes' characterization of Philip of Macedon's cruel treatment of Greeks. See Taddeo, "Signs of Demosthenes in Cicero's *Philippics*," 8.

84. Cicero taps into the "deepest passions and fears" of the Roman people. See Habinek, *Ancient Rhetoric and Oratory*, 28.

85. Translated by Manuwald in *Introduction and Texts*, 167.

86. Wooten, "On the Road to *Philippic* III," 3 passim.

87. Rowe, "Style," 134.

88. Manuwald, *Commentary*, 334.

89. The use of indignant rhetorical questioning (4c) in and of itself was meant to arouse the emotions of his audience. This type of questioning, which did not demand an answer, was probably "the most common means of conveying and evoking emotions in Greek oratory" (Wooten, "On the Road to *Philippic* III," 15).

90. On this, see Wooten, *Rhetoric of Crisis*, 63.

91. "A single detail is all that is required for a memorable, shocking effect" (Hall, "The *Philippics*," 285).

92. "To create emotion it is essential to be specific. General notions and abstract schemes have hardly any effect on the imagination." Whereas an audience will remain unmoved by the general carnage of a battle scene, they can be brought to tears by a small detail, such as the death of two young boys. See Perelman and Olbrechts-Tyteca, *The New Rhetoric*, 147.

93. This was Antony's third wife, Fulvia. Antony is also Fulvia's third husband; she had been married to P. Clodius Pulcher and then to C. Scribonius Curio. Cicero refers to Fulvia several times within his compositions and he is consistently critical of her. According to Cicero, she was greedy and involved in unsavory dealings along with Antony (see *Phil.* 2.11, 77, 95, 113; 3.10, 16; 5.11, 22; 6.4; 13.18). Cicero never refers to Fulvia by name, which is another way in which he indicates his contempt for her. See Manuwald, *Commentary*, 335.

94. "What Antony called the justifiable execution of traitors becomes in Cicero's hands a sadistic slaughter of innocents" (Hall, "The *Philippics*," 284).

95. Manuwald, *Commentary*, 335.

96. See Wooten, *Rhetoric of Crisis*, 63.

97. Rowe, "Style," 143.

98. Perelman and Olbrechts-Tyteca, *The New Rhetoric*, 116.

99. Perelman and Olbrechts-Tyteca, *The New Rhetoric*, 116–17. Perelman and Olbrechts-Tyteca credit Jean Piaget for this insight.

100. Francis Bacon states, "The affection beholdeth merely the present: reason beholdeth the future and sum of time. And therefore the present filling the imagination more, reason is commonly vanquished; but after that force of eloquence and persuasion hath made things future and remote appear as present, then upon the revolt of the imagination reason prevaileth." As quoted in Perelman and Olbrechts-Tyteca, *The New Rhetoric*, 117.

101. According to the historical record, Antony ordered many soldiers to death because they had defected. See Bailey in Cicero, *Philippics 1–6*, 180–81 n. 4. The

soldiers went to the side of Octavian. The latter may well have bribed them to abandon Antony. See Van der Blom, "*Officium* and *Res publica*," 306; Harries, *Cicero and the Jurists*, 219.

102. The more vivid the portrayal, the greater is the impact. Cicero aimed to provoke horrified outrage against Antony. See Hall, "The *Philippics*," 284.

103. Apparently, Antony was condemning the defection of two legions by killing a significant number of soldiers (see *Phil.* 3.10; 5.22; 13.18). On this see Bailey in Cicero, *Philippics 1–6*, 180–81 n. 4. In section 5.22, Cicero repeats the narration of this event and supplies a few more details. When the legions expressed their rejection of his promises, Antony ordered those whom he deemed disloyal to the Republic to come to his house and be slaughtered at his feet in the presence of his wife. Antony also distributed the soldiers' belongings to his own comrades and drinking companions (*comitibus compotoribusque*).

104. Manuwald, *Introduction and Texts*, 165.

105. Cicero, *Philippics 1–6*, 265, 267. Cicero backed Octavian as a practical matter. He hoped to gain his support in his own fight against Antony. While he praises Octavian in his *Philippics*, in his letters he describes Octavian as merely "the lesser of two evils in comparison with Antony." See Bailey in Cicero, *Philippics 1–6*, xxvii–xxviii. For more on the relationship between Cicero and Octavian, see especially Van der Blom, "*Officium* and *Res publica*," 294, 307–8. See also Harries in *Cicero and the Jurists*, 219 who remarks that Octavian bribed the Roman troops to gain their allegiance and pull them away from Antony.

106. "The traditional image of Tarquin is masterfully altered by Cicero; he appears as a slightly haughty king who nevertheless had Rome's interests at heart. It is rather Antony who is the villainous despot bent on destroying Rome" (Taddeo, "Signs of Demosthenes in Cicero's *Philippics*," 10).

107. "Tarquinius Superbus, Lucius," *Encyclopeida Britannica* 15th ed., 11.566.

108. On this, see also Hall, "The *Philippics*," 283.

109. Translated by Bailey in Cicero, *Philippics 1–6*, 185–87. Italics are the translator's.

110. By contrast, Jerise Fogel remarks that Cicero turns to Tarquin to encourage the senate to think of Antony as "extra-constitutional." See her "Cicero and the 'Ancestral Constitution,'" 248.

111. Wooten, "On the Road to *Philippic* III," 14.

112. For this view, see also Harries, *Cicero and the Jurists*, 216–17.

113. Wooten, *Rhetoric of Crisis*, 63–64. The use of the term *belua* and its cognates is common among Latin writers. Five and one-half pages of the *TLL* contain references of this term's use.

114. According to May, Cicero commonly depicted his enemies as beasts. He characterizes Verres as a monster (*In Verrem* 2.1.40, 1.42, 5.145, 5.146) and as a beast (*In Verrem* 2.1.121, 5.109). Similarly, he describes those involved in the Catiline conspiracy as monsters (*In Catilinam* 2.10) and beasts (*Pro Sulla* 76). Additionally, he depicts his enemies Clodius, Piso, and Gabinus as monsters and beasts (see *In Pisonem* 21, *De haruspicum responso* 59 and *Pro Milone* 85). See May, "Cicero and the Beasts," 143–47.

115. Indeed, such a characterization, while it can appear to be somewhat hackneyed, must have served Cicero's purposes quite well, as he employed this invective against his enemies more often than any other ancient writer of his time. See May, "Cicero and the Beasts," 147. See also Lévy's discussion of Cicero's use of the metaphor of a monster to characterize his political enemies in his "Rhétorique et Philosophie," 139–57. A monster wants to destroy close relationships, either through incest or assassination, and to dismantle the Republic and its institutions.

116. Cicero, *Philippics 1–6*, 51.

117. Van der Blom, "*Officium* and *Res publica*," 302–3.

118. Cicero wrote but never delivered his *Second Philippic*. See Manuwald, *Introduction and Texts*, 20.

119. A devouring monster leaves behind a trail of destruction, as Lévy remarks. See his "Monstruosité Politique chez Cicéron," 143.

120. Lévy cites Aeschines, *Against Timarchos* 96 and Aristophane, *The Frogs* 1466 in "Monstruosité Politique chez Cicéron," 143 n. 19.

121. *Phil.* 3.28 is not the only passage in which Cicero refers to Antony as a beast; the notion runs throughout the *Philippics* (see *Phil.* 4.12; 6.7; 7.27; 8.13; 13.15, 22). With regard to Cicero's use of the term "beast," May remarks that Cicero used this term more than any other ancient author of his time. According to May, Cicero's decision was serious and deliberate. To be a beast went against Cicero's core beliefs in what constituted being a human being. See "Cicero and the Beasts," 147. Similarly, Manuwald remarks that the term "beast" is not a random form of abuse. For Cicero, such a term had social and political ramifications. See her *Commentary*, 426.

122. *Phil.* 3.28 marks the start of the last argumentative section of the speech. The section ends at 3.36 with Cicero's "most emphatic appeal." According to Manuwald, the section under review marks the first time since the introduction (*Phil.* 3.1–2) that Cicero's own personality makes an appearance. Cicero appears to be personally threated by Antony. See *Commentary*, 425.

123. Manuwald translates *beluam* (28a) as "monster," but the word can easily be translated as "beast," its first lexical meaning. See ΛΟΓΕΙΟΝ, "belua," accessed August 20, 2014, http://logeion.uchicago.edu/index.html#belua.

124. Translated by Manuwald in *Introduction and Texts*, 181.

125. Cf. *Phil.* 10.22.

126. Lévy defines Cicero's beast (or monster) with the French word *gouffre* (abyss). See "Monstruosité Politique chez Cicéron," 143.

127. Elsewhere, Cicero claims that no one can understand what he says (*Phil.* 3.21). This is another way that Cicero distinguishes Antony from the rest of the human race, from those who speak intelligibly. Yet as Bailey points out, Cicero intentionally misinterprets Antony's statements and turns them into unintelligible ones. See Cicero, *Philippics 1–6*, 198 n. 27.

128. Manuwald, *Commentary*, 426; May, "Cicero and the Beasts," 147–53. On this point, see also Lévy, "Monstruosité Politique chez Cicéron," 143 passim.

129. In this treatise of 44, Cicero reprises the thoughts of his earlier and widely read work *De republica* (54–51 BCE). In both, he argues that morally reprehensible leaders pose a dire problem to the Republic. On this see Van der Blom, "*Officium* and *Res publica*," 312.

130. Cicero's belief in the power of reason and speech finds its basis in Greek sources such as Plato, Xenophon, Aristotle, Isocrates, and Sophocles. It is a Stoic notion that reason is what separates humans from beasts. Other traits assessed by Stoics as being solely human are the faculty of speech, the emotions, the knowledge of vice and virtue, free will and judgment, having laws, a sense of time, and the knowledge of the gods. See May, "Cicero and the Beasts," 147 n. 15.

131. See Manuwald, *Commentary*, 427–28.

132. That is, nouns or adjectives without intervening conjunctions.

133. Manuwald, *Commentary*, 427.

134. In *Phil.* 3.12—in a passage that leads up to Cicero's more full-blown depiction of Antony as a beast—he refers to Antony again in an asyndetic sequences, as

a filthy, shameless, and effeminate (*impuro, impudico, effeminate*) and then again, as naked, oiled, and drunk (*nudus, unctus, ebrius*).

135. According to Cicero, the tyrant who places his own desire for dominion and his own will above the voice of the people is nothing more than a beast. On this point, see May, "Cicero and the Beasts," 151.

136. The emotional sections gain in force and effectiveness because Paul alternates them with rational or explanatory passages. See Cronjé, "Defamiliarization," 223.

137. When discussing his opponents, Paul employs an "absolutely scathing tenor." Such a scathing tenor is present in Paul's remarks regarding those who trouble the Galatians (1:7, 5:10), bewitch them (3:1), and prevent them from obeying the truth (5:7). The opponents have dishonorable motives (4:17; 6:12–13). William Walker comments, "Apparently, in Paul's view, these opponents have no redeeming features at all" ("Does the 'We' Include Paul's Opponents?" 564).

138. The translation is my own.

139. Walker, "Does the 'We' Include Paul's Opponents?" 564; Betz, *Galatians*, 52.

140. Nanos remarks that Paul uses a combination of "negative stereotyping" and "excoriating polemics" against those influencing the Galatians. Paul's discourse is "hot." See *Irony of Galatians*, 27.

141. According to Roy Ciampa, with his double curse Paul appears to be echoing Deut 13:12–16. In those verses, the Israelites are told that should people attempt to lead inhabitants of their town astray by the worship of another god, they should be cursed with a curse. See his "Deuteronomy in Galatians and Romans," 99–100. See also Takaaki Haraguchi, "Words of Blessing and Curse," 40–43.

142. Betz remarks that with his curses Paul is employing "magical imperatives" (*Galatians*, 50). According to him, cursing and blessing directly pertain to the function of the letter. Paul carefully crafted the conditional curse at the start of the body of the letter and included a conditional blessing at its end (Gal 6:16). The presence of these curses and a final blessing indicates that the letter to the Galatians is not only a form of forensic rhetoric but also a "magical letter." According to Betz, magic supersedes the category of rhetoric (*Galatians*, 25). By contrast, see Penner and Lopez who remark, "There is no place outside rhetoric in Paul's letters" ("Rhetorical Approaches," 37).

143. The Greek noun ἀνάθεμα occurs in Theocritus (third century BCE) in his *Epigrammata*, the first-century BCE compilation of poems and epigrams *Anthologia Graeca* 6.162, in Philodemus (first century BCE) in his *de Musica*, and in inscriptions (*CIG26039d*). See LSJ 104. The Greek verb ἀναθεματίζω ("devote to evil") is found in epigraphs (*Tab. Defix. Aud.* 41A), in the sixth-century CE collection of legal codes (*Cod. Just.* I. I. 5. 3). See ibid., 105.

144. Kennedy explains, "Sacred language affects to be outside of time, but the very process of casting it into words casts it into history" (*New Testament Interpretation through Rhetorical Criticism*, 159).

145. Swartz, "The Aesthetics of Blessing and Cursing," 201–2.

146. In Galatians, Paul is not beyond wishing his opponents physical pain. See Gal 5:12.

147. Kennedy calls Gal 1:6–10 a *proem* (opening) and compares it to Cicero's vigourous attack against Catiline. See his *New Testament Interpretation through Rhetorical Criticism*, 148.

148. There is a connection between the emotion of anger and bewitchment in that they both concern the eyes. Historically, anger was commonly understood as the emotional response to "wicked stimuli" See Stearns, *Anger: Psychology,*

Physiology, Pathology, 5. The English word "anger" is etymologically derived from the Old Norse (eighth–fourteenth century CE) word "angre," which means "affliction." In Spanish, the verb for becoming angry is "enojar," and derives from "en" and "ojo," and literally means, "something that offends the eye." See ibid.

149. Nanos reads this section of Galatians as irony. See *Irony of Galatians*, 38.

150. The translation is my own.

151. The Greek verb βασκαίνω means "bewitch by the evil eye" or by other means. It occurs in Deut 28:56; Aristotle, *Problemata* 926^{b}24; and Philostratus (second–third century CE). See LSJ 301.

152. According to J. Louis Martyn, Paul is accusing the teachers (his term for Paul's opponents) of leading the Galatians into the realm of superstition (*Galatians*, 283). In general, Betz says little about Paul's use of a term for bewitchment. However, he claims that its purpose "was to characterize opponents and their sophistic strategies" (*Galatians*, 131).

153. Focusing on Paul's employment of bewitchment (3:1) and the presence of curses throughout Gal 3:1–14, Eastman argues that in these verses Paul employs an intertextual echo to Deuteronomy 28. The Greek verb Βασκάνειν ("to bewitch") occurs twice within Deuteronomy 28 (vv. 54, 56), and the chapter itself contains many references to curses that result from the disobedience of God's commandments (Deut 28:15–19). According to Eastman, in Galatians 3 Paul is alluding to a horrifying allegorical passage involving the evil eye and cannibalism (Deut 28:53–57) to further develop his theme of cursing and blessing. See her "The Evil Eye and the Curse of the Law," 71. Eastman goes on to remark that Paul's Galatian audience would have heard about cursings and blessings from these others, the teachers ("teachers" is a term used by Eastman but also by Martyn for Paul's opponents), and perhaps from Paul himself. Paul, then, was countering the arguments of the teachers, and employed echoes of the same passage from Deuteronomy that the teachers used but for his own and very different purpose. See ibid., 71.

154. For more on this verb, see Danker, "βασκαίνω," BAGD 171 and Delling, "βασκαίνω," TDNT 1.594–95. According to Nanos, Paul refers here to evil eye bewitchment, a widespread practice in the area around the Mediterranean and is still in use today. See Nanos, "Paul's Evil Eye Warning." See also Walter Burkert on rhetorical enchantment in his "ΓΟΗΣ," 36–55.

155. For more information on the evil eye and on Paul's use of it, see Elliott, "Paul, Galatians, and the Evil Eye," 262–73; Eastman, "The Evil Eye and the Curse of the Law," 69–87; Nanos, "Paul's Evil Eye Warning."

156. Nanos cites (Aristotle, *Rhet.* 2.10.1-2). See "Paul's Evil Eye Warning," 19.

157. Nanos, "Paul's Evil Eye Warning," 12.

158. Nanos, "Paul's Evil Eye Warning," 15.

159. Nanos, "Paul's Evil Eye Warning," 6.

160. Eastman, "The Evil Eye and the Curse of the Law," 82–83.

161. See Eastman, "The Evil Eye and the Curse of the Law," 84–85.

162. Elliott, "Paul and the Evil Eye," 264.

163. "Stronger condemnation of a false prophet can hardly be possible" (Cronjé, "Defamiliarization," 226).

164. "It is the fear of the effects of the evil eye that gives rhetorical power to Paul's use of βασκαίνω in Gal. 3.1" (Eastman, "The Evil Eye and the Curse of the Law," 84).

165. While his reasons for connecting Paul's own curses in 1:8–9 to this curse in 3:10 differ from my own, Betz also sees a necessary link between the two different references to curses. See *Galatians*, 144.

166. The translation is my own.

167. For the function and importance of repetition on oral discourse, see Lee and Scott, *Sound Mapping*, 135–56.

168. The text Paul quotes does not "fully correspond to the LXX or the MT." Betz wonders whether or not Paul quotes from a LXX unknown to us. See *Galatians*, 144–45.

169. Aptly, Francis Watson notes that Paul "universalizes a scriptural statement" that was meant in the original context to apply only to those who transgress the law. "Paul here appears to universalize a scriptural statement which refers *prima facie* to only one of the two main categories of those addressed by the law: *those who transgress it*, as opposed to those who observe it." See his *Paul and the Hermeneutics of Faith*, 427. (Italics are my own.)

170. According to Roy Ciampa, Paul is responding to a nearly universal understanding that a curse of the law had fallen on Israel and Judah in Paul's day. See "Deuteronomy in Galatians and Romans," 102. By contrast, I am arguing that Paul is manufacturing the curse of Torah and does so by modifying his scriptural source. Paul is the one claiming there is a curse of the Torah, yet no such curse was present either within the tradition or at the time of Paul.

171. Other ancient sources supply the ἐν absent in the Nestle-Aland 27th edition. These other ancient sources include A C D F G and latt.

172. The translation is my own.

173. Betz remarks, "On the surface, Deut 27:26 says the opposite of what he [Paul] claims it says." Betz lays out four proposed solutions aimed at trying to understand Paul's argument and concludes that none of the four is satisfactory. See *Galatians*, 145–46. "In the present verse Paul interprets Deut 27:26 in a way that is the precise opposite of its literal meaning" (Martyn, *Galatians*, 309). See also Stanley who comments, "Whereas the quotation pronounces a curse on the person who fails to abide by the requirements of Torah, Paul applies the curse to those who seek to *comply* with the laws of Torah" (as quoted in Ciampa, "Deuteronomy in Galatians and Romans," 101; italics are the author's).

174. Martyn, *Galatians*, 311.

175. Betz downplays the modifications Paul makes to his deuteronomic source. He mentions that Paul's text does not "fully correspond to the LXX or to the MT." He wonders whether Paul is quoting from a version of the LXX that is no longer extant. See his *Galatians*, 144–45. Martyn too does not discuss the detailed differences between the two verses and, like Betz, comments that Gal 3:10 is different from "all texts [LXX] known to us" (*Galatians*, 309).

176. Betz calls 3:13 Paul's final and most important proof from scripture, the last of a series of five proofs. This final proof commences in Gal 3:8. See *Galatians*, 19.

177. The translation is my own.

178. See Betz's discussion in *Galatians*, 149. (Italics are my own.) According to Betz, the expression "curse of the Law" is "strange and occurs only here in Paul" (ibid).

179. Hays, *Echoes of Scripture in the Letters of Paul*, 203–4 n. 24. (Italics are the author's.) Such a nuanced difference is difficult to appreciate. By contrast to Hays, Cohen refers to the section defined by Gal 3:10–14 as "the curse of the law." See "The Letter of Paul to the Galatians," 337.

180. Eastman, "The Evil Eye and the Curse of the Law," 72.

181. "amulet, n," OED Online, June 2015, Oxford University Press, http://www.oed.com/view/Entry/6778 (accessed July 9, 2015).

182. Once again, Betz remarks that while Paul pulls from Deut 21:23, his statement in Gal 3:13 does not "fully conform to the LXX" of Deuteronomy. See *Galatians*, 151.

183. The translation is my own.

184. According to Roy Ciampa, Paul's substituted word ἐπικατάρατος occurs very often in Deuteronomy 27–28. Instances of that verb in Deuteronomy suggest that Paul has those chapters in mind when composing this section of Galatians. See "Deuteronomy in Galatians and Romans," 104.

185. Betz, *Galatians*, 151. (Italics are my own.)

186. Martyn, *Galatians*, 320–21. By contrast, Ciampa sees nothing particularly problematic by the absence of the phrase "by God" in Paul's citation. According to him, in this passage the expression "cursed by God" is the same as "cursed of the law" ("Deuteronomy in Galatians and Romans," 104–5).

187. Eastman, "The Evil Eye and the Curse of the Law," 71–72.

188. "allegory, n," OED Online, http://www.oed.com/view/Entry/5230 (accessed August 5, 2014).

189. Dawson, *Allegorical Readers*, 3–4.

190. Dawson, *Allegorical Readers*, 3.

191. Dawson, *Allegorical Readers*, 3–4.

192. Castelli, "Allegories of Hagar," 231.

193. Dawson, *Allegorical Readers*, 8. Allegory challenges the prior meaning, the so-called "literal meaning." See ibid.

194. Dawson, *Allegorical Readers*, 16. Allegory not only reduces the original text—by eliminating elements that do not fit within the allegorical framework being created—but also privileges the allegorical meaning over the original one. See Castelli, "Allegories of Hagar," 231–39.

195. See Castelli, "Allegories of Hagar," 231. Dawson notes that allegory does not necessarily cancel out the prior literal meaning but instead suspends that prior meaning long enough to attach new non-scriptural meaning to it. See *Allegorical Readers*, 16.

196. Dawson, *Allegorical Readers*, 1.

197. The overriding goal of the authors David Dawson surveyed was "to convince readers that their allegorical interpretations tap directly into the original source of all meaning and truth, and, by contrast, to show up competing readings as mere derivations and deviations from this original authoritative wisdom" (*Allegorical Readers*, 18).

198. Dawson, *Allegorical Readers*, 1.

199. Allegory "promotes a set of new interpretive conclusions as both inherent to the tradition and inevitable results of the interpretive process" (Castelli, "Allegories of Hagar," 231).

200. Castelli, "Allegories of Hagar," 231.

201. Betz, *Galatians*, 239. According to Quintilian, the strongest argument should appear either at the beginning or the end of the section. Although J. Louis Martyn is critical of using categories of classical rhetoric to analyze Paul's letters, he too would place Paul's allegory (Gal 4:21–5:1) at the end of a larger section. See *Galatians*, 26. In both judicial and deliberative outlines for Galatians, this section falls under a section referred to as "proof." On this see Dewey et al., *The Authentic Letters of Paul*, 162.

202. "Paul is not interested in giving an historically accurate account of the Genesis narratives. He does not consider that Abraham had more than two sons (cf. Gen 25:1–6). . . . What concerns Paul here in 4:22 is the dualistic contrast between Hagar's son Ishmael and Sarah's son Isaac" (Betz, *Galatians*, 242).

203. According to Elizabeth Castelli, with his allegory Paul is seeking to build consensus for the "embrace" of the figure of Sarah and for the "rejection of the figure of Hagar." See "Allegories of Hagar," 231.

204. NRSV translation.

205. "Paul is not interested in the two women as historical persons, but in the two worlds they represent" (Betz, *Galatians*, 243).

206. By contrast, according to Susan Elliott, with his allegory Paul was cautioning against becoming enslaved to the cult of the Mother of the Gods and not against Torah itself. See "Choose Your Mother," 676–83.

207. Finding that Paul is in large measure reacting against Roman domination, Davina Lopez finds that with his allegory Paul is offering the Galatians two choices: a continuation under Roman rule, as depicted by the slave Hagar and her son, or "service to God and collective self-determination." See Lopez, *Apostle to the Conquered*, 162. Brigitte Kahl argues that the two women Sarah and Hagar represent allegorically "two contrasting theological and political conditions that are applicable to Israel as a whole and form the 'backbone' of the entire biblical tradition: exile and exodus" ("Hagar's Babylonian Captivity," 262). Like Lopez, Kahl also understands that Hagar represented for Paul subservience under Roman law and Roman rule, whereas Sarah was meant to characterize a rebirth of the nations through a God who leads out of that type of slavery (ibid., 269).

208. Castelli, "Paul on Women and Gender," 231. Martyn observes the built opposition between the present-day Jerusalem and the Jerusalem above. According to him, Paul is embroiled in a local conflict with Christian-Jewish evangelists (i.e., the Teachers) within Galatia, who advocate Torah observance in cooperation with the present-day Jerusalem church. See *Galatians*, 466. I agree with Martyn concerning the context as being one of conflict among leaders.

209. Much scholarship has been devoted to Paul and his use of Abraham. These works include Eisenbaum, "Paul as the New Abraham"; Eisenbaum, *Paul Was Not a Christian*, 200–207; Schliesser, *Abraham's Faith in Romans* 4; Koyzis, *Paul, Monotheism and the People of God*; Fee, "Who are Abraham's true children?"

210. According to Castelli, allegory "inscribes dualism at a conceptual level, setting up a clear opposition between the commonplace meaning and the privileged allegorical meaning and undergirding a whole series of further oppositions: literal-analogical, surface-depth, letter-spirit" ("Allegories of Hagar," 239).

211. Brendan Bryne observes how Paul "sidesteps" the fact that Isaac was also born "of the flesh." See his "Jerusalems Above and Below," 225.

212. According to Jennifer Glancy, the Hagar-Sarah allegory occasions the notion of the sexual vulnerability of Hagar the slave. See her *Slavery in Early Christianity*, 25.

213. This is a repetition of the same thought presented in different ways. Paul uses two different words to denote slavery, παῖς for the slave woman Hagar and δοῦλος for the state of slavery.

214. In Genesis, an angel grants Hagar many offspring (Gen 16:10), echoing the promise that Abraham receives.

215. Feminist interpreters have observed sexual overtones more generally in Galatians. Citing Brigitte Kahl, Joseph Marchal notes, "Feminist interpreters of this letter [Galatians] have been right to describe it as: 'the most "phallocentric" document of the New Testament. Nowhere else have we so much naked maleness exposed as the centre of a deeply theological and highly emotional debate: foreskin, circumcision, sperm, castration'" ("Bodies Bound for Circumcision and Baptism," 171).

216. According to Marchal, the two "female bodies are presented instrumentally, as receptacles for the delivery of sons and then as figures receptive to presentation of wider concepts (freedom/slavery, Jerusalem above/Jerusalem now, spirit/flesh)" ("Bodies Bound for Circumcision and Baptism," 175).

217. J. Louis Martyn notes the lack of mention of the term "Sinai" in the Genesis narratives that regard Hagar and Sarai/Sarah. No covenants at all are associated with women. Yet he remarks that Sinai does have a strong biblical association with the Mosaic covenant; the laws were first given on Mount Sinai (Exod 19 ff). This is also one of only three references to the word "Sinai" in the New Testament. "Sinai" occurs in Acts 7:30 and 7:38. See *Galatians*, 437, n. 129.

218. *Repotia* is the repetition of a phrase with a slight difference in style. In 4:24 Paul writes ὄρους Σινᾶ and in 4:25 Σινᾶ ὄρος, reversing the order of the words "mountain" and "Sinai."

219. According to Betz, verse 4:25 is a "real *crux interpretum*" (difficult or impossible to interpret). He points out that the Greek does not say that Hagar is located in Mount Sinai in Arabia, but that she *is* Mount Sinai in Arabia. Furthermore, Mount Sinai is not in Arabia but in Israel. See *Galatians*, 244. (Emphasis is my own.) By contrast, Elliott argues that Hagar is meant to represent the Mountain Mother, mother of the self-castrated *galli*. According to her, Paul is counseling the Galatians to avoid relations with this goddess. See "Choose Your Mother," 676–83.

220. According to Glancy, Paul "subordinates biological to spiritual" (*Slavery in Early Christianity*, 36).

221. Similarly, Elliott remarks, "Not naming Sarah allows for a freer variety of allegorical identifications of the 'legitimate wife' who bears children by means of the promise and the Spirit (4:28–29). Such identifications include the vaguely defined city above, Paul himself (cf. 4:19), and the 'Spirit of God's Son,' who bears by baptism and reception of the Spirit (4:6)" ("Choose Your Mother," 682).

222. Again, the Hagar-Sarah allegory occasions the notion of the sexual vulnerability of Hagar the slave. See Glancy, *Slavery in Early Christianity*, 25.

Paul is certainly not "above" using sexualized language against his opponents. In a sudden burst of anger, he hurls the not subtle invective that those unsettling (ἀναστατοῦντες) the Galatians with their alternative message castrate themselves (ἀποκόψονται; Gal 5:12). David Gilmore remarks that castration is a near-universal Mediterranean image of diminishment and disgrace. See "Introduction: The Shame of Dishonor," 10–11. Indeed, Joseph Marshal calls this verse "the most disturbing argumentative moment" in the letter ("Bodies Bound for Circumcision and Baptism," 173). With regard to Gal 5:12, Martyn writes, "Paul paints a rude, obscene, and literally bloody picture" (*Galatians*, 478). According to Bernard Scott, ἀποκόψονται (Gal 5:12) does not refer to castration but to cutting off the penis itself! See his *The Real Paul*, 19.

223. Indeed, the sexual exploitation of one's own slaves was widespread. On this point, see especially Glancy, "The Sexual Use of Slaves," 215–29. Elsewhere, Glancy comments, "Slaveholders had unrestricted sexual access to their slaves" (*Slavery in Early Christianity*, 9). According to Marshal, slaves were like dildos for the female elite class. See his "The Usefulness of an Onesimus," 753.

224. Here I cite from Kyle Harper's 2012 JBL article. Readers may also wish to consult his monograph on the same subject. See his *From Shame to Sin: The Christian Transformation of Sexual Morality in Late Antiquity*. See too Jennifer Wright Knust, who writes, "In the ancient context, sexual behavior was an important component in the production and maintenance of status" (*Abandoned to Lust*, 28).

225. Harper, "*Porneia*: The Making of a Christian Sexual Norm," 367.

226. Troy Martin argues that with his allegory Paul addresses not the Galatians but instead the agitators. See his "Apostasy to Paganism," 89.

227. See Betz, *Galatians*, 149.

4
Persuading through Disjuncture

1. Manuwald and Hall make this assessment with regard to Cicero, yet it applies to all three authors: Demosthenes, Cicero, and Paul. See Manuwald, *Commentary*, 305; Manuwald, *Introduction and Texts*, 112; Hall, "The *Philippics*," 284.
For general information on the use of disjunctive rhetoric in rhetoric-of-crisis authors, see Cicero, *Philippics 1–6*, xx. See especially Wooten's discussion on the disjunctive mode of rhetoric in Cicero and Demosthenes in *Rhetoric of Crisis*, 58–86.

2. Olson, "Dissociation," 196.

3. Perelman and Olbrechts-Tyteca, *The New Rhetoric*, 417.

4. Perelman, *The Realm of Rhetoric*, 126; Perelman and Olbrechts-Tyteca, *The New Rhetoric*, 415.

5. Perelman and Olbrechts-Tyteca, *The New Rhetoric*, 416. (Italics are the authors'.)

6. Perelman, *The Realm of Rhetoric*, 135.

7. Aristotle, *The "Art" of Rhetoric*, xxxvi.

8. Libanius (*hyp.* 6.42) remarks that a report from envoys sent to Athens by Philip prompted Demosthenes' *Second Philippic*. The envoys complained that the Athenians had misrepresented the promises Philip had made. See Markle, "Demosthenes' *Second Philippic*," 68. Such a context, however, is not at all apparent from the rhetoric Demosthenes employs. Demosthenes does not appear to be debating with envoys (implicitly or explicitly) but instead aims his discourse at his own political adversaries. On this latter point, see Mader, "Fighting Philip with Decrees," 367–86. See also John Sandys who comments, "The speech is not entirely suitable for delivery before the envoys of Philip or of the Peloponnesian states. Philip is described as breaking the terms of the Peace and plotting against all the Greeks" (*Demosthenes: Texts and Notes*, xxviii).

9. On this, see Wooten, *Demosthenes' Philippic I*, 124.

10. The embassy was troubled from the start, as those to whom Demosthenes and others were sent, namely, the Argies, the Messenians, and the Arcadians, distrusted Athens because it had formed an alliance with Sparta. For more on this, see Demosthenes, *Olynthiacs, Philippics*, 123.

11. For a discussion of Demosthenes' other political opponents, see Mader, "Fighting Philip with Decrees," 367–86.

12. Ryder, "Demosthenes and Philip II," 72.

13. In contrast to Demosthenes, who wished to form an alliance with the Thebans to combat Philip, Aeschines sided with Philip against the Thebans. See Markle, "Demosthenes' *Second Philippic*," 62.

14. That Aeschines is in view, as well as Demosthenes' other rival Philocrates, see Sandys, *Demosthenes: Texts and Notes*, xxxii–xxxiii. Sandys writes, "In the latter part of the *Second Philippic*, the orator, while abstaining from mentioning names, undoubtedly refers to Philocrates and Aeschines as responsible for the present state of affairs, and in its closing sentence, he who 'deserves death' is undoubtedly Aeschines" (ibid., xxxii).

15. In this speech (2.35–36) and at the trial of Aeschines a year later, Demosthenes lays the blame for Philip's incursion into Thermopylae at the feet of

Aeschines. While acquitted, at his trial Aeschines was accused of treason for siding with Philip and for believing in the latter's claim to faithfully implement the terms of the peace treaty. See Ryder, "Demosthenes and Philip II," 76.

16. Stirring up the public against Philip likely served Demosthenes' aim of combatting his internal political rivals. See Ryder, "Demosthenes and Philip II," 73. Although Demosthenes claims that Philip broke the terms of the peace treaty, in reality he did not. See ibid., 72.

17. Mader, "Fighting Philip with Decrees," 367.

18. According to Mader, this speech-within-a-speech says as much about Demosthenes and his own self-promotion as it does about the current situation with Philip. Mader writes, "The sequence is as much about Philip's tactics as it is about the role of Demosthenes himself in disclosing and interpreting those designs. The regressive *ordo artificiosus*—the Athenians (Demosthenes' present audience in the *Second Philippic*) are warned by the example of the Argives and Messenians, who had themselves failed to heed the earlier warning example of Olynthus—gives point to the role of the speaker who discerns the interconnectedness of the discrete events and sees present and future as a replay of the past" ("Foresight, Hindsight," 351).

19. Ronnet remarks that dialog brings a level of interest or sense of life to discourse. Yet she also comments that the technique is artificial. According to her, dialogue requires preparation and thus by its very nature it is less spontaneous and thus false. See her *Étude sur le style de Démosthène*, 125.

20. The translation is by Vince in Demosthenes, *Olynthiacs, Philippics*, 137. Quotation marks are found in the Greek text of the Loeb edition (ibid., 136).

21. Demosthenes places the three pronouns, ταύτην, ταύτης, and ταύτην, emphatically at the start of their respective phrases. See Sandys, *Demosthenes: Texts and Notes*, 131. Aeschines repeats the same pronoun four times in a row in his *Against Timarchus* (191), written two years before Demosthenes' *Second Philippic*.

22. See Sandys, *Demosthenes: Texts and Notes*, 130.

23. ἀντέχεσθε is a present middle-passive imperative from the verb ἀντέχω. Its root meaning (in the infinitive form) is "to hold out against," "to withstand." In the middle voice, ἀντέχεσθε means to "hold on by," or to "cling to." See ΛΟΓΕΙΟΝ, "ἀντέχεσθε," accessed April 28, 2015, http://logeion.uchicago.edu/index.html#ἀντέχεσθε.

24. For the influence of the author's present situation on rhetoric, see the well-known work Bitzer, "The Rhetorical Situation," 1–14.

25. While the Greek word for trust (πίστις) does not appear in this particular internal speech, Demosthenes does make use of the term "trust" with regard to his rivals earlier in his *Second Philippic*. At 2.6, he bluntly remarks to the Athenians, "If you think me the better prophet, adopt my advice; if you prefer those who have so confidently trusted him [Philip] (πεπιστευκότες αὐτῷ), give them your allegiance" (as translated by Vince in Demosthenes, *Olynthiacs, Philippics*, 127).

26. This is Vince's translation of θεωρεῖτε (2.23a).

27. θεωρεῖτε is a second-person plural present active indicative of θεωρέω. In its infinitive form and according to the present context, it means "to behold," "to gaze," or "to gape," as a spectator would do at a game. See ΛΟΓΕΙΟΝ, "θεωρεῖτε," accessed April 28, 2015, http://logeion.uchicago.edu/index.html#θεωρεῖτε.

28. ἰδεῖν is a present infinitive of the verb ὁράω, which has the basic meaning of "see," "look to," "take or give heed to," and "perceive." See ΛΟΓΕΙΟΝ, "ὁράω," accessed April 28, 2015, http://logeion.uchicago.edu/index.html#ὁράω.

29. Mader, "Fighting Philip with Decrees," 368–70. Cf. *Phil.* 2.1.

30. Mader writes, "The syndrome of symbolic action he [Demosthenes] describes needs to be seen in the context of competing domestic agendas" and must be treated with caution ("Fighting Philip with Decrees," 382).

31. Many material safeguards are being contrasted to the one moral imperative ("mistrust"). On this see Sandys, *Demosthenes: Texts and Notes*, 131.

32. *Polysyndeton* is present with the repetition of the conjunction "and" (καὶ).

33. Sandys, *Demosthenes: Texts and Notes*, 131.

34. Sandys comments, "After recounting the 'manifold contrivances for the guarding and defending of cities,' and describing them as merely material safeguards involving costly expenditure, the orator contrasts these with a moral safeguard inherent in the instincts of all sensible men" (*Demosthenes: Texts and Notes*, 131).

35. Sandys, *Demosthenes: Texts and Notes*, 131.

36. This is a form of *paronomasia*: a play on words that sound nearly the same but have distinctly different meanings. For this see Rowe, "Style," 132. Demosthenes intends the two words to be understood in contrast to each other.

37. The interjection is lost in Vince's translation. νὴ Δία is the most frequent interjection Demosthenes employs. See Ronnet, *Étude sur le style de Démosthène*, 11.

38. On arousing audience expectation, see Sandys, *Demosthenes: Texts and Notes*, 131.

39. See Sandys, who remarks that Demosthenes uses the expression seven times within sections 20–25 (*Demosthenes: Texts and Notes*, 131).

40. Demosthenes, *Olynthiacs, Philippics*, 141. See also the note on his page 140.

41. Vince translates τύραννος as "despot" (2.25c).

42. The quotation is from the 1872 *Works of Henry Lord Brougham: Dissertations and Addresses*, 52. Cited in Sandys, *Demosthenes: Texts and Notes*, xxxi.

43. Perelman and Olbrechts-Tyteca remark, "Undoubtedly in very many cases it [dissociative argumentation] is to the speaker merely a matter of a simple persuasive technique" (*The New Rhetoric*, 447).

44. For the importance of noble value for Roman elites, see Rosenstein, "Aristocratic Values," 365–82. Rosenstein remarks, "Honor was everything at Rome, every aristocrat's all-consuming ambition" (ibid., 365). There is considerable scholarship on this issue, see Rosenstein's bibliography, ibid., 381–82.

45. Manuwald, *Commentary*, 424.

46. Cicero, *Philippics 1–6*, 175–76.

47. The term *libertas* occurs more frequently in *Philippic Three* than in any other of the *Philippics*. See Fogel, "Cicero and the 'Ancestral Constitution,'" 249. On this point, see also Manuwald, *Commentary*, 428.

48. "Cicero may state these terms [*serviamus/libertatem/servituti*] for the Roman people and use them in his arguments as a premise because he can rely on the fact that this view is generally accepted and shared by his audience" (Manuwald, *Commentary*, 428).

49. For this view, see especially Cowan, "*Libertas* in the *Philippics*," 147. Nathan Rosenstein remarks, "for aristocrats, an essential component was the freedom of the city's public affairs from the control of a tyrant or a small clique (*factio*) and consequently the freedom of individual aristocrats to compete to serve the Republic through office holding, legislation, or participation in other public matters and to serve the interests of friends and clients through patronage" ("Aristocratic Values," 379). Rosenstein, however, appears to understand *libertas* literally, as a fixed notion, rather than as a metaphor. Following on Matthew Roller, I adopt a metaphorical understanding of the term "freedom."

50. "Cicero's political world is always bi-polar. There were always only two choices, good or bad" (Harries, *Cicero and the Jurists*, 218).

51. Translated by Manuwald in *Introduction and Texts*, 181, 185.

52. On how the term *libertas* largely remains undefined and takes on a metaphorical meaning as a contrast to its opposing term *servitus*, see Roller, *Constructing Autocracy*, 221–27. Jerise Fogel explains things differently. According to her, in Cicero's *Philippics*, the term *libertas* has one of two values: 1) the *libertas* of the senatorial elites to guide public policy by their constitution and 2) the *libertas* of the people to be interested in the public welfare and to "live under non-dictatorial regime" ("Cicero and the 'Ancestral Constitution,'" 249). See also Rosenstein, "Aristocratic Values," 379. Both Fogel and Rosenstein tend to tie down a meaning for *libertas*, whereas Roller takes it as a constructed category, as do I. According to Matthew Roller, with whom I am in agreement, in Roman culture, *libertas* was not a coherent category. See *Constructing Autocracy*, 232.

53. Manuwald, *Commentary*, 425. See also Donat Taddeo who remarks, "the image is emotional and vivid" ("Signs of Demosthenes in Cicero's *Philippics*," 19).

54. As Manuwald remarks, a sense of process "makes good sense here" (*Commentary*, 426).

55. On this, see Manuwald, *Commentary*, 426. Some editors, such as Ferrarius, emend the text and change the accusative noun *possessionem* to the ablative *possession*.

56. The OED defines the subjunctive mood as, "Designating or relating to a verbal mood that refers to an action or state as conceived (rather than as a fact) and is therefore used chiefly to express a wish, command, exhortation, or a contingent, hypothetical, or prospective event"(OED online, "subjunctive," accessed October 24, 2014, http://www.oed.com/view/Entry/192731).

57. Manuwald translates the subjunctives as exhortations, "let us" (3.29, 3.35, 3.36).

58. According to Manuwald, "The present condition is based on the combined efforts and the unanimity of all the bodies within the *res publica*, on the support of the immortal gods and on Cicero's preserving himself for this very moment" (*Commentary*, 425). Harries writes, "Part of Cicero's rhetorical strategy, familiar from the past, was to emphasize the 'agreement' (*concordia*) of all the sections of Roman society opposed to Antonius." This *concordia* did not exist in reality. See *Cicero and the Jurists*, 207.

59. Elsewhere, Cicero paints himself as the defender of freedom. See *Phil.* 2.118–19.

60. Religion was an important source of legitimacy for the ruling elites, as Jörg Rüpke remarks. See "Communicating with the Gods," 231.

61. Manuwald notes the presence here of Cicero's own personality (cf. *Phil.* 3.1–2). See her *Commentary*, 425.

62. Cf. *Phil.* 4.1. See Harries who remarks that Cicero claims that he alone is the "true defender" of the *Res publica* and of the freedom. See *Cicero and the Jurists*, 207.

63. On the topic of urgency within the unit, see Manuwald, *Commentary*, 424.

64. Cicero employs this same expression elsewhere (*Phil.* 3.11; 4.7; 7.11; 10.14). See Manuwald, *Commentary*, 429.

65. According to Manuwald, *libertas* would have resonated with "essential values of the Republican order" (*Commentary*, 306).

66. Manuwald, *Commentary*, 446.

67. See *Phil.* 2.7, 74; 5.10, 32; 6.3; 7.17; 13.16, 20. When used against Antony, the term may be a reaction to Antony calling Cicero a *lanista* (a trainer of gladiators; *Phil.* 13.40). See Manuwald, *Commentary*, 387. On Antony's invective against

Cicero, see Hall, "The *Philippics*," 287. For the use of this term within the writings of Cicero, see Jal, "'Hostis (Publicus),'" 67.

68. Cowan, "*Libertas* in the *Philippics*," 147.

69. Roller, *Constructing Autocracy*, 221.

70. Roller, *Constructing Autocracy*, 221.

71. Roller, *Constructing Autocracy*, 227.

72. See the discussion in Roller, *Constructing Autocracy*, 223–26.

73. Aristotle, *Nicomachean Ethics* 1161b.1.

74. Joshel, *Slavery in the Roman World*, 6. According to Joshel, slavery was widely accepted and in no place was it considered morally wrong.

75. Joshel, *Slavery in the Roman World*, 8.

76. Wiedemann, *Greek and Roman Slavery*, 1.

77. Joshel, *Slavery in the Roman World*, 38–40; Glancy, *Slavery in Early Christianity*, 9, 25–26, 35.

78. Aristotle, *Nichomachean Ethics* 1161a.6. Joshel remarks that slaves were equivalent to things. Joshel, *Slavery in the Roman World*, 38. Those captured in war became slaves and were considered as property. See Wiedemann, *Greek and Roman Slavery*, 15.

79. Roller, *Constructing Autocracy*, 223.

80. There are numerous anecdotes in Roman literature describing masters' cruelty to slaves. See Roller, *Constructing Autocracy*, 224.

81. Joshel, *Slavery in the Roman World*, 20, 40.

82. Wiedemann, *Greek and Roman Slavery*, 9.

83. Roller, *Constructing Autocracy*, 226.

84. Roller, *Constructing Autocracy*, 226. This is not to say that "warm and loyal" relationships did not exist between masters and slaves, only that elites did not consider cordial relationships to be the norm.

85. Joshel, *Slavery in the Roman World*, 9–10.

86. Translated by Manuwald in *Introduction and Texts*, 181.

87. With regard to Cicero's long list of the abuses of Antony, Manuwald remarks, "Cicero's questionable plan of fighting Antonius will sound more plausible and necessary when it is justified by the danger to public affairs posed by the person of Antonius" (*Introduction and Texts*, 106). Robin Seager finds that Cicero's invectives often include a characterization of the subject's "unique wickedness." According to Seager, there are three modes of attack within Cicero's invectives: 1) the claim that the conduct of the subject is unprecedented; 2) that the subject's behavior "reveals his unique wickedness"; and 3) "synkrisis with one or more individuals, whose conduct in a comparable context was conspicuously virtuous or at least not nearly as bad, as a foil for the target of invective" ("Ciceronian Invective," 25).

88. For the translation of *hostis* as "public enemy," see Manuwald, *Introduction and Texts*, 92. See also Jal, "'Hostis (Publicus),'" 53–79.

89. Hall, "The *Philippics*," 286.

90. Being termed a *hostis* carried a heavy penalty. As Jal comments, the declaration required a senatorial decree and, if granted, entailed the loss of constitutional guarantees, the confiscation of all goods, and a damned memory. A *hostis* was considered a foreigner and excluded from society. See Jal, "'Hostis (Publicus),'" 55, 78. Jal remarks that Roman authors employed this term to provoke hatred for their enemies. "La plupart d'entre eux aient voulu par là assouvir leur haine" ("'Hostis [Publicus],'" 59). Cicero is not the only Roman author to employ this term. Jal cites, for example, Seneca, Suetonius, and Augustine. See ibid., 54–55.

91. Manuwald, *Introduction and Texts*, 92.

92. Manuwald, *Commentary*, 483–85. Cicero attempts to convince his audiences that Antony should be declared a *hostis* by presenting the situation as pressing, making his allusions precise, and by employing terms for war (*bellum*) and public enemy (*hostis*) often. See Jal, "'Hostis (Publicus),'" 70. Jal is describing the rhetoric-of-crisis model of argumentation.

93. Manuwald translates *Quirites* as "Men of Rome."

94. Manuwald, *Commentary*, 463–64.

95. The role of the people in Roman decision-making is the subject of vigorous scholarly debate. See Yakobson, "Popular Power in the Roman Republic," 383–400. Yakobson's article includes an extensive guide for further reading. See ibid., 399. For additional bibliography see Steel, *The End of the Roman Republic 146 to 44 BC*, 257–58. According to Rosenstein, elites had a need to sway popular opinion. See his "Aristocratic Values," 376.

96. See Manuwald, *Commentary*, 464–65.

97. On this point, see Manuwald, *Commentary*, 467.

98. Manuwald, *Commentary*, 465. For this view, see especially Karl-J. Hölkeskamp, who writes, "It was the *contio* which was in fact one of the most important stages of politics and performance, communication, and interaction—indeed according to Cicero's much-quoted dicta, it was the *locus ad agendum amplissimus, ad dicendum ornatissimus* and indeed the *maxima scaena* of the orator, who 'can no more be eloquent without a large audience that a flute-player can perform without a flute' and who had 'to employ the more ornate kind of oratory' on this 'most important stage'" ("Friends, Romans, Countrymen," 17).

99. As Manuwald remarks, both the *Third* and *Fourth Philippic* function to motivate the audience to side against Antony. See *Commentary*, 473, 476.

100. It is worth mentioning that Cicero published his oral speeches after delivering them and likely made modifications to them in the process of doing so. Publishing or circulating the written text served to garner additional support for the orator's views. Cicero compiled a corpus of twelve speeches (the *Philippics*) and chose the name in imitation of the speeches Demosthenes delivered against Philip. The twelve begin with what we know as *Philippic Three* and end with (our) *Philippic Fourteen*. Cicero was also responsible for placing the speeches in a particular order, one intended to promote his views. He separately circulated single speeches of the *Philippics* to various individuals. Brutus received several of his speeches for comment including *Philippic Three* and *Five* and likely the two *contio* speeches, *Four* and *Six*. For a fuller discussion of Cicero's publication and circulation of the *Philippics* see Manuwald, *Introduction and Texts*, 54–90.

101. Cicero set the ultimate aim above the means. See Manuwald, *Introduction and Texts*, 97. He rarely used factual proof or arguments but instead relied upon "sophisticated considerations and conclusions" (ibid., 112).

102. "Cicero does not convey the Senate decree before the people objectively, but in his interpretation" (Manuwald, *Commentary*, 470).

103. Translation is by Manuwald in *Introduction and Texts*, 191.

104. Manuwald explains, "In the Senate Cicero has to make the senators realize these alternatives [*hostis* or *consul*] and decide for the 'right' one, which requires a more extended argument before this conclusion. When he talks to the People after the Senate decree has been passed, he simply has to make them approve of it by presenting it clearly and persuasively" (*Commentary*, 486–87). However, in this case, no such decree was passed, so Cicero is being deceptive.

105. "The consensus argument is quite empty here" (Fogel, "Cicero and the 'Ancestral Constitution,'" 251).

106. Fogel, "Cicero and the 'Ancestral Constitution,'" 251.

107. Manuwald, *Commentary*, 470. According to Fogel, the Senate was not yet ready to take such a step. See "Cicero and the 'Ancestral Constitution,'" 246.

108. Wooten, *Rhetoric of Crisis*, 70.

109. Manuwald, *Commentary*, 488. Cicero's claims the presence of large audiences at other of his own *contiones*, and he ridicules small turnouts at *contiones* of his opponents. See ibid., 487.

110. Manuwald, *Commentary*, 488. Cf. *Phil.* 6.18; *Fam.* 12.7.1.

111. Using these kinds of titles was the way in which Cicero tried to interact with his audience. See Manuwald, *Introduction and Texts*, 116.

112. Manuwald, *Commentary*, 488.

113. Hölkeskamp, "Friends, Romans, Countrymen," 20.

114. Manuwald, *Commentary*, 489.

115. Manuwald, *Commentary*, 489.

116. *Princeps* indicates Cicero's "temporal and qualitative prominence in defending the People's liberty" (Manuwald, *Commentary*, 489).

117. According to Fogel, this line (and term) marks the first important ideological argument of the speech. See "Cicero and the 'Ancestral Constitution,'" 250.

118. Manuwald remarks that with his two *contio* speeches (*Philippic Four and Six*), Cicero turns a defeat in the Senate (as is evident in his *Third* and *Fifth Philippic*) into a source of "increased authority in relation to the People" (*Introduction and Texts*, 81).

119. Manuwald, *Introduction and Texts*, 92; *Commentary*, 33.

120. Indeed, *Phil.* 4.2b is a prime example of the "fundamental disjunctive pair" that describes, according to Manuwald, the whole of Cicero's campaign: "either Antonius is consul and his opponents must be punished, or Antonius is a public enemy and his opponents have acted rightly" (*Introduction and Texts*, 112–13).

121. In their monograph *The Authentic Letters of Paul*, Dewey, et al. provide an example of the various oppositions Paul draws. They write, "Paul's argument throughout Galatians bears the note of radical discontinuity. . . . His contrasts are quite extensive: human/divine, temporal/eternal, human approval/divine favor, traditional religious practices/confidence in God, mediators/one God, uncircumcised/circumcised, the nations/Jews, old identity/new identity, written/oral, curse/blessing, promise/law, minor/adult, Jew/Greek, slave/freeborn, male/female, dominated/liberated, son of a free woman/son of a slave woman, Mount Sinai/heavenly Jerusalem, life of subjection/life of freedom, self-serving desires/living in God's power, present evil age/new world" (44–45).

122. Castelli, "Paul on Women and Gender," 230.

123. Castelli, "Paul on Women and Gender," 230.

124. Indeed, this was already an idea suggested by the nineteenth-century theologian F. C. Baur (1792–1860). Baur made the topic of opponents central for an understanding of the occasion of Paul's letters. According to him, Paul's opponents were Judaizers, defined as Jewish-Christians who demanded the continuing practice of Torah. The Judaizers contended that the first step toward salvation was circumcision. While I disagree with Baur that Paul's opponents urged circumcision for reasons that pertain to salvation, I do find that opponents are central to Paul's many arguments. For a good review of Baur's position, see Sumney, *Identifying Paul's Opponents*, 15.

125. In Rom 2:13, Paul writes that "doers" of the Torah will be justified. Elsewhere in the NT one sees that "works" are as important as "trust." James 2:24, for example, states that a person is justified by works and not by trust alone.

126. The fact that Paul does not clearly and consistently specify why he argues against Torah adoption for non-Jews accounts for the myriad of different reasons commentators advance to explain it: adopting the Torah means denying that God through God's grace provides justification; the Torah is too particular and only pertains to Jews; Paul was against boasting in the exclusive privilege of having the Torah, etc. For a very good summary of the various positions regarding Paul and Torah, see Zetterholm, *Approaches to Paul*.

127. The bibliography on Paul and "works of law" is enormous. The following website contains numerous entries that touch on this subject: http://www.thepaulpage.com/the-new-perspective-on-paul-a-bibliographical-essay/, accessed September 26, 2014.

Jacqueline de Roo reviews the scholarship on this term. Her survey covers twentieth-century interpreters. See "Concept of 'Works of the Law,'" 116–17. See especially her footnotes on those pages cited. James Dunn in turn argues that works of law (food laws, Sabbath observance and circumcision) served as badges to identify a person as a Jew, as distinct from other nations. According to him, Greco-Roman writers at the time of Paul characterized Jews by their distinctive customs. According to Dunn, Paul opposed Jewish distinctiveness and the accompanying sense of privilege Jews had on account of their unique customs. Dunn has written extensively on this subject. His work reflects the New Perspective on Paul. See, for example, "The New Perspective on Paul," 192; "Works of the Law and the Curse of the Law (Gal. 3.10–14)," 215–41. Paul, however, does not appear to be bothered by Jewish particularism.

According to Nanos, works of law are what "mark out those who are the people of the Mosaic covenant, Israelites, from those who are not" ("What was at Stake?" 315 n. 109). Joseph Tyson's 1973 essay has been quite influential. From the early stages of the debate on the meaning of this term, Tyson argued that with the expression "works of law," Paul was not referring to the accomplishment of multiple commandments, but instead a mode of existence. "Works of law" stands for a religious system, or nomistic service, and not commandments themselves. See "'Works of Law' in Galatians," 425, 429.

128. Following on the work of Martin Hengel, Betz comments that Paul may not have been the first to contrast "trust" with "works of Torah"; the opposition "may have its origin with the so-called movement of the 'Hellenists.'" Hengel claimed that prior to the Maccabean revolt and with an aim of ending Jewish particularism, 'Hellenists' wanted to abolish the Torah of Moses. See Betz, *Galatians*, 139.

Yet Betz also notes, "According to Pauline theology, Scripture says that the *concepts* of 'faith' and 'law' are opposites" (*Galatians*, 138 n. 8; italics are the author's). Furthermore, after surveying many New Testament texts, including all the canonical gospels, the Letter to James, the Letter to the Ephesians and the Pastoral Epistles, Heikki Räisänen remarks, "*Paul is alone* in early Christianity in setting up a contrast between the Torah with its demands on the one hand and God's grace or man's faith in Christ on the other" (*Paul and the Law*, 198; italics are the author's).

129. Italics indicate that scripture is being quoted.

130. Betz perceptively adds the words "By contrast" to his translation, which makes explicit the contrast Paul is making between "those of trust," who are blessed along with Abraham, and "those of Torah," who are cursed. See *Galatians*, 137.

131. The translation is my own, with some assistance from Betz. The SV translators render these verses as follows: "You're in the same situation as Abraham. [As scripture says]: 'Abraham put his trust in God, and God counted that the right thing to do.' From this you ought to draw the conclusion that Abraham's heirs are

those born of confidence in God. Indeed, scripture anticipated what is happening right now, namely that God acknowledges that the nations are right to put their confidence in God. Scripture announced this beforehand to Abraham when it says, 'Because of you all the nations will be blessed.' For that reason those who put their confidence in God are blessed just like Abraham. On the other hand, whoever relies on traditional religious practices is under a curse, because it is written, 'Everyone who does not honor all the things written in the book of the Law by observing them is accursed'" (Dewey et al., *The Authentic Letters of Paul*, 55–56).

132. With regard to the cogency of the section (Gal 3:6–14), Betz remarks that by the criteria of historical-critical exegesis, Paul's arguments appear "arbitrary in the highest degree." Betz adds that these verses are "extremely difficult to follow" (*Galatians*, 137). By paying attention to Paul's own historical-cultural setting, Betz attempts (unsuccessfully in my view) to make some logical sense of what Paul is saying. By contrast, I am arguing that Paul here and elsewhere is involved in polemics. Driving home his position over that of his opponents appears to be more important than cogency.

133. For scholarship on Paul and his use of Abraham, see especially Pamela Eisenbaum, "Paul as the New Abraham"; *Paul Was Not a Christian*, 200–207.

134. In the midst of his comments on Gal 3:6, Betz includes a long excursus on Abraham. I sense that Betz is grappling with Paul's severely limited treatment of Abraham. Betz begins his excursus by reminding his readers of the importance of Abraham for Judaism. He cites Sir 44:19–21, which begins "great Abraham was the father of many nations; no one has ever been found to equal him in fame. He kept the law of the Most High. . . . " Betz remarks, in contrast to Jas 2:21–33 Paul "separates Abraham's faith in God's promise from his obedience to the Jewish Torah." According to Betz, Abraham becomes a prototype for the "Christian" believer. See *Galatians*, 139.

135. The Genesis account concerns Abram and not Abraham; otherwise the two verses are identical.

136. Paul certainly knew of this particular episode in the life of Abraham, as he refers to it in his letter to the Romans (4:9–12).

137. "In Galatians, Paul manages to evade the fact that Abraham, too, was circumcised—a fact that might have proved embarrassing for Paul's cause in that letter" (Räisänen, *Paul and the Law*, 190).

138. See J. Louis Martyn, who comments that Paul selects the Gen 15:6 text "to establish rectification of faith as the point of departure for the exegetical section" (*Galatians*, 300).

139. These are passive verbs that indicate being blessed.

140. As Betz points out, although 3:8a is marked as a scriptural quotation, no such scriptural statement corresponds to it. "The words are clearly marked as a quotation, although they cannot precisely be identified with any LXX passage in which the blessing is found. Paul's words may therefore be his own" (*Galatians*, 142).

141. "To use them to depict relationships with people who were not blood relatives was to use the strongest possible analogy to depict their relationships" (Rhoads, "Children of Abraham, children of God," 285).

142. Räisänen remarks, "Paul thus makes a sharp distinction between two sets of concepts. On the one side stand the law and the works (of the law); on the other side Christ, grace, the Spirit, faith and promise. In fact, Paul's argument for the thesis that Christ, not the law, is the basis of salvation consists almost exclusively of a repetition of this basic contrast in numerous variations" (*Paul and the Law*, 163–64).

143. Troy Martin comments, "Throughout the letter, Paul describes the agitators as those who desire to be under law (2:4–5, 12; 3:1–2; 5:1, 4, 12; 6:12–13)." See
his "Apostasy to Paganism," 89.

144. For Betz's complete outline, see *Galatians*, 16–23.

145. The category *exhortatio* is itself problematic. As Martin remarks, exhorta-
tive passages are "unknown" as a separate part of a speech in classical rhetoric.
See "Invention and Arrangement," 72.

146. Kennedy, who unlike Betz finds that Galatians is best seen as deliberative
and not judicial rhetoric, regards the entirety of Gal 1:11–5:1 as the proof section.
Elliott understands 5:1 as the end of Paul's allegory that begins at 4:21; see "Choose
Your Mother," 661–83. According to Martyn, Gal 4:21–5:1 is a literary unit of its
own, in which Paul deals with the "genetic identity of the Galatian churches"; see
Galatians, 431.

147. The allegory officially begins in 4:24 and ends at 4:27. By contrast, Betz
finds that the allegory extends from 4:22–27. See *Galatians*, 243–48.

148. Brigitte Kahl cites the contrasts between "born according to flesh"
and "born according to spirit through the promise"; "out of the slave woman"
and "out of the free woman"; and "Hagar/Ishmael" and "Sarah/Isaac." See her
"Hagar's Babylonian Captivity," 261. J. Louis Martyn creates a two-column table
with contrasting data, one headed by Hagar and the other by Sarah. In the Hagar
column is "slave," "Ishmael," "the son begotten by the power of the flesh, that is
circumcision," "begetting father: circumcision of the flesh," "bearing mother: the
covenant from Mount Sinai." In the Sarah column are the terms "free," "Isaac,"
"the son begotten by the power of God's promise/the Spirit," "begetting father:
the promissory Spirit," "bearing mother: the covenant of God's promise." See
Galatians, 456. Betz also creates a table with two columns of contrasting data, one
headed by Hagar and the other by Sarah. In the Hagar column, he includes the
"old covenant," and in the Sarah column, the "new covenant." See *Galatians*, 245.

149. Paul's distinctions between slave and free, however, predominate (4:22, 23,
24, 25, 26, 30, 31; 5:1).

150. Hagar has traditionally stood for Judaism but with troubling ramifications. As Kahl remarks, the allegory has been a "blueprint" of Christian anti-Judaism. Medieval churches depicted Hagar as blindfolded and defeated, with the
books of the law falling from her arms. Opposite her is the church, *Ekklesia*, depicted as an upright and victorious woman. See "Hagar's Babylonian Captivity,"
258. For more on that particular image of Hagar, see Claman, *Jewish Images in the
Christian Church*.

The identification of Hagar is a matter of considerable debate within Pauline
scholarship. According to Martyn, Hagar represents the "the political-religious
institution of Judaism for which the Holy City stands as a symbol" (*Galatians*,
246). By contrast, Kahl argues that the allegory itself reflects enslavement not to
the Jewish Torah but to Roman rule. See her *Galatians Re-Imagined*, 356 n. 73. See
also, Kahl, "Hagar's Babylonian Captivity," 269. In her 2014 article, Kahl comments that Hagar represents the "perpetuation of slavery and idolatry through
practices of separation that appear to conform to God's law, but in reality comply
with the Roman master order" (ibid.). On the other hand, Elliott equates Hagar
to the Mountain Mother, mother of the self-castrated *galli*. According to her, Paul
objected not to the Jewish Torah but to the Galatians' association with the cult of
the Mother of the Gods. See her "Choose Your Mother," 676–83.

151. On this point, see Marchal, who argues that in Gal 4:12–15 Paul does not
ask his audience to distance themselves from him, even though he (Paul) has a
"weakness in the flesh." See "Bodies Bound for Circumcision," 176.

152. Later on in his own arguments (Gal 5:19–23), Paul defines two contrasting modes of behavior with the same terms. The behaviors associated with the term "flesh" are characterized by, among other things, fornication, impurity, and licentiousness. And the acts and actions defined by the term "spirit" regard such things as love, joy, peace, and patience. Thus, Paul reinforces the positive and negative values he first assigns in this section.

According to Stowers, when associated with desire (ἐπιθυμίαν; Gal 5:16), the term "flesh" also obtains a negative association. Desire was a passion that was to be brought under control. See Stowers, *Rereading of Romans*, 47. As Stowers remarks, as far back as Plato, a common way of speaking about the self was in terms of a battle, "self against self." It was a "struggle of reason to master the passions" (ibid.).

153. Betz calls the phrase Τῇ ἐλευθερίᾳ (For freedom) a dative of "destiny" and "purpose." See *Galatians*, 255.

154. The translation is my own.

155. According to Betz, verse 48 provides the "*consequences* of the Scripture proof (4:22–27)." See his *Galatians*, 249; italics are my own.

156. Betz remarks that the change to the first-person plural verb "assumes that the readers of the letter approve of Paul's final conclusion and, therefore, recognize the proofs as valid" (*Galatians*, 251).

157. The passive verb Paul employs to express the idea of being in a yoke (ἐνέχεσθε) denotes "be subjected to" and "loaded down with." See Betz, *Galatians*, 258.

158. The verse is in the form of *epiphonema*, defined as "a statement, often in the form of an exclamation, that concludes a line of argument or makes a comment about what has been narrated" (Rowe, "Style," 148).

159. Verse 5:1 is central for Betz, however, in that it speaks of the "indicative" of "Christian salvation." See *Galatians*, 255. For Betz, that 5:1 serves rhetorically as a dramatic opening for a new section in Galatians, likely pertains to the theological significance he assigns to it.

160. There is scholarly debate on how best to understand the dative expression Τῇ ἐλευθερίᾳ, which I have translated as "for freedom." Betz remarks that the dative is not one of cause or instrumentality but instead one of "destiny" and "purpose." I am following Betz's understanding of this dative clause. See *Galatians*, 255.

161. I have written elsewhere how the expression "yoke of slavery" refers to circumcision. See Livesey, *Circumcision as a Malleable Symbol*, 89.

162. Paul assesses circumcision in various ways throughout his writings. See Livesey, *Circumcision as a Malleable Symbol*.

163. See Tyson who writes, "Circumcision itself is not thought of as a single act but as a kind of existence, viz., existence as a Jew" ("'Works of Law' in Galatians," 428). Similarly, Sam K. Williams remarks, "Circumcision is the ritual of entrance into a distinctive people, and one who takes that step takes upon himself the obligation to live according to the Sinai covenant in every sphere of personal and communal existence. He adopts a complete way of life" (*Galatians*, 136–37).

164. Nanos, *Irony of Galatians*, 95.

165. Focusing on theological enslavement, J. Louis Martyn believes that to take up circumcision would be to return to the belief that the Jewish law is salvific. See *Galatians*, 447. Martyn's understanding is reminiscent of the Augustinian-Lutheran perspective on Paul. See Scott, *The Real Paul*, 182. See also Kahl, *Galatians Re-Imagined*, 256.

166. Circumcision has an association with Paul's opponents elsewhere as well. See Gal 2:3–5, 12; 5:11–12; 6:12–13. See especially Gal 5:12. Troy Martin remarks,

"This practice of circumcision is a distinguishing characteristic of the agitators (6:13; 2:12)" ("Apostasy to Paganism," 88). Similar to my arguments, Martin claims that Paul is not against circumcision in and of itself but instead against those who practice it. Yet, in contrast to how I assess the situation, Martin finds that Paul universally rejects those who practice circumcision. See "Apostasy to Paganism," 87–89.

167. Knust remarks that even the categories "free" and "slave" were themselves contested. "Ancient status positions—free, free noncitizen, citizen, freed, slave—were not based on inherent characteristics but discursively produced and maintained" (*Abandoned to Lust*, 26).

168. As Jonathan Z. Smith notes, "The wide range of uses and interpretations of circumcision as a taxic indicator in early Judaism suggest that, even with respect to this most fundamental division, we cannot sustain the impossible construct of a normative Judaism. We must conceive of a variety of early Judaisms, clustered in varying configurations" (*Imagining Religion*, 14). For a similar view, see McEleney, "Conversion, Circumcision and the Law," 332; Collins, "A Symbol of Otherness," 163–79.

169. Betz, *Galatians*, 255. Similarly, J. Louis Martyn remarks that the whole of the letter of Galatians concerns the topic of slavery and freedom. See *Galatians*, 219.

170. Betz, *Galatians*, 255. Significantly, Betz remarks that Gal 5:1 marks an "abrupt new start" and the beginning of the section marked by exhortation. See his *Galatians*, 255.

171. Betz, *Galatians*, 256.

172. Betz, *Galatians*, 256. Similarly, Martyn comments that in 5:1, "freedom" is a realm and a space. Yet he follows up with an elaboration of what "freedom" and "slavery" signify. According to him, "freedom" is "the result of God's act in Christ." God created this realm "by delivering human beings from slavery under the powers of specific slave masters—the Law's curse, Sin, the Law itself, the elements of the cosmos . . . and the Impulsive Desire of the Flesh" (*Galatians*, 447). Thus, Martyn, like Betz, understands the terms "freedom" and "slavery" as significant for their semantic meanings rather than as locations or catchwords representative of opposing positions.

173. Räisänen writes, "The Christ event stands out as a liberating event of supreme importance, an event with universal implications, bringing freedom and peace to everyone willing to accept the message. . . . But when it comes to a description of *what men [sic] were liberated from*, the picture becomes more or less confused" (*Paul and the Law*, 23; italics are the author's).

174. Betz, *Galatians*, 258.

175. Betz, *Galatians*, 246. Similarly, Räisänen asks if Paul's polemic between the law and Christ was brought about to combat the "false brethren" (Gal 2:4), who, according to Paul, were advancing a rival "soteriological" claim. See *Paul and the Law*, 182.

176. For more on the understanding of rhetorical situation, see Bitzer, "The Rhetorical Situation," 1–14.

Conclusion

1. Ungern-Sternberg notes that since the nineteenth century and based on the testimony of Cicero and Sallust as well as on modern problems, it has been common to understand the crisis of the Republic as a struggle between two parties, the *optimates* and the *populares*. Antony represented the *populares*, those who favor the people, and Cicero the *optimates*, the aristocrats. See "The Crisis of the Republic,"

95. For more on this see also, Steel, *The End of the Roman Republic 146 to 44 BC*, 226–53. See also W. Jeffrey Tatum who attributes the downfall of the Republic to "unrestrained sharp practices by the political elite in their contest for individual domination." See "The Final Crisis (69–44)," 209.

2. It is telling that Betz comes around to his fullest explanation of the purpose of Paul's letter to the Galatians when he discusses his opponents. See *Galatians*, 9.

3. Penner and Lopez, "Rhetorical Approaches," 41.

4. In the introduction, I review several dominant approaches to Paul and Torah. As you will recall, in the Augustinian-Lutheran perspective, adopting Torah without first recognizing that salvation is dependent solely on God's grace heaps sins upon the person. A Christian, then, could follow Torah but not for the purpose of achieving salvation. Magnus Zetterholm remarks, in Luther's interpretation, there was "no room left for Judaism." See his *Approaches to Paul*, 62. The well-known and highly influential twentieth-century New Testament scholar Rudolf Bultmann (1884–1976) carries Luther's views of Paul forward. Bultmann found that, according to Paul, the Torah gives the person "the knowledge of sin" and then leads humans to sin. See ibid., 75. According to Betz's reading of Paul, by adopting Torah, one falls into a life of slavery. See *Galatians*, 255–58. Brigitte Kahl argues that the nations' adoption of circumcision has the consequence of giving in to the imperial law, a law representative of violence against nations. See *Galatians Re-Imagined*, 245–75.

5. As I mention in the Introduction, according to Nanos, non-Jewish adoption of circumcision compromises God's oneness. Non-Jews should not have to become circumcised Jews to enjoy the full benefits of the God of Israel. God is God to both Jews and non-Jews. On this see Zetterholm, *Approaches to Paul*, 154–55.

6. See Wendt, "From the Herodians to Hadrian," 63–92.

7. Wendt, "From the Herodians to Hadrian," 64. Unlike authority figures, who had institutional affiliation, these self-authorized experts had to rely upon their own skills for recognition and legitimacy.

8. Wendt, "From the Herodians to Hadrian," 79. See too Joseph Tyson's and Dennis Smith's discussion of the competition that ensues during the first half of the second century in their *Acts and Christian Beginnings*, 335–38.

9. I am indebted to Christine Shea for these allusions.

Bibliography

Primary Sources

Aland, Barbara and Kurt, eds. *Novum Testamentum Graece.* 27th ed. Stuttgart: Deutsche Bibelgesellschaft, 1996.

Aland, Barbara and Kurt, Johannes Karavidopoulos, Carlo M. Martini, and Bruce M. Metzger, eds. *Novum Testamentum Graece.* 28th Rev. ed. Accordance Electronic ed. Stuttgart: Deutsche Bibelgesellshaft, 2012.

Aristotle. *The 'Art' of Rhetoric.* Trans. John Henry Freese. The Loeb Classical Library. Cambridge: Harvard University Press, 1991.

_____. *The Nicomachean Ethics.* Trans. Harris Rackham. The Loeb Classical Library. Cambridge: Harvard University Press, 1968.

Cicero, Marcus Tullius. Cicero, Marcus Tullius. *De Inventione.* Trans. H. M. Hubbell. The Loeb Classical Library. Cambridge: Harvard University Press, 2000.

_____. *The Fourteen Philippic orations of Marcus Tullius Cicero.* Oxford: James Thornton, 1878.

_____. *Philippics 1–14.* Trans. Walter C. A. Kerr. The Loeb Classical Library. Cambridge: Harvard University Press, 1995.

_____. *Philippics 1–6.* Trans. D. R. Shackleton Bailey. Rev. and aug. John T. Ramsey and Gesine Manuwald. The Loeb Classical Library. Cambridge: Harvard University Press, 2009.

_____. *Philippics 7–14.* Trans. D. R. Shackleton Bailey. Rev. and aug. John T. Ramsey and Gesine Manuwald. The Loeb Classical Library. Cambridge: Harvard University Press, 2009.

Demosthenes. *Demosthenes' On the Crown.* Trans. John J. Keaney. New York: Random House, 1967.

_____. *Olynthiacs, Philippics, Minor Public Speeches, Speech Against Leptines I–XVII, XX.* Trans. J. H. Vince. The Loeb Classical Library. Cambridge: Harvard University Press, 1930.

_____. *Olynthiacs, Philippics, Minor Public Speeches, Speech against Leptines I–XVII, XX.* Trans. J. H. Vince. The Loeb Classical Library. Cambridge: Harvard University Press, 1989.

Hermogenes. *Hermogenes' On Types of Style.* Trans. Cecil W. Wooten. Chapel Hill NC: The University of North Carolina Press, 1987.

Van der Horst, Pieter W. *Philo's Flaccus: The First Pogrom.* Trans. Pieter W. van der Horst. Philo of Alexandria Commentary Series. Leiden: Brill, 2003.

Josephus, Flavius. *The Jewish War.* Vol. 2. Trans. H. St. J. Thackeray. Ed. G. P. Goold. The Loeb Classical Library. Cambridge: Harvard University Press, 1990.

_____. *The Life. Against Apion.* Trans. H. St. J. Thackeray. Ed. T. E. Page. The Loeb Classical Library. Cambridge: Harvard University Press, 1966.

Philo. "On the Migration of Abraham (*De Migratione Abrahami*)." Pp. 123–267 in *Philo vol. 4.* Trans. G. H. Whitaker and F. H. Colson. The Loeb Classical Library. Cambridge: Harvard University Press, 2005.

_____. *Questions and Answers on Genesis. Philo Supplement 1.* The Loeb Classical Library. Trans. Ralph Marcus. Cambridge: Harvard University Press, 2002.

_____. "The Special Laws (*De Specialibus Legibus*)." Pp. 98–607 in *Philo* vol. 7. The Loeb Classical Library. Trans. F. H. Colson. Cambridge: Harvard University Press, 1998.

Plutarch. *Plutarch's Lives*. Vol 1. Trans. Bernadotte Perrin. The Loeb Classical Library. Cambridge: Harvard University Press, 1959.

_____. *Plutarch's Lives*. Vol 7. Trans. Bernadotte Perrin. The Loeb Classical Library. Cambridge: Harvard University Press, 1986.

_____. *Plutarch's Moralia*. Vol 11. Trans. Lionel Pearson. The Loeb Classical Library. Cambridge: Harvard University Press, 1965.

Polybius. *The Histories, Books 5–8*. Trans. W. R. Paton, The Loeb Classical Library. Cambridge: Harvard University Press, 2011.

Quintilian. *The Institutio Oratoria of Quintilian*. Trans. H. E. Butler. The Loeb Classical Library. Cambridge: Harvard University Press, 1985.

Trevett, Jeremy, ed. *Demosthenes, Speeches 1–17*. Austin: University of Texas Press, 2011.

Xenophon. *Memorabilia of Socrates*. Trans. R. D. C. Robbins. New York: D. Appleton and Company, 1871.

Yunis, Harvey, ed. *Demosthenes, Speeches 18 and 19*, The Oratory of Classical Greece. Vol. 9. Austin TX: University of Texas Press, 2005.

_____. *Demosthenes on the Crown*. Cambridge: Cambridge University Press, 2001.

Secondary Sources

Achard, Guy. *Pratique Rhétorique et Idéologie Politique dans les Discours «Optimates» de Cicéron*. Leiden: Brill, 1981.

Anderson, R. Dean. *Ancient Rhetorical Theory and Paul*. Rev. ed. Leuven: Peeters, 1999.

Arena, Valentina. "The Orator and His Audience: The Rhetorical Perspective in the Art of Deliberation." Pp. 195–209 in *Community and Communication: Oratory and Politics in Republican Rome*. Eds. Catherine Steel and Henriette van der Blom. Oxford: Oxford University Press, 2013.

Arendt, Hannah. *The Human Condition*. Chicago: The University of Chicago Press, 1958.

Badian, E. "The Road to Prominence." Pp. 9–44 in *Demosthenes: Statesman and Orator*, Ed. Ian Worthington. London: Routledge, 2000.

Badiou, Alain. *The Foundation of Universalism*. Trans. Ray Brassier. Stanford CA: Stanford University Press, 2003.

Bailey, D. R. Shackleton. *Cicero*. New York: Charles Scribner's Sons, 1971.

Barclay, John M. G. "Paul, the Gift and the Battle over Gentile Circumcision: Revisiting the Logic of Galatians." *Australian Biblical Review* 58 (2010) 36–56.

Baur, Ferdinand Christian. "Hebraists, Hellenists, and Catholics." Pp. 399–408 in *The Writings of St. Paul*. Eds. Wayne A. Meeks and John T. Fitzgerald. New York: W. W. Norton & Company, Inc., 2007.

_____. *Paul the Apostle of Jesus Christ*. Trans. A. Menzies. Peabody MA: Hendrickson Publishers, Inc., 2003.

_____. *Paulus, der Apostel Jesu Christi, sein Leben und Wirken, seine Briefe und seine Lehre*. 2d ed. Vol. 1. Liepzig: Fues's Verlag, 1866.

_____. *Paulus, der Apostel Jesu Christi, sein Leben und Wirken, seine Briefe und seine Lehre*. 2d ed. Vol. 2. Leipzig: Fues's Verlag, 1867.

BeDuhn, Jason D. *The First New Testament: Marcion's Scriptural Canon*. Salem OR: Polebridge Press, 2013.

Berchman, Robert M. "Galatians (1:1–5): Paul and Greco-Roman Rhetoric."
Pp. 60–72 in *The Galatians Debate*. Ed. Mark D. Nanos. Peabody MA:
Hendrickson Publishers, Inc., 2002.

Betz, Hans Dieter. *Galatians: A Commentary on Paul's letter to the Churches in
Galatia*. Hermeneia. Philadelphia: Fortress Press, 1979.

_____. "The Literary Composition and Function of Paul's Letter to the Galatians."
Pp. 3–28 in *The Galatians Debate*. Ed. Mark D. Nanos. Peabody MA:
Hendrickson Publishers, Inc., 2002.

Bitzer, Lloyd F. "The Rhetorical Situation." *Philosophy and Rhetoric* 1,1 (1968) 1–14.

Blaschke, Andreas. *Beschneidung: Zeugnisse der Bibel und verwandter Texte*, Texte
und Arbeiten zum neutestamentlichen Zeitalter. Tübingen: A. Francke, 1998.

Van der Blom, Henriette. "*Officium* and *Res publica*: Cicero's political role after the
Ides of March." *Classica et Mediavalia* 54 (2003) 287–320.

Bloomquist, L. Gregory. *The Function of Suffering in Philippians*. Journal for the
Study of the New Testament Supplement Series 78. Sheffield: Sheffield
Academic Press, 1993.

Borgen, Peder. "Paul Preaches Circumcision and Pleases Men." Pp. 37–46 in *Paul
and Paulinism*. Eds. M. D. Hooker and S. J. Wilson. London: SPCK, 1982.

Bornkamm, Günther. *Paul*. Trans. D. M. G. Stalker. New York: Harper & Row
Publishers, 1971.

_____. *Paulus*. Stuttgart: W. Kohlhammer GmbH, 1969.

Boyarin, Daniel. *A Radical Jew: Paul and the Politics of Identity*. Berkeley: University
of California Press, 1994.

_____. *Border Lines: The Partition of Judaeo-Christianity*. Philadelphia: University of
Pennsylvania Press, 2004.

Brandes, Stanley. "Reflections on Honor and Shame in the Mediterranean." Pp.
121–34 in *Honor and Shame and the Unity of the Mediterranean*. Ed. David D.
Gilmore. Washington DC: American Anthropological Association, 1987.

Braun, Maximilian. "Stabilisierung und Destabilisierung sozialer Werte in
Ciceros Reden." Pp. 71–91 in *O tempora, o mores!* Eds. Andreas Heil, Andreas
Haltenhoff, and Fritz-Heiner Mutschler. München: Leipzig, 2003.

Bryne, Brendan. "Jerusalems Above and Below: A Critique of J. L. Martyn's
Interpretation of Hagar-Sarah Allegory in Gal 4.21–5.1." *New Testament
Studies* 60,2 (2014) 215–31.

Buckler, John. "Demosthenes and Aeschines." Pp. 114–58 in *Demosthenes:
Statesman and Orator*, Ed. Ian Worthington. London and New York:
Routledge, 2000.

Bultmann, Rudolf. *Der Stil der paulinischen Predigt und die kynisch-stoische Diatribe*.
Göttingen: Vandenhoeck & Ruprecht, 1910.

Burkert, Walter. "ΓΟΗΣ." *Rheinisches Museum für Philologie* 105 (1962) 36–55.

Callan, Terrance. "The Style of Galatians." *Biblica* 88,4 (2007) 495–516.

Camus, Albert. *The Rebel*. Trans. Anthony Bower. New York: Alfred A. Knopf,
1954.

Carlier, Pierre. *Démosthène*. Paris: Librairie Arthème Fayard, 1990.

_____. "Démosthène par lui-même." Pp. 47–53 in *L'invention de l'autobiographie
d'Hésiode à Saint Augustine*. Ed. Marie-Françoise Baslez. Paris: Presses de
l'École Normale Supérieure, 1993.

Castelli, Elizabeth A. "Allegories of Hagar: Reading Galatians 4:21–31 with
Postmodern Feminist Eyes." Pp. 47–53 in *The New Literary Criticism and the
New Testament*. Eds. Edgar V. McKnight and Elizabeth Struthers Malbon.
Valley Forge PA: Trinity Press International, 1994.

_____. "Paul on Women and Gender." Pp. 221–35 in *Women and Christian Origins*. Eds. Ross Shepard Kraemer and Mary Rose D'Angelo. New York: Oxford University Press, 1999.

Charlesworth, James Hamilton. *The Old Testament Pseudepigrapha and the New Testament*. Cambridge: Cambridge University Press, 1985.

Chilton, Bruce D. "Paul and the Pharisees." Pp. 149–73 in *In Quest of the Historical Pharisees*. Eds. Jacob Neusner and Bruce D. Chilton. Waco: Baylor University Press, 2007.

Ciampa, Roy E. "Deuteronomy in Galatians and Romans." Pp. 99–117 in *Deuteronomy in the New Testament*. London: T&T Clark, 2007.

Claman, Henry N. *Jewish Images in the Christian Church: Art as the Mirror of the Jewish-Christian Conflict 200–1250*. Mason: Mercer University Press, 2000.

Classen, C. Joachim. "Paul's Epistles and Ancient Greek and Roman Rhetoric." Pp. 95–113 in *The Galatians Debate*. Ed. Mark D. Nanos. Peabody MA: Hendrickson Publishers, Inc., 2002.

_____. "St. Paul's Epistles and Ancient Greek and Roman Rhetoric." Pp. 265–91 in *Rhetoric and the New Testament: Essays from the 1992 Heidelberg Conference*. Eds. Stanley E. Porter and Thomas H. Olbricht. Sheffield: Sheffield Academic Press, 1993.

Cohen, Dov and Angela K.-y. Leung. "Violence and Character: A CuPS (Culture x Person x Situation) Perspective." Pp. 187–200 in *Human Aggression and Violence: Causes, Manifestations, and Consequences*. Eds. Phillip R. Shaver and Mario Mikulincer. Washington DC: American Psychological Association, 2011.

Cohen, Shaye J. D. *Beginnings of Jewishness: Boundaries, Varieties, Uncertainties*. Berkeley: University of California Press, 1999.

_____. "Crossing the Boundary and Becoming a Jew." *Harvard Theological Review* 82,1 (1989) 13–33.

_____. *From the Maccabees to the Mishnah*. Philadelphia: The Westminster Press, 1987.

_____. *Josephus in Galilee and Rome: His Vita and Development as a Historian*. Leiden: Brill, 1979.

_____. "The Letter of Paul to the Galatians." Pp. 332–44 in *The Jewish Annotated New Testament*. Eds. Amy-Jill Levine and Marc Zvi Brettler. Oxford and New York: Oxford University Press, 2011.

_____. "Respect for Judaism by Gentiles According to Josephus." *Harvard Theological Review* 80,4 (1987) 409–30.

_____. *Why Aren't Jewish Women Circumcised?: Gender and Covenant in Judaism*. Berkeley: University of California Press, 2005.

Collins, John J. "A Symbol of Otherness: Circumcision and Salvation in the First Century." Pp. 163–86 in *To See Ourselves as Others See Us*. Eds. Jacob Neusner and Ernest S. Frerichs. Chico: Scholars Press, 1985.

Corbeille, Anthony. *Controlling Laughter: Political Humor in the late Roman Republic*. Princeton NJ: Princeton University Press, 1996.

Corley, Kathleen E. *Maranatha*. Minneapolis: Fortress Press, 2010.

Cowan, Eleanor. "*Libertas* in the *Philippics*." Pp. 140–52 in *Cicero's Philippics: History, Rhetoric and Ideology*. Eds. Tom Stevenson and Marcus Wilson. Auckland: Polygraphia, 2008.

Craig, Christopher. "Audience Expectations, Invective, and Proof." Pp. 187–213 in *Cicero the Advocate*. Eds. Jonathan Powell and Jeremy Patterson. Oxford: Oxford University Press, 2004.

Cristofoli, Roberto. *Cicerone e la II Filippica: circostanze, stile e ideologia di un'orazione mai pronunciata.* Roma: Herder, 2004.

Cronjé, J. Van W. "Defamiliarization in the Letter to the Galatians." Pp. 214–27 in *A South African Perspective on the New Testament.* Eds. P. J. Hartin, Bruce Metzger and Kobus Petzer. Leiden: Brill, 1986.

Dahl, Nils A. "Paul's Letter to the Galatians: Epistolary Genre, Content, and Structure." Pp. 117–42 in *The Galatians Debate.* Ed. Mark D. Nanos. Peabody MA: Hendrickson Publishers, Inc., 2002.

Davis, Anne. "Allegorically Speaking in Galatians 4:21–5:1." *Bulletin for Biblical Research* 14,2 (2004) 161–74.

Dawson, David. *Allegorical Readers and Cultural Revision in Ancient Alexandria.* Berkeley: University of California Press, 1992.

de Roo, Jacqueline C. R. "Concept of 'Works of the Law' in Jewish and Christian Literature." Pp. 116–47 in *Christian-Jewish Relations through the Centuries.* Eds. Stanley E. Porter and Brook W. R. Pearson. Sheffield: Sheffield Academic Press, 2000.

_____. *"Works of the Law" at Qumran and in Paul.* New Testament Monograph Series 13. Sheffield: Sheffield Phoneix, 2007.

Dewey, Arthur J. "The Masks of Paul." *Forum* 7,2 (2004) 159–75.

Dewey, Arthur J., Roy W. Hoover, Lane C. McGaughy, and Daryl D. Schmidt. *The Authentic Letters of Paul.* Salem OR: Polebridge Press, 2010.

Dugan, John. *Making a New Man: Ciceronian Self-Fashioning in the Rhetorical Works.* Oxford: Oxford University Press, 2005.

Dunn, James D. G. *Jesus, Paul, and the Law.* Louisville KY: Westminster John Knox Press, 1990.

_____. "The New Perspective on Paul." Pp. 183–214 in *Jesus, Paul and the Law.* Louisville KY: Westminster John Knox Press, 1990.

_____. "Once More PISTIS XRISTOU." Pp. 61–81 in *Pauline Theology Volume IV.* Ed. E. Elizabeth Johnson. Atlanta: Scholars Press, 1997.

_____. ed. *Paul and the Mosaic Law,* Wissenschaftliche Untersuchungen zum Neuen Testament, 89. Tübingen: J. C. B. Mohr, 1996.

_____. *The Theology of Paul the Apostle.* Grand Rapids MI: William B. Eerdmans, 1998.

_____. "What was the Issue between Paul and 'Those of the Circumcision'?" Pp. 295–317 in *Paulus und das antike Judentum.* Eds. Martin Hengel and Ulrich Heckel. Tübingen: J. C. B. Mohr, 1991.

_____. "Works of the Law and the Curse of the Law (Gal. 3.10–14)." Pp. 215–41 in *Jesus, Paul, and the Law.* Louisville KY: Westminster John Knox Press, 1990.

Dunning, Benjamin H. *Specters of Paul: Sexual Difference in Early Christian Thought.* Philadelphia: University of Pennsylvania Press, 2011.

Eastman, Susan. "The Evil Eye and the Curse of the Law: Galatians 3:1 Revisited." *Journal for the Study of the New Testament* 83 (2001) 69–87.

Eckert, Jost. *Die urchristliche Verkündigung im Streit zwischen Paulus und seinen Gegnern nach dem Galaterbrief.* Regensburg: Pustet, 1971.

Eisenbaum, Pamela. "Paul as the New Abraham." Pp. 130–45 in *Paul and Politics: Ekklesia, Israel, Imperium, Interpretation.* Ed. Richard A. Horsley. Harrisburg: Trinity Press International, 2000.

_____. *Paul Was Not a Christian: The Original Message of a Misunderstood Apostle.* New York: HarperOne, 2009.

Eisenman, Robert. "'Sicarii Essenes,' 'The Party of the Circumcision,' and Qumran." Pp. 247–60 in *Defining Identities: We, You, and the Other in the Dead*

Sea Scrolls. Eds. Florentino García Martínez and Mladen Popović. Leiden: Brill, 2008.

Elliott, John H. "Paul, Galatians, and the Evil Eye." *Currents in Theology and Mission* 17,4 (1990) 262–73.

Elliott, Neil. *The Arrogance of Nations: Reading Romans in the Shadow of the Empire.* Minneapolis: Fortress Press, 2008.

_____. "Paul and the Politics of Empire: Problems and Prospects." Pp. 17–39 in *Paul and Politics: Ekklesia, Israel, Imperium, Interpretation.* Ed. Richard A. Horsley. Harrisburg PA: Trinity Press International, 2000.

_____. *The Rhetoric of Romans.* Journal for the Study of the New Testament Supplement Series 45. Ed. David Hill. Sheffield: JSOT Press, 1990.

Elliott, Neil and Mark Reasoner, eds. *Documents and Images for the Study of Paul.* Minneapolis: Fortress Press, 2011.

Elliott, Susan M. "Choose Your Mother, Choose Your Master: Galatians 4:21–5:1 in the Shadow of the Anatolian Mother of the Gods." *Journal of Biblical Literature* 118,4 (1999) 661–83.

Ellis, E. Earle. "Paul and His Opponents: Trends in Research." Pp. 264–98 in *Christianity, Judaism, and Other Greco-Roman Cults: Studies for Morton Smith at Sixty.* Eds. Jacob Neusner and Morton Smith. Leiden: Brill, 1975.

Elmer, Ian J. "Setting the Record Straight. Paul's *Narratio* (Gal 1:12–2:14) as a Response to the Galatian Conflict." Pp. 21–37 in *Religious Conflict from Early Christianity to the Rise of Islam.* Eds. Wendy Mayer and Bronwen Neil. Göttingen: De Gruyter, 2013.

Engberg-Pedersen, Troels. *Paul and the Stoics.* Louisville KY: Westminster John Knox Press, 2000.

Enos, Theresa, ed. *Encyclopedia of Rhetoric and Composition.* New York: Garland Publishing, Inc., 1996.

Eshleman, Kendra. *The Social World of Intellectuals in the Roman Empire: Sophists, Philosophers, and Christians.* Cambridge: Cambridge University Press, 2012.

Fairweather, Janet. "The Epistle to the Galatians and Classical Rhetoric: Parts 1 & 2." *Tyndale Bulletin* 45,1 (1994) 1–38.

_____. "The Epistle to the Galatians and Classical Rhetoric: Part 3." *Tyndale Bulletin* 45,2 (1994) 213–43.

Fee, Gordon D. *Philippians.* The InterVarsity Press New Testament Commentary Series. Downers Grove: InterVarsity Press, 1999.

_____. "Who are Abraham's true children? The role of Abraham in Pauline Argumentation." Pp. 126–37 in *Perspectives on our father Abraham: Essays in Honor of Marvin R. Wilson.* Ed. Steven A. Hunt. Grand Rapids MI: William B. Eerdmans, 2010.

Feine, Paul. *St. Paul as a Theologian, Parts 1 and 2.* New York: Eaton & Mains, 1908.

Fine, Steven. *Art and Judaism in the Greco-Roman World.* Cambridge: Cambridge University Press, 2005.

Finney, Mark. *Honour and Conflict in the Ancient World: 1 Corinthians in Its Greco-Roman Social Setting.* London: T&T Clark International, 2012.

Fitzmyer, Joseph A. *First Corinthians: A New Translation with Introduction and Commentary.* The Anchor Yale Bible. New Haven: London, 2008.

Fogel, Jerise. "Cicero and the 'Ancestral Constitution': A Study in Cicero's *Contio* Speeches." PhD diss., Columbia University, 1994.

Foley, John Miles. *Immanent Art: From Structure to Meaning in Traditional Oral Epic.* Bloomington: Indiana University Press, 1991.

Fowl, Stephen E. *Philippians.* Grand Rapids MI: William B. Eerdmans, 2005.

Fredriksen, Paula. "Judaism, the Circumcision of Gentiles, and Apocalyptic Hope: Another Look at Galatians 1 and 2." Pp. 235–60 in *The Galatians Debate*. Ed. Mark D. Nanos. Peabody MA: Hendrickson Publishers, Inc., 2002.

Frisch, Hartvig. *Cicero's Fight for the Republic: The Historical Background of Cicero's Philippics*. Trans. Niels Haislund. Copenhagen: Gyldendals, 1946.

Frey, Jörg. "Paul's Jewish Identity." Pp. 285–321 in *Jewish Identity in the Greco-Roman World*. Eds. Jörg Frey, Daniel R. Schwartz and Stephanie Gripentrog. Leiden: Brill, 2007.

Furnish, Victor Paul. *The Moral Teachings of Paul*. 3d ed. Nashville: Abingdon Press, 2009.

Gager, John G. *Reinventing Paul*. Oxford: Oxford University Press, 2000.

Galinsky, Karl. "The Augustan Programme of Cultural Renewal and Herod." Pp. 29–42 in *IJS Studies in Judaica, Volume 6: Herod and Augustus*. Ed. David M. Jacobson. Boston: Brill, 2009.

Garlington, Don B. *'The Obedience of Faith' A Pauline Phrase in Historical Context*. Tübingen: J. C. B. Mohr (Paul Siebeck), 1991.

Gaston, Lloyd. *Paul and the Torah*. Vancouver: University of British Columbia Press, 1987.

Gaventa, Beverly R. "Galatians 1 and 2: Autobiography as Paradigm." *Novum Testamentum* 28,4 (1986) 309–26.

Georgi, Dieter. *The Opponents of Paul in Second Corinthians: A Study of Religious Propaganda in Late Antiquity*. Philadelphia: Fortress Press, 1986.

Gibson, Twyla. "The Philosopher's Art: Ring composition and Classification in Plato's *Sophist* and *Hipparchus*." Pp. 73–109 in *Orality and Literacy: Reflections across Disciplines*. Eds. Keith Thor Carlson, Kristina Fagan and Natalia Khanenko-Friesen. Toronto: University of Toronto Press, 2011.

Gilmore, David D. "Introduction: The Shame of Dishonor." Pp. 2–21 in *Honor and Shame and the Unity of the Mediterranean*. Ed. David Gilmore. Washington DC: American Anthropological Association, 1987.

Glancy, Jennifer A. "The Sexual Use of Slaves: A Response to Kyle Harper on Jewish and Christian *Porneia*." *Journal of Biblical Literature* 134,1 (2015) 215–29.

_____. *Slavery in Early Christianity*. Oxford: Oxford University Press, 2002.

Goodman, Martin. "Religious Variety and the Temple in the Late Second Temple Period and its Aftermath." Pp. 21–37 in *Sects and Sectarianism in Jewish History*. Ed. Sacha Stern. Leiden: Brill, 2011.

Grimal, Pierre. *Cicéron*. Paris: Librairie Arthème, 1986.

Gruen, Erich S. "Herod, Rome, and the Diaspora." Pp. 13–28 in *IJS Studies in Judaica, Volume 6: Herod and Augustus*. Ed. David M. Jacobson. Boston: Brill, 2009.

Gunther, John J. *St. Paul's Opponents and Their Backgrounds: A Study of Apocalyptic and Jewish Sectarian Teachings*. Supplements Novum Testamentum. Leiden: Brill, 1973.

Habinek, Thomas. *Ancient Rhetoric and Oratory*. Malden MA and Oxford: Blackwell Publishing, 2005.

Hall, Jon. "The *Philippics*." Pp. 273–304 in *Brill's Companion to Cicero: Oratory and Rhetoric*. Ed. James M. May. Leiden: Brill, 2002.

Hall, Robert G. "The Rhetorical Outline for Galatians: A Reconsideration." Pp. 29–38 in *The Galatians Debate*. Ed. Mark D. Nanos. Peabody MA: Hendrickson Publishers, Inc., 2002.

Haraguchi, Takaaki. "Words of Blessing and Curse: A Rhetorical Study of
    Galatians." *Asia Journal of Theology* 18,1 (2004) 33–50.
Hammond, Nicholas. *Philip of Macedon*. Baltimore: The John Hopkins University
    Press, 1994.
Harnack, Adolf von. "The Founder of Christian Civilization." Pp. 419–24 in *The
    Writings of St. Paul*. Eds. Wayne A. Meeks and John T. Fitzgerald. New York:
    W. W. Norton & Company, Inc., 2007.
Harper, Kyle. *From Shame to Sin: The Christian Transformation of Sexual Morality in
    Late Antiquity*. Cambridge: Harvard University Press, 2013.
_____. "*Porneia*: The Making of a Christian Sexual Norm." *Journal of Biblical
    Literature* 131,2 (2012) 363–83.
Harries, Jill. *Cicero and the Jurists: From Citizen's Law to the Lawful State*. London:
    Duckworth & Co. Ltd., 2006.
Harris, Stephen L. *The New Testament: A Student's Introduction*. 7th ed. New York:
    McGraw-Hill Companies, Inc., 2012.
Harris, William V. *Restraining Rage*. Cambridge: Harvard University Press, 2001.
Hays, Richard B. *Echoes of Scripture in the Letters of Paul*. New Haven: Yale
    University Press, 1989.
_____. "ΠΙΣΤΙΣ AND PAULINE CHRISTOLOGY: What is at Stake?" Pp. 35–60 in
    Pauline Theology Volume IV. Ed. E. Elizabeth Johnson. Atlanta: Scholars Press,
    1997.
Heslop, G. H. *Demosthenis Orationes Publicae: The Olynthiacs; The Philippics*.
    London: Rivingtons, 1868.
Hill, Craig C. "On the Source of Paul's Problem with Judaism." Pp. 311–18 in
    Redefining First-Century Jewish and Christian Identities. Ed. Fabian E. Udoh.
    Notre Dame IN: University of Notre Dame Press, 2008.
Hodge, Caroline E. Johnson. *If Sons, Then Heirs*. Oxford: Oxford University Press,
    2007.
Hölkeskamp, Karl-J. "Friends, Romans, Countrymen: Addressing the Roman
    People and the Rhetoric of Inclusion." Pp. 11–28 in *Community and
    Communication: Oratory and Politics in Republican Rome*. Eds. Catherine Steel
    and Henriette van der Blom. Oxford: Oxford University Press, 2013.
_____. "History and Collective Memory in the Middle Republic." Pp. 478–95
    in *A Companion to the Roman Republic*. Eds. Nathan Rosenstein and Robert
    Morstein-Marx. Malden MA: Blackwell Publishing, 2006.
Horrell, David G. *An Introduction to the Study of Paul*. 2d ed. New York: T&T
    Clark, 2006.
Horsley, Richard A. "Introduction: Krister Stendahl's Challenge to Pauline
    Studies." Pp. 1–16 in *Paul and Politics: Ekklesia, Israel, Imperium, Interpretation*.
    Ed. Richard A. Horsley. Harrisburg PA: Trinity Press International, 2000.
_____. *Jesus and the Spiral of Violence: Popular Jewish Resistance in Roman Palestine*.
    San Francisco: Harper & Row Publishers, 1987.
_____. "Paul and Slavery: A Critical Alternative to Recent Readings." *Semeia*
    83–84 (1998) 153–200.
Hughes, Paul M. "Moral Anger, Forgiving, and Condoning." *Journal of Social
    Philosophy* 26,1 (1995) 103–18.
Hunn, Debbie. "Pleasing God or Pleasing People? Defending the Gospel in
    Galatians 1–2." *Biblica* 91 (2010) 24–49.
Jaeger, Werner. *Demosthenes: The Origin and Growth of His Policy*. Trans. Edward
    Schouten Robinson. Berkeley: University of California Press, 1938.
Jal, Paul. "'Hostis (Publicus)' dans la littérature Latine de la fin de la République."
    Revue des Études Ancienne 65,1–2 (1963) 53–79.

Jay, Timothy. *Why We Curse: A Neuro-Psycho-Social Theory of Speech.* Philadelphia: John Benjamins Publishing Company, 2000.

Jewett, Robert. "The Agitators and the Galatian Congregation." *New Testament Studies* 17 (1971) 198–212.

_____. *A Chronology of Paul's Life.* Philadelphia: Fortress Press, 1979.

_____. "Conflicting Movements in the Early Church as Reflected in Philippians." *Novem Testamentum* 12 (1970) 362–90.

Joshel, Sandra R. *Slavery in the Roman World.* New York: Cambridge University Press, 2010.

Judge, E. A. "St Paul and Classical Culture." *Jahrbuch für Antike und Christentum* 15 (1972) 19–36.

Kahl, Brigitte. "Hagar's Babylonian Captivity: A Roman Re-imagination of Galatians 4:21–31." *Interpretation* 63,3 (2014) 257–69.

_____. "Galatians: On Discomfort about Gender and Other Problems of Otherness." Pp. 755–66 in *Feminist Biblical Interpretation.* Eds. Luise Schottroff and Marie-Theres Wacker. Grand Rapids MI: William B. Eerdmans, 2012.

_____. *Galatians Re-Imagined: Reading with the Eyes of the Vanquished.* Minneapolis: Fortress Press, 2010.

_____. "No Longer Male: Masculinity Struggles Behind Galatians 3.28?" *Journal for the Study of the New Testament* 79 (2000) 37–49.

Kelber, Werner H. *The Oral and the Written Gospel: The Hermeneutics of Speaking and Writing in the Synoptic Tradition, Mark, Paul, and Q.* Bloomington IN: Indiana University Press, 1997.

Kennedy, George. *The Art of Persuasion in Greece.* Princeton: Princeton University Press, 1963.

_____. *New Testament Interpretation through Rhetorical Criticism.* Chapel Hill NC: The University of North Carolina Press, 1984.

Kern, Philip H. *Rhetoric and Galatians.* Cambridge: Cambridge University Press, 1998.

King, John R. *The Philippic Orations of M. Tullius Cicero.* Oxford: Clarendon Press, 1868.

Kinneavy, James L. *A Theory of Discourse: The Aims of Discourse.* Englewood Cliffs NJ: Prentice-Hall, Inc., 1971.

Kloppenborg, John S. *Q the Earliest Gospel.* Louisville KY: Westminster John Knox Press, 2008.

Knox, John. *Chapters in the Life of Paul.* New York: Abingdon-Cokesbury Press, 1950.

Knust, Jennifer Wright. *Abandoned to Lust: Sexual Slander and Ancient Christianity.* New York: Columbia University Press, 2006.

Koester, Helmut. "The Purpose of the Polemic of a Pauline Fragment." *New Testament Studies* 8 (1961–1962) 317–32.

Kohut, Heinz. *The Restoration of Self.* Madison CT: International Universities Press Inc., 1990.

Koptak, Paul E. "Rhetorical Identification in Paul's Autobiographical Narrative: Galatians 1:13-2:14." Pp. 157–68 in *The Galatians Debate.* Ed. Mark D. Nanos. Peabody MA: Hendrickson Publishers, Inc., 2002.

Kotrosits, Maia. *Rethinking Early Christian Identity: Affect, Violence, and Belonging.* Minneapolis: Fortress Press, 2015.

Koyzis, Nancy Calvert. *Paul, Monotheism and the People of God: The Significance of Abraham Traditions for Early Judaism and Christianity.* London: T&T Clark, 2005.

Kraemer, Ross Shepard. *Her Share of the Blessings: Women's Religions among Pagans, Jews, and Christians in the Greco-Roman World*. New York: Oxford University Press, 1992.

_____. "Women's Judaism(s) at the Beginning of Christianity." Pp. 50–79 in *Women & Christian Origins*. Eds. Ross Shepard Kraemer and Mary Rose D'Angelo. New York: Oxford University Press, 1999.

Kümmel, Werner Georg. *Introduction to the New Testament*. Trans. Howard Clark Kee. 17th ed. Nashville: Abingdon Press, 1975.

Kustas, George L. "Diatribe in Ancient Rhetorical Theory." *The Center for Hermeneutical Studies in Hellenistic and Modern Culture* 22 (1976) 1–49.

Lacey, W. K. *Cicero: Second Philippic Oration*. Warminster, Wiltshire England: Aris & Philipps Publishers, 1986.

Langton, Daniel R. *The Apostle Paul in the Jewish Imagination: A Study in Modern Jewish-Christian Relations*. New York: Cambridge University Press, 2010.

_____. "The Myth of the 'Traditional View of Paul' and the Role of the Apostle in Modern Jewish-Christian Polemics." *Journal for the Study of the New Testament* 28,1 (2005) 69–104.

Lee, Margaret Ellen and Bernard Brandon Scott. *Sound Mapping the New Testament*. Salem OR: Polebridge Press, 2009.

Levine, Amy-Jill and Marianne Blickenstaff, eds. *A Feminist Companion to Paul*. Cleveland OH: The Pilgrim Press, 2004.

Levine, Amy-Jill and Marc Zvi Brettler, eds. *The Jewish Annotated New Testament*. Oxford: Oxford University Press, 2011.

Lévy, Carlos. "Rhétorique et Philosophie: la monstruosité politique chez Cicéron." *Revue des Études Latines* 76 (1998) 139–57.

Lieu, Judith M. *Christian Identity in the Jewish and Graeco-Roman World*. Oxford: Oxford University Press, 2004.

Lightfoot, J. B. *Saint Paul's Epistle to the Philippians*. London: Macmillan and Co., Lt., 1913.

Livesey, Nina E. *Circumcision as a Malleable Symbol*. Wissenschaftliche Untersuchungen zum Neuen Testament 2 Reihe. Tübingen: Mohr Siebeck, 2010.

Long, George. *M. Tullii Ciceronis Orationes*. London: Whitaker and Company, 1858.

Lopez, Davina C. *Apostle to the Conquered: Reimagining Paul's Mission*. Minneapolis: Fortress Press, 2008.

Lüdemann, Gerd. *Paul Apostle to the Gentiles: Studies in Chronology*. Trans. F. Stanley Jones. Philadelphia: Fortress Press, 1984.

_____. *Paul, the Founder of Christianity*. Amherst NY: Prometheus Books, 2002.

Luther, Martin. *Lectures on Galatians 1535: Chapters 1–4*. Trans. Jaroslav Pelikan. Luther's Works. Vol. 26. Ed. Jaroslav Pelikan. Saint Louis: Concordia Publishing House, 1963.

Lyons, George. *Pauline Biography: Toward a New Understanding*. Atlanta: Scholars Press, 1985.

Mack, Burton L. *Rhetoric and the New Testament*. Minneapolis: Fortress Press, 1990.

Mader, Gottfried. "Fighting Philip with Decrees: Demosthenes and the Syndrome of Symbolic Action." *The American Journal of Philology* 127,3 (2006) 367–86.

_____. "Foresight, Hindsight and the Rhetoric of Self-Fashioning in Demosthenes' Philippic Cycle." *Rhetorica* 25,4 (2007) 339–60.

Malina, Bruce J. *The New Testament World: Insights from Cultural Anthropology*. Rev. ed. Louisville KY: Westminster John Knox Press, 1993.

Manuwald, Gesine, ed. *Cicero, Philippics 3–9: Commentary.* Vol. 2. Berlin and New York: De Gruyter, 2007.

_____. ed. *Cicero, Philippics 3–9: Introduction, Text and Translation, References and Indexes.* Vol. 1. Berlin and New York: De Gruyter, 2007.

_____. "Cicero Versus Antonius: On the Structure and Construction of the *Philippics* Collection." Pp. 39–61 in *Cicero's* Philippics: *History, Rhetoric and Ideology.* Eds. Tom Stevenson and Marcus Wilson. Auckland: Polygraphia Ltd., 2008.

Marchal, Joseph A. "Bodies Bound for Circumcision and Baptism: An Intersex Critique and the Interpretation of Galatians." *Theology & Sexuality* 16,2 (2010) 163–182.

_____. "The Usefulness of an Onesimus: The Sexual Use of Slaves and Paul's Letter to Philemon." *Journal of Biblical Literature* 130,4 (2011) 749–70.

Markle, M. M. "Demosthenes' *Second Philippic*: A Valid Policy for the Athenians against Philip." *Antichthon* 15 (1981) 62–85.

Martin, Dale B. *The Corinthian Body.* New Haven: Yale University Press, 1995.

Martin, Troy. "Apostasy to Paganism." Pp. 73–94 in *The Galatians Debate.* Ed. Mark D. Nanos. Peabody MA: Hendrickson Publishers, Inc., 2002.

_____. "Invention and Arrangement in Recent Pauline Rhetorical Studies." Pp. 48–118 in *Paul and Rhetoric.* Eds. J. Paul Sampley and Peter Lampe. New York: The Continuum International Publishing Group Inc., 2010.

_____. "The Syntax of Surprise, Irony, or Shifting of Blame in Gal 1:6–7." *Biblical Research* 54 (2009) 79–98.

Martyn, J. Louis. *Galatians,* The Anchor Bible. Vol. 33A. New York: Doubleday, 1997.

Mason, Steve. "Josephus's Pharisees: The Narratives." Pp. 3–40 in *In Quest of the Historical Pharisees.* Eds. Jacob Neusner and Bruce D. Chilton. Waco: Baylor University Press, 2007.

_____. "Josephus's Pharisees: The Philosophy." Pp. 41–66 in *In Quest of the Historical Pharisees.* Eds. Jacob Neusner and Bruce D. Chilton. Waco: Baylor University Press, 2007.

Matlock, R. Barry. *Unveiling the Apocalyptic Paul: Paul's Interpreters and the Rhetoric of Criticism.* Journal for the Study of the New Testament Supplement Series 127. Sheffield: Sheffield Academic Press, 1996.

May, James M. "Cicero and the Beasts." *Syllecta Classica* 7 (1996) 143–53.

_____. "Cicero: His Life and Career." Pp. 1–21 in *Brill's Companion to Cicero: Oratory and Rhetoric.* Ed. James M. May. Leiden: Brill, 2002.

_____. *Trials of Character: The Eloquence of Ciceronian Ethos.* Chapel Hill NC: The University of North Carolina Press, 1988.

McEleney, Neil J. "Conversion, Circumcision and the Law." *New Testament Studies* 20 (1974) 319–41.

Meyers, Eric M. "Sanders's 'Common Judaism' and the Common Judaism of Material Culture." Pp. 153–74 in *Redefining First-Century Jewish and Christian Identities.* Ed. Fabian E. Udoh. Notre Dame IN: University of Notre Dame Press, 2008.

Mitchell, Margaret M. *Paul and the Rhetoric of Reconciliation: An Exegetical Investigation of the Language and Composition of 1 Corinthians.* Louisville KY: Westminster John Knox Press, 1993.

Mitchell, Thomas N. *Cicero, the Senior Statesman.* New Haven: Yale University Press, 1991.

Mullins, Terence Y. "Formulas in New Testament Epistles." *Journal of Biblical Literature* 91,3 (1972) 380–90.

Murphy, James J., ed. *Demosthenes' On the Crown*. New York: Random House, 2009.

Nanos, Mark D. *The Irony of Galatians: Paul's Letter in First-Century Context*. Minneapolis: Fortress Press, 2002.

_____. *The Mystery of Romans*. Minneapolis: Fortress Press, 1996.

_____. "Paul's Reversal of Jews Calling Gentiles 'Dogs' (Philippians 3:2): 1600 Years of an Ideological Tale Wagging an Exegetical Dog?" *Biblical Interpretation* 17 (2009) 448–82.

_____. "The Social Context and Message of Galatians in View of Paul's Evil Eye Warning (Gal. 3:1)." 32 pages. Accessed on September 12, 2012. http://www.marknanos.com/EvilEyeWarning-6-20-03.pdf.

_____. "What was at Stake in Peter's 'Eating with Gentiles' at Antioch?" Pp. 282–318 in *The Galatians Debate*. Ed. Mark Nanos. Peabody MA: Hendrickson Publishers, Inc., 2002.

Nanos, Mark D. and Magnus Zetterholm, eds. *Paul within Judaism: Restoring the First-Century Context to the Apostle*. Minneapolis: Fortress Press, 2015.

Neusner, Jacob. *From Politics to Piety: The Emergence of Pharisaic Judaism*. Englewood Cliffs NJ: Prentice-Hall, Inc., 1973.

Neusner, Jacob and William Scott Green. *Dictionary of Judaism in the Biblical Period: 450 BCE to 600 CE*. 2 vols. New York: Macmillan Library Reference, 1996.

Niehoff, Maren. *Philo on Jewish Identity and Culture*. Tübingen: Mohr Siebeck, 2001.

Nietzsche, Friedrich. "The First Christian." Pp. 408–10 in *The Writings of St. Paul*. Eds. Wayne A. Meeks and John T. Fitzgerald. New York: W. W. Norton & Company, Inc., 2007.

Nolland, John. "Uncircumcised Proselytes?" *Journal for the Study of Judaism in the Persian, Hellenistic, and Roman Periods* 12 (1981) 173–94.

Novaco, Raymond W. "Anger." Pp. 170–74 in *Encyclopedia of Psychology*. Ed. Alan E. Kazdin. Oxford: Oxford University Press, 2000.

O'Brien, Peter T. *The Epistle to the Philippians: A Commentary on the Greek Text*. The New International Greek Testament Commentary. Grand Rapids: William B. Eerdmans, 1991.

Olson, Kathryn M. "Dissociation." Pp. 196–97 in *Encyclopedia of Rhetoric and Composition*. Ed. Theresa Enos. New York: Garland Publishing, Inc., 1996.

Oltramare, André. *Les Origines de la Diatribe Romaine*. Lausanne: Librairie Payot, 1926.

Ong, Walter J. *Orality and Literacy*. London: Routledge, 1982.

Osiek, Carolyn. *Philippians Philemon*, Abingdon New Testament Commentaries. Nashville: Abingdon Press, 2000.

Oesterreich, Peter L. "Irony." Pp. 404–6 in *Encyclopedia of Rhetoric*. Ed. Thomas O. Sloan. Oxford and New York: Oxford University Press, 2001.

Pagels, Elaine. *Revelations: Visions, Prophecy, & Politics in the Book of Revelation*. New York: Viking Penguin, 2012.

Patterson, John R. *Political Life in the City of Rome*. Bristol: Bristol Classical Press, 2000.

Penner, Todd and Davina C. Lopez. "Rhetorical Approaches: Introducing the Art of Persuasion in Paul and Pauline Studies." Pp. 33–52 in *Studying Paul's Letters: Contemporary Perspectives and Methods*. Ed. Joseph A. Marchal. Minneapolis: Fortress Press, 2012.

Perelman, Chaïm. *The Realm of Rhetoric*. Notre Dame IN: University of Notre Dame Press, 1982.

Perelman, Chaïm and Lucie Olbrechts-Tyteca. *The New Rhetoric: A Treatise on Argumentation.* Trans. John Wilkinson and Purcell Weaver. Notre Dame IN: University of Notre Dame Press, 1969.

_____. *Traité de l'argumentation: La nouvelle rhétorique.* Bruxelles: Éditions de l'Université de Bruxelles, 1988.

Pervo, Richard I. *Acts: A Commentary,* Hermeneia. Minneapolis: Fortress Press, 2009.

_____. *Dating Acts: Between the Evangelists and the Apologists.* Santa Rosa CA: Polebridge Press, 2006.

_____. *The Making of Paul: Constructions of the Apostle in Early Christianity.* Minneapolis: Fortress Press, 2010.

Porter, Stanley E., ed. *Paul and His Opponents.* Leiden: Brill, 2005.

Porter, Stanley E. and Thomas H. Olbricht, eds. *Rhetoric and the New Testament: Essays from the 1992 Heidelberg Conference.* Sheffield: Sheffield Academic Press, 1993.

Preuss, Siegmundus. *Index Demosthenicus.* Hildesheim: Georg Olms Verlagsbuchhandlung, 1963.

Price, Jonathan J. *Jerusalem Under Siege: The Collapse of the Jewish State 60–70 CE.* Leiden: Brill, 1992.

Räisänen, Heikki. *Paul and the Law.* Tübingen: J. C. B. Mohr (Paul Siebeck), 1987.

Ramsey, J. T. *Cicero, Marcus Tullius: Philippics I–II.* New York: Cambridge University Press, 2003.

Rajak, Tessa. *Josephus: The Historian and His Society.* London: Duckworth, 1983.

Rawson, Elizabeth. *Cicero: A Portrait.* London: Bristol Classical Press, 2001.

Reumann, John. *Philippians: A New Translation with Introduction and Commentary,* The Anchor Bible. New Haven CT: Yale University Press, 2008.

Rhoads, David M. "Children of Abraham, Children of God: Metaphorical Kinship in Paul's Letter to the Galatians." *Currents in Theology and Mission* 31,4 (2004) 282–97.

Riggs, James Stevenson. *A History of the Jewish People: During the Maccabean and Roman Periods (Including New Testament Times).* New York: Charles Scribner's Sons, 1921.

Robinson, James M. and Helmut Koester. *Trajectories Through Early Christianity.* Philadelphia: Fortress Press, 1971.

Roetzel, Calvin J. *The Letters of Paul.* Louisville KY: Westminster John Knox Press, 1998.

Roller, Matthew. *Constructing Autocracy: Aristocrats and Emperors in Julio-Claudian Rome.* Princeton: Princeton University press, 2001.

Ronnet, Gilberte. *Étude sur le Style de Démosthène dans les Discours Politiques.* Paris: E. de Boccard, 1951.

Rosenstein, Nathan. "Aristocratic Values." Pp. 365–82 in *A Companion to the Roman Republic.* Eds. Nathan Rosenstein and Robert Morstein-Marx. Malden MA: Blackwell Publishing, 2006.

Rowe, Galen O. "Style." Pp. 121–57 in *Handbook of Classical Rhetoric in the Hellenistic Period 330 BC–AD 400.* Ed. Stanley E. Porter. Boston and Leiden: Brill, Inc., 2001.

Rubenstein, Richard L. *My Brother Paul.* New York: Harper & Row Publishers, 1972.

Rüpke, Jörg. "Communicating with the Gods." Pp. 215–35 in *A Companion to the Roman Republic.* Eds. Nathan Rosenstein and Robert Morstein-Marx. Malden MA: Blackwell Publishing, 2006.

Russell, D. S. *The Method and Message of Jewish Apocalyptic: 200 BC–AD 100*. The Old Testament Library. London: SCM Press Ltd, 1964.

Ryder, T. T. B. "Demosthenes and Philip II." Pp. 45–89 in *Demosthenes: Statesman and Orator*. Ed. Ian Worthington. London and New York: Routledge, 2000.

Saldarini, Anthony J. *Pharisees Scribes and Sadducees*. Edinburgh: T&T Clark, 1989.

Sampley, J. Paul and Peter Lampe, eds. *Paul and Rhetoric*. New York and London: T&T Clark, 2010.

Sanders, E. P. *Paul and Palestinian Judaism: A Comparison of Patterns of Religion*. Minneapolis: Fortress Press, 1977.

_____. *Paul, the Law, and the Jewish People*. Minneapolis: Fortress Press, 1983.

Sanders, Jack T. "Circumcision of Gentile converts: the root of hostility." *Bible Review* 7,1 (1991) 20–25, 44.

Sandys, John Edwin. *Demosthenes: On the Peace, Second Philippic, On the Chersonesus and Third Philippic: With Introduction and Critical and Explanatory Notes*. London: Macmillan and Co., 1913.

Schliesser, Benjamin. *Abraham's Faith in Romans 4: Paul's Concept of Faith in Light of the History of Reception of Genesis 15:6*. Wissenschaftliche Untersuchungen zum Neuen Testament. Tubingen: Mohr Siebeck, 2007.

Schiffman, Lawrence H. *Who Was a Jew? Rabbinic and Halakhic Perspectives on the Jewish-Christian Schism*. Hoboken NJ: Ktav Publishing House, Inc., 1985.

Schmithals, Walter. *Paul and the Gnostics*. Trans. John E. Steely. Nashville LA: Abingdon Press, 1972.

Schnelle, Udo. *Apostle Paul: His Life and Theology*. Trans. M. Eugene Boring. Grand Rapids MI: Baker Academic, 2005.

_____. *Paulus Leben und Denken*. Berlin: De Gruyter, 2003.

Schüssler Fiorenza, Elisabeth. "Response to John R. Lanci: Transforming the Discipline—the Rhetoricity/Rhetoricality of New* Testament Studies." Pp. 165–99 in *Genealogies of New Testament Rhetorical Criticism*. Ed. Troy W. Martin. Minneapolis: Fortress Press, 2014.

_____. *Rhetoric and Ethic: The Politics of Biblical Studies*. Minneapolis: Fortress Press, 1999.

Schütz, John H. *Paul and the Anatomy of Apostolic Authority*. Cambridge: Cambridge University Press, 1975.

Schwartz, Daniel R. "'Judaean' or 'Jew'? How should we translate *Ioudaios* in Josephus?" Pp. 3–27 in *Jewish Identity in the Greco-Roman World*. Eds. Jörg Frey, Daniel R. Schwartz and Stephanie Gripentrog. Leiden: Brill, 2007.

_____. "One Temple and Many Synagogues: On Religion and State in Herodian Judaea and Augustan Rome." Pp. 385–98 in *Herod and Augustus*. Institute of Jewish Studies in Judaica. Vol. 6. Ed. David M. Jacobson. Boston: Brill, 2009.

Schweitzer, Albert. *The Mysticism of Paul the Apostle*. Trans. William Montgomery. London: A. & C. Black, 1931.

Scott, Bernard Brandon. *The Real Paul*. Salem OR: Polebridge Press, 2015.

_____. *The Trouble with Resurrection: From Paul to the Fourth Gospel*. Salem OR: Polebridge Press, 2010.

Seager, Robin. "Ciceronian Invective: Themes and Variations." Pp. 25–46 in *Cicero on the Attack: Invective and Subversion in the Orations and Beyond*. Ed. Joan Booth. Oakville CT: The Classical Press of Wales, 2007.

Sealey, Raphael. *Demosthenes and His Time: A Study in Defeat*. New York: Oxford University Press, 1993.

Segal, Alan F. *Paul the Convert: The Apostolate and Apostasy of Saul the Pharisee*. New Haven: Yale University Press, 1990.

_____. "Paul's Religious Experience in the Eyes of Jewish Scholars." Pp. 321–43 in *Israel's God and Rebecca's Children*. Eds. David B. Capes, April D. DeConick, Helen K. Bond and Troy A. Miller. Waco: Baylor University Press, 2007.

_____. "Response: Some Aspects of Conversion and Identity Formation in the Christian Community of Paul's Time." Pp. 184–90 in *Paul and Politics: Ekklesia, Israel, Imperium, Interpretation*. Ed. Richard A. Horsley. Harrisburg PA: Trinity Press International, 2000.

Sell, Aaron. "Applying Adaptationism to Human Anger: The Recalibrational Theory." Pp. 53–70 in *Human Aggression and Violence: Causes, Manifestations, and Consequences*. Eds. Phillip R. Shaver and Mario Mikulincer. Washington DC: American Psychological Association, 2011.

Setzer, Claudia. "Jewish Responses to Believers in Jesus." Pp. 577–79 in *The Jewish Annotated New Testament*. Eds. Amy-Jill Levine and Marc Zvi Brettler. Oxford and New York: Oxford University Press, 2011.

Sklar, Howard. *The Art of Sympathy in Fiction: Forms of Ethical and Emotional Persuasion*. Amsterdam: John Benjamins Publishing Company, 2013.

Smit, Joop. "The Letter of Paul to the Galatians: A Deliberative Speech." Pp. 39–59 in *The Galatians Debate*. Ed. Mark D. Nanos. Peabody MA: Hendrickson Publishers, Inc., 2002.

Smith, Dennis E. and Joseph B. Tyson, eds. *Acts and Christian Beginnings: The Acts Seminar Report*. Salem OR: Polebridge Press, 2013.

Smith, Jonathan Z. *Imagining Religion: From Babylon to Jerusalem*. Chicago: The University of Chicago Press, 1982.

Souter, Alexander. *The Earliest Latin Commentaries on the Epistles of St. Paul*. Oxford: Clarendon Press, 1927.

Sprinkle, Preston M. and Michael F. Bird. "Jewish Interpretations of Paul in the Last Thirty Years." *Currents in Biblical Research* 6,3 (2008) 355–76.

Stanley, Christopher D. "'Neither Jew nor Greek': Ethnic Conflict in Graeco-Roman Society." *Journal for the Study of the New Testament* 64 (1996) 101–24.

Steinmetz, David C. *Luther in Context*. 2d ed. Grand Rapids MI: Baker Academic, 2002.

Stendahl, Krister. "The Apostle Paul and the Introspective Conscience of the West." Pp. 78–96 in *Paul Among Jews and Gentiles and other Essays*. Philadelphia: Fortress Press, 1976.

_____. *Final Account*. Minneapolis: Fortress Press, 1995.

_____. *Paul Among Jews and Gentiles*. Philadelphia: Fortress Press, 1976.

_____. "Paul Among Jews and Gentiles." Pp. 1–77 in *Paul Among Jews and Gentiles and other Essays*. Philadelphia: Fortress Press, 1976.

Stearns, Frederic R., M.D. *Anger: Psychology, Physiology, Pathology*. Springfield IL: Charles C. Thomas, 1972.

Stevenson, Tom. "Antony as 'Tyrant' in Cicero's First Philippic." *Ramus* 38,2 (2009) 174–86.

_____. "Tyrants, Kings and Fathers in the *Philippics*." Pp. 95–113 in *Cicero's Philippics: History, Rhetoric and Ideology*. Eds. Tom Stevenson and Marcus Wilson. Auckland: Polygraphia Ltd., 2008.

Stowers, Stanley K. *A Rereading of Romans: Justice, Jews and Gentiles*. New Haven and London: Yale University Press, 1994.

_____. *Letter Writing in Greco-Roman Antiquity*. Philadelphia: The Westminster Press, 1986.

Strange, James F. "Archaeology and the Pharisees." Pp. 237–51 in *In Quest of the Historical Pharisees*. Eds. Jacob Neusner and Bruce D. Chilton. Waco: Baylor University Press, 2007.

Steel, Catherine. *The End of the Roman Republic 146 to 44 BC: Conquest and Crisis.*
    Edinburgh: Edinburgh University Press Ltd, 2013.
Sumney, Jerry. *Identifying Paul's Opponents: The Question of Method in 2 Corinthians.*
    Sheffield: Sheffield Academic Press, 1990.
_____. "Studying Paul's Opponents: Advantages and Challenges." Pp. 7–58 in
    Paul and His Opponents. Ed. Stanley E. Porter. Leiden: Brill, 2005.
Swartz, Michael D. "The Aesthetics of Blessing and Cursing: Literary and
    Iconographic Dimensions of Hebrew and Aramaic Blessing and Curse
    Texts." *Journal of Ancient Near Eastern Religions* 5,1 (2005) 187–211.
Taddeo, Donat Joseph. "Signs of Demosthenes in Cicero's *Philippics.*" PhD diss.,
    Stanford University, 1971.
Tatum, Gregory. *New Chapters in the Life of Paul: The Relative Chronology of
    His Career.* The Catholic Biblical Quarterly Monograph Series. Vol. 41.
    Washington DC: The Catholic Biblical Association of America, 2006.
Tatum, W. Jeffrey. "The Final Crisis (69–44)." Pp. 190–211 in *A Companion to the
    Roman Republic.* Eds. Nathan Rosenstein and Robert Morstein-Marx. Malden
    MA: Blackwell Publishing, 2006.
Tempest, Kathryn. *Cicero: Politics and Persuasion in Ancient Rome.* London and
    New York: Continuum International Publishing Group, 2011.
Theissen, Gerd and Annette Merz. *The Historical Jesus: A Comprehensive Guide.*
    Trans. John Bowden. Minneapolis: Fortress Press, 1996.
Thielman, Frank. *Paul and the Law: A Contextual Approach.* Downers Grove IL:
    InterVarsity Press, 1994.
Thiessen, Matthew. *Contesting Conversion: Genealogy, Circumcision, and Identity in
    Ancient Judaism and Christianity.* New York: Oxford University Press, 2011.
Thiselton, Anthony C. *The Living Paul: An Introduction to the Apostle's Life and
    Thought.* Downer's Grove IL: InterVarsity Press, 2009.
Thurén, Lauri. *Derhetorizing Paul: A Dynamic Perspective on Pauline Theology and
    the Law.* Tübingen: Mohr Siebeck, 2000.
_____. "Was Paul Angry? Derhetorizing Galatians." Pp. 302–20 in *The Rhetorical
    Interpretation of Scripture: Essays from the 1996 Malibu Conference.* Eds. Stanley
    E. Porter and Dennis L. Stamps. Sheffield: Sheffield Academic Press, 1999.
Tolmie, D. F. *Persuading the Galatians: A Text-Centered Rhetorical Analysis of a
    Pauline Letter.* Tübingen: Mohr Siebeck, 2004.
Turner, C. H. "Greek Patristic Commentaries on the Pauline Epistles." Pp. 484–
    531 in *A Dictionary of the Bible.* Ed. James Hastings. Edinburgh: T&T Clark,
    1909.
Tyson, Joseph B. "'Works of Law' in Galatians." *Journal of Biblical Literature* 92,3
    (1973) 423–31.
Udoh, Fabian E. "Paul's Views on the Law: Questions about Origin (Gal 1:6–2:21;
    Phil 3:2–11)." *Novum Testamentum* 42,3 (2000) 214–37.
Ungern-Sternberg, Jürgen von. "The Crisis of the Republic." Pp. 78–98 in *The
    Roman Republic.* Ed. Harriet I. Flower. Cambridge: Cambridge University
    Press, 2014.
Usher, Stephen. *Greek Oratory: Tradition and Originality.* Oxford: Oxford
    University Press, 2001.
VanderKam, James C. "The Pharisees and the Dead Sea Scrolls." Pp. 225–36 in
    In Quest of the Historical Pharisees. Eds. Jacob Neusner and Bruce D. Chilton.
    Waco: Baylor University Press, 2007.
Vos, Johan S. "Paul's Argumentation in Galatians 1–2." Pp. 169–80 in *The
    Galatians Debate.* Ed. Mark D. Nanos. Peabody MA: Hendrickson Publishers,
    Inc., 2002.

Waisanen, Don. "Political Conversion as Intrapersonal Argument: Self-dissociation in David Brock's *Blinded By the Night.*" *Argumentation and Advocacy* 47 (2011) 228–45.

Walker, William. "Does the 'We' in Gal.15–17 Include Paul's Opponents?" *New Testament Studies* 49,4 (2003) 560–65.

Watson, Francis. *Paul and the Hermeneutics of Faith.* London and New York: T&T Clark, 2004.

Weil, Henri. *Les Harangues de Démosthène.* 3d ed. Paris: Librarie Hachette, 1912.

Wendt, Heidi. "From the Herodians to Hadrian: The Shifting Status of Judean Religion in Post-Flavian Rome." Pp. 63–92 in *Fall 2015 Westar Christianity Seminar Papers.* Atlanta GA, 2015.

Westerholm, Stephen. *Israel's Law and the Church's Faith.* Eugene: Wipf and Stock Publishers, 1998.

_____. *Perspectives Old and New on Paul: The "Lutheran" Paul and His Critics.* Grand Rapids MI: William B. Eerdmans, 2004.

White, John L. "Introductory Formulae in the Body of the Pauline Letter." *Journal of Biblical Literature* 90,1 (1971) 91–97.

White, L. Michael. *From Jesus to Christianity.* New York: HarperOne, 2004.

Wiedemann, Thomas. *Greek and Roman Slavery.* Baltimore: The Johns Hopkins University Press, 1981.

Wiley, Tatha. *Paul and the Gentile Women: Reframing Galatians.* New York: Continuum, 2005.

Williams, Bernard. *Shame and Necessity.* Berkeley: University of California Press, 1993.

Williams, Guy. *The Spirit World in the Letters of Paul the Apostle.* Göttingen: Vandenhoeck & Ruprecht GmbH & Co. KG, 2009.

Williams, Sam K. *Galatians.* Ed. Victor P. Furnish. Abingdon New Testament Commentaries. Nashville: Abingdon Press, 1997.

Wills, Garry. *What Paul Meant.* London: Penquin Books, 2007.

Wilson, Bryan R. *Magic and the Millennium.* London: Heinemann, 1973.

Wire, Antoinette Clark. *The Corinthian Women Prophets: A Reconstruction through Paul's Rhetoric.* Minneapolis: Fortress Press, 1990.

Wooten, Cecil W. *A Commentary on Demosthenes' Philippic I: With Rhetorical Analyses of Philippics II and III.* Oxford: Oxford University Press, 2008.

_____. *Cicero's Philippics and Their Demosthenic Model: The Rhetoric of Crisis.* Chapel Hill NC: The University of North Carolina Press, 1983.

_____. "On the Road to *Philippic* III: The Management of Argument and the Modulation of Emotion in the Deliberative Speeches of Demosthenes." *Rhetorica* 28,1 (2010) 1–22.

Worthington, Ian, ed. *Demosthenes: Statesman and Orator.* London: Routledge, 2000.

Worthington, Ian. *Demosthenes of Athens and the Fall of Classical Greece.* Oxford and New York: Oxford University Press, 2013.

_____. Worthington, Ian. *Philip II of Macedonia.* New Haven: Yale University Press, 2008.

Wrede, William. *Paul.* Trans. Edward Lummis. London: Philip Green, 1907.

Wright, N. T. *The Climax of the Covenant: Christ and the Law in Pauline Theology.* Minneapolis: Fortress Press, 1991.

_____. "Paul's Gospel and Caesar's Empire." Pp. 160–83 in *Paul and Politics: Ekklesia, Israel, Imperium, Interpretation.* Ed. Richard A. Horsley. Harrisburg PA: Trinity Press International, 2000.

_____. *Paul and the Faithfulness of God*. Christian Origins and the Question of God. 2 vols. Minneapolis: Fortress Press, 2013.

Yakobson, Alexander. "Popular Power in the Roman Republic." Pp. 383–400 in *A Companion to the Roman Republic*. Eds. Nathan Rosenstein and Robert Morstein-Marx. Malden MA: Blackwell Publishing, 2006.

Yunis, Harvey. *Taming Democracy: Models of Political Rhetoric in Classical Athens*. Ithaca NY: Cornell University Press, 1996.

Zetterholm, Magnus. *Approaches to Paul*. Minneapolis: Fortress Press, 2009.

Index of Ancient Sources

Classical Sources

Anthologia Graeca
6.162   219n143

Aristotle
  Rhetorica
  1.2.2   131
  1.2.3   53, 131
  1.2.4–5   54
  1.10.4   197n131
  2.10.1–2   220n156
  3.7.4   87

pseudo-Aristotle
  Problemata
  926ᵇ24   220n151

Cicero
  De haruspicum responso
  59   217n114

  De officiis
  1.52   107

  De oratore
  2.189   87

  De republica
  2.48   105

  Epistulae ad Atticum
  14.9.2   186n76
  15.12.12   186n83
  16.9   186n83
  16.14.1   186n83

  Epistulae ad familiares
  10.1.1   100

  In Catalinam
  2.10   217n114

  In Pisonem
  21   217n114

In Verrem
  2.1.40   217n114
  2.1.42   217n114
  2.1.121   217n114
  2.5.109   217n114
  2.5.145   217n114
  2.5.146   217n114
  2.5.180   186n82

Orationes philippicae
  1.20   193n89
  1.29   193n89
  1.38   193n89
  2.1   204n77
  2.7   228n67
  2.11   216n93
  2.14   193n89
  2.19   193n89
  2.74   228n67
  2.77   216n93
  2.90   193n89
  2.95   216n93
  2.113   193n84, 216n93
  2.118   204n77
  2.118–19   228n59
  2.66–67   106
  3.1   28, 29, 30, 31
  3.1–2   191n56, 218n122, 228n61
  3.2   29–31, 50
  3.3   104, 216n82
  3.3–14   32, 216n82
  3.4   102–3, 216n82
  3.9–10   105
  3.10   104, 216n93, 217n103
  3.11   228n64
  3.12   218n134
  3.14   148
  3.15–27   32, 216n82
  3.16   216n93, 228n67
  3.19   193n84
  3.21   148, 218n127

Judaic Sources

17	120, 158
17:15–16	121
21	120, 124
21:1–7	121
22	158
22:12	158
25:1–6	222n202

Isaiah
2:2–4	6
49:1	207n127

Jeremiah
1:4–5	207n127

Judges
13:5	208n127

Micah
4:1–3	6

Philo
De migratione Abrahami
89–93	198n155

De specialibus legibus
1.4–10	198n155

Quaestiones et solutiones in Genesin
3.46–52	198n155

1 Samuel
11	208n127

Sirach
44:19–21	233n134

Zechariah
8:21–23	6

Christian Sources

Acts
7:30	224n217
7:38	224n217
9:3–22	210n163
17:22–31	177
22:3	4
22:6–16	210n163
26:12–18	210n163

1 Corinthians
1:1	70
1:20	206n112
2:6	206n112
2:8	206n112
3:18–19	206n112
5:1–2	114
5:9	114
7:18–19	182n34
7:19	49, 84

2 Corinthians
1:1	69, 205n96
4:4	206n112

Galatians
1:1	47, 67–71, 74–75, 78, 204n84, 205n92, 210n155
1:1–5	36, 67–68, 72, 75, 79, 205n86
1:1–12	210n155, 210n158
1:1–24	77, 210n158
1:2	68
1:3	68
1:4	68, 71, 206n112
1:6	36–41, 43, 45, 49–50, 194n101
1:6–7	45, 194n91, 194n101
1:6–9	14, 35–36, 39–41, 43–44, 67, 79, 110, 194n93, 196n125, 210n159
1:6–10	207n122, 219n147
1:6–11	207n122
1:6–2:21	194n94
1:7	36–39, 79, 82, 194n101, 196n117, 219n137
1:7–9	81
1:8	36–39, 79, 109, 118
1:8–9	109–10, 112, 124, 220n165,
1:9	36–39, 49, 79, 109, 207n122
1:10	73–75, 78, 81,

Index of Modern Authors

Index of Rhetorical Terms and Devices

About the Author

Nina E. Livesey (Ph.D., Southern Methodist University) is Associate Professor of Religious Studies and Interdisciplinary Studies in the College of Liberal Studies at the University of Oklahoma in Norman. A specialist in Jewish-Christian relations and Christian origins with an emphasis on Pauline studies, she is the author of *Circumcision as a Malleable Symbol* (2010) as well as many scholarly articles on Paul and on second-century Christianity. She serves as co-editor (with Clayton Jefford) of the academic journal *Forum*.

CPSIA information can be obtained
at www.ICGtesting.com
Printed in the USA
FFOW03n0505211016
28633FF